For Them's Return

Northchurch Folk Who Survived the First World War

Richard North

Paperback	978-1-80369-089-6
Hardback	978-1-80369-090-2

www.newgeneration-publishing.com

New Generation Publishing

Index

Forward

For Them's Sake, co-authored by Ray Smith and me, told the stories of the men from Northchurch Parish in Hertfordshire who died during the First and Second World Wars. Whilst researching the stories for the book we came across a local newspaper article from 8th September 1917 that made mention of a War Shrine inside St Mary's, Northchurch. No photograph of the shrine has so far come to light, but it is known that it was regularly adorned with freshly-cut flowers by the villagers. At the time of the article the names of two hundred and sixteen Northchurch servicemen were listed on the shrine, but unfortunately their names consisted solely of a surname and an initial, making their positive identification somewhat difficult. Fortunately, the majority were subsequently confirmed from the 1918 and 1919 Absent Voters Lists for Northchurch and Berkhamsted, together with the army service records that survived destruction during the Blitz in 1940. Of the remaining names seven have been identified, but lack any information on their military service, whilst a further twelve names remain unidentified. It is thought that some may be relatives of people living in Northchurch at the time, but with no specific link to the village, or men working on the estates of the local large houses who, by the nature of their work, did not tend to stay in a particular area for long.

Unlike *For Them's Sake*, which was based solely upon the names appearing on either the Northchurch War Memorial or other memorials in the village, the scope of this book has been widened to encompass the men who lived in the area covered by the Electoral Roll for the Parish of Northchurch at the time, together with that for Gossoms End, which until 1909 came under the jurisdiction of Northchurch Parish Council. As a result, the stories of most of the servicemen (and women) from Northchurch village and its surrounding area, the hamlets of Dudswell and Cow Roast, Gossoms End and a large area to the north and east of Berkhamsted, including the hamlets of Frithsden and Nettleden, together with areas further east known as Little Heath and Bourne End Lane, are included in this book.

As is well known, many of the servicemen who returned from the war rarely spoke of their experiences. Even during the war many of the letters and postcards they sent back to their families tended to give a positive gloss to events to lessen the worries of their loved ones. Only in their final years did some of the ex-servicemen finally reveal the true horrors and experiences they had endured.

Richard North, September 2021

Prologue

19th November 1919, No 1 Dispersal Centre, Purfleet, Essex

What was going through the mind of Sapper Joseph Hosier as he finally stood in line at the Dispersal Centre in Purfleet awaiting his demobilisation from the Royal Engineers? It was just over a year since the war had ended, and in theory he should have been demobilised long before now. The demobilisation process put in place by the British Government when the war ended was designed to give priority to those servicemen who had urgently-needed skills back in civilian life together with those that had served the longest. Joseph's older brother, Frederick, had already been demobbed the previous March and his younger brother, Arthur, a former prisoner of war, had been repatriated home from neutral Switzerland in 1917.

Back in 1914, Joseph Hosier had already been serving as a Special Reservist with the Bedfordshire Regiment for six years and had later fought in the trenches in France with the regiment's 2nd Battalion between November 1914 and October 1915. As such he was proud to be called one of the 'Old Contemptibles'[1].

Most of his old Bedfordshire comrades who had survived the war had already been demobilised and discharged from the army. Yet Joseph Hosier's war had been very different. He had already been discharged from the army on a previous occasion, in October 1915, due to a rule in the then current army regulations that allowed a serving soldier to be discharged at the end of his term of service, having continuously served for six years. The outbreak of war just before he was due to be discharged had, however, automatically extended Joseph's six-year term by a further twelve months. Having been discharged from the Bedfords, Joseph had returned to his home in Northchurch and resumed his former civilian occupation as a brickmaker.

A year later, with conscription now in force and considerable pressure being put on former soldiers to rejoin, Joseph found himself back in France serving as a Sapper in a Field Company of the Royal Engineers, whose work included digging trenches and dugouts, road repairs and the clearing of captured enemy defences whilst on the constant lookout for booby-traps.

---

[1] The name 'Old Contemptibles' arose from an Order of the Day issued by Kaiser Wilhelm of Germany which mentioned 'Sir John French's contemptible little army'. All soldiers serving with the British Expeditionary Force in France between 5th August and 22nd November 1914 were subsequently entitled to call themselves 'Old Contemptibles'.

Since the end of the war in November 1918, he had watched as some of his mates had started to be demobilised or posted to other units, whilst spending much of his own time endlessly filling in many of the trenches that he and his fellow sappers had dug since 1916 or repairing roads that had effectively ceased to exist after four years or warfare. He had then been sent to Limerick in Ireland for a short period. At least he had not been included with the men from his unit that had recently been sent to Russia to support the White Russians against the Bolsheviks.

Finally, it was his turn. Joseph had been given a medical examination before he left his unit, together with army Form Z18, which showed his army service since July 1916. At Purfleet he was given the all-important forms Z21(Certificate of Transfer to the Reserves on Demobilisation) and Z11, (Protection Certificate and Certificate of Identity). These two documents were effectively proof that he was at long last on his way back to civilian life. Finally, he was issued with a railway warrant to get him back to the nearest railway station to his home, which, in Joseph's case, was Berkhamsted.

Whilst in Northchurch on his final leave and awaiting his formal discharge from the army, Joseph was still technically a soldier, and until he was formally discharged he could still be recalled, although, with his low medical classification, this was unlikely. He was now allowed to wear civilian clothes, as opposed to his khaki army uniform, and receive his last instalments of army pay, which he collected on three occasions from the Post Office in Northchurch High Street.

Joseph was just one of over three hundred young men from Northchurch and the surrounding area who had served during the war. Of those, over fifty would never return. As the village of Northchurch in Hertfordshire was a typical small close-knit community, almost every inhabitant had at least one relative who had gone off to war, either voluntarily, or later having been conscripted. Many households, like that of the Hosiers, had three men who had served their country.

For many of the soldiers returning to Northchurch following their discharge the subsequent weeks, months and years back in civilian life would be difficult, and many never spoke in detail about their wartime experiences. Some returned home physically unscathed and resumed their former occupations, others could not settle back into familiar surroundings and chose to start a new life in Canada or Australia, whilst others suffered the ongoing effects of life-changing injuries. Some were to die early as an indirect result of the war; others would live on into their eighties.

1 – Your Country Needs You

Five years earlier, on 4th August 1914, whilst Joseph Hosier was serving as a Special Reservist with the Bedfordshire Regiment, Great Britain had declared war on Germany. Tension had been building in Europe over the previous five weeks after the assassination of Archduke Franz Ferdinand Carl Ludwig Joseph Maria, the heir presumptive to the throne of Austria-Hungary. Matters had been made worse by the complex network of treaties between the various European powers set up during the previous decade. Germany's invasion of neutral Belgium as part of their plan to defeat France made the declaration of war inevitable.

The day before Great Britain declared war on Germany, the annual camp of the local Territorial Force, which in 1914 was held on the Ashridge Estate two miles north of Northchurch, had ended early with the servicemen instructed to return home and await orders. Elsewhere, regular soldiers began to be mobilised and army reservists like Northchurch man Charlie Graham were recalled to active service. Some of the reservists were ordered to travel to Ireland to rejoin their battalions, only to return to England with them within hours of their arrival. Some battalions serving overseas on garrison duties were also recalled.

On 15th August 1914, a large advertisement appeared in the local press calling on men between nineteen and thirty years of age to volunteer to join the newly-appointed Secretary of War Lord Kitchener's 'New Army'. Former regular soldiers were also urged to join the Special Reserve to replace the men that had been mobilised. Recruiting centres were established in all the major towns, the nearest to Northchurch being in Berkhamsted, where nineteen-year-old Fred Carter and twenty-two-year-old Edgar Kempster were quick to volunteer. Other local men decided to volunteer in Hertford, Bedford or Watford.

Before being accepted, the volunteers had to meet strict age, height and nationality criteria, and undergo a medical examination to ensure that they could cope with the rigours of military life. Many of the Northchurch volunteers were farm workers or gardeners employed on the estates of the local large houses and so were used to heavy work. Consequently, they had no problem in passing the medical examination. The final stage was that of swearing an oath of allegiance to the King. With the formalities complete, they were marched off to start their training.

Most of the local men joined infantry battalions, whilst others with specialist skills like motorcycle builders, Cecil and Edward Burney, signed up as despatch riders for the Signal Corps. Many of the gardeners employed by Lieutenant Colonel Sir Charles Frederick Hadden RA at his home at

Rossway, one of the large houses to the south of Northchurch village, appear to have been encouraged by him to sign up with the Royal Artillery.

Within a month of the war starting, the *Berkhamsted Gazette* reported the Rector of St Mary's, Northchurch, Revd. RH Pope, as saying that some twenty-eight men from Northchurch had volunteered. He continued "*It must have given all a fearful shock to hear of war declared and one prays that it may soon cease. We must all try and do our little part at home to lessen the sufferings that go with war. 'Give Peace', must be our prayer*".

By the spring of 1915, with the number of volunteers beginning to decline, the British Government decided to ascertain the number of men of fighting age who had yet to volunteer and who could make up for the rising losses at the Front. This led to the passing of the National Registration Act, making it compulsory for all men and women resident in England, Scotland and Wales and aged between fifteen and sixty-five to provide their name, address, marital status, dependents, occupation and any specialist skills they may have. Within two months some five million men of military age not serving in the armed forces had been identified, most of whom were not working in key industries. That October Lord Derby became Director-General of Recruiting and within a week he set up a deferred enlistment scheme, which became known as the 'Derby Scheme'. Under this Scheme, men aged between eighteen and forty would voluntarily attest to join the Army Reserve, but would remain at home until they were called up. Married men were promised that single men would be called-up before they were. Even following the introduction of the Derby Scheme there were still not enough men volunteering, so the War Office announced that the Scheme would end on 15th December 1915 and that compulsory service, commonly known as 'Conscription', would follow. This move forced many Northchurch men, like Fred Grover, Fred Hales and James Waldron, who were still pondering what to do, into attesting under the Derby Scheme just before it ended.

The Military Service Act, which introduced conscription, came into effect in March 1916. Men between the ages of eighteen and forty-one on 2nd November 1915 were now liable to be conscripted unless they were married, widowed with dependent children, or else worked in one of the reserved professions. The following May, the Act was amended to treat married and unmarried men the same and extend the upper age limit to forty-five.

Military Service Tribunals were set up in the major towns to hear any appeals against conscription. In Berkhamsted, the Military Tribunal which also covered Northchurch, met in the Council Chamber. Made up of members from the area who understood local employment needs, together with a military representative, the Tribunals heard individual and employer appeals on the grounds allowed under the Act relating to personal hardship, infirmity and ill health, doing work in the national interest, and conscientious objection to military service. Applicants dissatisfied with the decision of the Berkhamsted Tribunal could appeal to the County Appeal Tribunal at Hertford, which either upheld the Berkhamsted Tribunal's decision, or sent the case back for reconsideration. Several men from Northchurch would appear before the Berkhamsted Tribunal during the final three years of the war to appeal against their conscription into the armed services.

Northchurch Servicemen and civilians in front of the Pheasant Public House
Courtesy of BLH&MS

2 – The Bedfordshire Battalions

The British infantryman, commonly known as 'Tommy Atkins', or just 'Tommy', was the backbone of the army during the First World War. The bulk of the infantry was made up of the Line Regiments with regional links, such as the Border Regiment, or with county allegiances, such as the Bedfordshire Regiment (which also included regular soldiers from Hertfordshire). Before the war most of the regiments only maintained two battalions, with one of the two often serving on garrison duty somewhere in the British Empire. Added to this were the local part-time volunteer soldiers that formed the Territorial Force, commonly known as 'Terriers' and who could be sent overseas to serve following prior agreement of the soldiers themselves. With the outbreak of the war and the call for volunteers each regiment subsequently created several additional battalions ready to serve their country.

In 1914 infantry battalions consisted of some 1,007 men, including 30 officers, under the command of a Lieutenant Colonel, and was made up of a headquarters section and four Companies, normally abbreviated as 'Coy', and identified by the letters A to D. Companies were further divided into Platoons of some 50 men each, which were split into four Sections. Additionally, until 1916, each battalion had its own machine gun section.

Infantry Brigades had an establishment of between 3,000 and 4,000 men and consisted of a brigade headquarters, 4 infantry battalions, as described above, and supporting horses under the command of a Brigadier General.

An Infantry Division had an establishment of between 16,000 and 18,000 men under the command of a Major General. The bulk of the

Kempston Barracks, Bedford circa 1914
Author's Collection

men in an infantry division were those made up from its three infantry brigades. To support the infantry, each division had artillery brigades, ammunition columns, engineers, field and signal companies, a cavalry squadron, a divisional train for transport, and field ambulances. Two or more Divisions of some 50,000 men would make up a British Corps, with two or more Corps forming an Army Group.

Not surprisingly, many of the Northchurch men serving in the regular army before the war were members of the Bedfordshire Regiment and had enlisted at their Barracks at Kempston.

George Bedford (1873 – 1939)
Private 20442, 1st Battalion, Bedfordshire Regiment

George Bedford was one of the oldest men from Northchurch to serve in the war, but, although he was in an infantry regiment, he did not serve on the front line. He was born in Ellesmere Road, Berkhamsted in 1873 to farm worker, Joseph Bedford and his wife, Catherine, and was their fourth son. At that time, Ellesmere Road was one of the Berkhamsted streets that formed part of the eastern section of Northchurch Parish and consequently George was christened at St Mary's in January 1874. By 1891, the Bedford family had moved to a cottage in Northchurch High Street, close to the *George & Dragon* public house, with George working for a local blacksmith.

On reaching the age of 19, George decided to join the army and enlisted with the Bedfordshire Regiment. His medical record of the time shows him as being 5ft 7¼ins tall, weighing 125lbs and with brown hair, brown eyes and a fresh complexion. His first year was spent with the Bedfords 2nd Battalion, but in February 1896 he transferred to their 1st Battalion, which was about to embark for India on garrison duties. George and his new battalion arrived there in March 1896, but it was to be a difficult time for him, as over the next two years he was admitted to the local military hospital on numerous occasions, complaining of pains in his chest and breathlessness. He was eventually diagnosed with a heart condition and returned to England for treatment at the Netley Military Hospital near Southampton. In July 1898, he was deemed unfit for further military service and returned to Northchurch and civilian life.

The 1901 Census shows George, aged 28, still living with his parents and family in a small terraced cottage in Bell Lane, Northchurch, and working as a farm worker on one of local estates, possibly alongside his father, Joseph. Six years later, George married Charlotte Elizabeth Hobbs from Woburn, and the couple moved into a four-roomed cottage in Gossoms End. Joseph Bedford died in 1911 and his widow and younger sister, Sarah, moved in with George and Charlotte. His mother died three years later.

The only record of George's war service comes from the 1918 Absent Voter's List which shows him serving as a Private with his old battalion at the regiment's Bedford depot. By then, he would have been 45 years old. Sadly, by the time George was demobilised following the end of the war, his wife had died during the influenza pandemic.

George returned to his old job as a farm worker and moved in temporarily with his recently-married sister, Sarah and her husband, Joseph Brooks, who lived in a cottage in Riverside Terrace, Gossoms End. In 1922, George remarried and he and his new wife, Mary Ann Duncombe, lived in a cottage in Gossoms End for many years before moving to nearby Norris's Terrace. George Bedford died in May 1939, aged 65.

Charles Graham (1882 – 1955)
Private 3/8398, 1st Battalion, Bedfordshire Regiment

Born in Northchurch in October 1882, Charles Graham, known as Charlie, was one of George and Jane Graham's eleven children. They formed part of the extensive Graham family who occupied three adjacent four-roomed cottages in New Road, Northchurch. By 1903, Charlie had started work as a bricklayer, but two years later he enlisted with 1st Battalion, Bedfordshire Regiment for the standard twelve-year term of duty, nine in the line, with the remaining three in the reserves. Charlie spent his first two years of army life on garrison duty in India before returning with his battalion to England in 1908. In 1911, the period a soldier had to spend in the line was reduced by two years and he became a reservist in the Bedford's 3rd Battalion, maintaining his link with his regiment by attending their annual training camps.

Back home in New Road, Charlie lived with his now widowed mother and two younger brothers and went back to bricklaying. Within months of his return, he met Ada Glenister, a domestic servant working at one of the local large houses, and the couple later married at St Mary's, Northchurch. Over the next three years he and Ada would become the parents of three children.

As a Reservist, Charlie was recalled to his regiment on the outbreak of war and after retraining at Kempston barracks in Bedford, he travelled to France in November 1914 as part of a small draft of men, joining 'A' Coy in his old battalion. By this time, 1st Bedfords had already become battle-hardened troops, having been in action on several occasions since their arrival in France. In January 1915, Charlie went down with influenza and was hospitalised for a short time in Rouen whilst he recovered.

Charlie was to remain with 1st Bedfords for the remainder of the war, becoming part of 'C' Coy, and would see action during the Somme Offensive, the Battle of Arras and the Third Battle of Ypres, before being sent to the Italian Front towards the end of 1917. The battalion was recalled to France following the German Spring Offensive in March 1918 and later took part in the allied advance that led to the signing of the Armistice the following November.

In 1919 Charlie was demobilised and returned home to his family in New Road and went back to bricklaying. His wife, would later give birth to two more children. In 1939, Charlie was still working as a bricklayer and living with his family in Tring Road, Northchurch. He died in 1955, aged 72.

George Henry Rickard, MM DCM (1893 -?)
Sergeant 9707, 2nd Battalion, Bedfordshire Regiment

George Rickard was born in the picturesque Hertfordshire village of Aldbury in February 1893, and was one of five children of William Rickard, a farm worker, and his wife, Ruth. The family later moved to Frithsden, then part of Northchurch Parish, where George became a farm labourer. On reaching the age of 18 in 1911, George decided to become a soldier, joining 2nd Bedfords at Kempston Barracks.

In 5th October 1914, George and 2nd Bedfords left Southampton on board the SS *Winifredian*, bound for Zeebrugge. Within days of their arrival they were in action at the First Battle of Ypres.

George remained with 2nd Bedfords throughout the war, rising to the rank of Sergeant. On 23rd October 1918, during one of the final battles of the war in France, 2nd Bedfords were north-east of le Cateau, some 15 miles from Cambrai. Leading his platoon during an advance, George found the way blocked by ten German soldiers manning a machine gun post. With seven of his men already dead or wounded, George grabbed a Lewis gun and, accompanied by an infantryman carrying some spare ammunition drums, crept forward until they were about six yards from the machine gun position. Opening fire, George killed or wounded all the German machine gunners enabling the advance to continue. In recognition of his action that day George was awarded both the Military Medal (MM) and the Distinguished Conduct Medal (DCM).

George returned home early in 1919 and within a few weeks he had married Jessie Owen in Croxley Green Church, near Watford. Settling in Nettleden, George worked on a local farm and he and Jessie started to raise a family together. Possibly because of his experiences during the war, George found settling back in England somewhat difficult, and he and Jessie soon started to discuss the possibility of starting a new life in Canada. Financed by an assisted package from the Canadian Government, George and his family left Southampton in April 1927 on board the SS *Arabic*, a passenger steamship which had served as an auxiliary cruiser in the Imperial German Navy during the war. The passenger list shows the family's destination as Toronto, Ontario.

In 1965, George was working as a farmer close to the township of Uxbridge, some 25 miles north-east of Toronto. It is not known when he died.

James Henry Waldron (1895 – 1963)
Private 25278, 4th Battalion, Bedfordshire Regiment

James Waldron was born in June 1895, the son of Joseph Waldron, a gardener and originally from Lambeth, and his wife, Annie. One of five children, James grew up in Gossoms End and later moved with his family to George Street, Berkhamsted. After leaving school he became a carman. By 1915, the Waldron family had moved again, and were living in Highfield Road, Berkhamsted.

In December that year, just before the introduction of conscription, James attested at Watford under the Derby Scheme. His medical record shows that he stood 5ft 10½ins tall, and weighed 149lbs. Passing with an A1 medical classification, James was sent home and told to await mobilisation. He did not have long to wait, and on 21st January 1916, James reported to the Bedford's depot at Kempston and was posted to their 9th (Service) Battalion, which was then based near Colchester, for training. Having completed his training, James then transferred to the Bedford's 4th Battalion.

The battalion left Southampton on the evening of 24th June on board the SS *Inventor* and arrived at Le Havre early the following morning. They would first see action during the Battle of The Ancre in November 1916, which effectively ended the Somme Offensive, and the following year would take part in the Battle of Arras and the Third Battle of Ypres, during which he was slightly wounded. The following year the battalion suffered heavily during the German Spring Offensive.

In April 1919, James's hopes of early demobilisation were dashed when he became one of 60 men from his battalion who were transferred to 2/4th Battalion, Oxford & Buckinghamshire Light Infantry and then, three months later, attached to 17th Battalion, Worcestershire Regiment. He finally returned to England in September 1919 and was demobilised the following month.

By the time James returned to England, his parents had moved to a cottage in Dudswell and this is where he spent the next few years. What he did for a living on his return, however, is currently unknown. In 1925, he married Ellen Parfitt Beeson from Watford. The newlyweds initially lived with James's parents before moving to a cottage in Belton Road, Gossoms End, the garden of which backed onto the Grand Junction Canal. Not long afterwards, his parents moved into an adjoining cottage.

By 1939, James was a father of three children and was living in larger accommodation in Granville Road, Northchurch and was working as a warehouseman. James Waldron died in 1963, aged 68.

Henry Hill Forsyth (1898 – 1967)
Private 201193, 1/5th Bedfordshire Regiment

Henry Forsyth was born in Carlisle in August 1898, the son of single mother, Sarah Forsyth. Within eighteen months of his birth, Sarah and Henry had moved south to Hertfordshire and were living in Boxmoor where Sarah married wood finisher, Frederick Margrave. Sarah and Frederick would raise several children together, but Henry retained his mother's maiden name. Growing up in Boxmoor, he attended the Two Waters School in Hemel Hempstead and later moved with his mother and stepfather to a cottage in Bourne End Lane.

In 1916, at the age of 18, Henry received his conscription papers. After completing his training in early 1917, he was posted to 1/5th Bedfordshire Regiment, which was then serving near Gaza in Palestine.

Following the Turkish surrender in October 1918, 1/5th Bedfords moved to Beirut where, in June the following year, they were disembodied and returned to England. Henry decided to remain in the army, however, joining the newly-created 2nd Beds & Herts Regiment in 1920 and within two years he had become a Lance Corporal. He left the army in 1923 and returned to Bourne End Lane.

The following year he married Ethel May Collier, whose family lived in Ellesmere Road, Berkhamsted. Settling in nearby George Street, Ethel gave birth to a daughter in 1925. In 1939, Henry and Ethel were still living in George Street, with Henry working as a car examiner for the London Passenger Transport Board, a forerunner of Transport for London. With another war with Germany having just broken, he was also serving as an air raid warden for his employers. Henry died in 1967, aged 68.

Alick Tattle Cousins (1895 – 1956)
Private 31364, 6th Battalion, Bedfordshire Regiment

Alick Cousins was an eighteen-year-old cowman working at Dudswell Farm when he was conscripted in February 1916. Born in 1895, in Stoke St Gregory, Somerset, Alick moved to Dudswell when his father, Walter, became the farm foreman there. After leaving school, he started working alongside his father as a cowman, but also attended the Northchurch Technical Institute in Bell Lane, where, in 1915, he won a prize for woodwork.

Three months after receiving his conscription papers Alick was told to report to the Regimental depot at Bedford where he was posted to the Bedford's 6th Battalion. Having completed his training, Alick was one of 50 new conscripts that joined the battalion near Hebecourt in the Somme sector on 11th January 1917.

During January and February 1917, 6th Bedfords received a substantial number of conscripted men like Alick, but there was little time to integrate them, as within days they had moved north to the trenches near Loos and almost immediately began to suffer casualties to German shellfire. That April, 6th Bedfords took part in the Battle of Arras, and later in the year saw action during the Third Battle of Ypres. Alick and his battalion remained in the Ypres area until the spring of 1918.

Following the failure of the German Spring Offensives, the British Army went through a substantial reorganisation. Alick's battalion was disbanded and most of the men were transferred to 1st Hertfordshire Battalion. Alick, however, was selected to be in a small group of soldiers from the battalion who were sent to train some of the newly-arrived American troops. By August 1918, with the training completed, he also transferred to 1st Hertfordshire Battalion.

Alick was demobilised in February 1919 and returned to Dudswell Farm. In 1922 he married Dorothy Fantham in St Mary's, Northchurch and later moved to a cottage in New Road. How long he remained at Dudswell Farm is uncertain, as by 1939 he was working for the local Co-operative Stores and living in Tring Road, Northchurch. Alick Cousins died in early 1956, aged 60.

Verulam William Arthur Forward (1880 – 1948)
Private 36656, Transport Workers Battalion, Bedfordshire Regiment

Details of Verulam Forward's early years are somewhat unclear. He was born in Highbury, Islington in March 1880, the son of James and Sophia Forward and was christened at Peter's, Hoxton Square, Shoreditch three months later. Sadly, Verulam's father died when he was just three years old and it appears that his mother later remarried. By 1891, ten-year-old Verulam was living with an aunt and uncle in Cowper Road, Berkhamsted, where he spent the remainder of his youth. He later became a general labourer at the William Cooper and Nephews chemical factory in Berkhamsted. September 1909 saw Verulam marry Kate Simmons at Tring Parish church, the newlyweds setting up home in a house in Cross Oak Road, Berkhamsted. Two years later they became parents upon the birth of a boy.

Verulam was probably conscripted in the summer of 1916, and, as he was subsequently posted to one of the Bedfordshire Regiment's two Transport Workers Battalions, it is likely that he was given a low grading following his medical examination.

The Transport Workers Battalion Scheme was created by the War Cabinet in May 1916 to supplement civilian labour vital to the war effort in the ports, railways, canals and iron and steel works to ensure that they were kept operating. The Bedfordshire Regiment had two Transport Workers

Battalions; 12th Battalion, raised in December 1916 worked in the ports of Folkestone, Chatham, Rochester, Sittingbourne, Weymouth and Newhaven whilst 13th Battalion, raised the following March, worked in Boston, Ipswich, London, Harwich and King's Lynn. Unfortunately, no information has come to light identifying in which of the two battalions Verulam served.

Men serving in the Transport Worker's battalions were not armed and had to pay for their own food and billets. By early 1917, the total number of men employed in these battalions had increased to around 5,000, and would eventually reach 35,000. Despite their hard work and the success of the scheme, at the end of the war all the men in the Transport Worker's battalions were demobilised and never received any form of medal from the army in recognition of their services.

By the time Verulam was demobilised and returned home, his wife and son had moved to Gossoms End where they remained for a number of years before moving to Holly Drive, Berkhamsted in the late 1920s. Whether Verulam went back to work at William Cooper and Nephews after his return from military service is currently unclear. In the 1939 Register, Verulam and Kate were recorded as still living in Holly Drive, but fifty-nine-year-old Verulam is shown as 'incapacitated'. He died in 1948, aged 68.

George Hayden Moore (1892 – 1955)
Lance Corporal 34582, 12th Transport Workers Battalion, Bedfordshire Regiment

Born in May 1892 in the village of Hawley, Hampshire, not far from the Royal Military Academy at Sandhurst, George Moore was one of seven children of James Moore and his wife, Emma. James Moore's work as a gardener seems to have resulted in him regularly moving around Surrey and Hampshire looking for work, before he and his family finally settled in a cottage in New Road, Northchurch. After leaving school, George started work as a gardener and later worked at a local nursery in Berkhamsted, presumably Lanes, which was located at the western end of Berkhamsted High Street. On 18th April 1915, George married Mary Emma Flitney, the daughter of a fellow gardener, at St Peter's, Berkhamsted. Following the wedding, George and Mary moved into a cottage on Northchurch High Street.

With no surviving service record, it is unclear when George joined the army, but like Verulam Forward, it is likely that he was conscripted during the summer of 1916, by which time Mary was pregnant with their first child. The Northchurch Absent Voters lists for 1918 and Spring 1919 show George serving with 12th Transport Workers Battalion, Bedfordshire Regiment, with the rank of Lance Corporal, so he would have worked in the ports of Folkestone, Chatham, Rochester, Sittingbourne, Weymouth and Newhaven.

After the war, George returned to his job as a gardener. Mary had given birth to a second child in the autumn of 1918 and a third child would be born four years later. The 1939 Register shows George and Emma living in Darrs Lane, Northchurch, with George working as a head gardener at one of the large houses in the area. Later retiring to a house in Berkhamsted, George Moore died in 1955, aged 63.

Fred Grover (1877 – 1935)
Private 355175, 53rd (YS) Battalion, Bedfordshire Regiment

Just before the introduction of conscription in 1916, Fred Grover, a 38-year-old wood sawyer from Gossoms End, attested in Berkhamsted under the Derby Scheme. Fred was born in Ellesmere Road, Berkhamsted, in the summer of 1877 to Walter and Maria Grover. His father worked as a labourer for the London & North Western Railway. By 1891, the Grover family were living in nearby Station Road, with Fred working as an errand boy. Sadly, his mother died in 1893 and Fred's maternal grandmother, Mary Graham, who lived in Gossoms End, helped to bring up his younger brothers and sisters.

In 1899, Walter Grover remarried. His new wife, Alice East, was the widow of Henry East, a hoop maker who lived in Berkhamsted High Street near the *Rose and Crown* public house. By then, Walter was also living in Gossoms End and Alice moved in together with her daughter, Kate, and son, Cornelius. Fred, was living with his grandmother a few doors away and was working at East & Son's timberyard.

Fred, and his new step-sister, Kate, subsequently fell in love and were married on 4th August 1902, the newlyweds settling in a small cottage in Thorns Yard, Northchurch. Over the next ten years Kate would give birth to five children, with one sadly dying in infancy.

When war broke out in 1914, Fred was 37 years old and had a family to support. It was not until the end of 1915, and facing the prospect of conscription, that Fred finally decided to attest under the Derby Scheme. The following year, he was posted to a reserve battalion of the Bedfordshire Regiment, but Fred's age meant that it was unlikely that he would serve overseas. He was subsequently placed on Home Service duties, possibly with 10th (Service) Battalion, Bedfordshire Regiment.

In 1914, as part of Lord Kitchener's creation of new army groups, 'Reserve Battalions' were created in each regiment, the Bedford's 10th (Service) Battalion being one of them. Often used for training, the units underwent several changes over the next few years as the need for manpower changed. Soon after Fred was called up, 10th (Service) Battalion was redesignated as 27th Battalion in the newly-formed Training Reserve and a year later it became 53rd (Young Soldiers) Battalion, Bedfordshire Regiment. In its new guise the unit provided three months of basic training for soldiers aged between 18 years and one month and 18 years and five months who were in the medical categories A4, B1 and C1 (see Appendix 3). Initially based at Clipstone Camp near Mansfield, the battalion later moved to Cannock Chase near Birmingham. It is unclear what role Fred performed in the unit, being some 20 years older than the recruits then under training.

In 1919, 53rd Battalion moved to Germany as part of the Army of Occupation, but by then Fred was over 40 years old and his services were no longer required. He returned home to Northchurch and, presumably, his job as a sawyer at the timberyard. Fred Grover died in the late winter of 1935, aged 57.

3 – Other Infantry Regiments

In 1914 men enlisting in the army could choose the regiment in which they wished to serve. As we have seen, many from Northchurch chose to join the Bedfordshire Regiment, but other regiments were often chosen because of family connections or their family history. This choice ended in 1916, following the introduction of conscription, with the conscript having no say in where he was posted. Similarly, soldiers in the field could be compulsorily transferred to another regiment to replace casualties at any time. If a soldier were himself a casualty, there was no guarantee that, having recovered, he would return to his original unit on his return to service.

Frank Percival Baker (1889 – 1970)
Private 20258, 14th Battalion Northumberland Fusiliers

Frank Percival Baker, commonly known as Percy, was the fourth child of Charles Baker, a gardener's labourer from Wigginton, and his wife, Phoebe, a straw plaiter. Born in February 1889, Percy grew up in Wigginton, living first in Bottom Row and later in Fox Road, and after finishing school he found work as a cowman on a local farm. By 1910 he had met and married Amy Davis from Northchurch, a daughter of Frederick and Mary Davis and the sister of Robert Davis. They subsequently moved into a cottage on Northchurch High Street, close to Amy's widowed mother and siblings who lived in New Road. At the end of 1910 Amy gave birth to her first child, with a second following in 1912.

Although Percy's service record has not survived, it appears that he enlisted soon after the start of the war, joining 14th Battalion, Northumberland Fusiliers. This battalion, formed in September 1914, was one of the first to be stationed in the Berkhamsted, Northchurch and Tring areas before moving to Halton Camp, which may have influenced Percy's decision to join it.

Landing in France on 9th September 1915, the Fusiliers first saw action during the Battle of Loos, where the Germans used gas shells for the first time, inflicting severe casualties on some members of the battalion. Percy, however, does not appear to have been injured. Later in the war, his battalion saw action during the Somme Offensive, the Battle of Arras, the Third Battle of Ypres and the Battle of Cambrai and, after the failure of the German Spring Offensive, the final push north-eastwards that slowly drove the Germans out of France and into Belgium.

By May 1919, the Fusiliers had been demobilised and Percy was back home with his wife and family who were now living in a cottage in New Road. That autumn Amy gave birth to a third child, whom they named Charles Percival[2].

In 1920, Percy moved with his family to a cottage in Little Heath, having obtained work as a cowman on a nearby farm. He remained there for the next few years, during which time Amy gave birth to three more children. By 1939, Percy and his family had moved to The Lodge at Hambleton, near Guildford, where he continued to work as a cowman. He died in 1970, aged 81.

Sydney William Beasley (1891 – 1958)
Private 241271, 2nd Battalion, East Kent Regiment
Vincent Beasley MM (1898 – 1962)
Corporal 46569, Dorsetshire Regiment

The Beasley family arrived in Dudswell around 1900 from Hagbourne, near Didcot, Berkshire. The head of the family, Vincent Beasley (snr), was a painter, and it was probably work that brought him, his wife Elizabeth, together with six of their seven children, to the area. Initially working as a painter on a farm, Vincent later became a house painter in the area. By 1911, the family were living in a cottage in New Road, Northchurch with only sons Sydney, Richard, Vincent (jnr) and John, still at home. Sydney was working on a local farm, Richard was a butcher, and the two younger brothers were still at school.

At the outbreak of war, both Richard and Sydney volunteered to join the Army. Richard joined the Bedfordshire Regiment, whilst Sydney joined 1/5th (Weald of Kent) Battalion, East Kent Regiment. Richard Beasley later went on to win a DSO and become a Lance Corporal, but was tragically killed in October 1917 during the Third Battle of Ypres[3].

Sydney Beasley's battalion was formed in Ashford in August 1914 as part of the Kent Brigade of the Home Counties Division. In October that year they left for India and were to remain there on garrison duty until November 1915, when they transferred to Mesopotamia, landing at Basra on 6th December. On their arrival, the battalion joined 35th Indian Brigade of the 7th (Meerut) Division, which had recently arrived from the Western Front with orders to proceed inland and relieve the siege of the town of Kut-al-Amara.

British troops had first landed in Mesopotamia in late 1914 to protect the Anglo-Persian oilfields from Turkish attack. With the oilfields secured,

---

[2] Charles Percival Baker was killed in the fighting in Italy during 1944 whilst serving with 8th Battalion, Manchester Regiment.

[3] Richard Beasley's story is told in *For Them's Sake*

the British troops, under Lieutenant General Sir John Nixon of the Indian Army, advanced inland with the ambitious aim of capturing Bagdad. The only viable route north, however, was via the Tigris and Euphrates rivers. As the troops advanced north, it soon became apparent that a highly organised supply line was required to keep them fed and watered and also provide for the evacuation of any sick or wounded soldiers. By the time the troops reached Kut-al-Amara, the supply line had stretched to almost 400 miles and was beginning to break down in places. Despite this, General Nixon decided to continue the advance north as Bagdad was only 120 miles away. On 22nd November 1915, the British attacked the Turkish defences at Ctesiphon, some 22 miles south of Bagdad, but the attack was badly planned and, despite capturing part of the Turkish front line, the British troops could not break through the Turkish second line of defence. A major German-led Turkish counterattack forced the British troops to retreat south towards Kut, and by the time they arrived there over half of Nixon's troops had become casualties. Four days after the British arrived at Kut, 12,000 Turkish troops surrounded the town and started a siege. On Christmas Eve 1915, the Turks made their only concerted effort to capture Kut, after which they left just enough troops to contain the garrison and sent the rest down the Tigris river to create a series of defensive positions to block the arrival of fresh troops sent to break the siege.

Conditions during the British relief force's advance north up the Tigris river was arduous and painful. Not only did the troops have to contend with the threat of Turkish attacks, but the hot climate, combined with the marshy ground in the area, made movement difficult and slow. Added to this was the problem of disease, as cholera was rife in the area. With the 7th (Meerut) Division unable to break through the Turkish lines, the besieged garrison at Kut eventually surrendered on 29th April 1916 with some 13,000 British troops going into captivity. Of these, about a third were later to die of disease and malnutrition.

In 1917, Sydney's battalion advanced north once again in an offensive that would eventually lead to the capture of Bagdad. That October Sydney was injured during a training exercise and was hospitalised. He appears to have made a full recovery, however, and after convalescing he was transferred to 2nd Battalion, East Kent Regiment in Salonika.

By the time Sydney arrived, British and French troops had been there for nearly two years, fighting a combination of the Bulgarian army, the extreme weather conditions and malaria, and to many serving there, it seemed to have become the forgotten front. During his time at Salonika Sydney was fortunate not to have become a victim to one of these three threats and he remained there until the war ended.

Sydney was demobilised in 1919 and returned to Northchurch, resuming his job as a farm worker. In the late autumn of 1919, he married Kate Welling, the widow of Walter Welling from Northchurch, who had been killed in September 1916 during the Somme Offensive[4]. Kate Welling had only been married to Walter for nine months and had subsequently given birth to his daughter. Having gained a daughter by marriage, Sidney was to become a father in his own right during the summer of 1920, with a further child being born in 1922. Initially, the family lived in New Road, Northchurch, but later moved to Wigginton. Sydney Beasley died in November 1958, aged 67.

Vincent Beasley, the youngest of the Beasley brothers to serve in the war, was born in May 1898 and spent most of his childhood in Northchurch. Unfortunately, Vincent's service record has not survived, so what he did in the four years between leaving school and being conscripted into the army in 1916 is currently not known. After his conscription Vincent was posted to 1st Battalion, Bedfordshire Regiment, but how long he remained with them is unclear, as sometime in 1917, now a Corporal, he was transferred to 12th Middlesex Battalion, 54th Brigade. That year, Vincent's new battalion moved from the Somme sector to Flanders where they took part in the Third Battle of Ypres, during which he learnt how to use a Lewis machine gun. Following an army reorganisation in February 1918 due to the shortage of new conscripts, 54th Brigade lost one of its four battalions and Vincent was transferred to 2/2nd Royal Fusiliers (City of London Regiment). Within weeks he and his new comrades experienced the full force of the enemy during the German Spring Offensive.

Early in the morning of 21st March, in an attempt to defeat the British and French armies before troops from the United States arrived in France, the Germans launched the first of a series of major offensives. Using new co-ordinated tactics which employed specially-trained stormtroopers, aircraft and, to a limited extent, tanks, the ferocity of the offensive took the British by surprise, although an attack had been anticipated for weeks and they were forced to retreat hurriedly, losing all the territory that had been recaptured in the Somme sector during the previous two years. Thousands of men were taken prisoner, and those who remained were forced to merge into composite battalions to make them effective fighting units. Vincent's battalion suffered badly and he found himself in a composite Fusilier battalion made up of men from 2/2nd, 2/4th and 3rd London Battalions, including the recently-arrived conscript, Charlie Mashford, from Gossoms End[5], who was the same age as him.

On 24th April, Vincent's battalion were holding the line at Hangard Wood, east of the strategic town of Villers-Bretonneaux. Here, early in the morning, the Germans launched a massive three-hour artillery barrage followed by an attack by stormtroopers supported by five A7V tanks.

---

[4] Walter Welling's story is told in *For Them's Sake*
[5] Charlie Mashford's story is told in *For Them's Sake*

British tanks drove off the German vehicles, but as the mist rose, Vincent's battalion saw that they were effectively surrounded on three sides, giving them the only option of retreating across sloping open ground in full view of the enemy. Realising there was no alternative, Vincent, carrying his heavy Lewis gun and equipment, made a dash for it, along with some of his comrades, and managed to escape. Writing to his mother in Northchurch a month later, Vincent's Platoon leader, who, coincidentally, came from Boxmoor, gave her the news that Vincent had been awarded the Military Medal for his action that day. Sadly, fellow Northchurchman, Charlie Mashford, did not survive the attack. After the German offensives had petered out, the British army underwent a significant reorganisation and Vincent was transferred to the Dorsetshire Regiment and following the end of the war, he spent a short period in the Labour Corps.

Demobilised in December 1919, Vincent returned home to New Road, but did not stay there long, moving to Hammersmith, West London. On 2nd September 1923, he married Elizabeth Sarah Chandler, the widow of Jim Chandler who had died of influenza in Germany whilst serving as a military policeman in the Army of the Rhine four years earlier[6]. In the process, Vincent became the second Beasley brother to marry a war widow.

In 1925, Vincent and Elizabeth were living in Watford before moving back to Berkhamsted a few years later. By 1939, the couple had moved to Hemel Hempstead, where Vincent worked as an electrical engineering inspector. Vincent Beasley died in 1962, aged 63.

Thomas Belshaw (1896 - 1954)
Private 27203, 1st Battalion, Dublin Fusiliers

The Belshaws were a Presbyterian family from Dublin who moved to Carlow, County Carlow, some 52 miles south of the city, in the mid 1890s. Thomas Belshaw was the third son of John Belshaw and his wife, Grace, and was born in Carlow in the spring of 1896. Two years later, soon after the birth of John and Grace's last child, Gilbert, John Belshaw died, leaving his widow to bring up their six young children as best she could. All four brothers later became members of the Carlow Boys Brigade. Like his older brothers, John and Robert before him, Thomas became a bicycle mechanic.

The family were still living in Carlow when war broke out in 1914. Thomas was the first of the brothers to enlist, volunteering to join the Royal Fusiliers with his medical examination taking place at Naas, the county town of Kildare. This described him as being 5ft 4¼ins tall, weighing 110lbs, with a fresh complexion, grey eyes and brown hair. No doubt because of his occupation, within three months of volunteering, Thomas

---

[6] Jim Chandler's story is told in *For Them's Sake*

had been transferred to 16th Division Army Cyclists Corps at Mallow, County Cork.

Each infantry division had one cyclist corps, their primary role being that of reconnaissance and ferrying messages between units, although they could also be used as fighting infantry as and when required. Thomas was to remain in Ireland for a further eight months before being sent to Pirbright, Surrey, in preparation for his unit's departure for France.

He left Southampton bound for Le Havre on 18th December 1915. By then the defensive trench system, which effectively stretched between the English Channel and the Swiss border, was nearly a year old and meant that the use of army cyclists in their normal role would not be very effective near the front line. Thomas and his mates therefore settled down to a quiet and mundane life of trench and barbed wire maintenance in the area near Béthune.

Being unable to fulfil their original function, Thomas's unit was eventually disbanded and the men were transferred as infantry into 8th (Service) Battalion, Royal Dublin Fusiliers and first saw action was during the latter stages of the Somme Offensive in 1916. A series of later reorganisations within the battalions resulted in Thomas being transferred to the Fusilier's 2nd Battalion in October 1917 during the Third Battle of Ypres. He was still serving with them when the Germans launched their Spring Offensive in March 1918. Facing overwhelming forces and incurring considerable casualties, Thomas and his surviving comrades were forced to retreat westwards until the German offensive lost impetus. His battalion later merged with the survivors of the Fusilier's 1st Battalion to form a cadre unit[7] and was removed from the front line shortly afterwards. With the unit rebuilt following the arrival of newly-trained conscripts and men transferred from other battalions, Thomas was again in action during advance north-eastwards during the summer and autumn of 1918, ending the war close to Courtrai in Belgium.

He remained at an army camp in Calais until March 1919 awaiting demobilisation. By now his mother had moved into a cottage in New Road, Northchurch, and this is where Thomas returned. It is not known how he initially spent his time in Northchurch, but by 1922 he had started working for the Post Office. In 1925, he and his mother were living in a cottage in Northchurch High Street. He later moved to the Harrow area, becoming a groundsman and was married in 1935. Thomas Belshaw died in the 1954 aged 57.

---

[7] A basic fighting unit formed from surviving members of other units

Herbert Samuel Bright (1880 – 1965)
Private 33106, 15th Battalion, Lancashire Fusiliers

At the start of the war Herbert Bright was working as a coachman for wealthy civil servant Walter Samuel Cohen at his recently-built home, Amersfort, in the eastern part of Northchurch Parish. Born on St Valentine's Day 1880 in Witham, Essex, Herbert was the son of Samuel Bright, a farm labourer and later farm bailiff, and his wife Phoebe, and the eldest of five children. By the age of eleven he was working at Troys Farm, Felstead, Essex, where his father had become bailiff. Enjoying working with horses, Herbert decided to become a groom and by 1901, aged 21, he had found work at Holmewood House, Huntingdonshire.

Holmewood House, was a large red-brick 'Tudoresque' mansion, situated in some 680 acres of parkland, and had 20 tenanted farms. It had recently been sold by Lord de Ramsey to John Ashton Fielden, a rather eccentric man with a passion for country sports. The estate employed around 100 people, among them Edward Cheek who, like Herbert, was born in Witham, so it is likely that it is through this connection that Herbert came to work there. Working alongside Edward Cheek, as caretaker, was his wife Ella, and sister-in-law, Janet Waltham, both of whom came from the nearby village of Barnack. Between them, they were responsible for running the house and stabling at Holmewood House. Three years later, on 11th July 1904, Herbert and Janet Waltham were married at St John the Baptist, Barnack, but by then, Herbert had found a new employer and was living in the village of Broughton, Northamptonshire, presumably working as groom at a large house in the area.

Herbert and Janet did not stay in Broughton for long, however, as in 1907 Janet gave birth to a son in the village of Milton, Berkshire. Four years later, he had changed employers again and was now working as a groom, and later coachman, for Walter Cohen at Fairhill on Berkhamsted Common, his family living in the accommodation adjacent to the stables there. About that time and just down the road, work had started on the building of Amersfort.

With the coming of war, Walter Cohen obtained a Commission with the 1/2nd Hertfordshire Yeomanry and Herbert, now 34 years old, decided to join 2/1st Hertfordshire Yeomanry, a home defence force formed in September 1914, so that he could continue working with horses. A year later the unit was attached to 69th (2nd East Anglian) Division based at Huntingdon, not far from where Herbert had met his wife. In April 1916, the Yeomanry moved again, this time to the Manningtree area of Essex, close to where Herbert grew up. He was not there for long, as within weeks the Yeomanry had moved again to Kent, firstly to West Malling near Tonbridge, and then to Sevenoaks. September 1917 saw the Yeomanry lose its horses, which were replaced by bicycles, the unit joining 13th Cyclist

Brigade, part of the Cyclist Division. The following month, the unit was transferred again, this time to 67th Division which was about to be sent to Murmansk in support of the Imperial Russian Army. The October Revolution of 1917 and the subsequent surrender of the Russian army, however, led to the cancellation of this move.

The high British casualty rate caused by the German Spring Offensive in March 1918 meant that all fit men, including Herbert, who were not serving in the front line were liable to be compulsorily transferred to fighting units and sent to the Western Front. As a result, Herbert became Private 33106, 15th Battalion, Lancashire Fusiliers, otherwise known as 1st Salford Pals. What he may not have known at the time of his transfer was that his wife was pregnant with their second child.

Herbert's new unit had been formed in Salford in September 1914 as one of the original 'Pals Battalions'. They moved to France in November 1915 and went into action for the first time at Thiepval Ridge on the opening day of the Somme Offensive. Within minutes, German machine gun and artillery fire had effectively annihilated the unit and by 1918 very few of the original 'Pals' remained. In the closing months of the war when Herbert was with them, 15th Battalion took part in the advance that recaptured all the territory the German army had taken during the Spring Offensive and on 1st November 1918, the battalion launched its last major attack of the war at Lappegarbes, close to the town of Landrecies, south-west of Mons.

Herbert was demobilised at the start of 1919 and returned to his job as coachman, and later chauffeur, at Amersfort and remained in the employment of the Cohen family for many years. He died in 1965, aged 85.

Walter Tyrwhitt Bromfield (1879 – 1953)
Lieutenant-Colonel, Leicestershire Regiment

Walter Tyrwhitt Bromfield was born in Chester in May 1879 into a family with a strong military tradition. His father, Francis William Bromfield, served with the Cheshire Regiment and later rose to the rank of Colonel. Walter's mother, Minnie Charlotte Eliza Tyrwhitt, whom his father met in India, was herself the daughter of a military officer.

Walter was educated at Bath College for Boys and in March 1898, following the family tradition, he obtained a Commission with 3rd Militia Battalion, The Loyal North Lancashire Regiment. The following year he was transferred to 2nd Battalion, Northumberland Fusiliers and embarked with them on board the SS *Kildonan Castle* for South Africa to fight in the Boer War. Walter returned from South Africa in July 1901, but went back in March the following year, two months before the Boers finally surrendered, to take command of a Company.

Promoted to Captain in 1906, Walter transferred to 2nd Battalion, Leicestershire Regiment, commonly known as 'The Tigers', which was then serving in India. It was here that he met Ethel Elizabeth Stubbs and they were married in Bangalore in November 1908. Two years later, Walter and his now-pregnant wife returned to England where he was assigned to the Leicestershire Regiment's Depot at Glen Parva barracks, just south of Leicester. The family set up home at Port Hill in the nearby village of Blaby. In 1912, Walter was appointed Adjutant of the Leicestershire's 1/5th Battalion.

Walter was still serving at Glen Parva barracks when war broke out in 1914. His battalion's war preparations took place in the Luton and Bishop's Stortford areas before departing for France in February 1915. After landing at Le Havre the battalion spent the first few months in the Armentières sector. Known as The Nursery, this area of France was frequently used by the army to familiarise newly-arrived battalions with the conditions of trench warfare. When out of the front line Walter, as the battalion's Adjutant, was responsible for regular inspections of the troops. In September 1915, he was promoted to Major and seconded to the Royal Naval Division.

The battalions of the Royal Naval Division, named after famous British naval heroes like Drake, Nelson, Hawke, Collingwood, Benbow, Hood, Howe and Anson, had been sent to the Dardanelles at the start of the Gallipoli campaign. By the September of 1915, however, it had become evident to the allies that the attempt to capture the Gallipoli peninsula and the Dardanelle Straights had failed and the main priority was now to keep the Turkish forces tied down and not moved to other fronts in the Ottoman Empire. Given command of one of the Royal Naval Division battalions, Walter remained on the Gallipoli peninsula until the allied forces were evacuated under great secrecy at the end of the year.

Walter returned to England in 1916 and he and his family moved to Denham in Dudswell. He now had the new role of setting up an Officer Cadet Battalion in Berkhamsted. This was one of twenty-seven training centres that would eventually be established in England following the high attrition rate suffered by subalterns in the field. Up until then there had been no standard approach to the selection and training of new officers and the Officer Cadet battalions were seen as the solution to resolve this problem. Coming mainly from the ranks, the officer candidates now had to be approved by their Commanding Officer and would retain their existing rank throughout their training in case they failed the course. The Berkhamsted Officer Cadet Battalion courses took place at Netherfield, a large house off Gravel Path, each course lasting for four weeks, and concentrated primarily on leadership skills and self-confidence. Strategic and technical matters were considered of less importance.

In September 1917, Walter became a brevet Lieutenant-Colonel and was seconded as Commanding Officer of 1/7th Manchester Regiment, which at the time was fighting in France. Arriving there at the end of the year, Walter assumed command of the battalion, replacing the previous commanding officer who had been taken ill. Returning to France in March 1918 following a short period of home leave, Walter became ill with influenza and was hospitalised. Fortunately, this turned out to be a mild form of influenza, not the deadlier type that would take hold later in the year.

It is not clear what role Walter took on after being discharged from hospital in the spring of 1918, for in April that year he was replaced as Commanding Officer of 1/7th Manchester Regiment and it was not until March 1919 that Walter rejoined the Leicestershire Regiment, becoming the Second in Command of their 2nd Battalion.

In July 1919, 2nd Battalion was sent to India and the following year, Walter became the battalion's Commanding Officer. Two years later the battalion was sent to Khartoum following unrest in the Sudan and took part in the suppression of a mutiny by Sudanese troops.

The battalion returned to England in 1925 with Walter remaining as its Commanding Officer whilst they were based in Colchester, and later in Germany as part of the occupation troops. He retired from the army in February 1930 and moved to a house in the small village of Gipping in Suffolk. Lieutenant-Colonel Walter Tyrwhitt Bromfield died in 1952, aged 73.

Albert Henry Bunker (1895 – 1966)
Private 23231, 3rd Battalion, Coldstream Guards

Albert Bunker was born in the hamlet of Winkwell, the easternmost part of Northchurch Parish, in December 1895, and was the fifth of ten children of William Bunker, a roadman working for the local council, and his wife, Frances. After leaving school, Albert started work at the brush making factory of GB Kent & Sons in Apsley, where his two older sisters worked.

It is unclear how long Albert spent there, however, as by the autumn of 1914 he was employed as a moulder at an ironworks working on a War Office contract. Despite this, on 16th November 1914, 18-year-old Albert decided to enlist at Kensington for a four-year-term with the 13th London Regiment. Passing his medical examination, Albert was assigned to the regiment's 2nd Reserve Battalion.

In November 1915, Albert was suddenly demobilised. The rush of men enlisting in the early months of the war resulted in a severe manpower shortage in the munitions industry which caused a severe impact on the production of artillery shells. Albert's civilian occupation as a moulder put him in a classification which was now exempt from frontline service and he returned to his former employer. A proviso of Albert's demobilisation was that, should his services be required in the future, he would be recalled to army service.

In June 1917, Albert married Ethel Lilian Welling, the 18-year-old daughter of a local gardener, at St John's, Bourne End, and the newly-weds moved into a cottage in Bourne End Lane. Albert continued as a moulder until the end of March 1918 when the aftermath of the German Spring Offensive resulted in many men in protected occupations being recalled to army service.

Albert was posted to 5th Reserve Battalion, Coldstream Guards at Windsor and became an unpaid Lance Corporal two months later and was to spend another three months in England before being sent to France. On 24th September, reverting to the rank of Private, Albert left Folkestone and after disembarking at Boulogne was sent to the nearby Guard's base depot before being posted to 3rd Battalion Coldstream Guards.

Joining his new unit in early October, Albert immediately went into action during the Battle of the Selle which saw the German army driven back from their rapidly constructed defensive line on the river Selle near Cambrai. A week before the signing of the Armistice, he was in action again at the decisive battle of the Sambre.

Albert was demobilised for a second time in April 1919 and returned home. He and Ethel would later raise three sons together. In 1939, the family were still living in Bourne End Lane, with Albert working as a foreman in a local sawmill. He died in 1966, aged 70.

Fred Carter (1894 – 1969)
Private 12210, 7th Battalion, Norfolk Regiment

Fred Carter, the third son of George Carter, a worker on a local watercress farm and his wife, Ellen, was born in Northchurch in November 1894. He grew up in a cramped cottage in New Road with his four brothers and four sisters and later followed his two elder brothers in becoming a domestic gardener. By 1911 the family had moved to a slightly larger cottage on Northchurch High Street. On 20th August 1914, nineteen-year-old Fred attested at Berkhamsted and was sent to Bedford for his medical examination where, standing 5ft 9ins tall, weighing 186lbs and with grey eyes and brown hair, he was declared fit by the medical officer. Expressing a wish to join the Norfolk Regiment, Fred travelled to Norwich where, two days later, he joined the newly-formed Norfolk's 7th Battalion.

Fred's army training took place at the large Shorncliffe Camp near Cheriton, Kent. On 1st October, he was appointed one of the battalion's drummers, and proudly wore a drummer's badge on his sleeve. Each infantry battalion at that time included sixteen drummers, four to a company, together with a sergeant drummer, and were paid an extra one penny a day. Drummers also played the bugle and were responsible for the 'sounding' of regimental calls giving instructions to the battalion's soldiers on the battlefield. In times of war, drummers were also trained to act as temporary stretcher bearers or orderlies.

Fred and his battalion left Folkestone in May 1915 on board the SS *Invicta* bound for Boulogne and first saw action in the trenches near Loos at the end of September. Sent south to the Somme sector the following year, the battalion was held in reserve during the first two days of the Somme Offensive and thus avoided the bloodbath that many other units experienced. The battalion attacked the German lines the following morning with mixed success, having incurred numerous casualties from incoming artillery shells even before their own attack had started. A second attack on 7th July was more successful, with the battalion capturing two lines of enemy trenches. Christmas 1916 saw Fred and his mates given two pairs of socks purchased from funds raised by friends of the battalion's officers back home.

Private Fred Carter
Courtesy of Roger Emery

Most of 1917 was spent back in northern France with the battalion taking part in the various operations around Arras and later during the Battle of Cambrai, suffering badly during the German counter attack following the stalling of the British advance. Fred was fortunate not to become a casualty, and he and the remnants of his unit spent Christmas 1917 recovering and regrouping well behind the lines.

The Norfolks were in northern France at the start of the German Spring Offensive and were immediately ordered to move south to help hold the line. On several occasions they were forced to retreat as the German troops continued to press forward, and at one point several the battalion's officers were captured when one of their outposts was cut off.

On 8th August 1918, Fred and his fellow Norfolks took part in the Battle of Amiens, which was the opening battle of the allied offensive that would eventually lead to the signing of the Armistice. The co-ordination of aircraft, artillery, tanks and infantry for the first time meant that by the end of the day 29,144 Germans had become prisoners of war, 338 guns had been captured and 116 towns and villages had been liberated. The German chief-of-staff, General Erich von Ludendorff, called 8th August 1918 *"the blackest day of the German army".* The allied offensive continued with Fred and the Norfolks reaching the Scheldt Canal on 27th October. Shortly afterwards, they were withdrawn and were in billets when the Armistice was signed.

Fred was demobilised at the end of March 1919 and returned home. In the spring of 1925 he married May Roff, a nursemaid, whose family lived in New Road, Northchurch. They moved into a cottage in Northchurch High Street. By 1939, they were living at Threeways in Dudswell with Fred working as a wheelwright. By then, a new war was looming, and he had become an Air Raid Precaution (ARP) Warden in Berkhamsted, supervising the recently introduced blackout. Fred Carter died in 1969, aged 74.

John Carvell (1890 – 1935)
Private 9625, 8th Battalion, King's Own Yorkshire Light Infantry

John Carvel was the only son of Edwin Carvell, a farm labourer and his wife, Ellen and was born in New Road, Northchurch, during the summer of 1890. The Carvel family later moved to a cottage in Orchard End where John's mother died in 1906 when he was just fifteen, leaving his elder sister, Ruth, to bring up his younger sisters.

Two years after Ellen's death, Edwin Carvell married Esther Holland, a widow with three children. Born Esther Bignell in 1874, John's new stepmother had married James Holland in 1892, and become a widow eleven years later. Esther and her children moved into Edwin Carvell's four-roomed cottage in Orchard End and around this time eighteen-year-old John decided to leave home and join the army.

Instead of one of the local regiments, John decided to join the King's Own Yorkshire Light Infantry and remained in England until his nineteenth birthday when he could serve overseas. Sailing to the British colony of Hong Kong at the end of 1909, John joined the regiment's 1st Battalion on garrison duty there. He was to spend the next three years in Hong Kong before the battalion sailed for Singapore and was still on garrison duty there in August 1914.

Having been recalled to England when war broke out, John and his battalion left Southampton onboard SS *Benares* bound for Le Havre on 15th January 1915. They headed north-eastwards by train towards the Ypres salient and entered the front line. Within days, John was wounded and admitted to No3 Casualty Clearing Station at Poperinghe. The station's medical log records John as suffering from a gunshot wound to his right arm, although most wounds at that time were simply recorded as 'gunshot wounds', no matter whether it was a bullet or a piece of shrapnel that caused the wound.

John had not rejoined his battalion by the time his battalion left for Salonika some five months later, so his wound was probably quite serious.

Unfortunately, as his service record has not survived, no clear information on his subsequent service with King's Own Yorkshire Light Infantry is available. According to his medal card however, John served in the regiment's 2nd, 9th and 8th battalions which all served on the Western Front until November 1917 when 8th Battalion was sent to Italy. It remained there until the surrender of Austria-Hungary the following year.

John was demobilised in April 1919 and returned to his father's home in Orchard End. Two years later, the family moved to one of the newly-built council houses close to the *Old Grey Mare* public house on the road to Tring. By then, John had started work delivering coal around Berkhamsted and Northchurch.

The spring of 1928 saw John marrying Violet Mary Delderfield, the widow of William Delderfield who had died four years earlier, aged just 26. John and Violet settled in Eddy Street, Gossoms End and the following year John became a father. Sadly, John was to die ten years later, aged just 45.

Ernest Chandler (1887 – 1950)
Private 52194, 9th Battalion, Cheshire Regiment

Ernest Chandler was born in Farnham, Surrey, in December 1887 and was one of George and Fanny Chandler's eleven children. George Chandler, a domestic gardener, regularly moved his family around Hampshire and Surrey looking for work, but around the turn of the century he finally settled in Northchurch. A few years after arriving in the Northchurch area, Ernest met Hilda Flitney, a laundress from Wilstone, and in 1908 they were married in Marylebone, London, where Ernest was working as a gardener. Their first son was born the following year, with another arriving in 1913.

With a young family to support, Ernest did not volunteer at the start of the war, but with the possibility of conscription looming, he decided to enlist in August 1915. After completing his initial training, Ernest was posted to the West Yorkshire Regiment.

Instead of immediately being sent to the front upon his arrival in France in 1916, the draft of new recruits, which included Ernest, was kept at an infantry base depot near the French coast. This decision probably saved their lives, as the West Yorkshire Regiment incurred severe casualties during the opening days of the Somme Offensive.

As a result, Ernest and his comrades were transferred to 9th Battalion, Cheshire Regiment, and it is likely that he saw action with them in the latter part of the Somme Offensive. The following year, 9th Cheshires took part in the Battle of Messines and the Third Battle of Ypres. In 1918, Ernest was wounded during the German Spring Offensive and spent some time recovering in hospital. His wounds healed, he returned to his battalion and was with them as they advanced north-eastwards in the closing weeks of the war. At the time of the Armistice, Ernest and his battalion were in billets near Bavay, just south of Mons.

Ernest was demobilised in April 1919 and returned home to Northchurch. He later became a market gardener and moved to Watford. He died in 1950, aged 62.

George Arthur Cooling (1891 – 1958)
Private 32200, 1st (Provisional) Battalion, Grenadier Guards

George Cooling, the Northchurch village policeman in 1915, was born in November 1891 in Fulbeck, Lincolnshire, where his father, Arthur, worked in an ironstone quarry. After leaving school, George decided not to follow his father and elder brother as ironstone miners and instead became a gardener at the local workhouse. After several other gardening jobs in Fulbeck, George moved south to Hertfordshire in the autumn of 1913 finding work as a gardener at Pendley Manor near Tring. Ten months later however, George travelled to Hatfield and applied to become a police constable with the Hertfordshire Constabulary, his medical record from this time showing him as standing 5ft 8½ins tall with a fair complexion, blue eyes and fair hair. Despite passing the medical examination, he was advised that there were no current vacancies in the Hertfordshire Constabulary and not to give up his job at Pendley Manor until a suitable vacancy arose.

In early October 1914, he was told to report to the Police headquarters at Hertford to start his probationer training on a weekly salary of £1 4s 6d. Completing his training in January 1915, PC 125 George Arthur Cooling, joined 'A' Division based at Hoddesdon. The following August, George wrote to the Superintendent of 'A' Division requesting permission to marry. George had met his intended bride, Annie Rawding, before he moved to Hertfordshire and she was currently working as a Lady's Maid in Caterham, Surrey. Having secured the necessary references as to the suitability of marrying a serving policeman, permission was granted and the marriage took place at the Parish Church in Leadenham, Lincolnshire on 18th October 1915.

Eleven days before his wedding, George was informed that he was being transferred from 'A' Division at Hoddesdon to 'D' Division at Northchurch to become the village policeman, replacing PC William Hunt, who had resigned from the Hertfordshire Constabulary in 1914 to join the Royal Engineers. Following their wedding, George and Annie set up home in the police cottage in New Road.

Serving as the village policeman, George was responsible for all general law and order matters as well as enforcing the blackouts, air raid warnings and licensing laws. Controlling blackouts was particularly important in the local area as German Zeppelin airships had on occasions passed directly over Northchurch during the night as they followed the railway line south to London.

Police Constables were not exempt from military service, and in December 1915 George decided to attest under the Derby Scheme. Mobilised four months later, he resigned from the police force and after completing his army training, he was assigned to 1st (Provisional) Battalion, Grenadier Guards, a newly established battalion based at the Senior Officers School at Aldershot. George was never sent abroad to fight, and remained at Aldershot until the war ended.

Following his transfer to the army reserve in January 1919, George rejoined the Hertfordshire Constabulary and returned to his role as the Northchurch policeman, earning £2 7s per week. By now he was a father, his wife having given birth to their son, Raymond, a few months earlier. Annie gave birth to a second son in 1923. In January 1924, George was transferred to 'E' Division at Datchworth and later promoted to Acting Police Sergeant following a transfer to Hitchin police station. Unfortunately, a disciplinary offence three months later resulted in George reverting to the rank of Police Constable.

George continued to be based at Hitchin police station and in 1939, having completed 25 years in the police force, applied for retirement. Although his request was initially approved, the outbreak of the Second World War delayed his actual retirement until June 1944.

George and Annie's elder son, Raymond, had joined the Royal Artillery at the outbreak of the Second World War and was captured by the Japanese Army whilst serving in Singapore in 1942. Held in a PoW camp in French Indo-China, (now Vietnam), Raymond Cooling was tragically killed during an air attack in April 1945.

George Cooling died in Wood Green, London in 1958, aged 67.

Alfred John Dancer (1899 – 1959)
Private G/68223, 8th Battalion, Queens, Royal West Surrey Regiment

Alfred Dancer was the fifth child of Thomas Dancer, a watercress worker, and his wife, Martha, and was born in the summer of 1899 in the family home in Bourne End Lane. Alfred was conscripted into the army in 1917 and posted to 8th Battalion, The Queens, Royal Surrey Regiment, but remained in England until the summer of 1918 and was probably part of a draft of 50 men that joined the battalion in France on 17th August.

The German army was now being slowly pushed back across France, having failed to make the hoped-for breakthrough before the arrival of thousands of American troops. Alfred's battalion had distinguished itself holding the line during the German Spring Offensives and was now in the forefront of the allied advance. By the time the Armistice was signed the battalion was just south of Mons.

The demobilisation of 8th Battalion troops happened relatively quickly, with the battalion ceasing to exist at the end of February 1919. Alfred was not immediately demobilised however; he had been appointed Lance Corporal and transferred to the Foot Branch of the Corps of Military Police. Known to the troops as the 'Redcaps' after the red-topped peaked caps they wore, the military police now had the unenviable task of keeping thousands of impatient British soldiers under control in the numerous army camps on the French coast whilst they awaited their demobilisation and return to civilian life.

Alfred returned home to Bourne End Lane in 1920. Four years later, he married Elsie Scott from Kings Langley and they would later have two children together. In 1939, Alfred and his family were living in Hemel Hempstead, where he worked as a bricklayer. Alfred died in Hemel Hempstead in 1959, aged 59.

Henry John Davis (1890 – 1964)
Private 51057, Gloucestershire Regiment

Henry Davis, the third of Thomas and Sarah Ann Davis's eleven children, was born in April 1890 in Eddy Street, Gossoms End, a few yards from the East & Son timberyard where Henry's father worked as a sawyer. After leaving school Henry started working for the Berkhamsted Co-operative Society as a coal deliveryman.

In the summer of 1915, Henry married Edith Coates, who worked as a cook in St Albans. The following year, with conscription extended to married men, Henry received his call-up papers and, despite an appeal to the Berkhamsted Military Tribunal by his employers, he was given no choice but to report to the local recruiting office.

Details of Henry's subsequent military service are somewhat unclear as his service record has not survived; the 1918 Northchurch Absent Voters List shows him serving with 3rd (Reserve) Battalion, Bedfordshire Regiment in England, whilst the medal roll produced in 1920 by the Gloucestershire Regiment, shows that he had previously served in France with both the Bedford's 6th and 7th battalions. The Bedford's 6th Battalion took on several drafts of men in February 1918 just prior to the anticipated German offensive and Henry was probably in one of them. Following the failure of the offensive, it is likely that Henry was transferred to the Bedford's 7th Battalion, which was disbanded soon afterwards following a major reorganisation of the army. Most of the battalion's troops then transferred to the Bedford's 2nd Battalion, while the remainder were employed training newly-arrived American troops. They, in turn, later joined 2nd Battalion when the training programme ended. It is therefore unclear when and why Henry was transferred to the Gloucestershire Regiment around this time.

Following his demobilisation towards the end of 1919, Henry returned to Northchurch and his old job as a coal deliveryman for the Berkhamsted Co-op. In 1920 he and Edith were living in a cottage in New Road, Northchurch, where, over the next six years, Edith would give birth to three children. By 1939 Henry and his family had moved to a larger house in Granville Road, Northchurch and he was still working for the Co-op. He died in the late winter of 1964, aged 73.

Ernest Frederick Dell (1899 – 1934)
Private 25180, 1st Provisional Battalion, Coldstream Guards

Ernest Dell, like Alfred Dancer, was one of the last Northchurch men to be sent abroad to fight during the war. One of five children, he was born in the family home in Northchurch High Street in the spring of 1899 and was the son of Johnson Dell, a general labourer, and his wife Louisa.

Being too young to volunteer for service when war broke out in 1914, it was Ernest's thirty-seven-year-old father, Johnson, who decided to enlist, joining the Bedfordshire Regiment in January 1915. Johnson remained on home duties in England until May 1916 when he was declared no longer physically fit for service and was consequently discharged from the army.

Two years later, aged 18, Ernest received his conscription papers and was posted to the recently formed 1st Provisional Battalion, Coldstream Guards at the Senior Officers School at Aldershot where the former Northchurch village policeman, George Cooling, was also serving. Several men from 1st Provisional Battalion were later sent to France at the start of November 1918, and, as Ernest was subsequently awarded both the British War and Victory medals, he must have been one of them. The Coldstream Guards formed part of the Guards Division, and by the time the war ended they were stationed around Maubeuge, due south of Mons.

In December 1918, the Guards were ordered to cross the Rhine into Germany to become part of the British Army of Occupation. Ernest's unit was only to remain in Germany for a short period, however, and returned to England in February 1919.

During the war, Ernest's parents had taken over the running of the Canal Stores at Dudswell, but they were not to stay there for long. In 1921, they moved into a cottage at Hill Farm, just the north of Northchurch village and later to a cottage at the nearby Ashridge woodyard before settling at Keepers Cottage on Northchurch Common.

Around 1928, it appears that Ernest moved to Thornhill Farm at Malmesbury, Wiltshire, where he had obtained work. Unfortunately, Ernest's health soon began to decline and by 1930 he had returned to his parents who were now living in Potten End. Treated at the Ware Park Sanatorium in Hertford, he died at his parent's home in May 1934, aged just 34. Ernest's death certificate states that he died of cardiac failure, pulmonary tuberculosis and chronic nephritis (a kidney disease). His occupation was simply described as Army Pensioner.

Ernest Walker Dell (1898 – 1964)
Private 55861, 8th (Service Battalion) Yorkshire Regiment

Ernest Walker Dell, known during his time in the army as Walker Ernest Dell, was born at his maternal grandparents' home in Wigginton in June 1898. His father, George Dell, was a casual labourer and came from Northchurch. In 1901, no doubt looking for work at the busy London docks, George Dell was living with his growing family in a cramped terraced house in Alnwick Road in Canning Town, just north of the river Thames. How long they remained in docklands is unclear, as all of Ernest's later siblings were either born in Wigginton or Northchurch. By 1911, George Dell, his wife, Lucy, and their nine surviving children were living in a four-roomed cottage in Orchard End with Ernest's two older sisters working at the paper mill at Apsley.

Ernest was conscripted aged 18, and posted to 11th (Service) Battalion, The Sherwood Foresters (Nottinghamshire & Derbyshire Regiment). As Ernest's service record has not survived, it is unclear when he joined his battalion in France, but it was highly likely that he was serving with them during the Third Battle of Ypres. In November 1917, Ernest's battalion was withdrawn from the Western Front and sent to Italy to support the Italian Army which had suffered a major defeat at the hands of the Austrian army. He was to remain in Italy for the remainder of the war, transferring to 8th (Service) Battalion, York & Lancaster Regiment in September 1918.

Ernest returned to civilian life in Northchurch towards the end of 1919 and in 1926, he married Alice Edith Smith, the daughter of a railway foreman, at St Peter's, Berkhamsted. He later became the manager of a butcher's shop belonging to the local Co-operative Society in Hemel Hempstead. He died in 1964, aged 65.

Daniel Diplock (1884 – 1973)
Private 97283, 1/7th Battalion, Royal Welsh Fusiliers

One of many of the gardeners working at the local big houses in the Northchurch area in 1914 was Daniel Diplock. Born in Ringmer, Sussex, in November 1884, Daniel was the son of a shoemaker. After leaving school he took up gardening and in 1901 he was working as an undergardener at one of the large houses in Ringmer. By 1912, he had moved north and was working as a gardener at Langley House in Abbots Langley.

Around 1913 Daniel started work as an assistant gardener at Rossway, the home of Major General Sir Charles Frederick Hadden, working under head gardener, Oliver Hayles. Within months, Daniel had met Ada Curl from Orchard End, Northchurch, and they were married at St Mary's, Northchurch, in January 1914. They moved to a house in the High Street, where Ada gave birth to a son the following November.

With the coming of war, unlike many of his fellow gardeners working at Rossway, Daniel did not sign up, and it is likely that he was conscripted under the Military Service Act in the summer of 1916. It was a further six months before he was called up and, wishing to join the Royal Garrison Artillery, Daniel asked his employer, Major General Sir Charles Frederick Hadden, to write to the Recruiting Officer at Watford to press his case. The letter proved unsuccessful however, as he was subsequently posted to an infantry unit, the Bedford's 1st/5th Battalion. In April 1917 and now a Lance Corporal, he left England as part of a new draft of men for his battalion on board the HT *Abbassieh*, bound for Egypt.

The Bedford's 1st/5th battalion had been in Palestine fighting the Turkish army since March 1917 and had taken part in the First and Second Battles of Gaza, both of which had ended in stalemate. By the time Daniel arrived in Palestine at the end of May, the battalion was in training for a large raid on the Turkish positions near Gaza called Umbrella Hill. The raid in July 1917 was successful and was used as a model for subsequent raids in the area. It was not until the following November, however, that Gaza was finally captured.

1918 saw the Turks retreating, having lost Jerusalem the previous December. Bad weather prevented further action taking place and there was further disruption when the Germans launched their Spring Offensive on the Western Front, which resulted in the withdrawal of some troops from Palestine. Daniel and the 1st/5th Bedfordshire remained in Palestine, however, moving to the Jordan Valley to take part in further operations against the Turks between February and May. In August 1918, he was admitted to the local Field Ambulance where "ICT R leg", an inflammation of the connective tissue in his right leg, was diagnosed. This description covered anything from cartilage injuries and torn ligaments, to skin problems, and if left unattended in the difficult desert conditions could prove extremely serious. Daniel was later transferred to a military hospital at Giza, near Cairo, and did not return to his unit until December 1918, by which time the war was over.

It would be another year before he was demobilised. During this time, he was transferred twice following the disbandment of his old unit, firstly to 1/5th Battalion, Suffolk Regiment, and then 1/7th Battalion, Royal Welch Fusiliers.

Daniel was finally demobilised at Shrewsbury in December 1919 and returned to Northchurch. Whether his job as assistant gardener at Rossway was still available is unclear, but within months he and his family had moved to the village of Mickleham on the North Downs, where presumably he had found new work. Ada Diplock died suddenly in 1925 and Daniel later remarried and moved to the Guildford area. By 1939 he was living in Cheam, Surrey, and working at nearby Raynes Park for the seed company, Carters Tested Seeds, one of the major seed companies in the country at the time. Daniel Diplock died in 1973 aged 89.

Percy Dwight (1886 – 1946)
Lieutenant, 25th Battalion, Middlesex Regiment

In 1914 the surname Dwight in the local area was synonymous with pheasants. The Dwights were one of the largest pheasant breeders in the country with their farm located to the north-east of Berkhamsted, in what was in the eastern part of the Northchurch Parish electoral district.

The Dwight family originally came from the Chesham area, and one of the earliest references to their association with the game bird dates from January 1828 when it was reported that William Dwight, a local pheasant breeder, died suddenly on his way home from the *Waggon and Horses* public house in the town. Over the coming years, various members of the Dwight family bred their own pheasants, but it was not until Matthew Dwight settled at a farm in Northchurch Parish did breeding, on what would later become an industrial scale, begin. By 1881, Matthew Dwight had retired as a pheasant breeder and his business was being run by his sons William and Frederick. William, his wife, Jane, and his family lived at the 320-acre Ivy House Farm where he employed a workforce of eleven men and three boys. The farm would later become better known as The Pheasantries. Within a few years, William Dwight had become so successful in running one of the largest pheasant nurseries in the country that he was able to employ two full-time servants and a parlour maid.

In 1901, William Dwight had some 4,000 pheasants on his farm which by now had now grown to over 1,000 acres. The stock birds were kept in large pens, each pen containing one cock and five hens, surrounded by an 8ft high fence intended to keep the birds in and the local predatory wildlife out. As a further precaution, the wings of each bird were clipped to prevent them flying over the fence. The egg-laying season commenced in April and lasted for three months, with each hen laying an average of thirty to forty eggs during this period. Many of the eggs were then sent by Dwights to other farmers all over the world, carefully wrapped in soft hay and placed in hampers. Those eggs that were kept by the farm were collected and taken to a nursery where some six hundred brooding hens would incubate them in boxes placed in tiers in a large barn, with each hen incubating around fifteen eggs. After twenty-four days, the eggs would hatch and the hen and her 'foster' pheasant chicks were moved to a large meadow containing coops, again surrounded by a large wire fence. Here the young pheasants would grow up. To discourage poaching, large dogs and noisy guinea fowl were employed, and it was not unknown for the Dwights to prosecute anyone attempting to steal their birds. In 1909, William Dwight became one of the first churchwardens of the newly-consecrated church of St Michael and All Angels, Sunnyside, which was not far away from the farm.

Percy Dwight was born in April 1886 and was the seventh of William and Jane Dwight's children. With the profits from the pheasant breeding business growing, the family were able to send Percy to Berkhamsted School where he soon joined the school's Officer Training Corps. Leaving Berkhamsted School in 1902, aged 16, Percy started work on the farm where he remained until the outbreak of war.

On 15th September 1914, Percy and his younger brother, Sidney, answered an appeal in the newspapers to join a new unit made up of former public school and university-educated men. They travelled together to Westminster and were enlisted into 19th (Public Schools) Battalion, Royal Fusiliers. Percy was given the service number PS287, whilst Sidney became PS288.

Percy's medical record shows him as standing 5ft 11ins tall, weighing 149lbs, a fair complexion, hazel eyes and brown hair. 19th (Public Schools) Battalion was effectively an officer training corps and, although it was sent to France in November 1915, it did not see active service, being attached to the headquarters of 33rd Division.

Just over two months after arriving in France, Percy, like most of his contemporaries, applied for a Commission, showing an interest in serving in a cavalry unit, or in one of the Sussex, Hampshire or Middlesex infantry regiments. His application accepted, Percy returned to England and was sent to No2 Officers Cadet Battalion, based at Pembroke College, Cambridge, to complete his officer training. Lieutenant Percy Dwight was subsequently posted to 25th Battalion, Middlesex Regiment. Percy's brother, Sidney decided not seek a commission however, and later served in the Royal Engineers.

In December 1916 Percy and his unit, now renamed 25th (Garrison) Battalion, Middlesex Regiment, left Devonport bound for the British colony of Singapore. The journey there was to prove eventful, as in February 1917, whilst rounding Cape Agulhas, some 108 miles south-east of Cape Town, the battalion's transport ship, SS *Tyndareus,* struck a mine laid by a German raider. The ship rapidly began to fill with water and started going down by the bow. Urgent orders were given to the battalion to line up in parade order on deck whist the lifeboats were lowered. Nobody was lost during the incident and King George V later wrote a message to the battalion expressing his appreciation for the way they handled themselves. The battalion finally reached Singapore at the end of March 1917 where half of them remained, the other half travelling on to Hong Kong. It is not clear in which colony Percy served during the following months, and it was only in July 1918 that the two parts of the battalion were reunited in Hong Kong on board the SS *Ping Suey*. Their destination was not England, however, but the Russian port of Vladivostok.

In February 1917, with the cost of the war crippling the Russian economy, food riots and army mutinies led to the abdication of the Russian Tsar, Nicholas II. Although a new Soviet government was set up, the war continued, but unrest in the army continued to be rife and anarchist and Bolshevik agitators promoted this for their own aims. Following a disastrous summer campaign and a failed military coup, the new government was in chaos and in October 1917, the Bolsheviks led by Vladimir Ilyich Ulyanov, better known as Lenin, seized power virtually unopposed. Shortly afterwards, they called for an armistice on the Eastern Front and negotiations with the Germans and Austrians began. The signing of the Treaty of Brest-Litovsk in March 1918 formally ended the war between Russia and Germany and its allies.

With Russia out of the war, thousands of German troops were transferred from the Eastern Front to the Western Front and planning for a major offensive in the spring of 1918 commenced, the aim being to end the war before the arrival of fresh troops from the United States of America[8]. Meanwhile, the punitive conditions imposed by the Germans under the peace treaty resulted in the outbreak of civil war in Russia with the opposing sides becoming known as the Bolshevik 'Red Army' and the 'White Russians'.

Fear of revolution following the events in Russia was rife among the western governments who decided to support the White Russian forces against the Bolshevik's Red Army. The only available way to get support to the White Russians was via the Pacific port of Vladivostok, at the eastern end of the Trans-Siberian railway. In December 1917 Pro-Bolshevik forces had seized the port where thousands of tons of allied military equipment, meant for the Russian Imperial army, had been stockpiled whilst awaiting shipment westwards. In June 1918, the Czecho-Slovak Legion, a strong anti-

British Troops at Vladivostok 1918
Author's Collection

---

[8] The USA had entered declared war on Germany in April 1917, but had yet to fully mobilise its army in significant numbers

Bolshevik force of former prisoners of war and other groups, had taken back control of the port and the following month the British Government authorised the creation of a Siberian Expeditionary Force to support the White Russians. Among the allied troops sent to Russia in 1918 were men from Great Britain, Canada, China, Italy, Japan and the United States. The British force consisted of two battalions – 1/9th Battalion, Hampshire Regiment and 25th Battalion, Middlesex Regiment, Percy's battalion, which was the first to arrive, landing at Vladivostok on 3rd August 1918.

This battalion, under the command of Lieutenant-Colonel John Ward, a former MP and Trades Union leader, left Vladivostok to support the Czecho-Slovak Legion along the line of the Trans-Siberian railway. It soon became apparent that the Red Army forces were advancing quickly towards Vladivostok, with additional support being provided by an armoured train. With the British and Czecho-Slovak Legion forces coming under heavy and increasingly accurate artillery fire, Ward requested assistance from the captain of the armoured cruiser, HMS *Suffolk*, which was moored in Vladivostok Harbour. The artificers on board the *Suffolk* quickly assembled their own armoured train, mounting two 12-pdr naval guns and two machine guns from the ship onto railway wagons and sent them forward. A second similarly-armed train later followed. A fierce firefight between the opposing trains ensued and ended with a well-positioned shot to the Red Army locomotive.

Over the subsequent weeks the Czecho-Slovak Legion and the British troops slowly advanced eastwards along the railway, securing it from Red Army attack, but distrust among the 'allied' forces started to grow, particularly with the Japanese, who had landed 70,000 troops close to the border with Manchuria. Within months, the various factions fighting the Red Army were fighting among themselves and in the summer of 1919, except for the Japanese, the allies decided to withdraw their troops. Percy left Vladivostok with his battalion for England.

The following October, Percy left the army and relinquished his Commission, retaining the honourary rank of Lieutenant. He returned to The Pheasantries and resumed his pheasant breeding. He was to remain there until his death in 1946, aged 59.

Charles Eggleton (1889 – 1936)
Private 19792, 2nd Battalion, Northamptonshire Regiment

Very little is known about the detail of Charles Eggleton's military service. Born in the hamlet of Hawridge in 1889, Charles was the son of farm worker, Harry Eggleton, and his wife, Sarah. By 1901 the Eggleton family had moved to Holiday Street, Berkhamsted, at which time Charlie's older sister was working for Messrs Hughes, Hawkins and Co, at what was commonly called the 'Mantle Factory' in Lower Kings Road. Sarah

Eggleton sadly died in 1909, and shortly afterwards the family moved to a five-roomed cottage in Gossoms End. Charles was then working as a cowman on a local farm, possibly the same one where his father worked.

In April 1914, Charles married Gladys Grace Hoddy, a domestic servant in one of the local large houses and the following year Gladys gave birth to a boy.

Although Charles's military service record has not survived, it is known that he did not volunteer when war broke out and it is likely that he was conscripted in the summer of 1916. After completing his training, Charles was posted to 2nd Battalion, Northamptonshire Regiment which had been serving on the Western Front since November 1914. If Charles joined his battalion at the end of 1916, he would have seen action during the German retreat to the newly-built Hindenburg Line in 1917 and have been amid the fighting during the German Spring Offensive the following year and the final allied advances across France.

Following his demobilisation, Charles returned to Gossoms End and later moved to Unity Cottages in Berkhamsted High Street. He died in 1936, aged 48.

Lawrence Herbert George Girling (1897 – 1982)
Lieutenant, Middlesex Regiment

Lawrence Girling was born in West Hampstead in late December 1897. His father, John Henry Girling, came from Derbyshire and worked as a banker's clerk, presumably in the City of London, and was wealthy enough to employ a domestic servant. By 1909, the Girling family had moved from London to a large ten-roomed house in Kitsbury Road, Berkhamsted and it is here that Lawrence's mother, Emma, gave birth to his sister. Little is known about Lawrence's early years in Berkhamsted, but is likely that he went to Berkhamsted School and joined their Officer Training Corps. In due course the Girling family moved to The Wycke a large house in Shootersway.

In July 1915, aged eighteen, Lawrence obtained a Commission with the Middlesex Regiment. Seventeen months later, he was promoted to Lieutenant, but it was not until Christmas Eve 1917 that he finally arrived in a war zone, being posted to 3rd Battalion, Middlesex Regiment which was fighting at Salonika.

Lawrence's battalion had been in Salonika for two years and had faced the triple enemies of the Bulgarian army, disease and extremes of weather. By the time of his arrival, the fighting there was at an effective stalemate and the main task was to keep warm and healthy. April 1918 saw him attached to the Signals Service in Salonika and he was serving with them during the major offensive the following September that led to the surrender of the Bulgarian army and the end of the fighting in the area. Following the end of the war, Lawrence decided to continue in the army and remained with the Signal Corps, later renamed the Royal Corps of Signals, until June 1920. Three years later, he was promoted to Captain and transferred to the King's (Liverpool) Regiment, spending much of his time serving in the Mediterranean area.

In 1927, Lawrence retired from the army. Whilst serving with the King's Regiment, he had married Mary Scott and became a father. Looking for a new career, he decided to train as a teacher, and by 1932 he had become the headmaster at Southlea, a small private preparatory school in Malvern, Worcestershire.

It appears that the school closed soon after the start of the Second World War and the Girling family later moved to London to live in a town house in the prosperous area of Westborne Terrace, Paddington. Lawrence Girling died in Oxford in 1982, aged 84.

Charles W Gladwell (1884 – 1965)
Private 40, 10th Hussars

What brought Charles Gladwell and his wife, Elizabeth, to Northchurch is a mystery. He is registered at a cottage in New Road in the 1918 Absent Voters List, but he does not appear to have any previous link with the area. Although fighting as an infantryman during the war, he was not a member of an infantry battalion, but a cavalryman serving with 10th Hussars.

Charles Gladwell was born in Cambridge in April 1884, the fifth child of Thomas Gladwell, a bricklayer from Suffolk, and his wife Lydia. He grew up in Cambridge and after leaving school became a baker's assistant. Wanting more excitement than baking loaves of bread, in January 1907, then aged 22, Charles joined 10th (Prince of Wales Own) Royal Hussars, a cavalry regiment dating back to the time of the Jacobite Rebellion in 1715. After completing his training, he left for Rawalpindi, India where the 10th Royal Hussars were then based. Within weeks of his arrival, Charles saw action on the Northwest Frontier helping to suppress a local uprising amongst the local tribal forces. He remained at Rawalpindi with the Hussars until October 1912 before travelling with them to Bloemfontein, in the recently-formed Union of South Africa, where he remained until news of the outbreak of war in Europe was received.

10th Hussars sailed from Cape Town on 24th August on board RMS *Balmoral Castle* bound for Southampton where they arrived on 19th September. Making their way to Ludgershall, 16 miles north-east of Salisbury, they joined 6th Cavalry Brigade, 3rd Cavalry Division. With the BEF in full retreat after the Battle of Mons and with the Channel Ports in the sights of the advancing German Army, 6th Cavalry Brigade were quickly entrained to Southampton where on 6th October they boarded ships bound for Ostend.

Landing two days later, 6th Cavalry Brigade made its way eastwards towards Lille to help stem the German advance. Forced back to Ypres by the sheer strength of the German army, however, 10th Hussars were forced to dig in and fight as dismounted cavalry. The unit was to suffer badly during the First Battle of Ypres. By 17th November, with new troops arriving from England, the German advance had been stopped. Sir Douglas Haig, the Commander of the BEF's First Army Corps, sent the following telegram *"Please congratulate 6th Cavalry Brigade from me upon the excellent fight they put up. I regret to hear your losses were so heavy but it is very satisfactory to know that the enemy's casualties were so much heavier…"*.

Having recovered from the heavy fighting, February 1915 saw Charles and his unit back at Ypres, again acting as dismounted cavalry. The trenches 10th Hussars occupied at this time were only 12 to 15 yards away from the German trenches, and it was not unknown for the troops to exchange messages in matchboxes thrown over the parapets. One matchbox thrown by the German troops at this time contained the message *"We are a battalion of an Alsace Regiment; don't shoot us and we won't shoot you. Vive La France, but Germany comes first"*[9]. The unit continued to fight as dismounted cavalry during the Second Battle of Ypres in April 1915 and the Battle of Loos the following September.

At the start of the Somme Offensive the following year 10th Hussars were held in readiness with its horses for the expected breakthrough. Day after day Charles and his comrades were told to "stand to" whilst based at Bonney, 26 miles east of Amiens, but the call never came. The scale of the casualties and the failure to break through the German lines meant that the skills of the British cavalry units went totally unused.

For the next ten months, 10th Hussars remained far behind the front line. It was not until early April 1917 that orders came to "saddle up" and move to Arras where the next British offensive was being planned. To the east of Arras, on high ground overlooking the town was the village of Monchy-le-Preux at the northern end of the Hindenburg Line. The task of the 10th Hussars and the Essex Yeomanry was to charge the German lines on horseback and, having gained the element of surprise, seize the high ground, capturing Monchy in the process. As soon as the attack started on 11th April, the German Artillery and machine-guns opened fire. 10th Hussars managed to ride into the centre of Monchy, but at some cost. As the infantry arrived the Germans started shelling the town and casualties among the men and horses began to escalate. Despite this, the British troops successfully hung on, but by the following day Monchy lay in ruins and littered with dead and injured horses and men. The engagement cost 10th Hussars 27 men

---

[9] Alsace and Lorraine were part of France until the Franco-Prussian War of 1870 when they were ceded to the newly formed Imperial Germany.

and officers killed with a further 157 wounded and 5 missing. Overall some 600 cavalrymen became casualties. Among those wounded was Charles Gladwell.

Charles was sent back to England to recover from his wounds. Three months later, on 24th July 1917, he married Elizabeth Smith at Camden Parish Church in London. He did not return to frontline duties but was fit enough to start work at No1 Cavalry Cadet School at Netheravon, Wiltshire where he remained until the end of the war. His discharge from the Hussars on grounds of being no longer fit for military duty came in April 1919.

Following his demobilisation, Charles became a railway porter for the London & North Western Railway and joined the Watford branch of the National Union of Railwaymen.

Sadly, Elizabeth Gladwell died in the late summer of 1931. Four years later, Charles married Annie Dell and in 1939 they were living in Greenway, Berkhamsted, and he was still working as a railway porter. Charles Gladwell died in 1965, aged 81.

Fred Hales (1884 – 1939)
Lance Sergeant 47614, 1/4th Northamptonshire Regiment

Fred Hales was born in April 1884, the first son of Joseph and Elizabeth Hales's ten children, two of whom would die in infancy. His father, Joseph Hales, worked as a platelayer with the London & North Western Railway and originally came from Ivinghoe. Among Fred's surviving male siblings who grew up alongside him in their New Road cottage in Northchurch were William, Jack, Joseph and George, all of whom would serve during the war. After leaving school, Fred started working locally as a carter and labourer.

Fred was not one of those to volunteer early in the war and it was only with the threat of conscription looming that in November 1915 he decided to attest under the Derby Scheme. By then he was 31 years old and, like his father, he was now working as a platelayer for the London & North Western Railway. Fred's medical record from the time he attested shows him as being 5ft 4½ins tall, weighing 132lbs and with perfect vision.

It was not until April 1917 that he was mobilised and told to report to Bedford where he was posted to 3rd (Reserve) Battalion, Northamptonshire Regiment. He was later transferred to the regiment's 1/4th Battalion and placed in 'H' Coy and on 18th July 1917, he left Southampton bound for Alexandria in Egypt.

Fred's battalion had been away from England since being sent to Gallipoli during the summer of 1915 and had remained there until being evacuated to Egypt at the end of the year. Initially assigned to garrison duty near the Suez Canal, it later moved north during the allied advance into Palestine. During the first two battles of Gaza the battalion had suffered badly, and Fred was just one of many fresh soldiers posted to Palestine at the time to bring it back up to fighting strength.

It was during the Third Battle of Gaza on 3rd November 1917, that Fred was shot in his right leg. He was evacuated from the battlefield and sent to a field hospital at Kantara, Egypt, for treatment. After making a full recovery, he was able to rejoin his unit at the end of the year and remained with them for the rest of the war. By the time of the Turkish armistice in October 1918 his unit had advanced as far as Beirut.

It would be another year before Fred and his comrades would return home, by which time he had been promoted to Lance Sergeant. He left Alexandria on board HT *Caledonia* bound for England on 8th October 1919 and on his return home to Northchurch was granted four weeks leave followed immediately by his demobilisation.

Fred did not stay long in Northchurch and soon moved to London, still working for the London & North Western Railway. In 1928 he was married and living in the St Pancras area where he would remain for the rest of his life. By 1939 Fred was seriously ill with tuberculosis and he died in Highgate Hospital that December, aged 55.

George Hales (1900 – 1972)
Lance Corporal 151103, 23rd (Service) Battalion, Royal Fusiliers

Born in May 1900, George Hales, the youngest of Joseph and Elizabeth Hales's boys, was among the final men in Northchurch to be conscripted. By 1918, when his conscription papers arrived, George had already seen all his older brothers go off to war and an uncertain future, and he was still under training with 23rd (Service) Battalion, Royal Fusiliers at an army camp in England when the Armistice was signed.

Otherwise known as the First Sportsman's Battalion, the unit had an unusual background. Back in 1914 when substantial numbers of men were enlisting with the army, Mrs Emma Cunliffe-Owen, the daughter of the curator of the Victoria and Albert Museum in Kensington, frequently challenged her male friends to join up. Often met with the response 'why don't you form your own battalion?' she did just that, sending a telegram to Lord Kitchener asking for permission to create a battalion of 'middle and upper-class men, physically fit and able to shoot and ride'. Mrs Cunliffe-Owen's request was accepted and she hired the India Room at the Hotel Cecil in London's The Strand for the interviews, placing advertisements in the appropriate national newspapers. Other recruiting events took place across the country, all with the proviso that applicants had to be 'upper or middle class'. Within four weeks, there were enough applicants to form her first battalion, which later became 23rd (Service) Battalion, Royal Fusiliers. Training initially took place on The Strand, where traffic was disrupted on a frequent basis, but later moved to a specially constructed camp in

Hornchurch, Essex. Many sportsmen joined the embryo unit, but the ability to play sports was never a prerequisite of applying. Soon there were enough numbers for a second battalion to be raised which became 24th (Service) Battalion, Royal Fusiliers. Both battalions went off to fight in France in 1915 and were to suffer severe losses in the Somme Offensive the following year.

By the time George joined 23rd Battalion in 1919, most, if not all, of the original men were no longer serving, having either been killed or wounded during the war, or in the process of being demobilised following the signing of the Armistice. The original selection criteria for joining the battalion had also vanished. George was one of several fresh, new recruits posted to the battalion, which now formed part of the British Army of Occupation in Cologne.

Under the terms of the Armistice, Belgium, France, Great Britain and the United States would send troops into Germany and they would be located on the eastern bank of the River Rhine. The British forces would be centred around Cologne, with the Belgians to the north and the French and American troops to the south. By March 1920, however, most of the units had been dissolved, leaving a small force which became known as the British Army of the Rhine. George's battalion were one of the last to leave Germany in March 1920, by which time he had risen to the rank of Lance Corporal.

Returning home to Northchurch, George stayed with his parents until 1926 when he married Eva Fowler. In 1939, George and Eva were living in a cottage in New Road, and he was working as a painter and decorator, whilst also serving as a member of Berkhamsted's Auxiliary Fire Service. George Hales died in the late summer of 1972, aged 72.

Ernest Thomas Holland (1897 – 1982)
Private 50676, 9th Battalion, Gloucestershire Regiment

Ernest Holland was born in Boxmoor on Guy Fawkes Night 1897 and was the second son of James Holland, a labourer and carter from Boxmoor. James died in 1903 aged just 33, leaving his widow, Esther, to bring up her two young boys alone. In 1910 Esther married Edwin Carvell, a widower from Northchurch, and the Holland family moved into their new family home in Orchard End.

Ernest's older brother, Alfred (but known as James), joined the Royal Field Artillery soon after the outbreak of war, but being younger, Ernest faced the prospect of conscription. In 1916, his papers arrived and he was posted to 8th Battalion, Norfolk Regiment. Ernest's service record has not survived, but it is likely that he joined the Norfolk's during the spring of 1917 and served in the Somme sector and later during the Third Battle of Ypres. By the Autumn of 1917 however, he was serving in 1/7th

Worcestershire Regiment, probably because of being wounded in action or becoming sick. That November, Ernest was admitted to hospital suffering from pneumonia and by the time he was fit enough to return to active duty, his battalion had been posted to Italy. Consequently, he found himself transferred again, this time to the Worcestershire's 4th Battalion.

Serving with his new battalion in Flanders during the spring of 1918, Ernest was amid the battle to hold the third of the German Spring Offensives that aimed to break the British supply line and cut off the British Second Army at Ypres. The battalion later participated in the advance into Belgium, ending the war at Lessines, some 36 miles south-west of Brussels. After the war, Ernest was transferred to 9th Battalion, Gloucestershire Regiment and was not demobilised until late 1919 when he returned to Orchard End.

In 1922, Ernest moved into one of the newly-built council houses near the *Old Grey Mare* public house in Northchurch and was probably working as a gardener. He remained there until about 1926, but his movements after this date are uncertain. He next appears in north Kent in the late summer of 1932, where he married Sarah Jane George from mid Wales. Seven years later, Ernest, Sarah and their two children were living in Huntingdon, where he was working as a gardener's handyman. Ernest Holland died in 1982, aged 84.

Edward George Hooper (1897 – 1944)
Lieutenant, 2nd Battalion, The Loyal North Lancashire Regiment

Edward Hooper was born in Berkhamsted in January 1897, the son of John Hooper, a domestic coachman from Devon, and his wife, Annie. Edward was initially brought up along with his older brother, Henry, and sister in his parents' home in Berkhamsted High Street before his father became the estate steward at Woodcock Hill, Northchurch. With the new job came a new home, and John Hooper and his family moved to The Lodge at the bottom of what is now Durrants Lane, but at that time a private road leading up the hill to the main house. The Woodcock Hill estate had been purchased in 1907 by Robert McVitie, the owner the McVitie and Price biscuit company, who regularly travelled by train from Berkhamsted station to the company's factory near Willesden Junction in north London.

Like his older brother, Henry, Edward attended Berkhamsted School and it is likely that their school fees were paid by the McVitie family. At Berkhamsted School, he became a keen sportsman and a member of the school's Officer Training Corps as well as a skilled bugler. Edward had intended to continue his studies in chemistry, but following the outbreak of war in 1914 he decided to enlist as a trumpeter with the Hertfordshire Yeomanry.

In early 1915 Edward applied for a Commission with the Loyal North Lancashire Regiment and the following year, having completed his training and reaching the age of nineteen, he was posted to the regiment's 2nd Battalion, which was then fighting the German colonial forces in East Africa.

During the late 19th century many of the European powers vied for power and territory in the newly-opened continent of Africa. What started as a 'free for all' ended with the Congress of Berlin of 1885, which

Lieutenant Edward Hooper
Courtesy of Jane Cook

brought some order to the territorial disputes by formalising the existing spheres of influence. Great Britain's territory now included Egypt and British East Africa in the north, and numerous adjacent colonies in the south. Between them, breaking a continuous line of red down the map of Africa, lay the territory of German East Africa, comprising today's countries of Rwanda, Burundi and Tanzania. On the west coast of Africa, to the north of the Cape Colony, Germany also acquired German West Africa (now Namibia).

Following the outbreak of war, British Empire forces attempted to dispossess Germany of her overseas territories, and seize the ports on the coast of German East Africa from where enemy warships could threaten ships carrying troops and supplies from India and Australia to Europe via the Suez Canal. In November 1914, allied troops, including 2nd Battalion, The Loyal North Lancashire Regiment, attempted an amphibious attack on the town of Tanga in German East Africa, only to be routed by the local protection force, the *Schutztruppe*, under its experienced German commander, Colonel Paul von Lettow Vorbeck who, realising that it would only be a matter of time before his East African *Schutztruppe* would face overwhelming British Empire forces, decided to adopt guerrilla-style tactics and started raiding communications, ambushing supply columns and patrols, avoiding pitched battles and only fighting when he had the stronger force. In so doing and for the remainder of the war, he managed to keep tied down in Africa a considerable number of Empire troops who might otherwise have been sent to the Western Front. It was not just the *Schutztruppe* in German East Africa that caused the British forces significant problems, however; the hot and steamy subtropical conditions meant that mosquitos and tsetse flies reigned supreme. More troops became casualties from illnesses like malaria and dysentery than from battle wounds. The Loyal North Lancashire Regiment was one of many regiments to be withdrawn from the fighting due to their inability to continue under such severe conditions and in June 1916 they were sent to South Africa to recover and rebuild. It was here that 2nd Lieutenant Edward Hooper joined them.

Hooper's battalion returned to East Africa in September 1916, but it was only there for a few months before being withdrawn for a second time and sent to Egypt. Now part of the Egyptian Expeditionary Force, the battalion joined General Edmund Allenby's troops that would slowly advance northwards out of Egypt and would eventually lead to the capture of Jerusalem in December 1917.

Hooper, now a Lieutenant, and his battalion were transferred to the Western Front in May 1918 as part of the rebuilding of the British army after the mauling it had received during the German Spring Offensives. The following August, during the Battle of Amiens, the battalion incurred heavy casualties, including the loss of their commanding officer, but pressed on with Hooper's conduct during the battle resulting in him being Mentioned in Despatches.

With the war over, Hooper's battalion became part of the new Army of Occupation and moved into the Rhineland. In July 1919, Hooper was back in England where he married Veda Mary Jenkins at St Mary Magdalene, Addiscombe, Surrey. Veda gave birth to a daughter the following year. Deciding to remain in the army, Hooper served with his battalion when they were sent to Ireland during the Irish War of Independence.

During his subsequent years with the Loyal North Lancashire Regiment Hooper became an expert in firearms, and during the early 1930s, now promoted to Captain, represented his regiment on several occasions at shooting competitions at Bisley, becoming one of the best shots in the country.

Hooper applied to serve overseas once again during the Second World War, but was retained on home service due to his experience with small arms. In 1943 he was promoted to Lieutenant Colonel.

Tragically, the following year both Hooper and his wife were killed during the last German bombing raid on England. His home at Yewlands, near Hoddesden, Hertfordshire, lay directly under the flight path of the German bombers and a stray bomb fell on the property and exploded. He was 47 years old.

William Frederick Hunt (1886 – 1921)
Lieutenant, Royal Inniskilling Fusiliers

William Hunt was the Northchurch village policeman when war broke out in August 1914. Born in Bushey in January 1886, he was the son of Thomas and Emily Hunt. Thomas Hunt worked as a labourer on the railway but sadly died when his son was just two years old. William was subsequently brought up in Watford by his maternal aunt and uncle, who worked as a platelayer with the London & North Western Railway. After completing his schooling William started work as a general labourer, but later followed his uncle in becoming a platelayer for the railway and also joined the local militia.

In September 1905, nineteen-year-old William enlisted at Hounslow for a twelve-year term of duty with the 21st Lancers. His service record shows William as standing 5ft 11ins tall, weighing 137lbs with a fresh complexion, brown eyes and black hair. He did not stay with 21st Lancers for long, however, as the following April he managed to purchase his discharge from the army to join the Hertfordshire Constabulary as a police constable, taking his medical examination at Hertford a few days later.

William spent the next four years as a police constable with 'C' Division at Watford, during which time he met Alice Mary Sibley, the daughter of a Watford train driver and the couple were married in the summer of 1910. Later that year William was transferred to 'F' Division at Hertford, where he and Alice became parents upon the birth of a daughter. October 1911 saw William transferred to 'G' Division at Wheathampstead where he spent the next two years before joining 'D' Division to become the Northchurch village policeman. In November 1913 William and his family moved into the police cottage in New Road.

Deciding not to volunteer upon the outbreak of war, he remained as the village policeman until January 1915 when he enlisted with the Royal Engineers. It is not known in which branch of the Royal Engineers William served, other than that he arrived in France to join his unit on 30th September 1916. By then, his wife and daughter had left Northchurch to make way for PC George Cooling, William's replacement as village policeman, and probably moved back to her parents' home in Watford.

Following the loss of many officers earlier in the war and having been promoted to the rank of Corporal, in 1917 William applied for a Commission, and on 28th August 1917 he joined the Royal Inniskilling Fusiliers as a Temporary Second Lieutenant in their 12th (Reserve) Battalion, based at Finner Camp, near Ballyshannon, County Donegal. William remained in Ireland until May 1918 when he was attached to the Royal Army Medical Coops training facility at Weeton Camp, Blackpool, becoming their Company Commander. Leaving Blackpool in August 1918, William's final army posting was to Burma, where he served until his demobilisation in December 1919 with the rank of Lieutenant.

After leaving the army he applied to rejoin the Hertfordshire Constabulary, but, having failed the subsequent medical examination, his application was rejected and he was awarded a police pension of £117 per annum. The 1920 Electoral Roll for Watford shows William and Annie living in Chester Road, Watford, but they did not stay there long, as in

August that year he applied to join the Auxiliary Division of the Royal Irish Constabulary (ADRIC).

The relationship between the Irish people and the Royal Irish Constabulary had been deteriorating for some years and had gained pace following the suppression of the Easter Rising in 1916. In the Irish election of December 1918, the Irish nationalist party *Sinn Féin* won by a landslide and the following month declared independence, setting up their own government, the *Dáil Éireann*. Within hours, two policemen had been killed by *Sinn Féin* members and over the next few months the violence escalated. As a result, the *Dáil Éireann,* together with *Sinn Féin* and its military wing, the Irish Republican Army (IRA), were outlawed and the British government sent newly-recruited auxiliary troops to Ireland to support the Royal Irish Constabulary in an attempt to restore law and order. Bearing the brunt of a new IRA offensive, many policemen serving in the Royal Irish Constabulary decided to resign to protect their families, or were intimidated into leaving. The resulting manpower crisis led to the creation in June 1920 of the Auxiliary Division of the Royal Irish Constabulary (ADRIC), a paramilitary unit of the Royal Irish Constabulary which recruited mainly former British army officers recently returned from the war. To encourage recruitment, ADRIC offered a lucrative basic pay of £1 per day with generous allowances. William exactly fitted the profile of a typical ADRIC recruit of the time – a former army Lieutenant, born between 1885 and 1899, who had been commissioned around 1917 having previously served in the ranks, and with no previous family tradition of military service and a working class background.

Divided into Companies of about 100 men each, ADRIC was based throughout Ireland and formed a series of heavily armed, mobile para-military troops focused on the elimination, by whatever means, of members of the IRA. William became an Intelligence Officer and a Platoon Commander with ADRIC's 'B' Coy, based at Templemore Abbey, County Tipperary[10]. The surrounding area was a hotbed of republican activity and William was frequently involved in the interrogation of prisoners, apparently gaining a reputation for his aggressive style and as a result, his name was added to the IRA's death list of ADRIC members. In November 1920, following an intelligence lead, men from 'B' Coy raided a public house in County Limerick and shot dead an IRA volunteer. Whether this had any bearing on William's decision in February 1921 to relinquish his role of a Platoon Commander in 'B' Coy and become a Temporary Cadet is unclear, but between then and the following June he was moved four times between different ADRIC units.

---

[10] After ADRIC left Templemore Abbey in the Spring of 1921 it was destroyed by the IRA as an act of vengeance

On 26 June 1921, William and a fellow ADRIC member visited their wives who were then lodging at the Mayfair Hotel, Lower Baggot Street, Dublin. Whilst having supper together in the hotel dining room four IRA men entered and opened fire. Caught by surprise, William was shot in the chest and died instantly, whilst the other ADRIC member was seriously wounded. William's ten-year-old daughter, who was also in the dining room at the time, received a gunshot graze to her leg and the two women were uninjured. A few hours later, one of the IRA men was arrested by ADRIC men and was identified by Annie Hunt as one of the assassins. The other men escaped.

William's body was returned to England and, following a military funeral, his body was laid to rest in Watford Cemetery.

William Howlett (1892 – 1969)
Private 26862, 9th Battalion, West Riding Regiment

William Howlett, known as Will, was born in Orchard End, Northchurch, in April 1892, the son of William Howlett, and his wife Lucy. After leaving school he worked alongside his father at Lanes Nurseries in Berkhamsted High Street.

Will's 18-year-old brother, Walter, was the first of his two brothers to join the army, enlisting in 1915 with 7th (Service) Battalion, Bedfordshire Regiment. Walter would later be tragically killed the following year on the first day of the Somme Offensive[11]. It was not until December 1915, with the introduction of conscription imminent, that twenty-three-year-old Will attested at Watford under the Derby Scheme. It would be a further two months before he was mobilised and told to report to the Bedfordshire Regiment's base at Kempston where he was posted to the Bedford's 3rd (Reserve) Battalion for training.

Private William Howlett
Courtesy of Julie Blackley

Three days after the death of his brother and his training now complete, Will was transferred to 1/4th Battalion, Royal Welch Regiment. Soon afterwards, he left Southampton as part of a draft of 199 men, bound for Rouen, joining the battalion at Bois de Bouvigny, south of Béthune. This

---

[11] Walter Howlett's story is told in *For Them's Sake*

battalion had become a pioneer battalion the previous September and the men now spent most of their time digging new trenches and dugouts as well as merging captured German trenches into the extensive British trench network. Much of this work took place at night-time when it would go unobserved. Any work done during the daytime frequently put the pioneers at greater risk and several of Will's comrades became casualties. Away from the front line, the pioneers were responsible for the repair and improvement of the local roads and light railway lines that brought the troops close to the front line. On occasions, pioneers were also seconded to assist tunnelling companies, mainly formed of Canadian troops, in the preparation of tunnels under the German lines where large explosive mines would be placed. Will spent much of 1917 in the area around Ypres.

At the start of November 1917, he was granted two weeks home leave and returned to Northchurch for the first time since leaving for France. Within a month of returning to France, Will was transferred to 19th Battalion, Royal Welch Fusiliers. His new unit originated as a Bantam Battalion created specifically for men under the minimum height of 5ft 3ins, which was only one inch shorter that Will's own height, and were mostly former miners. Used as pioneers, Will was to be with them for only a few weeks before the unit was broken up and the men dispersed to other pioneer units.

At the start of April 1918, Will found himself posted to 'D' Coy, 9th (Service) Battalion, The Duke of Wellington's (West Riding Regiment). He was now in the front line and expected to fight. The launch of the German Spring Offensive ten days earlier had resulted in the British incurring substantial casualties which were quickly replaced by men like Will with limited fighting experience. By the time he joined his new unit, however, the German offensive had lost momentum and the entrenched British forces in the area were stalling any further advance.

Despite the intense pressure the men had been put under over the previous few weeks, army discipline was still strictly enforced. On 13th May, whilst away from the front line with his battalion, Will was found to have a dirty uniform and bayonet whilst on Church Parade and was duly confined to barracks for three days.

On 26th August, during the allied advance following the Battle of Amiens, Will was shot in his right leg. Taken to No34 Causality Clearing Station at Fienvillers, he was put in a convoy of injured men and sent to 53rd Field Ambulance where it was decided that he should be returned to England. He spent the next few weeks at 5th Northern General Hospital in Leicester, followed by a spell in a convalescent home. By the time he returned to duty at the West Riding Regiment's base at Halifax, the war was over. In July 1919, Will was transferred to the regiment's 2nd Battalion and demobilised two months later. He returned home and resumed his job at Lane's nursery.

Before the war, Will had been courting Lydia Dealey, one of twin daughters, born to Joseph and Martha Dealey in 1891, who lived in Red Lion Yard, Berkhamsted. Both Lydia and her sister, Elizabeth, known as Lizzie, worked as domestic servants in one of the large houses in the area. On 24th September 1921, Will married Lydia and set up their family home at 4 Alma Road, Northchurch.

Lydia and Will did not have any children, but as many of their family lived locally they were regularly invited along to their home. Christmas afternoons were often spent there with sandwiches and cake, and a bran tub for the children. By 1939, Lydia's unmarried twin sister, Lizzie, who was still in service, had moved in with them. Later, Will, Lydia and Lizzie moved into one of the newly-built council bungalows in Lagley Gardens, Gossoms End.

In 1962, Lydia died, aged 71. Three years later, Will married his sister-in-law, but sadly, Lizzie was to die after only two years of marriage. Will Howlett died in 1969, aged 77.

Sidney Albert Lay (1899 – 1962)
Private 442591, 4th Battalion, North Staffordshire Regiment

Sidney Lay was born in Northchurch in June 1899. His father, also called Sidney, and mother, Annie Bignell, had married at St Mary's, Northchurch, during the summer of 1898 and Sidney was their first child. Sidney (snr) was a former labourer, but around the time of his son's birth he started working for the General Post Office installing telegraph poles, which resulted in the family moving to Hillingdon, London. By 1911 however, the family had returned to Northchurch and were living in Orchard End, although Sidney (snr) was still working away from home and sadly died three years later, leaving Annie to bring up Sidney and his younger brother.

Sidney was conscripted in June 1917 and although his service record has not survived, it is known that after completing his training he was posted to one of the Leicestershire Regiment's battalions. Sometime in 1918, he transferred to 4th Battalion, North Staffordshire Regiment, most likely because of the British army reorganisation following the German Spring Offensive, and was serving with the North Staffordshires at the time of the Armistice.

At the end of January 1919, units from 4th Battalion, which may have included Sidney, were sent to the holding camp at Valdelièvre, near Calais, where a mutiny had broken out among British troops awaiting transit back to England. Conditions and discipline in the transit camp were extremely poor and reports had already reached the British press. Several demonstrations had subsequently taken place and following the arrest of an army private called John Pantling, one of the leading demonstrators, a riot broke out. The rioters released Pantling from his prison cell and set up a soldiers' council. A call then went out for a general strike and within three days, some 20,000 troops had joined the mutiny. The mutineers then seized control of the army headquarters in Calais and in England sympathy strikes broke out at several army bases. Initially, the British authorities were slow to react, but within days units of troops, including sections of Sidney's battalion, were sent to Calais to restore order, installing machine guns at prominent positions as a show of strength. Fortunately, by the end of the month the mutiny at Calais had collapsed without any shots being fired. The protests led to improvements being put in place with the time taken to repatriate soldiers back home being reduced. No significant action was ever taken against the leaders of the mutiny.

Not long after, Sidney was demobilised and returned to Orchard End. He later found work at the Berkhamsted gasworks in Billet Lane. In 1925 he married Gertrude Shaw and in 1939 they were living in Norris's Terrace, Gossoms End, with Sidney also serving as an ARP warden at the nearby Berkhamsted gasworks. Sydney Lay died in the late winter of 1962, aged 61.

David Allen Mapley (1892 – 1972)
Private G/32279, 17th Battalion, Royal Sussex Regiment

Born in the family home in New Road, Northchurch in April 1892, David Mapley was the son of George Albert Mapley and his wife Esther, both originally from the nearby village of Wigginton. One of nine children, David grew up in Northchurch and, like his elder brother, Ernest, became a bricklayer after leaving school.

Although David's service record has not survived, it appears that he spent much of the war in England serving with 5th (Reserve) Battalion, Royal Fusiliers, possibly due to being given a low medical category. His subsequent posting to 9th (Service) Battalion, Royal Fusiliers in France in 1918 probably came about as a result the army restructuring following the German Spring Offensive. Before being demobilised at the end of 1919, David was transferred to 17th Battalion, Royal Sussex Regiment. Whether this took place before or after the Armistice is uncertain. He spent the last few months of his army service in a camp in the Dunkirk area awaiting repatriation to England.

After returning home to this parent's home in New Road, David resumed to his job as a bricklayer. In November 1936, aged 44, he was out rabbiting on the railway embankment just before Northchurch railway tunnel with his friend, Charles Eggleton. From the newspaper reports of the time, it appears that Eggleton lost his footing on the slope just as a train was passing below and was killed instantly. David later gave evidence at the inquest where a verdict of 'accidental death' was recorded. Charles Eggleton left a wife, Gladys and a grown-up son.

Three years later, David was still working as a bricklayer and living in Eddy Street, Gossoms End with Charles Eggleton's widow, Gladys and they were married a year later. David Mapley remained in Eddy Street until his death in 1972, aged 80.

Daniel Meager, MM (1888 – 1971)
Corporal 32327, 1st Battalion, Grenadier Guards

The Meager surname is one of the long-established Northchurch names, along with those of Dell, Delderfield and Monger. Daniel Meager was born in Northchurch in November 1888 and was Frederick and Lucy Meager's fifth child. With his father and older brothers, Henry and Frederick, all working as bricklayers, it was not surprising that after leaving school Daniel joined them, starting work for a Mr Smith in Tring.

In December 1907, having just passed his eighteenth birthday, Daniel travelled to Bedford to enlist for six years with the local Militia battalion, 4th Battalion, Bedfordshire Regiment, joining their 'C' Coy. His medical record shows him standing at 5ft 5½ins tall, weighing 128lbs with brown hair and blue eyes. Following his enlistment Daniel started 49 days of basic drill with further training due to start a few weeks later. The following April, he received instructions to report to Hertford no later than 10:00 on 4th May 1908 where his training would recommence. Whether Daniel ever made the journey to Hertford is unclear, however, as his service record shows that he was discharged from the army on 4th May following the receipt of the required discharge payment of £20, a not insubstantial amount in those days and which would be equivalent to £2,400 in today's money. Unfortunately, Daniel's attestation papers provide no further information as to why he left the Militia, nor who paid for his discharge.

Daniel's war service record has not survived, but it is known that he did not volunteer at the start of the war, and it is likely that he was conscripted in early 1916 and then posted to 10th Battalion, Essex Regiment. During the final weeks of the Somme Offensive in the autumn of 1916 Daniel was one of number of men from his battalion to receive the Military Medal and this is probably related to the capture by British and Canadian troops of the heavily defended Regina Trench system near Thiepval. Soon afterwards he became a Lance Corporal.

In September 1917, he was officially reported as being wounded, but the details of injuries, or when they happened, are not known. By the spring of 1918, however, he had recovered and was able to return to full duty, but, as was quite normal, Daniel was now posted to a new battalion, joining '4' Coy, 1st Battalion, Grenadier Guards. He remained with the Grenadier Guards until the end of the war.

Daniel was demobilised in the Autumn of 1919. Shortly afterwards, he moved to London, where he had found work as a bricklayer. Here he met

Mercilla Prudence Fox, who in 1911 was working as an attendant at St Olave's Union Workhouse in Lewisham. They married in the autumn of 1920 and over the next three years Mercilla would give birth to three children at the infirmary at St Olave's. A fourth child was registered in Berkhamsted in 1928, following the family's move to a cottage in New Road, Northchurch. In 1939, Daniel and Mercilla were living in a cottage in Gossoms End with Daniel still working as a bricklayer. He died in 1971, aged 81.

Jack Roy (1882 – 1959)
Private GS/3009, 2nd Battalion, Royal West Kent Regiment

Like at least four of his five siblings, Jack Roy was born in Brockley, in what was then Kent, in December 1882 and was the son of a naval pensioner from Ireland. Details of Jack's early life are somewhat unclear and it not certain when the Roy family moved to Bourne End Lane in the eastern part of Northchurch Parish. In early 1901, Jack was working as a timber carter whilst his younger brother, William, was a carpenter's labourer. Later the same year, Jack's father, James, died.

Sometime before 1911 Jack and his brother William left home. William emigrated to Queensland, Australia, whilst Jack moved to London and in 1914 was lodging in Norwood. It was here, on 5th September 1914, aged 31 years and 8 months, that Jack volunteered to join the army, stating that he wished to join the Royal West Kent Regiment. His medical examination took place the same day in Maidstone and his medical records show him as being 5ft 5ins tall, with a fresh complexion, brown eyes, brown hair and weighing 130lbs. Passing the medical with an A1 classification, Jack began his military training with the newly-formed Kent Regiment's 7th Battalion.

Meanwhile, in Queensland Jack's brother William volunteered to serve with the Australian Infantry Force. After completing his training William was posted to 15th Battalion AIF and sent to Gallipoli. Sadly, he was killed there on 8th August 1915.

Jack's army training took place at Maidstone, Purfleet and Colchester. On 1st June 1915, shortly before 7th Battalion was sent to France, Jack was transferred to the regiment's 9th Battalion and remained in England pending reassignment to another battalion. The following December, he was transferred to 2nd Battalion, Royal West Kent Regiment and left Bristol as part of the Indian Expeditionary Force in a draft of reinforcements bound for Basra in Mesopotamia.

Before the war, 2nd Battalion had served at Multan, India and was sent to Mesopotamia in February 1915. Two of its companies were attached to 30th Brigade, 6th (Poona) Division the following November and became part of the ill-fated British troops that were besieged at the town of Kut-al-

Amara. Jack and his comrades in the new draft were part of the relief force that was being assembled in the unsuccessful attempt to break the siege.

About the same time as the Turkish army captured Kut-al-Amara, Jack was taken ill with colitis and was invalided back to India onboard the hospital ship HMHS *Varsova*. It would be six months before he made a full recovery and returned to Basra and made his way north to where 2nd Battalion were still fighting the Turks.

In June 1918, he was granted a month's leave and returned to India. Two months after his return to Mesopotamia, Jack's battalion was in action for the last time during the Battle of Sharqat. During the fighting, he was shot in his right thigh and was treated at 36th Combined Field Ambulance. By the time he had recovered the war was over.

Jack's battalion later returned to India to become part of the Northwest Frontier Force tasked with restoring order following a rebellion among the local Afghan tribes. He spent four months in the area before leaving for home.

Back in Bourne End Lane, Jack returned to working as a general labourer and in 1921 he married Jane West. In 1939, Jack and Jane were still living in the cottage in Bourne End Lane with Jack now working as a roadman. He died in 1959, aged 77.

Harry Scott (1886 – 1941)
Private 41837, 12th Battalion, Norfolk Regiment

Harry Scott was born in a cottage on Northchurch High Street in July 1886 and was the second son of James Scott, a general labourer and bricklayer from Ley Hill, Chesham, and his wife, Emma. Three years after his birth Harry was christened alongside his brother, Charles, at St Mary's, Northchurch. Harry's first job after leaving school was working as a ploughboy on a local farm, but by 1911 he had become a bricklayer, possibly working alongside his father. The same year he married Rebecca Wesley at St Peter's, Berkhamsted, and moved to Highfield Road, Berkhamsted.

Although Harry's service record has not survived, it appears that he was conscripted in the spring of 1916 and posted to 2nd Bedfords. He joined them in France in the following September. Two months later Harry was admitted to 18th General Hospital in Camiers where he was treated for bronchitis and then spent a short period convalescing in the small town of Doulens, south-east of Arras.

After returning to duty, Harry saw action with 2nd Bedfords during the German retreat to the Hindenburg Line, the Battle of Arras and the Third Battle of Ypres. In January 1918, he was admitted to 11 Casualty Clearing Station at Godewaersvelde suffering from a typical complaint of solders eating food in the unhygienic conditions of the trenches – diarrhoea.

Harry later was transferred to the 12th Battalion, Norfolk Regiment, which arrived in France in the May of 1918 from Mesopotamia to help rebuild the British army following the German Spring Offensive and remained with them until the end of the war.

Harry was discharged from the army around the summer of 1919 and returned home. In 1920 he and Rebecca were living in Northchurch High Street, where Rebecca gave birth to their only child. The family later moved to Orchard End, but it is not currently known whether he returned to bricklaying after the war. They were still living in Orchard End in 1939, but by that time Harry was classed as 'incapacitated'. Harry Scott died in the late winter of 1941, aged just 54.

Robert Charles Talbot (1899 – 1973)
Private 50129, 1/1st Huntingdonshire Cyclists

Born in December 1899 in Northchurch, Robert Talbot was one of the youngest men from the village to serve in the war. His mother, Louisa, was a single parent and the younger sister of Charles Talbot, who was killed in France in 1914[12]. Robert grew up in his widowed grandmother's home, firstly in Gossoms End and later in Bell Lane.

Following his conscription, Robert was posted to the Huntingdonshire Cyclist Battalion, probably 2/1st Battalion, and began his training at Hinchingbrooke Park, Huntingdon, and continued it in Lincolnshire. Assigned mainly to reconnaissance and messenger roles, the men serving in the army's cyclist battalions were armed as infantry and, where local circumstances allowed, could provide mobile firepower, although many in the front line ended up serving as basic infantrymen. At the end of his training in 1918, Robert was transferred to 1/1st Battalion ready to be sent to France, but the war ended before he could be posted there.

Robert decided to remain in the army after the war and in 1919 he transferred to the Argyle & Scottish Highlanders, remaining with them until 1921, including a tour of duty in Ireland during the Irish War of Independence. He returned home to Northchurch in 1922 and became a gardener. In 1929, he married Louisa Elizabeth Freeman from Potten End, and later moved to one of the newly-built houses in Bridgewater Road, Berkhamsted. In 1939 Robert was still working as a gardener. He died in 1973, aged 73.

---

[12] Charles Talbot's story is told in *For Them's Sake*

Anthony William Tuke (1897 – 1975)
2nd Lieutenant, 4th Battalion, Scottish Rifles

In 1725, Mary Tuke, a member of the Quaker community in York, opened a grocery shop specialising in tea, coffee and the increasingly popular cocoa in the city's Walmgate. The business flourished and moved into larger premises with Mary later being joined by her nephew, William Tuke. After her death in 1752, the business passed to William Tuke who diversified the business into the manufacture of chocolate, which was by then becoming increasingly popular.

With the success of the business the Tuke family became an established part of the York community, and particularly in its social causes. When a fellow Quaker, Hannah Mills, died in York Lunatic Asylum in 1790, the resulting scandal led to William Tuke and other local Quakers looking at how the mentally ill were being treated in the city. As a result, he was able to raise enough money and support to found The Retreat, a dedicated home for mentally ill Quakers in the area. The revolutionary approach to caring for the patients at The Retreat, where they were treated as human beings in friendly surroundings and given decent food in accordance with Quaker beliefs, led to many similar improvements being introduced elsewhere in the country.

William Tuke's son, Henry, and grandson, Samuel, continued the association with The Retreat whilst still running the chocolate and tea business. Under Samuel Tuke, the firm became tea and chocolate merchants and in 1849 opened an office in London in conjunction with his son, William Murray Tuke. Back in York, in 1832 Samuel founded the Friends Provident Institution with fellow Quaker, Joseph Rowntree, which later became known as Friends Life. Outside of York, Samuel Tuke took an interest in prison reform, visiting several prisons with fellow Quaker, Elizabeth Fry.

In 1862, Joseph Rowntree bought the Tuke family's chocolate business and started the well-known Rowntree chocolate manufacturing empire. The following year, William Murray Tuke, who was now living in Saffron Walden, Essex, used some of the proceeds from the sale of the business to join his brother-in-law, George Stacey Gibson, to become a partner in the banking firm of Gibson, Tuke & Gibson, which was also known as the Saffron Walden and North Essex Bank. In 1880, the bank became closely involved with another bank, Fordham, Gibson & Co of nearby Royston. William Murray Tuke's son, William Favill Tuke, later joined the Saffron Walden and North Essex Bank and in 1896 the bank merged with Fordham, Gibson & Co to become Barclay and Co Ltd. On 24th February the following year, William Favill Tuke's son, Anthony William Tuke, was born in Saffron Walden.

Anthony William Tuke was educated at Winchester College and joined its Officer Training Corps, rising to the rank of Corporal. He left Winchester in June 1915 and started work as a clerk in the Transport Department of the Admiralty. By now, his father had moved to Norcott Court, a large detached property with substantial grounds, situated to the north of Dudswell, which belonged to the Loxley family, its former owner, Captain Arthur Noel Loxley, having been killed the previous January following the sinking of his ship, HMS *Formidable* by a German submarine[13].

The following year, Anthony Tuke was conscripted and told to report to the Recruiting Officer at Watford. Sent home to await his call-up, three months later Anthony's medical report described him as being 5ft 9¾ins tall, weighing 168lbs and with perfect vision. Shortly afterwards, he applied for a Commission, stating that his preferred unit was The Kings Royal Rifle Corps. In October 1916, having been temporarily assigned as a Private in the Essex Regiment, he joined No3 Officer Cadet Battalion at Bristol for training. Earlier that year, a new system of prospective officer training had been introduced which meant that temporary commissions could now only be granted if a man had previously been through an Officer Cadet Unit. Entrants had to be aged over 18½ and to have served in the ranks, or to have been with a school or university Officer Training Corps; Anthony met both criteria. The training course at Bristol lasted four and a half months and on 24th January 1917 he was granted a Commission with 4th Battalion, The Scottish Rifles, based in Greenock.

It was not until the following December that Anthony left for France where he joined his new unit near Cambrai. Less than a month later however, he reported to 27th Field Ambulance suffering from a problem with his foot which was initially diagnosed as Inflammation of the Connective Tissue (ICT) a parasitic infection which, if left untreated, could lead to gangrene, Anthony was transferred to 55th Casualty Clearing Station and then to No2 British Red Cross Hospital in Rouen suffering from sepsis. He remained there under treatment for four weeks before being invalided back to Norcott Court to recover.

Initially given two months' leave, a series of Medical Boards were later held to assess Anthony's health and the probability of him returning to frontline service. The first of these took place at Caxton Hall, London where, although not considered fit to return to the front line, Anthony was given the medical category of C1. A second review in May 1918 found that the injury had healed sufficiently to enable him to be fit enough to return to duty.

Ordered to report to duty at the Scottish Rifles depot at Dunbar, Scotland, Anthony was to remain there for the remainder of the war. On 2nd

---

[13] Arthur Noel Loxley's story is told in *For Them's Sake*

July 1919, he was demobilised. That same year, he joined Barclays Bank and married Agnes Edna Gannaway, the daughter of a ship's draughtsman from Jarrow. In 1920, Anthony relinquished his Commission with the Scottish Rifles, but retained the honorary rank of Lieutenant.

1920 was to be an eventful one in the Tuke family; during the summer Agnes gave birth to their first child, Anthony Favill Tuke jnr. and Anthony's father, William Favill Tuke was elected to the main board of Barclays Bank, having become a General Manager in 1916. Two years later William Favill Tuke was instrumental in the creation of the Northchurch Working Men's Club in New Road which enabled ex-servicemen to meet, play games and chat. The Tuke family continued to live at Norcott Court for some years before moving to Ayot St Lawrence, near Welwyn, Hertfordshire.

Within four years of joining Barclay's Bank, Anthony William Tuke had become a local director at Luton. In 1925, his father became Vice-Chairman of the bank and in 1931 became a General Manager at its head office. The following year he became Deputy Chairman and served as Chairman between 1934 and 1936. Anthony followed in his father's footsteps, joining the bank's main board as Vice-Chairman in 1946 and becoming Deputy Chairman in 1947 and finally Chairman in 1951.

By the time Anthony William Tuke stepped down as Chairman in 1962, Barclays had become the largest bank in the United Kingdom. He retired as a member of the board in 1972 and died three years later[14].

Arthur James Weedon (1887 – 1964)
Private 612871, 19th Battalion, The London Regiment

Although Arthur Weedon did not move to Northchurch from north London until after the war, he had strong links with the area via both his parents. Arthur's father, James Weedon, was a carman from Wilstone, whilst his mother, Sarah, came from nearby Aldbury. Both had moved to Kentish Town soon after their marriage in 1883 which was where Arthur was born in July 1887. On leaving school Arthur started work as an office boy, and later became a clerk.

March 1909 saw Arthur marrying Arabella Louisa Phillips, the daughter of a fisherman from East Boldre, Hampshire, at St Cuthbert's, Hampstead. At first the newlyweds lived with Arthur's parents in their two-story Victorian terraced house, which was big enough to accommodate both couples. By 1911 however, Arabella had given birth to her first son, and

---

[14] Anthony William Tuke's eldest son, Anthony Favill Tuke (jnr), joined Barclays Bank after serving in the Second World War, and became Chairman of the bank between 1973 and 1981.

with Arthur earning more money working as a financier's clerk, they moved to a house nearby where two more children would later be born.

With a young family to provide for, 27-year-old Arthur did not volunteer to join the army when war broke out and he was probably conscripted during the summer of 1916. After completing his training, he was posted to 'A' Coy, 19th Battalion, The London Regiment, and sent to France. By this time Arabella was pregnant with their fourth child.

On 7th June 1917, 19th Battalion were in reserve during the opening phase of what was later to be called the Battle of Messines, an attempt to prevent the German forces taking the high ground near Ypres. It was hot and dry, and Arthur and his colleagues were forced to wear gas masks for lengthy periods of time for fear of the Germans using gas shells. The hot, dry conditions also gave a perfect opportunity for German aircraft to view the allied advance from the air, providing details to the enemy artillery as well as the chance to fly low over the trenches and strafe the British troops below. It was during one such attack on 13th June, which specifically targeted 'A' Coy's position, that Arthur was shot in the forearm. Three days later, having receiving initial treatment at a Casualty Clearing Station, Arthur boarded 31st Ambulance Train at Hazebrouck which took him and other wounded soldiers to one of the military hospitals in Étaples. Oddly, the records for the military train show Arthur, along with five other soldiers from various other regiments, as all having 'self-inflicted' wounds.

How long Arthur was out of action is not known, but it is likely that he returned to England for a short period of leave in early 1918. By now, his parents and wife had moved to a cottage in Northchurch High Street where his father, James Weedon, was now running an Off-licence. In the autumn of 1918, Arabella gave birth to her last child, but it would be some months before Arthur was able to see it following his demobilisation at the end of 1919.

The extended Weedon family were to remain in Northchurch High Street for several years. Arabella gradually took over the running of the Off -licence, branching out to also sell haberdashery and second-hand clothes. In the 1939 Register, she is described as a 'dealer'. Arthur, meanwhile, became a civil servant. They later left Northchurch and moved to George Street, Berkhamsted. Arthur Weedon died in January 1964, aged 76.

Harvey Welling (1899 – 1983)
Rifleman 44339, 11th Battalion, Kings Royal Rifle Corps

Harvey Welling was born in April 1899. His father, Harvey Welling (snr), was a labourer from Berkhamsted whilst his mother, Janet Ellen, came from Cumberland. In 1901, the Welling family were living in Great Gaddesden, but not long after moved to a cottage at Little Heath, in the eastern part of Northchurch Parish. By 1911, Harvey Welling (snr) had become a domestic coachman at one of the local large houses and the family cottage had also become very crowded, as the four-roomed building was now home to nine people, including Harvey's paternal grandfather. After leaving school he joined his older brother, Stanley, working at one of the local sawmills.

Harvey was conscripted into the Kings Royal Rifle Corps in April 1917, and was later posted to their 11th Battalion, joining them in France the following November, just prior to the start of the Battle of Cambrai. The following year this battalion helped to hold the German Spring Offensive and took part in the slow advance across France following the Battle of Amiens. The battalion ended the war close to the French / Belgian border at Le Quesnoy.

With the war over, and when weather permitted, Harvey and his battalion comrades spent much of their time with the unenviable task of filling in some of the trenches that now dominated northern France, returning it to farmland. This was a still a highly dangerous job as unexploded shells and mortar bombs were frequently unearthed. By now, the demobilisation process had started, but Harvey remained with the Kings Royal Rifle Corps until January 1920, possibly as part of the newly-formed Army of Occupation based at Cologne. He later returned home, but he had found a taste for adventure whilst in the army, so later that year, still only 21, he applied to join the Royal Air Force. He was accepted and joined them on 27th October 1920 as an Aircraft Hand, signing up for a total of twelve years, six of which would be in the reserves. His RAF service record from that time shows Harvey as being 5ft 8½ins tall, with dark brown hair, brown eyes and a fresh complexion.

He was posted to one of the many airbases in Essex that had been built during the war following the threat of Zeppelin raids on the country. In 1925, having obtained permission from the RAF, Harvey, now a Corporal, married 19-year-old Gladys Ethel Sell at Newport Parish Church, Essex. Two years later, he became a father and transferred to the RAF reserves. Moving with his family to a house in Berkhamsted it is likely that Harvey once again started work at a local sawmill. In June 1930, he was discharged from the RAF having served nearly 10 years with them. Two years later he became a father for a second time.

With the possibility of a new war with Germany breaking out, Harvey decided to rejoin the RAF Reserve in March 1938. The 1939 Register shows Gladys living in Hazel Road, Berkhamsted with her two sons and Harvey absent, presumably having already been recalled to duty. After the war, he became a foreman at the sawmill. He died in the autumn of 1983, aged 84.

4 - The Terriers

In 1908, significant reforms were introduced to the British Army by the then Secretary of State for War, Richard Burden Haldane. These reforms enabled the creation of an Expeditionary Force to be sent overseas during wartime, whilst a newly-created part-time Territorial Force (TF) would provide home defence. The men serving in the Territorial Force would soon become known as 'Terriers', or by the more unflattering name of 'Saturday Night Soldiers'. Apart from the Guards, the Irish regiments, the King's Royal Rifle Corps and Rifle Brigade, the newly-formed Terriers were organised along county lines and replaced their existing Militia units. In the local area, the Bedfordshire Regiment's 1st and 2nd (Hertfordshire) volunteer battalions were merged to form a single Hertfordshire battalion. Two years later, the new battalion left the Bedfordshire regiment and was renamed 1st Battalion, Hertfordshire Regiment (TF), commonly known as the 'Hertshires'. Men from Hemel Hempstead, Berkhamsted, Northchurch, Tring and Ashridge joining the Hertshires were posted to 'F' Coy.

Those joining the Terriers normally did so for a minimum of four years, which could be then extended in blocks of four years. Whilst continuing with their civilian occupations, the men were expected to meet for monthly drill sessions with their unit and to attend the annual army camp. Additionally, they were not obliged to serve overseas, although they could agree to do so, should the need arise.

At the end of July 1914, it was the turn of the Ashridge Estate, just to the north of Northchurch, to host the annual two-week Territorial Camp of the East Midland Brigade, which incorporated the Terriers serving in units in Cambridgeshire, Bedfordshire, Northamptonshire and Hertfordshire. Over a period of several days some 4,000 men descended on the large tented camp that had been erected in Ashridge Park facing the main house and was probably the largest body of men ever housed under canvas on the estate.

Despite glorious weather and the

Ashridge Territorial Camp, July 1914
Courtesy of BLH&MS

65

numerous sporting activities available, not everyone at the camp was happy; a drummer with the Northamptonshire Regiment wrote a postcard home complaining about the fact that nearby Berkhamsted had only one 'picture house' and saying that 'it is very dull here'!

Three days before Britain declared war on Germany, the *West Herts and Watford Observer* commented that *'... it is possible in view of the military movements on the Continent that the Brigade may not break up at the end of the Camp'*. This prediction proved true and at 05:00 on 3rd August the men of the Hertfordshire Regiment were ordered to strike camp and return home to await further orders. War was declared at 23:00 the following day.

On 5th August, the Hertshires were embodied for war service and those that volunteered to serve overseas were sent with others from the East Midland Brigade to the Romford area where they prepared to leave for France. In the event, they had to wait a further two months before sailing for France and spent their time training in the area around Bury St Edmunds. In November 1914, the Hertshires were transferred to 4th (Guards) Brigade, 2nd Division, and left England on board the SS *City of Chester* bound for Le Havre.

Robert Davis (1892 – 1958)
Private 265427, 1st Battalion, Hertfordshire Regiment

Robert Davis joined the Hertshires in 1913. Born in Northchurch in December 1892 to farmworker, Frederick Davis and his wife Mary Ann, he spent his early years living in a cottage at Shooterways Farm where his father and grandfather both worked. After his grandfather's retirement and his father's early death in 1908, aged just 40, Robert's mother moved to a four-roomed cottage in New Road, Northchurch, where, to make ends meet, she took in washing and rented out one room to a lodger. Robert meanwhile, started work as a farm labourer.

It is not clear whether Robert attended the 1913 Annual Territorial Force Camp at Dibgate Farm, near Sevenoaks, Kent, but he was certainly present at the following year's event on the Ashridge Estate. As one of the men that volunteered to serve overseas, Robert sailed to France with his battalion in November 1914 and appears to have survived the war unscathed apart from spending a short spell under treatment for scabies at the start of 1917.

Following his demobilisation in 1919, he returned to his New Road home and the following year married Susan Violet Dean, the daughter of a Berkhamsted carpenter, the couple later setting up home in Clarence Road, Berkhamsted. In 1939, Robert was working as a bricklayer and living with his wife in a cottage in Darrs Lane, Northchurch. At that time, he was also serving in the local auxiliary fire service. He died in 1958, aged 65. His wife, Susan, was to live for a further 38 years, passing away in 1996, aged 100.

John Duncombe (1869 – 1915)
Private 3914, 1st Hertfordshire Regiment

At the age of 45, John Duncombe was one of the oldest Northchurchmen to enlist in the army. He was born in Lambeth in 1869, to Tring-born labourer Henry Duncombe and his wife, Ellen. Soon after his birth the family moved back to Hertfordshire, settling in The Wilderness, Berkhamsted, before moving into a cottage in Ellesmere Road.

By 1890 the Duncombe family had moved to Provident Place, Berkhamsted, with John now working as a gardener. That November, he travelled to Bedford where he attempted to enlist with the Bedfordshire Regiment for the standard twelve-year term of service. John's enlistment papers show that for some reason he stated that he was over a year younger than he actually was. The document also shows, him as standing 5ft 6ins tall, weighing 124lbs, with a fresh complexion, grey eyes and brown hair. The doctor conducting John's medical examination noted however that he considered him to be of '*short sight, under chest for height and seems deficient in intelligence*'. John's application to join the army was consequently rejected.

Four months later, however, and now working as a labourer at Coopers chemical factory in Berkhamsted, John applied to join the local Militia, 4th Battalion, Bedfordshire Regiment, for a six-year term. This time, John gave his correct age on his enlistment papers, but explained that his previous rejection by the Bedfordshire Regiment was down to 'skin disease'. Passing the medical examination at Hertford, John started his Militia training. His time in the Militia, during which he attended all bar one of the annual training camps, ended in 1897.

In March 1900, John, now working as a bricklayer's labourer for James Honour, a building contractor in Tring, married Mary Ann Bignell at St Peter's Church, Berkhamsted, and moved into a cottage at the bottom end of Upper Kings Road. Two years later Mary gave birth to a daughter, with a son being born in 1904. John attempted to rejoin the Militia in 1905, but was rejected after failing the medical examination. Sometime between 1906 and 1910 the Duncombe family moved to a cottage in Norris's Terrace, Gossoms End and during that period Mary Duncombe gave birth to two further children.

The coming of war in 1914 saw 45-year-old John enlisting as a Terrier with 1st Battalion, Hertfordshire Regiment. The maximum age that former soldiers were allowed to join the Territorial Force was 45, which meant that 72 days after enlisting, John was discharged from the Hertshires deemed 'no longer fit for military service'.

Three months later he died at his home in Gossoms End following a stroke and pneumonia. His widow, Mary, later received a small pension from the army to help support her young family.

Sidney Wilfred Frank Holland (1898 – 1979)
Private 268273, 1st Battalion, Hertfordshire Regiment

Sidney Holland, commonly known as Frank, only spent a short time living in Northchurch Parish. Born in Watford in July 1898, Frank was one of six children of miller, John Holland, and his wife Elizabeth, who in 1911 were living at Mill Cottage in Bourne End.

Although underage, early in 1915 Frank managed to enlist with 22nd (Kensington) Battalion, Royal Fusiliers and in August that year, he moved with his battalion to Tidworth Camp, Wiltshire, where final preparations were being made for their move to France.

Frank's service record has not survived, but it is likely that he was wounded or fell sick sometime in 1917, and had to return to England for treatment. By December that year, he had fully recovered and had been posted to the Bedfordshire Regiment's 5th (Reserve) battalion at Crowborough Camp, Sussex. On 11th December he was posted to the Hertshires and left for France, joining them near Ypres two days later. He remained with the Hertshires for the rest of the war.

Frank was demobilised in April 1919 and returned home to Mill Cottage. It appears that he did not stay there long, however, moving to Wealdstone in north London, where he became a clerk. In July 1932, he married fellow clerk, Edna Lillian Rogers, in St Dunstan's, Acton, and was later to become the father of two children. In 1939, Frank and his family were back in Watford, where he worked as a district auditor. He died there in 1979, aged 80.

Ernest Waterton, MM (1894 – 1950)
Private 266017, 1st Battalion, Hertfordshire Regiment

Ernest Waterton was born in Little Heath in August 1894 and was one of twelve children of road worker, Samuel Abiathar Waterton, and his wife, Ellen. After leaving school in 1908, he started work as a cowman on a local farm.

Unlike his cousin, Harry Waterton, Ernest did not join the Hertshires before the war and it was only its outbreak that prompted him to do so. Enlisting in either September or October 1914, he joined them in France in July the following year as part of a draft of 70 men. Details of Ernest's subsequent service with the battalion is not known, except that in September 1918 he was awarded the Military Medal but, unfortunately, no citation has been found.

Ernest was demobilised in February 1919 and on returning home started working for a local nursery, possibly the same one where his uncle, Jabez Waterton, worked. By 1922, he was living in Great Gaddesden where he married Ethel Lily Spurr from the nearby hamlet of Piccotts End. The couple later moved to a house in Berkhamsted High Street, and in 1939, Ernest was working as a lorry driver for the London & North Western Railway. He died in 1950, aged 56.

Harry Waterton DCM (1892 – 1968)
Sergeant 265170, 1st Battalion, Hertfordshire Regiment

Harry Waterton, Ernest Waterton's cousin, joined the Hertshires in 1912. Born in July 1892 in Potten End, Harry was one of nine children of Jabez Waterton and his wife, Kezaher. Jabez worked as a farm labourer and later as a nurseryman. Shortly after Harry's birth, Jabez moved his family into a cottage in Frithsden, where Harry grew up and later became a farm labourer. His first annual camp with the Hertshires was in 1913 at Dibgate Farm, near Sevenoaks.

Harry was another of the men who volunteered to serve overseas, leaving for France in November 1914, and spent the next eighteen months taking part in the major battles in northern France before moving south in 1916 to take part in the Somme Offensive.

On 12th November 1916, the Hertshires left their billets and moved to the former German-held *Schwaben* Redoubt near the river Ancre. At 05:45, with thick mist sweeping the valley, the British artillery opened fire on what was to be the last major battle of the Somme Offensive. Advancing under artillery cover, Harry, now an acting sergeant and armed with a machine gun, advanced with the troops some 1,600 yards and captured a German trench system. Over 250 enemy prisoners were taken, and despite several German counter-attacks, the line held. For his role during the advance and helping to fend off the counter attacks, Harry was later awarded the DCM.

After being demobilised in the spring of 1919, he returned home to Frithsden. He was not to stay there long however, as by 1921 he had moved to the village of Ewelme in south Oxfordshire where he had obtained work as a gardener. That same year he married Mary Ellen Lowe in the 12th Century Cotswold church of St Mary's, Charlbury. In 1939, Harry was still working as gardener and living with his family in Abingdon, Oxfordshire. He died there in 1968, aged 75.

Arthur William Wright (1897 – 1957)
Private 266713, 1st Battalion, Hertfordshire Regiment

One of eight children, Northchurch-born Arthur Wright, son of blacksmith, George Wright and his wife Annie, joined the Hertshires in June 1915. Born in Norris's Terrace, Gossoms End in August 1897, the Wright family later moved to Shrublands Avenue, Berkhamsted.

Arthur served with the Hertshires in France from 1916 until the end of the war. In March 1918 he reported to 34th Casualty Clearing Station at Marchélepot complaining of a problem with this right foot and he was sent to 14th Field Ambulance, where he was treated for ICT. Although the treatment was successful the problem would return nine months later, just after the war had ended.

Demobilised in early 1919, Arthur returned home to Gossoms End and later became a painter and decorator. In 1926, he married Mabel Parker from Haddenham, Buckinghamshire. Arthur Wright died in early 1957, aged 59.

---oOo---

In November 1915, 24th (Home Counties) Battalion, Rifle Brigade, was formed at Halton Camp, near Wendover. One of seven new Territorial Force battalions created around this time by the Rifle Brigade, it was made up of drafts of supernumeraries from units based in Great Britain on garrison duties. The men serving in 24th Battalion came from several regiments including the Queen's, Norfolk, Suffolk, Bedfordshire, Royal Sussex, East Surrey, Essex, Royal West Kent and Hertfordshire. Soon after their creation the new Rifle Brigade battalions were posted overseas on garrison duty, with 18th, 23rd and 24th Battalions being sent to India. Among the territorial soldiers serving with 24th Battalion were four men from Northchurch – Fred Carter, Charles Hinton, James Honor and Walter Duncombe, and all would spend the next four years in various parts of India.

Fred Carter (1875 – 1951)
Rifleman 206424, 24th Battalion, Rifle Brigade

Fred Carter was born in September 1875 in the hamlet of Hudnall near Little Gaddesden. His father, Henry Carter, worked on a nearby farm. After leaving school, Fred became a farm labourer and later worked as a general handyman and gardener for Edward Bovill at Norcott Court.

On 7th April 1900, Fred married Beatrice Rance at St Mary's, Northchurch. Beatrice gave birth to a daughter the following year, with a son being born in 1902. He continued working at Norcott Court for at least another ten years and, at some point, he became a Terrier.

With the coming of war, Fred, being nearly forty years old, did not volunteer to serve overseas and so remained in England on garrison duties with the Hertfordshire Regiment, becoming one of those who were later transferred to 24th Battalion, Rifle Brigade and sent to India. It was not until November 1919, a year after the war ended, that he returned home.

By now, Fred's family were living in Middle Road, Berkhamsted, and it is unlikely that he returned to his job at Norcott Court, with the estate now being leased to the Tuke family. Fred later moved to Bennetts End Lane in Leverstock Green and in 1939, he and Beatrice were still living in the Hemel Hempstead area, where he was working as an engineer at the local waterworks. He died in 1951, aged 75.

Charles Court Hinton (1878 – 1946)
Rifleman 206469, 24th Battalion, Rifle Brigade

Charles Hinton was born in September 1878 at the family home in George Street, Berkhamsted. Despite this being in the parish of St Peter's, Berkhamsted, when he was three months old, his parents, Frederick and Alma Hinton, arranged for him to be christened at the same time as his older siblings Arthur and Beatrice at St Mary's, Northchurch. Seven years later Frederick Hinton died, leaving Alma to bring up her family. By 1891 she was living with her children in Holliday Street, Berkhamsted and working as a needlewoman repairing items of clothing. Charles was still at school, whilst his two older brothers were now working.

After leaving school Charles started work at the William Cooper & Nephew chemical factory in Berkhamsted, but on reaching the age of 18 he decided to sign up for the local militia, only to change his mind shortly afterwards and enlist with the Rifle Brigade. Charles was 5ft 6½ins tall, weighing 119lbs with a fresh complexion, grey eyes and brown hair. Unfortunately, his service record for this period with the Rifle Brigade has not survived, but it is known that he served with them for a short period during the Boer War.

By the time of the 1901 Census, Charles was back in Berkhamsted working as a general labourer and living with his mother in Gossoms End. Later that year he married Louisa Rance at St Mary's, Northchurch. Louisa gave birth to their first child the following year, with another arriving two years later.

In October 1914, now aged 36, Charles decided to rejoin his old regiment, but, possibly because of his age or a low medical classification, he initially remained in England was later transferred to 24th Battalion going with them to India. Sometime during his time there he was taken ill and it is likely that he was sent home. Awarded a Silver War Badge, he was demobilised in October 1919.

Charles later became a painter, but by 1939 he had become unemployed. His wife, Louisa had died four years earlier and Charles was now living with his son and daughter-in-law in Gossoms End. He died seven years later, aged 67.

James Honor (1880 – 1958)
Rifleman 206470, 24th Battalion, Rifle Brigade

James Honor was born in Bell Lane, Northchurch, in June 1880, the son of local bricklayer, Fred Honor, and his wife, Annie. The family later moved to a cottage in nearby Orchard End. James became a tailor and in 1905 he married Annie Meager at St Mary's Northchurch. Having settled in a 4-roomed cottage in Bell Lane, close to where James was born, Annie gave birth to a son two years later.

It appears that James joined the Rifle Brigade around the same time as Charles Hinton as their original service numbers are adjacent, but it is unclear whether James served alongside him during the Boer War. James was later transferred to 24th Battalion and was to remain in India with this unit until May 1919 when he returned home.

It is not currently known whether James resumed his job as a tailor on his return to Northchurch, but in 1939 he and Annie were living in a recently-built bungalow in New Road with James described as a coat presser. He died in 1958, aged 77.

Frederick Stevens Pocock (1888 – 1957)
Sergeant 206508, 24th Battalion, Rifle Brigade

Frederick Pocock was the only child of coal depot manager, Fred Pocock and his wife Louisa. Born in Berkhamsted in July 1888, Frederick later became a railway clerk, a job he retained for the rest of his working life. He also joined the Rifle Brigade as a Territorial solder, eventually rising to the rank of sergeant.

In the autumn of 1915, shortly before 24th Battalion was sent to India, Frederick married Ethel Aldridge, a dressmaker from Gossoms End, and it was at Ethel's parents' address that Frederick was registered in the 1918 and 1919 Absent Voters Lists. Frederick returned from India towards the end of 1919 and was demobilised. By 1921, Frederick and Ethel were living in Montague Road, Berkhamsted and would later raise two boys. In the early 1930s, the family moved to West Road, Berkhamsted. Frederick Pocock died in 1957, aged 68.

Walter George Duncombe (1888 – 1965)
Private 241964, Royal West Kent Regiment

Born in Berkhamsted in April 1888, Walter Duncombe was one of George and Sarah Duncombe's nine children. A general labourer, George and his growing family lived in a house in Berkhamsted High Street before moving to Gossoms End. After leaving school, Walter became one of the many gardeners working in the local area.

Walter enlisted as a Terrier in October 1914 and later became a member of 24th Battalion, Rifle Brigade and posted to India. At some stage during the war, Walter left 24th Battalion and was transferred to 1/5th Royal Kent Regiment (TF). Later, like many of the servicemen serving in India, he became sick, but it appears that Walter remained in India until early 1919. Within months of returning to Gossoms End Walter married Lydia Franklin, a children's nurse from Banbury, the wedding taking place at St Peter's Berkhamsted. Soon afterwards, he was formally discharged from the army and awarded a Silver War Badge on the grounds of sickness.

By 1921, Walter and Lydia had left the area with Walter now working as a gardener for Reginald Charles Hart Dyke, a wealthy retired solicitor, who owned a red-brick Jacobean house near Hatfield called Great Nast Hyde. They lived at the Lodge on the estate and it was here over the next three years that their two children were born. By 1939, Walter had become the estate's head gardener, and it is assumed that he retained his post when the house was requisitioned shortly afterwards by the nearby de Havilland aircraft manufacturers who used Great Nast Hyde to house visitors to the company. Walter Duncombe died in 1965, aged 77.

Charles Bignell (1889 – 1926)
Private 241961, 4th Reserve Battalion, Royal West Kent Regiment

Charles Bignell was born in the family home in Northchurch High Street in July 1889, the fourth child of George and Elizabeth Bignell. His father, originally from New Mill, Tring, worked at William Cooper & Nephew's Chemical factory in Berkhamsted. Growing up in Northchurch, Charles later became a gardener. On 27th April 1912, he married Elsie Goodege, at St Peter and St Paul's, Little Gaddesden. Elsie came from Little Gaddesden and worked as a parlour maid at Boxwell House in Berkhamsted. The newlyweds moved into a cottage in New Road, Northchurch and Elizabeth later gave birth to twin girls, but unfortunately one died shortly afterwards.

Charles's military service record has not survived, but like his older brother, Alfred, it appears that he joined the

Private Charles Bignell, his wife and daughter
Courtesy of Vivienne Beaumont

Territorials before the war. A photograph of Charles with his wife and young daughter shows him wearing a Hertfordshire Regiment badge and dates from late 1913. Details of his army service following the outbreak of the war are also somewhat unclear, but, unlike Alfred, it appears that he did not volunteer for overseas service, and initially remained as a Territorial soldier assigned to home defence. Charles was certainly in England until the late spring of 1915, as Elsie gave birth to another daughter in March the following year. He was later sent to India along with other Terriers.

The 1918 Absent Voters List for Little Gaddesden shows Charles as registered at Ringshall, a small hamlet close to Little Gaddesden, and serving with 4th Reserve Battalion, The Queens Own (Royal West Kent) Regiment. This home-based unit had its headquarters near Maidstone, Kent, so it is possible that Charles returned from India because of sickness and having recovered, was subsequently transferred to 4th Reserve Battalion.

Charles was demobilised early in 1919. At that time, Elsie and her daughters were still living in Ringshall, but when Charles found work at William Cooper & Nephew in Berkhamsted the family moved back to New Road, Northchurch. Here, in 1921, Elsie gave birth to another set of twins.

Charles was to continue working for Coopers until his untimely death in 1926, aged 37.

Francis Drake Hugh Brockman (1884 – 1969)
Captain, 1/4th The Buffs (East Kent Regiment)

Francis Drake Hugh Brockman was born at Beachborough, a large country estate close to the village of Newington-next-Hythe, Kent, in August 1884 and was the second son of Francis Drake Brockman, a wealthy land owner, and his wife, Margaretta. His older brother, William, had been born at Beachborough two years earlier.

The Brockmans were a long-established Kent family, owning land in the county since the 14th century and had acquired the 300-acre estate during the reign of Elizabeth 1. The most famous member of the family, Sir William Brockman (1595–1654), was appointed Sheriff of Kent in 1642 and was later imprisoned by Oliver Cromwell during the English Civil War for attempting to start a rebellion in Kent against the Parliamentary forces. Following his release from gaol in 1645, Sir William Brockman was unrepentant and played a significant part in the defence of Maidstone in 1648. After the town's surrender, he was arrested and later gaoled in Dover Castle. Another William Brockman was Member of Parliament for Kent between 1690 and 1695. In the mid-18th century, Beachborough was inherited by a near relative named Drake, who then legally assumed the name and arms of the Brockman family. From then on, the owners of Beachborough and their male heirs added Drake to their names, although the ladies of the family did not.

In 1876, Francis's father, Francis Drake Brockman, inherited Beachborough on the death of his uncle, Revd. Frederick Brockman. By all accounts, his father took his responsibilities as the local Squire very seriously, repairing the local churches, building schools, serving as a Justice of the Peace and becoming Chairman of the local Parish Council.

In 1901, Francis and his older brother, William, were both attending Tonbridge School. Nine years later however, hard times and heavy death duties had forced his father to lease Beachborough to Sir Arthur Markham, a British industrialist and politician. The Brockman family moved to Oaklands, an eight-bedroomed house in Cranleigh, Surrey. Here, in 1910, one of Francis's sisters, Phyllis, became heavily involved in the suffragette movement, becoming the Secretary of the Cranleigh branch of the National Union of Women's Suffrage Societies. He meanwhile, was living at Oaklands with his parents whilst working as an architect in London with Sir Edwin Landseer Lutyens.

It is unclear when the Brockman family took possession of Exhims, the former home of John Forster Alcock, which still stands at the junction of Northchurch High Street with Darrs Lane. In 1914 the house was occupied by a Miles Hopkinson, but by May 1915, Francis's father was already active in local matters, when he gave out the prizes at the Northchurch Technical Institute's exhibition of work.

At the outbreak of war, Francis quickly obtained a Commission with 1/4th The Buffs (East Kent Regiment), the local Territorial Force for the Beachborough estate. On 29th October 1914, he left Southampton for India with his battalion, part of the Home Counties Division. The battalion arrived at Bombay on 2nd December and was sent to Kamptee, a small military town located in the Nagpur District of Maharashtra, some 10 miles north-east of Nagpur. It is likely that Francis was a member of 'D' Coy, which was made up of men from Hythe and Folkestone, some of whom probably worked on the Beachborough estate. The battalion remained at Kamptee until the end of July 1915, when it sailed for Aden for a further period of garrison duties. It returned to India the following February.

In August 1916, Francis was attached to 'C' Coy of 1/5th, (Weald of Kent) Battalion, and posted to Mesopotamia where he joined his new battalion at Es Sinn. Es Sinn had been the site of a major battle between Anglo-Indian and Turkish forces in September 1915, which led to the defeat of the Turks and the recapture of the town of Kut-al-Amara. On 1st October, Francis was appointed an Orderly Officer in 35th Brigade, but two weeks later he was admitted to hospital suffering from what his service record describes as 'NYD [Not Yet Diagnosed] – neurasthenia?', a condition characterised by physical or mental exhaustion. As a result, at the end of October, Francis was invalided back to India where he rejoined his former battalion at Bareilly, a district in the northern Indian state of Uttar Pradesh.

In May 1917, Francis was promoted to Lieutenant, backdated to 1st June the previous year, and shortly afterwards to Acting Captain and put in charge of a Company. Within weeks however, Francis became ill once again, which forced him to return to the rank of Lieutenant. He was to remain in India until early 1919 when he relinquished his Commission, but retained the honorary title of Lieutenant. He left India for the last time on 10th March on board the SS *Ellora* and returned to the UK and the family home in Northchurch.

During the war, the Brockman's former family home at Beachborough became The Queen's Canadian Military Hospital. Its location close to Folkestone made it an ideal site for treating wounded Canadian soldiers returning from France.

Queen's Canadian Military Hospital
Author's Collection

In 1921, the Brockman family left Exhims, and moved to Bargrove, a large house in Green End Road, Boxmoor. Francis Drake Hugh Brockman never married and died in St Albans in 1969, aged 84.

George Robert Engeldow (1889 – 1966)
Lieutenant, Indian Army Reserve of Officers

George Engeldow was born in Marylebone, London, in September 1889 into a family with a strong metalworking tradition. Both his father, Frederick, and his grandfather had jobs as zinc workers in an area of Marylebone where many artisan workers lived. When George was about five years old, Frederick Engeldow and his family moved to Gossoms End, where he set up a new workshop and started advertising for work in the local trade directories.

Unfortunately, Frederick died in the summer of 1904, aged just 44, and, once his schooling was over, George decided to maintain the family metalworking tradition, becoming a whitesmith[15]. It also appears that sometime after 1911 George moved to Hampshire and became a member of 1st Wessex Brigade, Royal Field Artillery TF, which was based at a drill

---

[15] A person who worked with "white" or light-coloured metals such as tin and pewter

hall in Portsmouth. The 1st Wessex Brigade consisted of three batteries, each made up of four obsolete 15-pounder field guns.

In December 1914, George and his brigade were sent to India to relieve troops of the Regular Army, serving there on garrison duty. By 1916, he had become a sergeant and decided, like several other non-commissioned officers serving in India, to apply for a commission. By that time, the Indian Army had expanded rapidly and this had resulted in a severe shortage of trained officers. In May 1917, his application was approved and he became a member of the Indian Army Reserve of Officers. A year later and now a Lieutenant, he was posted to the Northwest Frontier and attached to 35th Scinde Horse. His new unit had been raised in 1838 to protect traders along the old Spice Route between India and Afghanistan and had continued in that role ever since.

Following the end of the war the Indian Army began to return home from the battlefields and most of the British officers were released from duty. Having relinquished his commission, George returned to his mother's home in Gossoms End, where he restarted his career as a whitesmith. In the autumn of 1919, he married Ethel Louisa Flitney, and by the summer of 1923 Ethel had given birth to two children.

George and his family continued to live in Gossoms End until at least the outbreak of the Second World War. He died in 1966, aged 77.

Frederick Fisher (1885 – 1981)
Private 241278, 1/5th Battalion, East Kent Regiment

Born in November 1885, Frederick Fisher was one of William and Elizabeth Fisher's nine children. He grew up in the family home in Kitsbury Road, and later Middle Road, Berkhamsted, and on leaving school he became an errand boy, before turning to gardening. By 1911 the Fisher family had moved to Gossoms End, and William was working as a house painter. Twenty-five-year-old Frederick had, however, moved away and was working as a gardener at Tresco Abbey on the Scilly Isles, which was leased from the Duchy of Cornwall by the Dorrien-Smith family. How long he spent there is unclear, as in 1914 he joined the Territorial Force and became a soldier with 1/5th Battalion, East Kent Regiment, which formed part of the Home Counties Division.

This battalion, along with other battalions in the Home Counties Division, was sent to India at the end of 1914, but at the end of 1915, the East Kent's was one of the battalions transferred to the India Army and sent to Mesopotamia. Frederick remained in Mesopotamia for the rest of the war and was demobilised in 1919.

Returning to his widowed father's home in Gossoms End, he resumed his job as a gardener, possibly still with the Dorrien-Smith family at their Berkhamsted home at Haresfoot. In 1921, Frederick married Elsie

Channing, whose family lived in Hunton Bridge near Watford, and they set up home next door to his father's house in Gossoms End. In September 1939, he was still working as a gardener and living in the same house. Sadly, Elsie had died earlier in the year, aged just 59. Frederick Fisher died in 1981, aged 95.

Nigel Keith Farrar Porter (1895 – 1968)
Lieutenant, 1/28th London Regiment (Artists Rifles)

Nigel Porter was born in Streatham in January 1895, the younger brother of Royden Spencer Bayspool Porter[16]. Nigel's father, George Joseph Bayspool Porter, was a partner in the busy firm of London solicitors, Farrar, Porter & Co which had offices close to St Paul's Cathedral.

Educated at Marlborough College, Nigel joined the college's Officer Training Corps in 1909 and excelled at musketry. By the time he left in 1913 he had risen to the rank of Cadet 2nd Lieutenant. Upon leaving Marlborough, Nigel decided to follow his father and elder brother in the City, becoming a stockbroker's clerk in the City of London at Messrs Holland and Balfour in Cushion Court, Old Broad Street.

Within days of the war breaking out, Nigel volunteered to join the army, having his medical on 12th August, before formally enlisting as a private with 28th (County of London) Battalion, The London Regiment (Artists Rifles), a Territorial unit. His medical record shows him as being 5ft 10½ins tall and with excellent eyesight. Such was the demand to join the Artists Rifles following the outbreak of war, that in due course it had to be split into three battalions, and Nigel became part of 1/28th London Regiment. Initially based at the Tower of London, the battalion spent much of October 1914 practising route marches before moving to Abbots Langley, Hertfordshire, prior to leaving for France. Marching to Watford Junction station at the end of the month the battalion entrained for Southampton where they boarded the SS *Australind,* bound for Boulogne. On their arrival in France the battalion moved to Bailleul in northern France where it became an Officer Training Corps.

It was not until March 1916 that Nigel finally obtained his Commission, but he remained with the Artists Rifles. In June 1917, his battalion was assigned to 190th Brigade, 63rd Royal Naval Division and prepared for the forthcoming offensive at Ypres.

On 26th October, Nigel and his battalion arrived at Reigersberg Camp, close to the Yser Canal, where final preparations for the attack on the nearby German lines were being made. The attack started at 05.50 on 30th October and over the next hours the Artists Rifles suffered significant casualties before they were relieved by the Royal Naval Division's Nelson

---

[16] Royden Porter's story is told in *For Them's Sake*

Battalion. Nigel Porter was one of four officers wounded during the attack, having been hit by a piece of shrapnel that caused a 6-inch wound to his right thigh and injured his elbow. He was rushed to a Casualty Clearing Station and then to the Liverpool Merchants Hospital at Étaples where the shrapnel was removed from his thigh. On 9th November, he was invalided to England and transferred to the Fishmongers' Hall Hospital near London Bridge. The wound refused to heal however, and he developed sepsis. A second operation took place on 13th December, during which a further piece of shrapnel, missed during the original operation, was found and removed. However, the wound continued to haemorrhage after the operation and required plugging.

Nigel was still recovering in the hospital on 19th December 1917 when his case was first considered by a Military Medical Board, which resulted in his case being deferred for four weeks. The next Board, held on 16th January 1918, heard that Nigel's wound had healed and that he was undergoing treatment to restore the functionality in his thigh muscle. Movement in his elbow joint was however, somewhat limited. It was therefore agreed that his case should be reviewed again after three months. By this time, Nigel's parents had moved from London to Fendley House at Cow Roast, outside Northchurch, and consequently he was transferred to Cross Oaks, a large house in Berkhamsted recently converted to a convalescent hospital. By April 1918, his thigh wound had healed, but he still had difficulty in using his arm for throwing as a result of the elbow injury. The Medical Board therefore decided to defer a further month before deciding whether he was fit to return to active service.

On 13th May 1918, Nigel was ordered to report to the Unity Hall in Berkhamsted, complete with Camp kit, and sent to No15 Officer Cadet Battalion at Hare Hall. This camp was run by the Artists Rifles and was in the grounds of Gidea Park, Romford. Here he became an instructor on the standard 18-week officer training course and was still there when the war ended. In January 1919, he requested to be seconded to 3rd Reserve Battalion, Royal West Surrey Regiment, a Territorial Army training unit based in Sittingbourne, Kent. He was demobilised in April 1919, but remained a member of the Territorial Army with the rank of Lieutenant.

Nigel later resumed his solicitor training and joined his father's firm. In 1920 he resigned his Commission, citing his legal studies. He continued to live with his parents at Fendley House until July 1927 when he married Kathleen Eve, a solicitor's daughter, at St Peter's, Berkhamsted. They later set up home in Hemel Hempstead. In due course Nigel became a successful solicitor in his own right and a partner in Farrar, Porter & Co. After retiring to Sussex, he died in London in 1968, aged 73.

5 – The Yeomanry

The Hertfordshire Yeomanry dates to 1794 and the Napoleonic wars against France, but as soon as the fear of a French invasion had passed it was disbanded. In the early 1830s the Yeomanry was reformed with seven troops of cavalry, four in the south of the county and three in the north. By 1871, only the North Hertfordshire Troop was still in existence and that year it was amalgamated with the South Hertfordshire Corps to become the Hertfordshire Yeomanry Cavalry and first saw active service during the Boer War some thirty years later. In 1908, following the Haldane reforms, the Hertfordshire Yeomanry became part of the Territorial Force.

The outbreak of war saw many of the men serving in the Hertfordshire Yeomanry volunteering for overseas service and being assigned to 1/1st Hertfordshire Yeomanry. Those who decided to remain on home duty were assigned to 2/1st Hertfordshire Yeomanry.

In September 1914, Eastern Mounted Brigade, which now included 1/1st Hertfordshire Yeomanry, left England for Egypt where it arrived the following November. In 1915, the unit was sent to the Gallipoli peninsula without their horses to serve as dismounted infantry and suffered substantial casualties. After the evacuation of the peninsula in December 1915, the Yeomanry returned to Egypt where they were reunited with their horses and became part of the Western Frontier Force. Shortly afterwards, the Hertfordshire Yeomanry was split into several squadrons. 'A' Squadron remained in Egypt and later fought in Palestine; 'B' Squadron was sent back to England before returning to Egypt in 1917 and later joined 'A' Squadron in Palestine; 'D' Squadron was sent to Mesopotamia.

John William Barnes (dates unknown)
Private 105021, 1/1st Hertfordshire Yeomanry

One of those who volunteered to serve overseas with 1/1st Hertfordshire Yeomanry was John Barnes. Very little is known about him, other than his original service number of 1104 indicates that he joined the Hertfordshire Yeomanry during 1909 and was one of the men that arrived in Egypt in November 1914. The 1918 and spring 1919 Northchurch Absent Voters Lists show him registered at a Cottage at Amersfort, owned by Walter Samuel Cohen, so it is likely that he worked there as a gardener or a groom before the war. John did not return to Amersfort after his disembodiment from the Yeomanry and the details of his subsequent life are currently unknown.

Charles Brazier (1888 – 1962)
Private 105255, 1/1st Hertfordshire Yeomanry

Another member of the 1/1st Hertfordshire Yeomanry to arrive in Egypt in November 1914 was Charles Brazier. He was born in St Albans in May 1888, the son of Thomas Brazier, a farm hand, and his wife, Elizabeth. Having completed his education, Charles initially found work as a printers' apprentice, but later became a warehouse clerk. Although his original service number of 1777 indicates that he enlisted in early September 1914, he was already proficient with horses, probably because of working with his father on a farm during his youth.

It is thought that Charles was a member of 'B' Squadron, 1/1st Hertfordshire Yeomanry, which returned to England in 1916, as on 9th December that year, he married Jenny Hales, a tailoress working in the Mantle factory on Lower Kings Road. Jenny's family home was in Northchurch High Street and this is where Charles was subsequently registered in the 1918 Absent Voters list. In 1917 he returned to Egypt with his squadron and later saw service in Palestine.

After his disembodiment, Charles returned to his old job as a warehouseman in St Albans. In 1939, he and Jenny were still living there with Charles now having the additional responsibility of being a fireman at his warehouse. He died in 1962, aged 74.

Frank Bunker DSM (1879 – 1961)
Captain, Hertfordshire Yeomanry

Frank Bunker was born at Hill Farm on Northchurch Common in May 1879, the fifth child, and only son, of Joseph Bunker and his wife Charlotte. The Bunkers were well-to-do farmers, originally from Chesham, who moved to the 240-acre Hill Farm in the 1870s where they employed 7 men and 5 boys. Although Hill Farm was part of the parish of Greater Berkhamsted, the Bunkers considered St Mary's Northchurch, just down the hill from their farm, as their local church. It was here that Frank was baptised on 2nd September 1879. He was later educated at the Bedford County School.

The Bunker family played a central part in Northchurch village life, allowing cricket matches to be played on their land and taking part in local agricultural shows. In 1902 Frank took part in a concert for parents of the children at the village school.

Frank grew up on the farm working alongside his father and on reaching the age of 18 in 1897 he joined the Hertfordshire Imperial Yeomanry, initially signing up for a period of 3 years. He continued in the Herts Imperial Yeomanry rising to the rank of Sergeant until April 1908 when, following the army reforms, it became part of the Territorial Force. His terms of service in the Territorials were set at one year and Frank renewed this annually until 1914. One condition of becoming a Territorial was the attendance at the annual camp for two weeks' training. This Frank did every May, attending the camps in Hertford in 1908, Berkhamsted in 1909, Patcham near Brighton in 1910, Broxbourne in 1911 and 1912

Captain Frank Bunker with his father, Joseph Bunker
Courtesy of Tim Warnock

and Patcham in 1913. The 1914 annual camp was at Luton Hoo, but his Service Record makes no mention of his attendance that year. Frank also was a keen rider and regularly went out with the local hunts and took part in a number of horse races.

Following the outbreak of war, Frank, like many of the men serving in the Yeomanry, volunteered for service overseas. This resulted in splitting the force into two parts - the 1/1st Hertfordshire Yeomanry who would serve overseas and 2/1st Hertfordshire Yeomanry who would serve at home. On 9th September 1914 Frank embarked at Southampton with members of 1/1st Battalion, Hertfordshire Yeomanry, bound for Egypt arriving at Alexandria on 26th September. In January 1915, the Hertfordshire Yeomanry joined the Yeomanry Mounted Brigade and seven months it later moved to Gallipoli to help replenish the losses of the previous few months. Here Frank's unit fought as dismounted infantry and in September 1915 he received a promotion to Squadron Sergeant Major. Two months later Frank was taken ill and evacuated to 1st Canadian Stationary Hospital at Mudros. Having recovered he was sent back to Egypt to await the return of the remainder of his unit from Gallipoli.

It was not long before Frank was back in action as part of the newly-created Western Frontier Force fighting the Senussi on the Egyptian /

Libyan border. During one of the engagements with the Senussi, he was wounded by an artillery shell but refused to report sick, his action later resulting in the following commendation appearing in the *London Gazette* the following June: *"260 Sqdn. S./M. F. Bunker, Hert. Yeo., T.F. - For conspicuous devotion to duty. When wounded by shrapnel he refused to report himself sick, and stuck to his duties in the trenches. He has done fine work with stretcher-bearers. ".* A Distinguished Service Medal was to follow.

Frank was commissioned into 1/1st Hertfordshire Yeomanry on 1st March 1916 and remained in Egypt with the unit until granted five weeks' leave. He left Alexandria on 14th September 1916 on board the *Caledonian* bound for England. His leave was later extended and he returned to Egypt joining 'A' Squadron, Hertfordshire Yeomanry at El Kubri, just north of Suez on 9th November as part of the Suez Canal defences.

Frank remained at El Kubri until April 1917, when he fell ill with a high fever and was admitted to 53rd Casualty Clearing Station and then No2 Australian Stationary Hospital at El Arish. Four days later he was transferred to 21st General Hospital at Alexandria. He had caught influenza, but fortunately it was not the same version that was to hit Europe and the Middle East with disastrous effects the following year and he quickly recovered. Just over two weeks after being taken ill, he was able to return to duty.

On 9th August 1917 Frank, now an acting Captain, was granted three weeks' leave and left Alexandria about the HT *Abbassieh*. A one-month extension of leave followed. He was needed back at Hill Farm and the Board of Agriculture applied to the Army Council to release him from military service on 'Agricultural Grounds'. The Army Council agreed to an extension until 6th May 1918, which was later amended to 13th August, with Frank then being struck off the strength of the Egyptian Expeditionary Force.

He was demobbed at the end of February 1919 and remained at Hill Farm for some years until moving to Aldbury. In 1939 he was working as the manager of a hunting stables in the village.

Frank Bunker died at the West Hertfordshire Hospital at Hemel Hempstead on 28th August 1961, aged 82.

Walter Samuel Cohen (1870 – 1960)
Captain, 1/2nd Hertfordshire Yeomanry

Walter Samuel Cohen was a descendant of an illustrious Dutch merchant called Levi Barent Cohen who was born in Amsterdam in 1747. The Cohen family had been prominent merchants in Amsterdam for several generations and had built up a substantial trading business in various commodities, including tobacco, in both Amsterdam and the city of

Amersfoort. Sometime before 1778 Levi Barent Cohen moved to England, setting up in business in Bevis Marks, near the centre of the City of London, and later moved to Angel Court, close to the Bank of England. In 1800 he became a naturalised British citizen. With a prospering business, Levi Barent Cohen played a prominent part in the local Jewish community and became the Presiding Warden at the Great Synagogue in Sandy's Row in Spittlefields, East London, and a founding member of many Ashkenazi charities. Being in such a high-ranking position, Levi Barent Cohen knew all the prominent Jewish families of the time in London. His eldest daughter married Nathan Mayer Rothschild, who in 1811 founded the London branch of the family's banking business, making his initial fortune trading government bonds. His next daughter married Sir Moses Montefiore, who make his fortune as a broker on the London Stock Exchange, before retiring at an early age to devote the rest of his life as a benefactor to poor and oppressed Jews. The remaining daughters also married into influential Jewish families providing a strong family link between them over the succeeding generations.

At the time of Walter's birth in November 1870, the Cohen family was living at 25 Montagu Square, a large townhouse in the fashionable area of Marylebone. His father, Levi Barent Cohen's great-grandson, Lionel Louis Cohen, was a wealthy stockbroker and a founder of the Jewish Board of Guardians, and had recently helped found the United Synagogue in London. Walter was the fifth of six children born to Lionel and his wife, Esther. In 1885, his father became Conservative Member of Parliament for North Paddington, but died two years later.

Walter was educated at Clifton College, Bristol and later at Trinity College, Cambridge, where, in 1893, he graduated with a BA. Deciding not to follow in the family tradition of finance, he looked to start a career in the law. Having become a member of the Inner Temple in London he was called to the bar in 1898. The following year he gained an MA.

Two years later in October 1900, Walter boarded the SS *Moor*, a Union-Castle Mail Steamship Company Ltd passenger ship, bound for Cape Town, intending to join the growing band of volunteers ready to fight the Boers. The Second Boer War had broken out in 1899 following the breakdown in talks between the Boers and the British Government. After some initial setbacks, the British forced the Boers to withdraw from territory they had captured, but by the end of 1900 the Boers had changed tactics and had started a guerrilla war against the British forces. Walter arrived in Cape Town in January 1901 and immediately volunteered to join the Western Province Mounted Rifles with the rank of Trooper, serving in what the Boers called the Orange Free State. His time with the Western Province Mounted Rifles was short-lived, however, as he returned to England the following April.

Back in England, Walter met Lucy Margaret Cobb, who was known as Margaret, the daughter of Henry Payton Cobb, a banker and solicitor, and former Liberal Party Member of Parliament for Rugby. He married Margaret in Highgate, London in August 1903. By then Walter had obtained a new post as a civil servant with the newly-formed Land Settlement Department of the now renamed Orange River Colony.

Following the end of the Boer War in May 1902, the British took control of the former Boer Orange Free State, renaming it the Orange River Colony and setting up its own civil service. Much of the land in the Orange River Colony had been devastated during the war and it was imperative to bring it back into use as quickly as possible. Consequently, as in the other former Boer territory, the Transvaal, a Land Settlement Department was created. The department's main responsibilities were to administer the land and to encourage English settlers to purchase or lease some 1,500,000 acres via a series of loans.

In 1904 Walter was appointed as Secretary to an Industrial Commission which looked at setting up or rejuvenating industry in the Orange River Colony. That same year Walter and Margaret's first child was born. In 1906, Margaret returned to England for the birth of their second child and later returned to the Orange River Colony where Walter had remained. Although the Colony achieved self-government in November 1907, he continued to work in Bloemfontein as a civil servant until April 1909, a few months before the Orange River Colony became part of the newly-formed Union of South Africa.

On his return to England, Walter joined the Board of Trade in London and was given responsibility for establishing Labour Exchanges in London and the South East. The Cohen family initially stayed with a family at The Kraal, White Hill, Berkhamsted, where Margaret had twin sons in October 1909, though one sadly died a few months later. In 1910 Walter moved to Fairhill, a large property on Berkhamsted Common which fell into the eastern part of Northchurch Parish. By the following year the family were employing eight servants as well as coachman, Herbert Bright.

Soon after moving to Fairhill, Walter commissioned the building of a new house close by, employing the architect Ernest Willmott, whom he had met in the Orange River Colony and who had designed many of the new government buildings in both Bloemfontein and Pretoria. The house he designed was in the Queen Anne style and consisted of two stories and attics in a symmetrical 'H plan'. Separate to the house was a stable block and lodge in matching bricks. He also designed the surrounding landscape complete with ornamental trees of thorn, crab, cherry and plum, together with a pool and statue, pergola and tennis court. To complement Willmott's landscape, Walter commissioned Gertrude Jekyll to design the formal gardens, as well as a kitchen garden, to provide year-round interest. Walter named his new home Amersfort after the city in Holland where many of his ancestors used to live. In May 1912, Margaret Cohen gave birth to a second daughter, who only lived five days.

When the war broke out in August 1914 Margaret was again pregnant and would give birth to another daughter in March the following year. Despite this, Walter, now aged forty-four, sought a commission with the recently-formed 1/2nd Hertfordshire Yeomanry. He remained in England, based at Huntingdon, until the end of 1915, being promoted to Lieutenant that April and passing a Musketry Course at Hythe in Kent. As he was fluent in modern Greek, as well as French and German, it was decided to second Walter to the British Salonika Force. He arrived at Salonika on 28th December 1915 as an Officer Interpreter, becoming a temporary Captain two days later.

In September 1916, Walter was appointed to the Intelligence Corps at Salonika, where he put his language skills to good use whilst interrogating captured enemy troops, as well as gaining information from the local people. All the information gleaned, including enemy troop movements and sightings, together with reports of interrogations, was collated into the daily reports for the General Staff. Walter remained in the Intelligence Corps until May 1918 when he became Acting Captain of 16 Corps Agricultural Company. Forming part of the Labour Corps, one of the roles of the agricultural companies in Salonika was to provide thousands of freshly-baked bread loaves for the troops and provision of other rations, much of which had to be grown locally due to the constant threat to supply vessels by German and Austrian U-boats in the Aegean Sea. The war in Salonika effectively ended in September 1918, following the defeat of the Bulgarian Army at the Battle of Doiran. Walter remained at Salonika until January 1919, however, returning home before being seconded to the newly-created British Army of the Rhine the following March. Two months later he was demobbed and went back home.

After the war Walter became a highly respected financier and company director and continued to live at Amersfort. With contacts throughout Europe, it is not surprising that he and his wife closely watched the unfolding events in Germany following the election of Adolph Hitler's National Socialist Party in 1933. The persecution of the German Jews reached a pre-war peak in November 1938 with *Kristallnacht*, the Night of Broken Glass, which saw some 100 people killed, thousands put in concentration camps, windows in buildings belonging to Jewish people smashed and many synagogues destroyed. Soon afterwards in Great Britain the Movement for the Care of Children from Germany and the British Committee for the Jews of Germany were set up with the aim of bringing children at risk out of Germany and offering them foster homes. On 25th November 1938 the BBC Home Service put out an appeal for people to take in these refugees, and Walter and Margaret Cohen were among those who answered the call.

In exchange for a guarantee that the prospective foster parents would provide for each child's care, education, and eventual emigration to reunite them with their natural parents, the British Government agreed to allow each child to enter Great Britain with a temporary visa.

Having been successfully vetted, the Cohens were put in contact with Dr Hanns Fischer and his wife who had two daughters, Konstanze and Marianne, who were at school in East Prussia, Germany. The German authorities had already refused permission for the family to emigrate as a unit and consequently Dr Fisher applied to send just his two children to England. In January 1939, Margaret Cohen wrote to the girls in Germany saying how much she and Walter were looking forward to their arrival. Two months later, Konstanze and Marianne Fischer arrived at Harwich as part of the scheme that later became known as the *Kindertransport*, or Children's Transport.

After their arrival at Harwich, Konstanze and Marianne were taken to London where they met Walter and Margaret for the first time and were then taken to their temporary home at Amersfort. Walter had previously arranged for both girls to be sent to Berkhamsted School and regularly communicated with their parents, who had managed to leave Germany and emigrate to Bolivia just before the war started. It had initially been hoped that the two girls would be able to rejoin their parents in Bolivia, but the deteriorating war situation meant that any crossing of the Atlantic was extremely risky and they both continued their studies in Berkhamsted. Margaret Cohen died of heart failure in 1942 and one of Walter's nieces took over her responsibilities. Konstanze later studied at Cambridge university and then violin at the Guildhall School of Music and became a violin teacher. Her younger sister, Marianne, studied singing and became a dancer and actress. It was not until 1948 that they were eventually reunited with their parents in New York.

Walter Cohen remained at Amersfort for the rest of his life, dying there in the summer of 1960, aged 89.

Ronald Selby-Smith (1898 – 1983)
Lieutenant, 1/2nd Hertfordshire Yeomanry

Ronald Selby-Smith came from a wealthy brewing family and was born in February 1898 at Pouchen End Hall at the easternmost extremity of Northchurch Parish. His father, Edward Selby-Smith was a director of the brewery whilst his paternal grandfather, Edward Howard Smith, was the owner of Barncroft, a large house in Berkhamsted situated on the parish boundary with Northchurch. By 1911 Ronald's parents had moved to The Fryth a large house on Berkhamsted Common where they employed three domestic servants whilst Ronald was sent to Harrow School, where he became a keen sportsman.

Upon leaving Harrow School in 1915, he immediately applied for a commission with the Hertfordshire Yeomanry. His application was granted on 1st January 1916 and he joined 1/2nd Hertfordshire Yeomanry. Ronald remained in England for the duration of the war and after it ended he retained his commission. On 23 January 1921 *The Times* announced his engagement to Miss Honor Scott Fergusson, the daughter of a wealthy Welsh merchant. They were married the following year at St Peter's, Berkhamsted.

They later became hotel proprietors, purchasing the Treyarnon Bay Hotel, near Padstow, Cornwall. Ronald remained in the west country for the rest of his life and died in 1983, aged 85.

John Arthington Bright (1891 – 1955)
Lieutenant, Royal East Kent Yeomanry

John Arthington Bright's name appears in the Northchurch Absent Voters List for 1918 and also spring 1919. In both lists, he is registered at Exhims, the Northchurch home of the Brockman family. Born in September 1891, he came from a wealthy Quaker family of carpet makers and politicians.

In the late 1700s, John's great-grandfather, Jacob Bright, had been apprenticed to a family friend, William Holme, who had a small farm and looms near Coventry. Having learnt to weave wool during his apprenticeship, Jacob soon became familiar with cotton spinning and when two of William Holme's sons moved to Lancashire, Jacob followed. Acquiring the necessary finance from friends to start a mill, Jacob founded what was later to become the carpet manufacturers, John Bright and Brothers Ltd.

The business prospered, with the spun cotton, sourced from plantations in the United States, being passed to local weavers who worked from home. It was then sent for sale in Manchester, which quickly became the cotton capital of England. It was a highly profitable business, and soon Jacob was able to repay his friends and start building the family fortune. He retired in 1839 and was succeeded by his three sons, John, Thomas and Jacob. Although John was the eldest brother, it was Thomas who was the driving force behind the business and under his direction the cotton mills expanded and later introduced steam-driven machines.

John Bright, John Arthington Bright's grandfather, had other ideas however. Born in Rochdale in 1811 and educated at a Quaker school in York, he joined the family business at the age of sixteen, but soon developed a passion for politics. It was at local temperance meetings in Rochdale that John Bright learnt the skill of public speaking and in 1839 he was invited to join a nationwide tour in support of the recently formed Anti-Corn Law League that promoted free trade, cheaper food and opposed capital punishment. Proving to be a popular speaker at rallies, John Bright entered Parliament in 1843 as the Liberal MP for Durham and in 1847 became the MP for Manchester. Being a Quaker and a pacifist, he was fiercely opposed to the Crimean War (1853 – 1856) against the Russians, and supported religious freedom. His unpopular views on the Crimean war, which he called a 'terrible crime', led to John Bright losing his seat in Manchester in 1857, but within months he was elected as one of the two MPs for Birmingham. In 1867, his brother Jacob joined him in Parliament as the Liberal MP for one of the Manchester seats. John Bright held his seat in Birmingham until his death in 1889, although he hardly ever visited the city, and as a member of various Liberal cabinets under Prime Minister William Gladstone, he became a very influential politician, holding the posts of both Chancellor of the Duchy of Lancaster and President of the Board of Trade. He is also reputed to have been responsible for coining the phrases 'the mother of all parliaments' and 'to flog a dead horse'.

John Arthington Bright's father, John Albert Bright, known as Albert, was born in London in 1848, the eldest son of John Bright and his second wife, Margaret[17]. Educated at the Quaker school in Tottenham and later at University College, London, Albert had no wish to follow his father into politics and later moved to Rochdale to help his uncle with the running of John Bright and Brothers Ltd and where he subsequently became a Borough Councillor and Justice of the Peace. In 1883, he married Edith Shawcross. John Bright's death in 1889 brought Albert into politics as he was asked to stand for his father's now vacant seat of Birmingham Central.

The government of the time was an alliance of Liberal Unionists and Conservatives and was close to breaking down and consequently a dispute arose over which party should provide the candidate for the vacancy. The Conservatives put forward Lord Randolph Churchill, the father of the future Prime Minister, Winston Churchill, as their candidate, whilst the Liberal Unionists, led by Joseph Chamberlain, suggested that Albert Bright stand for his late father's seat. With some reluctance the Conservatives backed down and Albert Bright was duly elected. It was during his father's time as the Member of Parliament for Birmingham Central that John Arthington Bright was born.

In 1901, Albert Bright and his family were living in a large house in the popular resort of St Leonards-on-Sea, East Sussex, his occupation being shown on the Census as 'Cotton and Carpet Manufacturer'. He returned to Parliament as Liberal MP for Oldham in 1906, before stepping down at the 1910 General Election. For the remainder of his life, Albert devoted himself to the family firm and became a director of the London & North Western Railway. It is uncertain whether the Bright family continued to use the house at St Leonards as a second home as, by 1911, they were living in

---

[17] John Bright's first wife, Elizabeth Priestman, died of tuberculosis two years after they were married

Rochdale at the 20-roomed old family home of One Ash, once owned by John's grandfather. By then, nineteen-year-old John was beginning to learn the family business. The following year, having learnt to drive, he was caught speeding at 25mph in a 10mph zone and fined at Ambleside magistrates court.

June 1914 saw the announcement of the engagement between Margerie Brockman, second daughter of Mr & Mrs Brockman of Beachborough, Folkestone and Cranleigh, and John Arthington Bright, the son of Mr & Mrs John Albert Bright. Shortly afterwards the Brockman family moved to Exhims. Despite his Quaker background, John immediately enlisted with the army and in December 1914 started his officer training as a private in the Inns of Court Officer Training Corps at Berkhamsted.

On 27th March 1915, having completed his training and been appointed as a 2nd Lieutenant with the Royal East Kent Yeomanry (the Duke of Connaught's Own) (Mounted Rifles) the previous month, John married his fiancée at St Mary's, Northchurch. The official history of the Inns of Court gives John's home address as 5 Hampstead Hill Gardens, Hampstead, a Georgian-style detached property close to the fashionable Hampstead Heath.

Although John's service record cannot be traced, from his medal record it appears that he was not posted to Egypt until February 1917 when the dismounted East Kent Yeomanry and the West Kent Yeomanry Regiments merged to become 10th (Royal East Kent & West Kent Yeomanry) Battalion, Territorial Force. At this time, John was attached to the Remount Depot, responsible for the provision of horses and mules to the new unit.

In May 1918, following the losses incurred by the allies during the German Spring Offensive, several secondary units were sent to France to provide emergency support. One of these was John's battalion, which arrived in Marseilles at the start of May and later took part in the allied offensive and advance that resulted in the signing of the Armistice the following November. Unfortunately, although being an officer, he is not specifically mentioned by name in the unit's war diary, so it cannot be established whether he travelled to France with them, or remained with the Remount Depot in Egypt.

John next appears in 1926 when he is recorded as living with his wife, Margerie, at Bright's Farm in Christian Malford, near Chippenham, Wiltshire and it seems that he was now living on the income received from the family firm. In the early 1930s John and Margerie moved to a town house in the fashionable West End of London. Within a few years, however, they were divorced and, in the spring of 1939, John remarried. By then, war was looming, and John had joined the Royal Air Force with the rank of Flying Officer, later becoming a Flight Lieutenant. After the end of the Second World War John and his wife left London and moved to Burwash Common in East Sussex. He died there in 1955, aged 59.

6 – The Machine Gun Corps

Initially, unlike the German army, the British did not fully appreciate the effectiveness of the machine gun as a weapon of war. The first self-powered, water-cooled machine gun was invented by Sir Hiram Maxim in 1885, and with the support of Vickers, it was developed it into a highly effective weapon. The British Army accepted the machine gun in 1891 and two years later used it for the first time during the Matabele Wars in Africa. In 1896 Vickers bought the patents for the gun from Maxim and developed a lighter version, which became known as the Vickers Machine Gun.

Following the end of the Boer War, during which both sides made use of machine guns, the British Army requested additional guns from the Government, but their request was refused on grounds of cost, with only two guns per infantry battalion being authorised. Although the Vickers machine gun was adopted by the British in 1912, the BEF went to war in 1914 mainly armed with the older, slower, Maxim machine guns.

The German army took a very different approach. In 1908, they adopted their own version of the Maxim machine gun and started full-scale production at a factory in Spandau, Berlin. Like the British, the Germans also allocated two guns per infantry battalion, but as they went to war in 1914 with more battalions, they had more machine guns. It was not long before they realised that machine guns worked best when organised into dedicated companies, as opposed to individual units led by specialist officers, and re-organised accordingly.

Battle experience, particularly during the First Battle of Ypres in the Autumn of 1914, led the British to re-evaluate their use of the machine gun and the first Machine Gun School was established at Wisques, near St Omer in northern France. Additionally, in February 1915, the number of machine guns in each infantry battalion was doubled to four. The following October, a dedicated Machine Gun Corps (MGC) was created, with a new base at Belton Park and a depot and training school on the French coast at Camiers. Belton Park, near Grantham, Lincolnshire, was the family seat of Lord Brownlow, the owner of the Ashridge estate near Northchurch.

Military Camp at Belton Park circa 1915
Author's Collection

Following the creation of the MGC, the existing machine gunners were organised into Brigade Infantry Machine Gun Companies, with three companies per division. New Machine Gun Companies were later formed at Belton Park and by 1917, a fourth company was added to each division. New Cavalry Machine Gun Squadrons and Motor Machine Gun Batteries also came into being, with each cavalry brigade being allocated a Machine Gun Squadron, whilst the Motor Branch included motor cycle batteries and light armoured cars. In March 1916, a Heavy Section was formed which in due course would evolve into the Tank Corps.

A new training course, which normally lasted for around 70 days, was also introduced based around the standard Vickers machine gun, and ran at both Belton Park and Camiers. The course comprised two parts, the first being mainly instructional, with the second being practical and points based. Failure to achieve the required number of points meant rejection and immediate transfer out of the Corps.

Each Infantry Machine Gun Company had sixteen Vickers machine guns, split into four Sections each containing two subsections. Each subsection was made up of six men, with each man being capable of taking over from a fellow team member in case of need.

Later in the war, Lewis machine guns were introduced. These were much lighter that the Vickers machine gun and were shoulder-held and could be carried by one man, although another gunner was required to carry and load the ammunition. Faster than the Vickers gun, it was capable of firing at a rate of 500 - 600 rounds per minute, the ammunition being contained in circular magazines, each containing 47 rounds.

Some 170,000 officers and men served in the MGC during the war, of which 62,049 became casualties with 12,498 being killed. Not surprisingly, the Corps was sometimes known as the 'Suicide Club'. Seven men from Northchurch joined the MGC, five later returned home, but not unscathed by their experiences; the other two, William Waite and Arthur Welling, were killed in action.[18]

William Drake Brockman (1882 – 1970)
Private 26168, Machine Gun Corps

William Drake Brockman, the first son of Francis Drake Brockman and his wife, Margaretta, was born in October 1882 at the family home of Beachborough, close to the village of Newington-next-Hythe, Kent. Like his younger brother, Francis Drake Hugh Brockman, William was educated at Tonbridge School.

Around 1910, William left home and the following year he was working as a 'French Gardener' at Offenham, a village near Evesham,

---

[18] William Waite and Arthur Welling's story is told in *For Them's Sake*

Gloucestershire. The 'French Gardening' system, which William employed, became very fashionable in the late Edwardian era, particularly in the Evesham area, and was based on a system of forcing vegetables under glass cloches using the heat generated by rotting manure. As a result, grocers' shops were able to sell the early-maturing vegetables at a higher price. Heavily promoted by *The Daily Mail*, 'French Gardening' became a craze among the middle and upper classes and only died out following the outbreak of war.

William's service record has not survived, but his medal record shows that unlike his younger brother, Francis, he did not seek a commission and later joined the Machine Gun Corps. As such, he would have gone through the standard training for all machine-gunners at Belton Park and Camiers. William's medal record also shows that he was later transferred to the Labour Corps, which would indicate that he was either wounded, or taken sick during his time with the MGC and consequently unable to continue as a valuable machine-gunner. After his demobilisation in 1919, William returned to Northchurch.

Following the death of his father in 1931, William inherited the land he owned in Hythe and which was subsequently sold. William never married and lived for the rest of his life at the family home at Bargrove Avenue, Boxmoor, which his father had purchased in 1921. He died in 1970, aged 88.

William Hales (1893 – 1952)
Private 165644, 101 Battalion, (Bucks and Berks) Machine Gun Corps

William Hales was the second eldest son of Joseph and Elizabeth Hales. Born in New Road, Northchurch, in December 1893 he later started work as a bricklayer's labourer. Sometime between 1911 and 1915 William left Northchurch and later met his future wife, Winifred Manning, the daughter of a local lino cutter from Camden.

Although William's service record no longer exists, by the time he and Winifred were married at Camden Parish Church in July 1915, he had enlisted as a Trooper with the 1st/1st Battalion, Royal Buckinghamshire Hussars and was based at Mooltan Barracks at Tidworth, Wiltshire. Four months after his marriage, and having completed his army training, William left England for Egypt where his battalion were just about to arrive after suffering badly during the Gallipoli campaign.

Army reorganisations during the next two years, and the resulting merger of several units, saw William become a member of 6th Mounted Brigade which served on the Libyan frontier and later in 1917 took part in the fighting around Gaza and the capture of Jerusalem. A further reorganisation in the late spring of 1918 saw the merger of the Buckinghamshire Hussars and the Berkshire Yeomanry to become a battalion of the MGC under the title 101 Battalion (Bucks and Berks) Machine Gun Corps. It then moved to the Western Front to help rebuild the British forces that had been badly mauled during the German Spring Offensive.

On 26th May 1918, the SS *Leasowe Castle* left Alexandria as part of a convoy of ships with 2,900 troops on board, including William's battalion, bound for Marseilles. At 00:30 the following day, on a bright moonlit night with a calm sea, the German submarine UB-51 launched a torpedo at the troopship hitting her on the starboard side. With the engines stopped the *Leasowe Castle* settled slightly to stern and as many troops as could rushed to their emergency stations. Orders were given for the lifeboats to be lowered. After about 90 minutes some 800 to 1,000 troops remained to be evacuated, the explosion having destroyed several lifeboats on the ship's starboard side. Most of the men were picked up by HMS *Lily* which came alongside, but at 02:00 the *Leasowe Castle* suddenly started to sink, leaving the remaining men on board to jump into the sea as she went down. William was among the survivors of the sinking, but a total of 101 soldiers lost their lives in the incident, including one officer and 3 men from his unit.

The survivors returned to Alexandria and were sent to the Sidi Bishir transit camp where they remained until 18th June before boarding HMT *Caledonia* bound for Taranto, Italy, from where they travelled to their destination of Étaples by train. This time the voyage across the Mediterranean was uneventful and William's unit finally arrived at Étaples on 28th June.

The next two months saw a period of intensive training before the unit was ready to participate in the attack on the German defences on the River Scarpe the following August, fighting alongside Canadian troops. At the time of the Armistice, William's unit had been placed in reserve having advanced north into Belgium between Ypres and Ghent.

With the war over, the demobilisation of the unit started just before Christmas. William was demobilised on 28th January 1919 and returned to his home in London. His wife, Winifred, gave birth to their first child in the summer of 1920 with another following three years later.

It is currently not known whether William resumed his occupation as a bricklayer on his return to civilian life, but by 1939, and still living in London, he had become a police officer. He died in 1952, aged 58.

Horace Augustus Frederick Kempster (1893 – 1962)
Lance Corporal 83891, Machine Gun Corps

Horace Kempster was born in Northchurch in July 1893, the only son of Harry Kempster, a cattleman, and his wife Georgina, and grew up in the family home in the High Street with his five sisters. In 1907 he won a prize for his work at the Technical School in Bell Lane and later became a gardener.

In September 1914, shortly after war was declared, the Banns of Marriage were read out at the parish churches of Tring and Northchurch for the wedding of Horace Augustus Frederick Kempster and Ada Nellie Harding. Ada Harding's father was a gardener, but by now Horace had changed professions and was working as a storeman. With a young wife to consider, Horace did not volunteer to join the army at the outbreak of war and by December 1915 he was also the father of two children. Sadly, within weeks of the birth of their second child, Ada died and was later buried in St Mary's churchyard. With two very young children to bring up, Horace called on his mother to help, although by now his father was in declining health. Horace also changed jobs to bring in more money and became a delivery man for mineral water suppliers, Messrs Lee & Sons.

The extension of conscription in the early summer of 1916 meant that Horace could no longer avoid the war. Despite his personal circumstances, and his employers appealing to the Berkhamsted Military Tribunal, Horace was conscripted and travelled to Hertford. His subsequent medical record described him as being 5ft 11ins tall, weighing 163lbs and with blue eyes.

On 29th November 1916, Horace was mobilised and reported to the Recruiting Office at Watford where he was assigned to 3/5th Bedfordshire Regiment, although he had previously expressed a desire to join the Royal Garrison Artillery. His two young children were left with his mother to bring up until he returned. Two months later, he was transferred to 3rd Battalion MGC and was sent to Belton Park for training.

In November 1917, Horace was sent to Egypt and posted to 158th Battalion MGC which formed part of 53rd Division. Over the previous months, 53rd Division had been advancing north into Palestine and had just defeated the Turkish Army at the Third Battle of Gaza. Within a month of arriving, Horace took part in the capture of Jerusalem and the defence of the city against a subsequent Turkish counterattack.

Following the Turkish surrender later that year, Horace, now a temporary Corporal, was transferred to No1 Depot at Helmia, near Cairo. In April 1919, and still in Egypt, he was admitted to No 27 General Hospital at Abbassia for two weeks' treatment for a shoulder and back injury. Shortly afterwards, he was granted three-weeks' home leave and left Port Said on 2nd May 1919 on board the SS *Burma*, arriving at Plymouth eleven days later. He returned to Northchurch to find that his ailing father had suffered a stroke and had now become mentally incapacitated, whilst his mother was also in poor health and was only just managing to look after his two children as well as her sick husband. With the war over, and no sign of Horace's imminent demobilisation, the only solution was for Horace's mother to write to the MGC headquarters at Belton Park, asking for his early release on compassionate grounds.

At the end of his three-week leave, Horace was ordered to return to Belton Park where he was posted to 6th Reserve Battalion to await reassignment. He was then told that he would shortly be returning to the Middle East. At this time, the letter that Horace's mother had written was still being reviewed and under normal circumstances, a soldier whose case was under review was not sent overseas. Unfortunately, due to an administrative error, this did not happen and Horace returned to Egypt where he was assigned to 12th Light Car Patrol MGC, Motor.

Once the error was discovered, the officer in charge at Belton Park was apparently 'relieved from his duties' and urgent cables were sent to Egypt requesting Horace's immediate return. Two months later however, still nothing definite had been heard, and Horace's mother contacted the Northchurch Soldiers & Sailors Families Committee, chaired by the Rector of St Mary's Northchurch, Revd. RH Pope, who wrote on her behalf to Belton Park asking for clarification. It took a further month before Horace's release was finally confirmed, by which time he had been appointed Lance Corporal. On 17th November 1919, he finally left Port Said on board the HT *Assaye* and returned home. He was finally demobilised on 28th December 1919.

Horace's father died in 1921, aged 56, and for the next few years, Horace and his two children continued to live with his widowed mother in Northchurch High Street. On 14th April 1929, Horace married Clara Shuter at St Peter's, Berkhamsted, and would subsequently become the father of two more children. In 1939, he was working in the Berkhamsted area as a gardener and serving as a Special Constable. Horace Kempster died in 1962, aged 68.

Robert William Kempster (1897 – 1962)
Private 72430, 17th Battalion, MGC

Robert William Kempster was the youngest son of William Henry Kempster and his wife, Emily. He was born in June 1897 and like his siblings grew up in Hog Lane on the southern border of Northchurch Parish and went to school at nearby Ashley Green. After leaving school in 1911 Robert started work as a gardener.

On 18th June 1915, aged 19, Robert attested at High Wycombe and the following day he travelled to Winchester where he joined the Rifle Brigade. Following the completion of his training he was allocated to 9th Battalion and he arrived in France on 7th October. 9th Battalion had been in France since May and first saw major action against the German army during the Battle of Hooge in July. It was here that they were the first battalion to face the full effect of the new weapon, the *Flammenwerfer*, or flamethrower. Although few of the battalion's soldiers were burnt, the impact of the F*lammenwerfer* had a considerable demoralising effect on the troops.

It is likely that Robert was included in a draft of 20 men that joined 9th Battalion on 17th October at Houtkerque on the French / Belgium border.

The following day the battalion returned to the front line at Ypres. Over the next few days the battalion alternated in the front line with the Kings Royal Rifle Corps. The weather at this time was particularly bad with heavy rain followed by hard frost. The result was that the trenches needed constant repair and the men got very little sleep. To make things worse, constant fire from the German trenches resulted in casualties being incurred on most days.

On 4th December 1915, Robert's battalion re-entered the Popijze trenches at Ypres. Within 24 hours Robert had been arrested and charged with being found asleep at his post. Three weeks later, on 27th December, Robert appeared before a Court-Martial at Houtkerque. He was found guilty and sentenced to 2 years imprisonment with hard labour. He was then taken to one of the military prisons near the British depot at Camiers where he would serve his sentence.

The British military prisons in France were all located close to depots and railheads where the prisoners' labour could be used best. Food only consisted of basic rations i.e. tinned beef and hard biscuits, made from salt, flour and water which were produced under government contract by Huntley & Palmers. The biscuits were so hard that they could crack teeth if not soaked first in tea or water.

On 5th January 1916 Robert heard that his sentence had been suspended, subject to a review after three months, and that he would be returning to his battalion. By now the British Army had started to suspend more and more convictions as it was realised that a fit soldier would be of more use in the front line. Robert did not return to his battalion, however, as within five days he had been diagnosed with 'trench foot' at the hospital at Camiers.

Robert's condition had been caused by standing for hours on end in the cold, wet and muddy conditions in the trenches in late October and November. Under such conditions, the blood vessels in the feet contract and result in a reduction of oxygen and nutrients to the affected area. The symptoms are normally cold swollen feet, which look a greyish colour and feel numb, heavy and painful. If left untreated, nerve damage results together with more swelling, blisters, peeling skin and finally gangrene, which normally required the toes or the complete foot to be amputated. What was not realised at the time was that it only takes one day for trench foot to develop.

On 17th January, Robert was invalided back to England for treatment on board the SS *Brighton*. Taken to the Northumberland War Hospital in Gosforth, Newcastle on Tyne, he was to spend the next three months being treated and recovering from his injury. After his discharge he was sent to the Rifle Brigade Depot at Winchester and returned to France at the start of October.

On 26th December 1916, Robert was transferred to the 60th Company, Machine Gun Corps and the following month he started his course at their base at Camiers. Ten days later, however, he was admitted to 20th General Hospital with a recurrence of trench foot and was invalided to England for a second time. His treatment this time was at York, where he remained until 19th March. After a short furlough he sailed for France on 11th April and returned to Camiers and rejoined his unit.

At the end of June 1917, Robert reported to 45 Casualty Clearing Station at Achiet-le-Grand suffering from impetigo, and syphilis, both common infections caught by troops of all nations during the war, but due to different circumstances. Transferred to hospital at the large British base at Étaples he found that his army pay had been stopped for a month whilst he was there. Under British military law, the concealment of venereal disease was a punishable offence, not the contraction of the disease. However, it was common practice at that time for men suffering from venereal disease to help pay for their treatment under what became known as a 'hospital stoppage', which was in effect a fine.

Robert returned to Camiers on 18th August. He later saw action with 60th Machine Gun Company during the latter stages of the Third Battle of Ypres and at Cambrai and the German Spring offensive in 1918. Following the heavy fighting much of the army was re-organised and he was transferred to 17th Battalion, MG Company, part of 17th Division. With them he took part in the fighting as the allies drove the German army back towards their homeland. He was on leave in England when the Armistice was signed in November 1918.

He returned to a peaceful France on 15th November, having no doubt experienced the celebrations back home. Four months later, on 21st March 1919 Robert was demobilised and he returned home.

In early 1927, Robert married Irene Fordham in north London. By then he had started working as a railway locomotive fireman. The newlyweds set up home in Edgware and remained there until his death in 1962.

Stanley Welling (1896 – 1980)
Sergeant 5225, 59th Machine Gun Corps

Stanley Welling was born in December 1896 in the hamlet of Winkwell, near Bourne End in the easternmost part of Northchurch Parish. The eldest son of Harvey and Janet Welling, Stanley and his elder sister, Ethel, were christened together in February the following year at Bovingdon parish church. Stanley grew up in Little Heath and in 1911 he was still living there with his parents and five younger siblings, including brother, Harvey. After leaving school Stanley began working at a nearby sawmill.

He enlisted with the Bedfordshire Regiment in 1915, but was not sent to France until the following year. Although Stanley's service record has not survived, it is known that he was later transferred to the 59th Battalion, MGC which was formed in March 1916. In the early autumn of 1917 he appears to have been taken sick and for some time was seriously ill and under treatment at No12 General Hospital in Rouen, subsequently making a full recovery.

In March 1918, Stanley was back with his unit at Mory, just north of Bapaume, awaiting the expected offensive by the Germans. A total of 60 machine-guns were positioned in a series of defensive positions to a depth of 6,000 yards behind the front line. A further four machine-guns were held in reserve at the rear. Each machine-gun was positioned in a specially designed small open emplacement linked by trenches and underground communication lines which protected the gunners from all bar a direct hit from artillery fire. The positions located to the rear were specifically designed to protect the emplacements in front of them.

The Germans launched the first of their Spring Offensives in the early hours of 21st March. By midday, reports were received that the advancing German stormtroopers had reached the village of Écoust-Saint-Mein, some two miles away from Stanley's position. Throughout the attack, the men of 59th Battalion put up fierce resistance, and many emplacements continued to fire on the German troops, even after they were surrounded. With ammunition running out, orders finally came to withdraw. During the attack Stanley's battalion suffered heavily, with over 350 officers and men becoming casualties or listed as missing in action.

As the German offensive ground to a halt, Stanley and the remnants of his battalion were moved north, setting up camp south-west of Lens. Here they spent much of the next few weeks rebuilding and training whilst new machine-gun emplacements were built to the east. The unit advanced north-eastwards in the final weeks of the war reaching Cambrai in October 1918 and were about to move further north when the Armistice was signed.

Stanley was demobilised on 14th March 1919 and returned home to Little Heath, starting work as a painter. On 4th September 1920 he married Ivy Barnwell at St Mary's, Summerstown, south London, and the newlyweds set up home in Bovingdon. In 1939, they were still living in Bovingdon and Stanley was working as a foreman at a local wood mill. He died in Enfield in 1980, aged 83.

7 – The Gunners

Formed in 1716, the Royal Regiment of Artillery, commonly known as 'The Gunners', is one of the oldest regiments in the British army. At the outbreak of the war in 1914, it comprised three distinct elements – the Royal Horse Artillery (RHA), the Royal Field Artillery (RFA), and the Royal Garrison Artillery (RGA).

In the twelve years between the end of the Boer War in 1902 and the start of the First World War the artillery pieces used by the British Army changed significantly. The batteries of both the RHA and RFA that had fought in the Boer War used guns dating from the 1880s. The RHA used the 12-pdr gun, whilst the RFA used the heavier 15-pdr gun, both breach-loaded, and mounted on carriages made of wrought iron and their overall design would have been familiar to those fighting in the Battle of Waterloo almost a century earlier.

Both guns suffered from one major problem – on firing, the recoil pushed the mobile gun platform out of position requiring the gunners to push it back before the next round could be fired. Guns manufactured after 1899 were fitted with a spade to improve their stability, but they still required precise repositioning after each shot.

In the late 1890s Vickers developed 'Quick-Fire', or QF, guns for naval and coastal defence use, specifically against fast moving naval vessels. To reduce the recoil, these guns allowed the barrel to travel backwards in a jacket or cradle, slowed by a hydraulic buffer, which then returned to the firing position using specially designed springs. This enabled the gun and its carriage to remain in place and considerably reduced the need for repositioning. Together with other improvements to the breach loading mechanism, these developments saved valuable time that enabled the artillerymen to reload and fire another salvo.

Overall research and development of the artillery pieces used by the British army was the responsibility of the Ordinance Committee, based at the Royal Artillery Headquarters at Woolwich. One of its leading members in the years before 1914 was Lieutenant-Colonel Charles Frederick Hadden (1854 – 1924), who lived at Rossway in Northchurch Parish.

The Hadden family's association with Northchurch began in the mid-1860s when Charles Stanton Hadden, Charles Frederick Hadden's father, purchased the Rossway estate to the south of the village and commissioned the building of an Italianate-style Victorian country house to replace the old manor house on the site.

Charles Frederick Hadden was born in Nottingham in June 1854, where the Hadden family ran a well-established hosiery business. Educated at

Elstree School and Cheltenham College, he received his military training at the Royal Military Academy at Sandhurst and after passing out in 1873 he joined the Royal Artillery. He quickly moved up through the ranks, becoming a Captain in 1882 and the Assistant to the Superintendent, Royal Laboratory in 1885. Three years later, he was appointed Inspector of Laboratory Stores and became a Major in 1890. 1893 saw him become Chief Inspector at the Royal Arsenal at Woolwich. Promoted to Lieutenant-Colonel in 1899, Hadden joined the Ordnance Committee in 1901, just at the time when the British army's artillery requirements were under review.

Looking for suitable replacements for the existing artillery, the Ordinance Committee purchased several *Ehrhardt* 7.5 cm Model 1901 field guns from the German weapons manufacturer *Rheinische Metallwaren und Maschinenfabrik,* renaming them 15-pdr field guns. Using the experience gained from the *Ehrhardt* guns, named after the company's founder, Heinrich Ehrhardt, specifications for new British-built QF guns were drawn up, and resulted in the

Training on an 18-pdr QF gun
Author's collection

production of the new 13-pdr and 18-pdr QF guns, together with the 4.5-in. howitzer. These guns were at the core of the Royal Artillery when it went to war in 1914.

In 1904, Lieutenant-Colonel Charles Frederick Hadden was appointed Commandant of the Ordnance College and Director of Artillery and three years later became Master-General of the Ordnance. In 1909, in his new role, he became a member of a new committee set up by the Prime Minister, Herbert Asquith, to exploit links between artillery and aerial observation using balloons and aircraft, something that would later feature significantly in the war. Hadden later became a member of the Army Council, and in 1908 received a KCB in the King's Birthday Honours. Promoted to Major-General in 1913, he was subsequently appointed President of The Ordnance Board and Royal Artillery Committee, a role he retained until his retirement in 1915.

Supplying ammunition to the various RFA batteries, as well as small arms ammunition to the troops, was the responsibility of the ammunition columns. At the start of the war, each of the four artillery brigades within an infantry division had its own ammunition column, with a separate one at divisional level. The ammunition columns themselves were formed of specially designed horse-drawn ammunition wagons or general service wagons.

Arthur William Badrick (1886 – 1951)
Gunner 42423, 42nd Brigade, RFA

Arthur Badrick was born in Wilstone, near Tring in January 1886, and was the son of farm worker, James Badrick, and his wife, Mary Ann. During her marriage to James, Mary Ann gave birth to a total of 16 children, but only eight would survive childhood.

James Badrick and his family remained in Wilstone until around 1894 when they moved to Bierton near Aylesbury. It was here in 1899, that Arthur's younger brother, Horace, was born. James Badrick died in 1906, aged 47, leaving Mary Ann to bring up the members of her family still living at home.

In October 1905, Arthur enlisted with the local Aylesbury regiment, the Oxfordshire and Buckinghamshire Light Infantry. His service papers describe him as being 5ft 3¼ins tall with light brown hair and brown eyes. Soon after enlisting, Arthur transferred to the Royal Regiment of Artillery, becoming a shoesmith as well as a gunner. In 1911, Arthur entered the Reserves and began working for Aylesbury Council as a carter at the local sewage works. The same year he married Alice Archer, the daughter of a farm worker from nearby Bierton. The married couple set up home at 2 Bell Yard, a small four-roomed terraced cottage in Walton Street, Aylesbury.

Following the outbreak of war, Arthur was mobilised and posted to 29th Battery, 42nd Brigade. His unit arrived in France on 19th August, too late to take part in the initial fighting at Mons, but their six 18-pdr field guns were put to good use during the BEF's retreat south.

Arthur's battery spent much of the next two years in the area around Ypres, providing artillery support to the infantry. In early July 1916 during the Somme Offensive, the battery moved south to increase the artillery support to the troops fighting around Delville Wood and Longueville. The following year a reorganisation of the RFA resulted in 42nd Brigade becoming a more mobile unit, moving between locations for short periods of time as the need arose. The same year Arthur's battery took part in the Battle of Arras and later formed part of the massive artillery and tank attack at Cambrai.

April 1918 saw 42nd Brigade in retreat during the German Spring Offensive and they were later withdrawn to Béthune to recover. In December 1918, the brigade crossed the German border and moved to Minden in the Rhineland as part of the Army of Occupation. It was here that Arthur ended his military career and returned to England to be demobilised.

In 1920, Arthur and Alice were living in Eddy Street, Gossoms End and it is likely that he was now working at East's timberyard. Six years later, they had moved to Castle Street, Berkhamsted and were still living there in 1939. At that time Arthur was working as a timber haulier. Arthur Badrick died in Berkhamsted in the late winter of 1951, aged 65.

Horace Frederick Badrick (1899 – 1935)
Gunner 286024, 326th Brigade, RFA

Arthur Badrick's younger brother, Horace, was born in Bierton, in late 1899. On 20th May 1915, fifteen-year-old Horace, attempted to join the Bucks Battalion of the Oxfordshire and Buckinghamshire Light Infantry, declaring himself to be aged nineteen. It was not long before Horace's ruse was discovered, however, and he was discharged under Paragraph 392 (iii) (c) of the Kings Regulations 1912 as he was 'found unlikely to become an efficient soldier'. Not deterred by his first failure to enlist, four months later Horace travelled south to Portsmouth and on 9th September he joined the Royal Artillery at Hilsea, Portsmouth, again giving his age as 19 and his occupation as groom. With no further questions asked he was posted to 19th Heavy Battery, Royal Garrison Artillery.

After completing his training, Horace was sent to France to join the battery in the Somme sector. During the Third Battle of Ypres in 1917 Horace's battery suffered heavy losses following German retaliatory fire, but he fortunately escaped injury. In early 1918 the battery was transferred to the Italian front.

Italy had joined the war in 1915 on the side of Great Britain, France and Russia, and saw it as a chance to expand their recently unified country by gaining territory from Austria to the north. Initially, the Italian army made several gains, mainly north of Trieste, but in 1917, following the collapse of the Russian Army, Germany was able to send more troops to the area to aid their struggling ally. The Battle of Caporetto in October 1917 proved a turning point, with the Austrians and Germans using poison gas shells to force the Italians to retreat from the mountains and south towards Venice and the banks of the River Piave. The Italians had no alternative but to seek help from the French and the British, who were at the time still heavily engaged in the Third Battle of Ypres.

Allowing the Italians to seek terms with the Austrians would mean that considerable numbers of Austrian and German troops would become available for redeployment on the Western Front. Faced with this dilemma, the French were the first to send reinforcing troops. The British followed later, sending what units they could as the fighting around Ypres died down. At the start of 1918 the German troops in Italy were withdrawn in readiness for their Spring Offensive on the Western Front, leaving their Austrian ally still in place.

The Austrians, wanting to finish the war as soon as possible, launched their own offensive in June 1918, but were held by the Italians, assisted by the French and British troops. The Italians did not immediately follow up their success however, and it was not until October 1918, with the Austro-Hungarian Empire breaking up, that they launched their own offensive with the help of their Anglo-French allies. On 3rd November 1918, a week before the German Armistice, the Austrians sued for peace.

By now Horace was serving with 542nd Howitzer Battery, 326th Brigade, RFA. He returned to England in January 1919 for demobilisation, but almost immediately he decided to re-enlist for a further four years. The Northchurch Absent Voters List shows him registered at this time at 5 Bell Lane, which was where his mother, Mary Ann was now living and her next door neighbour was his brother, George. In 1923, Horace re-enlisted for a further three years and finally left the army on 1st January 1926.

Settling in Chesham, Horace became a general labourer, but within a few years his health had started to deteriorate and he was diagnosed with tuberculosis. At that time, the only treatment was fresh air and rest. Horace was sent to Preston Hall, near Aylesford, Kent, which was a sanatorium for discharged soldiers. It contained several specially built cottages within its grounds, each one having a veranda so that tuberculosis patients' beds could be pushed outside to enjoy the fresh air. The cottages were also large enough to allow the patients' families to stay with them if necessary. Sadly, Horace Badrick was to die at Preston Hall in April 1935, aged just 35.

George Percy Cosmo Blount (1873 – 1954)
Lieutenant Colonel, Royal Artillery

The Blount family has a long tradition of providing officers to the armed forces dating back to at least the early 1800s, and continues to do so to this day. In 1836, Lieutenant Commander William Simpson Blount, married Leonara Anne Clavell, the daughter of Captain John Clavell, an experienced naval officer, who had fought against the French during the Battle of Trafalgar in 1805. He was the commander of the Sloop HMS *Hermes*, a wooden paddle steamer, which operated with the Royal Navy in the Mediterranean. In 1838 while based at Malta, Leonara gave birth to the first of their children, and named him George Bouverie Blount. Three years later, William Simpson Blount, now commander of HMS *Pluto*, played an important part in negotiating an anti-slavery deal with King Bell of the Bell River in the Cameroons, thus ending the slave trade in that area. In 1843, however, feeling depressed following the Admiralty's refusal to confirm his posting as commander of the new Royal Yacht, the *Victoria and Albert*, he committed suicide. Leonara, was due to give birth to their fourth child the same day.

Following her husband's suicide, Leonara returned to England with her children. Her eldest son, George, was later educated at the Royal Naval School in Greenwich and became a Civil Servant at the Admiralty. In 1866, he married Annie Christina Attenborough, and they would go on to have nine children – Rose Leonara, Edith Annie, George Hugh, George Bertie Clavell, George Percy Cosmo, Minna Bertha, George Ronald Beddard,

Oswald and Harrold. The first three children were born in Barnes, Surrey, but just after George Hugh's birth in 1870, the family moved to Woodside, a larger house on Picardy Road in the recently-built commuter village of Belvedere near Erith, Kent, where the remaining children were born. At Woodside, the family employed a cook and two maids together with a nurse to look after the younger children. The nearby railway also made it an easy journey for George Blount to commute to London each day. Some years later the family moved to Stanwell, Middlesex.

After his retirement as Deputy Accountant General of the Royal Navy around the turn of the century, George Blount and his family moved again, this time to the vacant large Rectory at Northchurch which was leased from the Diocese of St Albans, the then Rector of St Mary's, Revd. RH Pope, deciding to live elsewhere in the village. George Bouverie Blount died in the summer of 1910 and was buried in the churchyard of St Mary's, Northchurch. His widow, Annie, died six years later.

George Percy Cosmo Blount, known in the family as Percy, the third of George Bouverie Blount's sons, was born in November 1873. Educated at the Plymouth Army Department School, Blount passed the army examinations and entered the Royal Military Academy at Sandhurst in 1891 as a Gentleman Cadet. A keen sportsman, Blount excelled at cricket and football, representing Sandhurst as part of winning teams on numerous occasions. Percy Blount graduated from Sandhurst at the end of 1894 and joined the Royal Artillery. In 1897 he became a Lieutenant and was posted to the Royal Artillery gunnery base at Shoeburyness on the Thames Estuary.

The gunnery ranges at Shoeburyness were built in the late 1840s to replace the ranges at Woolwich which had become increasingly difficult to use due to their proximity to the busy London docks. The facility at Shoeburyness expanded considerably in the 1850s after the Crimean War and in 1859 a dedicated School of Gunnery was established. Not only were Royal Artillery gunners trained there, but Shoeburyness also acted as an experimental base for different types of guns, rockets and explosives located in specially built casements.

It was while Blount was at Shoeburyness in 1900, that he met, and later married, Bridget Constance Bally, the daughter of Major General JF Bally. The same year, he was promoted to Captain and within three years, Blount had become an Instructor at the artillery ranges. In 1907, Bridget gave birth to a son, Bertie Kennedy Blount, who would later serve with the Special Operations Executive during the Second World War.

In 1910, Blount transferred to the Royal Garrison Artillery at Gibraltar and that November he left England on board the SS *Egypt* with his wife and son. He would later become Brigade Major for the Royal Artillery on Malta and was based there when war broke out.

Recalled to England, Blount was to remain at Woolwich until July 1915 when he left Devonport on board the HMT *Karoa* en-route to Gallipoli. He landed at Suvla Bay on 9th August, with the 120 men, 70 horses and four 60-pdr guns of 15th Heavy Battery. A month later, the 60-pdrs and their gunners were withdrawn and sent to the recently opened front at Salonika. Blount however, remained at Gallipoli and in November he was promoted to the temporary rank of Lieutenant Colonel, becoming the Assistant Adjutant and Quartermaster General of 53rd Division. As such, he was responsible for the supervision of stores and the distribution of supplies and provisions under the most trying of circumstances. The conditions at Gallipoli had now become intolerable with 53rd Division incurring significant casualties to enemy action or sickness which reduced the division to just 162 officers and 2,428 men, about 15 per cent of its full strength. The following month and due to the decision to extract the troops from the peninsula, Blount and 53rd Division were evacuated to Mudros and then to Alexandria.

He remained with 53rd Division in Egypt whilst it prepared for the campaign in Palestine, firstly securing the Suez Canal from Turkish attack and then participating in the advance up the coast towards Gaza and the eventual capture of Jerusalem in December 1917. That year, Imperial Russia awarded Blount the Order of St Anne 3rd class. A DSO was to follow in the 1918 King's New Year's Honours List.

In June 1923 he was promoted to Colonel, Royal Artillery. He retired five years later. By this time his family had moved to Blandford, Dorset, where they continued to play a full and active part in the social life of the local community, with Blount becoming Assistant Commissioner for the Scouts. Colonel George Percy Cosmo Blount died in August 1954, aged 80.

William James Delderfield (1896 – 1971)
Gunner 93159, 58th Brigade, RFA

The name Delderfield is one of the most common surnames in the Northchurch and Berkhamsted areas, with most long-standing local families having at least one Delderfield in their family tree. William Delderfield was born during the autumn of 1896 in Orchard End, Northchurch and was one of eleven children born to Samuel Delderfield, a hay and straw dealer, and his wife, Emma. The 1911 Census records William, who had now left school, as doing jobbing work. Two of his older brothers were both working on local farms and it is likely that William later followed in their footsteps. Another older brother, John Delderfield, had emigrated to Canada in 1906 to become a farmer.

William's service record has not survived, but the 1918 Absent Voters list for Northchurch records him as a gunner serving with 58th Battery, RFA. His medal card however, shows that William arrived in France on 17th November 1915 and describes him as Driver, a highly skilled role. Drivers had to work closely with the team of six horses that pulled the battery's 18-pdr field guns, each driver being responsible for two horses each. As well as fulfilling the role of driver, William could also act as a gunner in case of need.

At the time William joined his unit 58th Battery was serving with 35th Brigade, 7th Division and had been in France for five months. During the winter of 1915/16 they provided artillery support to the troops in the trenches at Loos, close to the formidable *Hohenzollern* Redoubt. The following June his battery moved south to the Somme sector and provided artillery support during the Somme Offensive. In 1917, the battery took part in the fighting during the German retreat to the heavily fortified Hindenburg Line, the Battle of Arras and later, the Third Battle of Ypres.

Like Horace Badrick, William was sent to the Italian Front at the end of 1917. Having spent the last two years on the Western Front, and more recently in the mud and squalor that was the Third Battle of Ypres, the move to cold Alpine air made a complete contrast. By January 1918, William and his battery were helping to hold the line along the River Piave. The following October the Austrians lost the Battle of Vittorio Veneto, in which 58th Brigade played a major part. This led to the destruction of the Austro-Hungarian army and the subsequent end of its Empire.

By 1920, William had returned home after demobilisation and was living with his father, Samuel, in Thorns Yard, Northchurch. On 30th April 1921, William left England on board the SS *Minnesdosa* bound for Canada, taking advantage of a Canadian Government scheme for assisted passage for farm labourers. There he joined his older brother, John, who had emigrated to Canada fifteen years earlier and now had a farm in Leeds County in the Province of Ontario. On 5th December 1924, William married Violet Curtis and remained in Canada for the rest of his life. He died in January 1971, aged 74.

Fred Dwight (1886 – 1971)
Sergeant 22547, 102 Siege Battery RGA

Fred Dwight was born in the family home in Eddy Street, Gossoms End, in December 1886, and was the son of William Dwight, a labourer from Chartridge and working at East's timberyard, and his Aldbury-born wife, Mary. On completing his education, he initially became a gardener, but soon decided to join the RGA. The 1911 Census shows Fred living in the RGA Clarence Barracks in Portsmouth which housed six battalions. Unfortunately, no record has been found to identify to which battalion Fred was posted.

August 1913 saw Fred, now an Acting Bombardier, marry 20-year-old Kate Burley at St Stephen's church, Portsmouth. Kate worked at a dye works and was the daughter of a local builder. Two years later she gave birth to a daughter. Although his service record has not survived, other records indicate that Fred remained in Portsmouth until 1916 when he transferred 102 Siege Battery, RGA.

Formed in Portsmouth in the spring of 1916, 102 Siege Battery, consisting of 5 officers and 133 other ranks, departed for France on 18th May on board the SS *King Edward*, whilst the guns, lorries and stores sailed from Avonmouth on board the SS *Avenden*. Having landed, the battery moved to Bienvillers, 12 miles south west of Arras, where new defences were constructed. The battery's 6-inch howitzers were first used in action during the massive artillery barrage that preceded the Somme Offensive at the end of June. The following year Fred and his battery took part in the Battle of Arras. That September he received the sad news that his younger brother, Alfred, had been killed during the Third Battle of Ypres[19].

During the Battle of Cambrai in November 1917 the battery suffered a number of casualties when its four guns were captured during a surprise attack by German troops. Fred, however, appears to have escaped uninjured. Withdrawn from the front line to recover, the battery received four new 26cwt 6-inch howitzers the following month.

Fred remained with the battery for the remainder of the war and after his discharge moved to London with his family where he joined the Metropolitan Police. In 1925, he became a father for the second time with a second son being born in 1931. The 1939 Register shows Fred and his family living in Hammersmith. He died in 1971, aged 85.

Alfred James Holland (1894 – 1965)
Gunner 16402, 104th Brigade, RFA

Alfred James Holland, known as James, was born in Northchurch in March 1894 and was the eldest son of James and Esther Holland. When he was seven years old his father died, aged just 33, and in 1909 his mother married Edwin Carvell, a farm worker from Orchard End. Esther moved into Edwin Carvell's four-roomed cottage with her three children with James later starting work on a local farm. By 1914 James had changed occupations and moved away to become an asylum attendant, possibly in Exeter, Devon.

It was at Exeter on 31st August 1914 that James enlisted with the RFA, joining 18th Reserve Battery at Topsham Barracks. His service record shows him as being 5ft 11ins tall, weighing 126lbs, with brown eyes, fresh complexion and brown hair. After completing his training as a gunner, he was posted to 'B' battery, 104th Brigade, RFA.

On 29th August 1915, James arrived in France with his battery, which at that time consisted of four 18-pdr guns. The following month, 104th Brigade entered the front line near Armentières and remained in northern France for several months providing defensive support during the German attack on

---

[19] Alfred Dwight's story is told in For Them's Sake

Vimy Ridge in May 1916 and the British counter-attack the following month. After a short period of training, his battery was once again in action during the Somme Offensive. In 1917, following the reorganisation of the Royal Artillery, 104th Brigade became 104th Army Brigade and later that year took part in the Third Battle of Ypres.

In February 1918, 104th Army Brigade moved south to the Somme Sector. On 21st March, following the launch of the German Spring Offensive, James and his brigade were forced to withdraw west to newly prepared positions from where they provided covering fire to the retreating troops of the New Zealand Division and by the end of the month five of the brigade's six guns were out of action due to their constant use. With the failure of the German offensive, the front began to stabilise and 104th Army Brigade was given the task of providing harassing artillery fire on the German lines whilst the British forces regrouped. At the end of May, James and his brigade were withdrawn from the front line and entered the 3rd Army Reserve. Two months later 104th Army Brigade transferred to the British 5th Army in preparation for the major offensive that the allied armies were about to launch.

At 04:20 on 8th August 1918, the Battle of Amiens commenced with Australian, Canadian, British and French forces launching a surprise attack on the German lines. James and his brigade were ordered into action at midnight, relieving some of the artillery that had been firing their guns since the start of the attack.

By September 1918, 104th Army Brigade had reached the Hindenburg Line and on 16th September, German artillery targeted the brigade's 'B' and 'D' batteries, with high explosive and gas shells causing several casualties. Among those wounded during the attack was James Holland, whose name appeared in the weekly Casualty List published the following month. The extent of James' injury is not known, but it appears that he recovered and was later able to rejoin his unit.

Following the signing of the Armistice, his unit returned to England and was based at Catterick Camp, Yorkshire. Here he was transferred to 'F' battery. James was not demobilised until March 1920 when he returned to Orchard End. In 1921 he married Maud Shenton in Wandsworth, south London. Maud gave birth to a son the following year. By 1939 James and his family were living in Tring Road, Northchurch, close to the *Old Grey Mare* public house and he was working as a sawyer at a local timberyard. He died in 1965, aged 71.

Frederick George Fenn (1882 – 1949)
Driver 210508, 41st Divisional Ammunition Column, RFA

Frederick Fenn was born in the autumn of 1882 in Aldbury. The son of Edwin Fenn, a farm labourer from Cheddington, and his wife Elizabeth, he grew up in Aldbury and later became a horseman on a local farm. On 4th March 1905, he married Alice Parmenter at St Mary's, Northchurch, and the newlyweds set up home in nearby Dudswell. Over the next four years Alice would give birth to three children.

With a young family to support, Frederick did not volunteer to join up at the start of the war and was conscripted in June 1916. On 2nd February 1917, he was mobilised and underwent a full medical examination at Watford. Described as being 5ft 5ins tall and weighing 125lbs he passed with an 'A1' category. The following day the remainder of the conscription process was completed, with Frederick stating that, given the choice, he would like to serve with the Army Veterinary Corps. The Army, however, had other ideas, in view of his horse-handling skills, and posted him to the RFA as a driver. Following his army training, Frederick was sent to France on 25th June 1917 joining 25th Reserve Battery. Two months later, he was posted to 41st Divisional Ammunition Column.

This Ammunition Column had been in France since May 1916 and had supplied the division's batteries during the Somme Offensive and was soon to do the same during the Third Battle of Ypres. In 1917, a Divisional Ammunition Column consisted of fifteen officers and around seven hundred men. Its role was simple; collect ammunition from the Divisional Ammunition Parks run by the Army Service Corps and transfer it to collection points some five to six miles from the front line. From there the ammunition was collected by the ammunition wagons belonging to the individual gun batteries.

In November 1917, 41st Division was transferred to Italy to bolster the Italian army on the River Piave where it remained until February 1918, when it was ordered to return to France. Frederick arrived back on in the Somme Sector on the Western Front on 9th March, shortly before the German army launched its Spring Offensive. Later, the ammunition column moved north to Flanders where it continued to supply the division's batteries following the Battle of Amiens. Frederick was granted two weeks' leave in early September 1918 and returned to England to see his family. He was back in France later that month for the final advance that threw the German army out of France.

Following the signing of the Armistice, 41st Division was one of those chosen to form part of the Army of Occupation and moved to Cologne in January 1919. The following month, Frederick returned to England and was demobilised. In 1927, the family moved to a house in Seymour Road in Northchurch. He, Alice and one daughter were still living there in 1939 and he was now working as a gardener. Frederick Fenn died in 1949, aged 66.

Robert Henry Haynes (1887 – 1936)
Gunner 39731, 34th Divisional Ammunition Column, RFA

Robert Haynes was born in Shoreditch, east London in 1887, the son of Robert Haynes, a porter working for a piano factory, and his wife, Jane. The Haynes family later moved to the Islington area where all of his brothers and sisters were born.

After leaving school, Robert started working as a carman for a railway company, collecting and delivering goods. In 1905, aged 18, he enlisted for three years with the Royal Artillery at St George's Barracks in Orange Street, London, just south of Leicester Square. His medical record from that time describes him as being 5ft 3½ins tall, weighing 114lbs, with a fresh complexion, blue eyes and light brown hair. He would later extend his term of service in the artillery by a further nine years.

Assigned to 59th Battery RFA, Robert's initial training took place at Weedon Barracks near Northampton, and later at Deepcut Barracks, Camberley, Surrey where he joined 99th Battery, RFA. November 1908 saw him and his battery embarking for Harrismith in the Orange River Colony for a four-year term on garrison duty. On his return to England in 1912 he entered the Army Reserves.

Moving to Northchurch, Robert started work as a coachman for the Hadden family at Rossway and living in rooms over the stables on the estate. In February 1914, he married Annie Lay, sister of Alfred and Arthur Lay, at St Mary's, Northchurch.

On the outbreak of war, Robert was recalled and embarked for France on 16th August with 34th Brigade, RFA. This brigade consisted of the Divisional Ammunition Column, to which he had been posted, together with 22nd, 50th and 70th Batteries and formed part of 2nd Division. On arrival in France, the brigade headed towards the Belgian frontier, but the rapid German advance meant that they were only able to provide covering fire for the British troops retreating south from Mons. The brigade was again in action during the Battle of the Marne, the Battle of the Aisne and the First Battle of Ypres.

1915 saw Robert supporting the brigade's batteries during the Battles of Festubert and Loos in northern France and that April he was promoted to Acting Bombardier. The following year, 34th Brigade took part in the massive artillery bombardment which preceded the opening of the Somme Offensive and provided artillery support in wire cutting and firing at the German trenches during the ongoing assaults by the infantry. Throughout October 1916, whilst based at Mailly-Mallet, the brigade's 18-pdr and 4.5in howitzers fired an average of 800 rounds each day, putting immense pressure on Robert's Ammunition Column to keep them restocked.

He was promoted to Corporal in February 1917 and two months later, 34th Brigade became an Army Field Artillery Brigade and moved between various army divisions as required. Each gun was now supplied with a minimum stock of 2,000 rounds, but due to the severe shortage of horses, the movement of the ammunition was only possible at night time. 34th Brigade took part in the artillery barrage on the opening day of the Battle of Arras later that month, its twenty-four guns firing some 14,000 rounds in support of the advancing troops. Later that year, it provided artillery support during the battles at Messines and the Third Battle of Ypres. In October 1917 Robert was promoted to Sergeant.

His ammunition column was at Morlincourt, south-east of Amiens on the day the Germans launched the Spring Offensive, whilst the brigade batteries were further north at Villers-Plouich, to the south of Cambrai, close to the Hindenburg Line. The German offensive forced 34th Brigade to fall back towards the River Ancre, as did Robert's ammunition column, eventually arriving at Senlis, just north of Paris.

Robert was discharged in April 1919 and returned to Northchurch and soon after moved to Gossoms End. It is currently uncertain whether he resumed his job as coachman at Rossway. He died in the summer of 1936 aged 48.

Frank Parsley (1891 – 1982)
Driver 209979, London Divisional Ammunition Column, Army of the Rhine, RFA

Frank Parsley was born in the spring of 1891 and was the last child of Charles Parsley and his wife, Amelia. Shortly before Frank's birth, Charles died leaving Amelia to bring up her three other children, Archibald, Frederick and Emily, with only 14-year-old Archibald, who had just left school, bringing in any money to the family home in Orchard End, Northchurch. Living a few doors away were Amelia's elderly parents, William and Ellen Honor.

Growing up in Northchurch without a father would have been difficult for Frank. By 1901, his grandmother, Ellen Honor, had died and Amelia and her children had moved in with her widowed father. To make ends meet, Amelia was now working as a straw plaiter and Archibald had become a general labourer, but fifteen-year-old Emily had yet to find work. Ten years later, Emily had married and left home and Frank's grandfather had died. Amelia, Archibald and Frank had now moved into a small four-roomed cottage in Gossoms End, with Frank now working as a general labourer.

Frank's service record has not survived, but the Northchurch Autumn 1919 Absent Voters List shows his home address back in Orchard End and him serving with the RFA as a driver with No 2 Section of the London Divisional Ammunition Column, Army of the Rhine. The London Division was formed in March 1919 from units of 41st Division, so it is likely that Frank served with them in the latter part of the war, initially in France and then, following a short spell on the Italian Front, returning there following the German Spring Offensive.

At the end of the war 41st Division was selected to join the Army of the Rhine. The division's artillery contingent now consisted of 187th and 190th Brigades as well as the Frank's divisional ammunition column. He was to remain in Cologne with the occupation troops until September 1919 when his ammunition column returned to England for demobilisation.

On 23rd December 1922, Frank married Annie Elizabeth Warren, the daughter of a silversmith, at Christchurch, Somerstown, London. By then, he was living nearby in Charlton Street, midway between Euston and St Pancras stations and working as a labourer. In 1939, Frank and Annie were living in Watford and he was working as a labourer for a railway company. Later moving to Devon, he died there in the autumn of 1982, aged 91.

Ralph Pidgley (1896 – 1968)
Lance Bombardier 203031, Royal Horse Artillery

Ralph Pidgley was one of the men named on the war shrine in St Mary's, Northchurch. From what little information is known about him, it appears that he was probably working as a groom at one of the local large houses when war broke out.

Born in Wingrave, near Aylesbury in 1896, his father, Thomas, worked as a groom for a local hunt. Surrounded by horses from an early age it is not surprising that Ralph followed his father and older brothers to become a groom. As such, sometime between 1911 and 1914 he found employment in the Northchurch area.

Although Ralph's service record has not survived, from his medal record it is known that he did not serve abroad until after 1915 and employed his skill with horses becoming a driver and later a Lance Bombardier with the RHA. Unfortunately, no further details of where he served, or in which unit, are known.

Following his demobilisation, Ralph did not go back to his job in Northchurch and returned to Wingrave. By 1923 he was living at the stables at Ascott, near Wing, Buckinghamshire, where, presumably, he was still working as a groom. He stayed there for some years before moving to the Wolverton area, where in 1939 he was working as a groom, gardener and domestic servant at a large house near the village of Calverton. Ralph Pidgley remained single for all his life and died in 1968, aged 72.

---ooo---

The Royal Garrison Artillery (RGA) came into being in 1899 with the responsibility of manning the large artillery pieces located in fixed positions in the forts and fortresses across the British Empire. Its scope later expanded to include the heavy gun batteries attached to each infantry division, together with the guns of the siege artillery

The Siege and Heavy Batteries of the RGA were responsible for destroying enemy artillery positions, strongpoints, ammunition dumps, railway lines and roads located well behind the front line. The main weapons they employed were the 60-pdr, 6-inch, 9.2-inch, 12-inch and 14-inch guns, as well as the 6-inch, 8-inch, 9.2-inch, 12-inch and 15-inch howitzers. The 60-pdr gun dated from 1905 and was developed following experiences gained during the Boer war. By 1914 it was the main heavy gun in the British army and weighed 4.5 tons and capable of firing a 60lb high explosive or shrapnel shell over a range of 10,000 yards. Initially drawn by a team

60-pdr gun
Author's collection

of eight shire horses, improvements made during the war increased its weight and necessitated the use of petrol-driven Holt artillery tractors. In 1914, each infantry division was equipped with four 60-pdr guns, which was increased to six in 1916.

The 6-inch howitzer weighed 26-cwt and was the most numerous of the heavy howitzers used by the RGA. It was introduced in 1915 and could fire a 100lb shell at a steep angle reaching a range of 10,000 yards. Each howitzer had a detachment of 10 men and was initially drawn by a team of horses which was replaced later in the war by four-wheel drive 3-ton lorries.

Unlike the 60-pdr gun and 26-cwt howitzer, the 9.2-inch howitzer had to be disassembled into three loads when on the move. Capable of firing a 290lb shell up to a range of 13,935 yards, the 9.2-inch howitzer dated from 1913 and was designed by the Coventry Ordinance Works. It was one of the most accurate of the howitzers used by the RGA during the war.

In 1917, a major reorganisation of the British artillery resulted in the removal of the RGA guns from their dedicated infantry divisions, to join what were eventually called Heavy Artillery Groups (HAG), each with several batteries of different types of gun. Initially divided into Heavy and Siege Batteries, as the war progressed these names became interchangeable.

Ernest Batchelor (1893 – 1965)
Gunner 87103, 2/104th Heavy Battery, RGA

Ernest Batchelor was born in a four-roomed cottage in Gossoms End in July 1893, the third child of Thomas Batchelor, a gardener, and his wife, Rosetta. After leaving school, he became a printer's apprentice.

Although Ernest's service record has not survived, his medal record shows that he was not sent overseas until at least 1916. In 1918, he was serving in Mesopotamia with 2/104th Heavy Battery, RGA. The unit was raised as a replacement for 1/104th Coy which surrendered to the Turks following the fall of Kut-el-Amara. Armed with four 60-pdr guns, on arrival in Mesopotamia the battery was transported up the Tigris river and first went into action against the Turkish army at Orah and later participated in the recapture of Kut-el-Amara, thus avenging the loss of its predecessor battery[20]. In March 1917 it took part in the capture of Bagdad. Ernest remained in Mesopotamia with his unit until the campaign ended in 1918.

Demobilised in 1919, Ernest returned to Gossoms End. In the Autumn of 1920, he married May Grace, whose family lived in George Street, Berkhamsted. Soon after their marriage they moved to Crewe where Ernest had found work as a compositor in a printing works. They would later raise three children together.

In 1939, he and his family were still living in Crewe and he was now a foreman at the printing works. He died in 1965, aged 71.

Oliver Hayles (1878 – 1935)
Gunner 125535, 295th Siege Battery, RGA

Oliver Hayles was born in the small village of Binstead, on the Isle of Wight, in September 1878 where his father, George, worked as a gardener. His mother, Hannah, came from over the other side of the Solent in Fawley, Hampshire. In due course Oliver also became a gardener, and by 1901 he had left the Isle of Wight and was working as an undergardener at Longwood House in the village of Titchborne, Hampshire, the gardens of which had been designed by Gertrude Jekyll.

Oliver later moved to Northchurch and became the head gardener for Sir Charles Fredrick Hadden at his home at Rossway, living in a four-roomed cottage on the estate. In 1908, he married Annie Millard at St John the Baptist, Biddisham, Somerset. Oliver and Annie had met some years earlier on the Isle of Wight, when she was working as a domestic servant at Nunwell House, Brading. The following year, they became parents.

---

[20] One of the 60-pdr guns used by 2/104th Heavy Battery in Mesopotamia is currently on display at the Imperial War Museum at Duxford.

In 1914, Oliver was approaching his 36th birthday and was still the head gardener at Rossway. His service record has not survived, but he was probably conscripted in the summer of 1916. The Northchurch 1918 Absent Voter List shows him serving as a gunner with 295th Siege Battery, RGA.

This battery was formed in Hartlepool in November 1916 and sailed from Southampton for France the following March on board the paddle steamer *Mona Queen II* together with 294th and 296th Siege Batteries. On their arrival at Le Havre, the 6-inch howitzers of the Siege Battery were placed under the command of 17th HAG, which at that time formed part of 2nd Australian & New Zealand Army Corps (ANZAC). Moving to 52nd HAG the following month, Oliver's unit took part in the massive artillery barrage during the Battle of Messines. The battery later participated in the Third Battle of Ypres, during which several of Oliver's fellow gunners were killed. Moved to the Italian Front at the end of 1917, 295th Battery later took part in the key Battle of Piave.

Following his demobilisation, Oliver returned to Northchurch, and his job as head gardener at Rossway. He remained there until his death in 1935, aged 59.

Henry John Hooper (1885 – 1961)
Lieutenant, 157th Heavy Battery, RGA

Henry Hooper came to the RGA via another branch of the army. The elder brother of Edward Hooper, Henry was born in Berkhamsted in September 1885 and was the son of John Hooper, a domestic coachman, and later estate steward at Woodcock Hill, and his wife, Annie. Educated at Berkhamsted School, Henry later studied teaching at St Johns College, Battersea.

His first teaching experience was at the Abbey National School in St Albans, where he spent a year during his training. Returning to St John's College in 1905, Henry joined the 2nd (South) Middlesex Rifle Volunteers, rising to the rank of Sergeant. In 1908, he moved to Blackford, Somerset, where he spent a year teaching at Sexey's School, named after the 16th Century lawyer, Hugh Sexey. He then moved to the Isle of Wight, becoming an Assistant Master at the County Secondary School at Sandown. It was during his summer break in 1914, when he was staying with his parents in Northchurch and studying for a BSc, that war broke out.

It is likely that Henry returned to the school at Sandown at the end of the summer holidays, but he must have been considering what to do, as on 23rd December 1914, he attested at the Duke of York's Headquarters in Chelsea, joining the Royal Army Medical Corps (RAMC) as a Territorial, becoming Private 236 in 1st London (City of London) Sanitary Company, RAMC (T). The RAMC preferred educated and skilled men in their Sanitary companies, and being a teacher, Henry was well suited. He spent the next three weeks training at the Duke of York's Headquarters, attending numerous lectures as well as undergoing rigorous physical training sessions.

His training complete, he was posted to 15th Sanitary Section and boarded the SS *Atlantian* at Southampton on 18th January 1915 bound for Le Havre. Henry's unit consisted of one officer, two sergeants, two corporals, twenty privates and one batman. Its role was to provide, as far as possible, hygienic conditions for the soldiers, working closely with the local field ambulances, paying attention to all water supplies and containers and checking them regularly to ensure they were safe for drinking. Where the water was found to be contaminated portable 'Horrocks Boxes', which used sand filtration and chlorine sterilisation, were employed.

The provision of baths for the soldiers was another responsibility of the Sanitary Section, and something much longed for by the men whilst serving in the trenches. The baths were normally set up close to the soldier's billets, and enabled them to take off their dirty uniforms for cleaning, delousing and disinfection and then enjoy a hot shower or bath. Another responsibility was the regular inspection of billets which ranged from cellars, stables, sheds and houses, to temporary structures like Nissen huts. Rats and other vermin were another issue to deal with, which required the use of traps wherever possible. This did not solve the problem of the rats in the trenches however, some of which grew to the size of cats having fed off unburied corpses and discarded food. Then there was the provision of latrines, which were constructed well away from the billets and were also supposed to prevent the build-up of flies which carried diseases like typhus. Lice were another major problem, which frequently set up colonies in the soldier's uniforms, particularly in the seams, and caused typhus and 'Trench Fever'. Soldiers tended to run a candle flame against the uniform's seams to kill as many of the lice as possible, but it was only through a thorough delousing process that the uniforms could be completely cleared.

Henry and his unit remained in France until October 1915, when they embarked at Marseilles on board the SS *Transylvanian* bound for Salonika. In July 1916, Henry was promoted to Acting Corporal and two months later to Lance-Sergeant. The conditions at Salonika were abysmal as dysentery and other diseases were rife. More soldiers went down with illnesses than were killed or wounded in the campaign and Henry was no exception; in December 1916, he contracted jaundice and was admitted to a local Field Hospital. Fortunately, he made a good recovery and was able to rejoin his unit the following month. In March 1917, he was appointed Corporal.

By now, Henry had had enough of working in a Sanitary Unit. The same month that he was appointed Corporal, he applied for a commission with the Royal Garrison Artillery. Among the names he gave as referees were the Dean of London and Charles Henry Greene, the Headmaster of Berkhamsted School and father of the writer, Graham Greene. In his application, Henry was described as standing 5ft 6ins tall and weighing

133lbs. Before being approved to attend an officer training course, he had to spend six weeks attached to 127th Battery, RGA which was then serving at Salonika.

At the end of July 1917, following the completion of his period attached to the battery, Henry left Salonika for a period of home leave in Northchurch before starting his officer training course. Whilst in Northchurch, he met a fellow teacher, Elsie Popple, who was teaching in an elementary school in Berkhamsted, and the couple later became engaged. Henry and Elsie were married the following spring.

Henry's officer training commenced in November 1917 and took place at No2 RGA Officer Cadet School at Maresfield Park, near Uckfield, Sussex. He was Commissioned on 24th August 1918 and left England shortly afterwards for Mesopotamia to join his new unit, 157th Heavy Battery, 38th Brigade. Within days, however, he went down with influenza, which by then was sweeping across the world, infecting servicemen and civilians alike. Admitted to a hospital in Kut-el-Amara for treatment, he was fortunate to make a full recovery. On his discharge from hospital in October 1918, Henry joined his battery, but within days the Turkish government signed the Armistice of Mudros, ending the war in Mesopotamia.

In March 1919, he left Basra bound for England and decommissioning. Henry and Elsie moved to Southampton in 1920, where he became an Assistant Master at Southampton Itchen Secondary School. The following year, they moved again, to Sandy, Bedfordshire, where Henry taught at the Central School, becoming Headmaster in 1923. He remained at Sandy for six years before becoming Headmaster at a school at nearby Kempston, where he stayed until his retirement. In 1939, he was also serving as one of the local Air Raid Wardens in Kempston. Henry Hooper died in 1961, aged 76.

Edgar Leonard Kempster (1892 – 1964)
Wheeler Gunner 174675, 494th Siege Battery, RGA

Edgar Kempster was born in Ashley Green, Buckinghamshire in July 1892 and was the son of John Kempster, a general labourer, and his wife, Louise. On leaving school, Edgar started work as a gardener and by 1911 he was working locally as an undergardener, possibly for Head Gardener, Oliver Hayles, at Rossway.

A few days after the war started, Edgar enlisted at Berkhamsted, expressing an interest in serving with the Royal Artillery. His service record shows that he stood 5ft 7ins tall, weighed 130lbs and had hazel eyes and dark brown hair and spoke with a slight stutter. The day after his medical examination, Edgar formally joined the RGA at Woolwich and was posted to 21st Reserve Battery for training, which he later continued with 12th Reserve Battery at Brighton. In May 1915, he was transferred to the Royal Artillery's School of Instruction at Shoeburyness where he remained for two years. In June 1917, having completed a short course at Woolwich, he became a skilled wheelwright and was later posted to 494th Siege Battery, RGA.

On 10th April 1918, Edgar was sent to France along with his battery, probably as replacements for the batteries lost during the German Spring Offensive. On their arrival, 494th Siege Battery became part of the British 14th Garrison Artillery Brigade, which fell under the command of an Australian Heavy Artillery Corps. The Brigade's impressive firepower consisted of fourteen 6-inch howitzers, six 8-inch howitzers and two 12-inch howitzers. At 04:20 on 8th August 1918, at the start of the defining Battle of Amiens, Edgar's battery, located near Corbie in the Somme sector, was one of the many batteries that targeted the German artillery and provided a creeping barrage for the allied infantry and tanks to advance.

Gunner Edgar Kempster
Courtesy of Roger Emery

Edgar returned to England in March 1919 and within days he married Edith Ethel Dell at St Mary's, Northchurch. Two months later, Edgar was demobilised and awarded a Silver War badge. Whether this was because of an injury or illness during his time with 494th Siege Battery is unclear.

Soon afterwards, Edgar and Ethel moved to Caldecott House near Abingdon, Oxfordshire, where Edgar had found work as a gardener. Four years later he and Ethel and their two boys moved to the village of Walton-in-Gordano in north Somerset where in 1939, he was running his own market garden business. Edgar Kempster died in 1964, aged 71.

Henry (Harry) Rance (1878 – 1935)
Gunner 120091, 67th Siege Battery, RGA

Henry Rance, commonly known as Harry, was born in River Terrace, Gossoms End, in the early summer of 1878, the son of Amos Rance, a sawyer, and Sarah, a baker's daughter from Tring. Sadly, within weeks of his birth, Harry's father died, aged just 33, leaving his mother to bring up three young children. Sarah Rance herself died in 1888 and so his older sister became head of the household. After leaving school he started work as a general labourer.

On 4th August 1900, Harry married Elizabeth (Lizzie) Munday at St Mary's, Northchurch, and later moved to Battersea, south London where he had found work at a brewery. During their time in Battersea, Lizzie gave birth to four children - one son and three daughters.

Harry was 36 years old when war broke out, and with a wife and young family to support he did not join the rush to volunteer. By 1916, he and his family had moved back to Gossoms End and he was working as a carman. His conscription papers arrived that June and he duly reported to the Recruiting Officer at Watford. Aged nearly 38, he was now at the upper end of men being conscripted and his medical record shows him as being 5ft 8ins tall and weighing 149lbs. Mobilised three months later, Harry travelled to Bedford and, following another medical examination, he was posted to the RGA and sent to Clipstone Camp near Mansfield, Nottinghamshire, for training. The following month, he travelled higher up the country to Tynemouth, joining 339th Siege Battery RGA. Later transferred to 67th Siege Battery, RGA, Harry left for France in June 1917.

His battery was equipped with six 8-inch howitzers and had been in France since March 1916 and had taken part on the first day of the Somme Offensive. In April of the following year the battery moved north, taking part in the Battle of Arras, and by the time Harry joined them south of Ypres in June 1917, the men in the battery had gained three Military

Two 8-inch howitzers
Author's collection

Crosses, two DCMs, nine Military Medals and was twice 'Mentioned in Despatches'. Employed in counter-battery firing, i.e. the deliberate targeting of German artillery batteries, 67th Siege Battery fired some 7,200 rounds in July 1917 alone as part of the Third Battle of Ypres and on 1st October, during the same battle, the battery fired some 1,149 rounds. Casualties among the gunners were frequent, not just from enemy counterfire, but also due to accidents when defective explosive cartridges ignited whilst being handled. During the final days of the battle the following month, the battery fired 9,021 shells against the enemy lines. December 1917 saw Harry and his battery withdrawn from the front line to Poperinghe. For the men it meant a time of rest after the stress of the previous months, and for guns it meant a trip to the workshops for repair and maintenance. The same month, 67th Siege Battery came under the control of 62nd Brigade, RGA.

February 1918 saw the batteries of 62nd Brigade moving south from the Ypres Salient to Morlancourt in the Somme Sector. The German Spring Offensive the following month forced the brigade to retreat some 25 miles westwards, losing one gun in the process due to lack of transport. Wherever possible, Harry's battery provided harassing fire to cover the retreating British troops, many of the barrages being fired in co-operation with observation aircraft. On 5th April, its position having being detected, one of the battery's guns was put out of action by enemy artillery. By June 1918, Harry's battery was up to full strength again and on 20th July, he was given three weeks' home leave whilst the battery was out of the front line.

He returned to France on 10th August and shortly afterwards his battery rejoined 62nd Brigade, going into action at Courcelette. By the end of the war Harry's battery was at Bermerain, midway between Cambrai and Mons, where it halted.

Harry was demobilised on 24th February 1918 and returned to River Terrace, becoming a nursery gardener. He died in 1935, aged 54.

Charles Albert Sear (1895 – 1965)
Bombardier 56714, 2nd Siege Battery, RGA

Charles Sear, was born in Watford in May 1895. His father, also called Charles, came from Northchurch and worked locally as a milkman. Sometime between 1901 and 1911 the Sear family moved to a cottage in Gossoms End and probably started working for Arthur Sear, who ran a small dairy in Northchurch. By 1911, Charles jnr had started work as a presser at the Mantle factory in Lower Kings Road, Berkhamsted.

Little is known about his service in the RGA. His medal record shows that he was not sent abroad until after 1915 and the 1918 Northchurch Absent Voters List shows him as serving as a Gunner with 2nd Siege Battery, RGA. This unit was equipped with heavy 60-pdr guns and was one of the first batteries to be sent to France in 1914, where it remained for the rest of the war. During his time serving with the RGA Charles was promoted to Bombardier.

Soon after his demobilisation in early 1919, he married Wigginton-born Louise Nellie Reynolds at St Peter's, Berkhamsted. The couple settled in a cottage in Gossoms End, close to his parents and they would later raise four children together. In 1939, Charles and Louise were living in Hazel Road, Berkhamsted. He was working as a house painter and also serving as one of the local ARP wardens. Charles Sear died in 1965, aged 69.

George Simmonds (1882 – 1937)
Gunner 78927, 316th Siege Battery, RGA

George Simmonds was born at Shootersway Cottage on the Rossway estate in the late autumn of 1882, where his father, Charles Simmonds, worked as the estate carpenter. The following year on 25th July, a quadruple baptism took place at St Mary's, Northchurch, when George was christened along with his older siblings Ellen, Herbert and Minnie. George grew up on the Rossway estate and succeeded his father as estate carpenter after he retired. In 1911, George's brother, Herbert, also worked at Rossway as one of the gardeners.

In early 1916, George, now aged 33, received his conscription papers and was told to report to the Berkhamsted recruitment office. Here, on 26th February, he had a medical examination and was declared fit for duty. His records show that he stood 5ft 8½ins tall, weighed 178lbs and had grey eyes.

The following April, he was mobilised and travelled to Bedford where he was posted to the RGA. Two days later, at the RGA's Woolwich depot, George was classified as a skilled carpenter. Following his initial training at Woolwich, he was posted to 33 Coy, RGA at Portsmouth and then to 141st Siege Battery. After three months, and just before 141st Siege Battery left for France, George was transferred to 196th Siege Battery and so remained in England. The same thing happened two months later, just before 196th Siege Battery was due to move to France, he was transferred to 37 Coy, RGA and then 42 Coy, RGA, both home defence units based at Portsmouth.

Just before Christmas 1916, George was transferred yet again, this time to 316th Siege Battery which was armed with four 6-inch howitzers. He finally left Southampton on 14th April 1917, bound for the Italian Front. By the following July, 316th Siege Battery was on the Izonso River in Northern Italy as part of 94th HAG and was to remain in Italy until the end of the war.

In April 1919, the battery returned to England and George was demobilised five months later. He returned to his home on the Rossway estate and in the spring of 1920, aged 38, he married Laura Annie Rowe from Wigginton. They would later raise two children together. George Simmons died in 1937, aged 55.

Harold Edgar Smith (1895 – 1954)
Gunner 65786, 29th Siege Battery, RGA

Harold Smith was born in Ellesmere Road, Berkhamsted, in August 1895, in what was then part of Northchurch Parish. He was the third of four sons born to Walter Smith, a sawyer, probably at the nearby timberyard at Alford Wharf, and his wife, Mary Ann Smith.

After leaving school Harold became a doctor's houseboy and later moved to Desborough, Northamptonshire where he found work as a grocer's assistant. It was not until November 1915, with the introduction of conscription imminent, that Harold attested under the Derby Scheme at Market Harborough, asking to join the RGA. His medical record shows him as being 5ft 6¾ins tall and weighing 126lbs. The following month, he was mobilised and reported to the RGA Depot at Bexhill, where he was posted to 89th Siege Battery, RGA.

Two weeks later, Harold was back in Berkhamsted, where on 18th January 1916, he married Violet Ethel Mustill at St Mary's, Northchurch. Violet's brother, William, had recently returned to the family home at Cow Roast Lock, having been released in a prisoner of war exchange. Just over three months later, Harold and 89th Siege Battery left Southampton on board the SS *Viper* bound for Le Havre. In July, whilst Harold was serving in France, Violet, gave birth to a son.

89th Siege Battery was equipped with two brand new British Ordnance BL 12-inch howitzers, mounted on specially designed railway carriages built by the Elswick Ordinance Company. Each BL 12-inch howitzer sat in the middle of the four-axle railway carriage which, when fired, was lowered and fixed to the ground using cables or outriggers to provide extra stability. The howitzer and carriage combined weighed over 57 tons, with the gun having a range of over 11,000 yards.

Arriving at Le Havre on 30th April 1916, Harold and his battery were sent to the area south of Ypres where over the next few weeks they fired shells on the German lines daily, often working in conjunction with Royal Flying Corps observation aircraft. In 1917, the battery took part in the massive bombardment of the area surrounding the German-held Vimy Ridge, north of Arras that fell to Canadian troops on 12th April. Two months later, Harold's battery was in action at Messines and around this time he qualified as a gunner/layer, meaning that he was now part of the gun crew responsible for setting up and aiming the 12-inch howitzer.

His battery supported the British troops at the Third Battle of Ypres, during which each gun fired an average of 7 rounds per hour at specific targets. By August 1917, however, both of the battery's guns were worn out, having fired 2,794 and 2,502 rounds respectively, and were removed from the front line. They were later replaced by new models of the 12-inch howitzer. In December 1917, with the battle over, Harold returned home on leave where he saw his son for the first time. 29th Siege Battery moved south to the Somme sector in early 1918, but its movements in the subsequent months are unclear.

The day after the Armistice was signed, Harold again returned to England on leave, but shortly after his arrival he contracted influenza, and was admitted to hospital in Aylesbury. Fortunately, he had contracted a mild strain of the virus and recovered within a few days. Returning to France in early December, he was again in need of medical attention, this time for an abscess on his foot and he spent several days under treatment at the 3rd Australian Hospital in Abbeville.

He was demobilised in March 1919 and returned home, resuming his job as a grocer. In 1939, he was working as a grocery store manager in Chesham and also serving as a local ARP Warden. Harold Smith died in Chesham in 1954, aged 59.

Edward Infield Willis (1898 – 1983)
2nd Lieutenant, 440th Siege Battery, RGA

Edward Infield Willis was born in Kensington in November 1898. His father, Frederick James Willis, was a senior clerk at the Ministry of Health in London, whilst his mother, Agnes Maud Willis, was the daughter of wealthy newspaper proprietor Henry John Infield, who owned the Southern Publishing Company, based in Brighton.

By 1911, Edward, his parents and younger brother had moved to Shootersway House on the southern borders of Northchurch Parish. Here, Frederick Willis, now an Assistant Secretary at the Ministry of Health, employed a French governess to look after his two boys, together with a cook and a housemaid and it is likely that Edward later attended Berkhamsted School. In the King's New Year's 1914 Honours, his father was appointed a Knight Commander of the Bath.

The late summer of 1917 saw Edward going up to New College Oxford. He was not there long however, as on 25th January 1918, he obtained a commission with the RGA, and in due course was posted to 440th Siege Battery in Palestine.

Edward's battery, comprising four 6-inch howitzers, had arrived in Palestine the previous year to take part in the Battle of Nebi Samwil that led to the fall of Jerusalem. Unfortunately, Edward's service record has not survived, so it is unclear when he travelled to Palestine to join his unit, or what part he took in the final battles against the Turkish army during 1918.

On returning home in 1919 he resigned his commission and went back to New College, Oxford, to complete his studies. He later joined the Southern Publishing Company, which was now being run by his uncle, Henry Infield's son, Jonathan. In the summer of 1926, Edward married Winifred Edith Alice Upfield and the couple settled in Brighton.

In 1939, they were living at a house in Brighton's fashionable Marine Drive, his occupation being described as Newspaper Manager. Three years later, his uncle died and Edward took over as Chairman and Managing Director of the company. In 1965, the Westminster Press purchased 70% of Southern Publishing Company, with Edward remaining as Chairman. Following his retirement, the Westminster Press acquired the remaining 30% of the company. Edward Infield Willis died in 1983, aged 84.

8 – The Territorial Force Gunners

Following the creation of the Territorial Force in 1908, two artillery gun batteries were set up within Hertfordshire. 1st Hertfordshire Battery was based in St Albans, with drill stations in St Albans, Hatfield and Harpenden. 2nd Hertfordshire Battery was based at Watford, with drill stations in Hemel Hempstead, Berkhamsted, Tring and Kings Langley. Both batteries, together with the Northamptonshire battery, and a Brigade Ammunition Column based at Hertford, formed 4th East Anglian Brigade, RFA. Each battery had four guns, but a slow trickle of new recruits meant that it would only come up to full strength following the outbreak of the war.

From the information that still survives, it appears that none of the Territorial Force artillerymen from the Northchurch area who served during the war were members of the two batteries before 1914.

Francis (Frank) Harold Baldwin (1897 – 1980)
Gunner 890477, 386th Battery RFA(T)
Alfred Lay (1888 – 1959)
Gunner 890813, 386th Battery RFA(T)
Arthur Lay (1890 – 1951)
Driver 890866, 386th Battery RFA(T)

In Tring in December 1897, unmarried mother, Elizabeth Baldwin, gave birth to a son whom she named Francis Harold. Francis, or Frank as he later became known, grew up on Poor's Land Farm at Hastoe, a small hamlet to the south of Tring, which was run by his grandfather, Edward Baldwin, and his uncle, Frederick. In 1902, Frank's mother married William Dell, and in 1911 they were living with Frank in a 5-roomed cottage in Dudswell, along with two new daughters. By now, Frank had started work on a nearby a farm. His service record has not survived, but his service number indicates that he became a member of 4th East Anglian Brigade, RFA.

Alfred and Arthur Lay were two of James and Clara Lay's eight children. Arthur was the older brother by just over a year, being born in Orchard End, Northchurch, in November 1888, with Alfred following in February 1890. Their father, James Lay, was a general labourer who sometimes turned his hand to bricklaying. By 1891, the Lay family were living in a cottage in Thom's Yard, adjacent to the *George & Dragon* public house and later moved to Gossoms End. After leaving school both Alfred and Arthur started work at the William Cooper & Nephew chemical factory in Berkhamsted.

Following the outbreak of war, it was former Militia volunteer, fifty-six-year-old James Lay, who would volunteer to join the army. Thirty-seven days after enlisting, James was politely told that his services were not required.

Neither Alfred nor Arthur's service records have survived, but it is likely that they attested under the Derby Scheme towards the end of 1915 and were mobilised the following year, joining 4th East Anglian Brigade, RFA. Before mobilisation, both Alfred and Arthur took the opportunity to marry their girlfriends; Alfred married Edith Potten who worked at the Mantle Factory in Lower Kings Road, whilst Arthur married Elizabeth Cook, a leather factory worker.

Not only did the brothers work for the same company, get married within weeks of each other, but once their basic army training was complete, they later served together in the same artillery unit - 386th Battery, RFA, 30th Brigade.

Frank Baldwin, Alfred Lay and Arthur Lay, left England in September 1917 as part of 386th Battery bound for Mesopotamia. Their battery was equipped with six 18-pdr guns and on their arrival at Basra they moved north to set up new defensive positions at Shahroban, ready to protect the city of Bagdad which had been captured by the British earlier in the year.

All three men had different roles within the battery. Frank Baldwin, apart from being a gunner, also acted as a signaller for his unit. This was a highly dangerous role, with signallers being responsible for maintaining communication between forward observation posts, and the artillery positions. They were also responsible for repairing damaged telephone lines, often in the open, whilst under enemy fire. Where telephone lines were not practicable, the signallers resorted to the use of semaphore flags to pass on the information, which unless hidden from enemy forces, would easily attract their attention. Alfred Lay served as a gunner, whilst Arthur, was a driver responsible for hauling the guns.

With the fighting in Mesopotamia effectively over by July 1918, the men of the battery spent most of their time on gunnery practice, whilst trying to avoid both sandfly fever and heatstroke. The men of 30th Brigade remained in Mesopotamia until February 1919, when they began their long trip home and demobilisation.

In the autumn of 1921, Frank married Emmeline Honey from Berkshire. In 1939, they were living in at cottage at Callipers Hall Farm at Chipperfield near Watford, where he worked as a cowman. Frank Baldwin died in spring of 1980, aged 82.

Following their demobilisation, Alfred and Arthur Lay both returned to their jobs at the chemical factory. Arthur died in 1951, aged 62, whilst Alfred died eight years later, aged 69.

Harry Carter (1892 – 1971)
Gunner 890737, 54th Divisional Ammunition Column, RFA(T)
Leonard William Mapley (1894 - 1964)
Gunner 890736, 270th Brigade, RFA(T)
Jack Hales (1896 – 1966)
Gunner 895995, 54th Divisional Ammunition Column, RFA(T)

Harry Carter, Leonard Mapley and Jack Hales had one thing in common - they all joined 4th East Anglian Brigade, RFA, within days of each other and it is possible that they enlisted on the same day as their original service numbers, 951, 948 and 955, are so close together. Unfortunately, only Jack Hales's service record has survived. Another man from Northchurch, Ernest Frederick Delderfield, who initially served in the same unit, is covered separately.

Harry Carter was the oldest of the three men, and was born in Northchurch in August 1892, the fourth child of George Carter, a local watercress labourer, and his wife Ellen. After leaving school, he became a gardener and by 1911 all his brothers were doing the same type of work. During the second week of September 1914, Harry travelled to Hertford where he enlisted as a gunner.

Leonard Mapley was two years younger than Harry Carter. Born in Northchurch in August 1894, Leonard was the son of 19-year-old Leah Mapley, an unmarried domestic servant. A year after his birth, Leah married Raymond Bignell at St Mary's, Northchurch. Raymond was a former soldier and was now working as a general labourer. Their first child, Lucy Elsie, was born during the late winter of 1896 and was christened at St Mary's Northchurch, on 1st March 1897 at the same time as Leonard. When they moved to Pinner in Middlesex some time later, Leonard stayed in Northchurch to be raised by his maternal grandparents, George and Esther Mapley, who lived in a cottage in New Road. After leaving school, Leonard became a butcher's assistant, possibly working for John Ashby in his shop just around the corner in Northchurch High Street. He later left Northchurch and moved to Old Street, London, but when war broke out he travelled to Hertford to enlist as a gunner with the 4th East Anglian Brigade.

Jack Hales was the youngest of the three men. Born in March 1896 in New Road, Northchurch, he was the fourth son of Joseph Hales and his wife Elizabeth. He grew up in the village and became a gardener after leaving school. On 14th September 1914, he travelled to Hertford and attested for 4 years' service with 4th East Anglian Brigade's Ammunition Column. At that time, he stood 5ft 11ins tall and weighed 135lbs.

On the day that war was declared, 4th Brigade was at its annual camp in Northumberland. Orders quickly came for them to return south to their designated war base at Warley, near Brentwood, Essex. A few weeks later, just before Harry, Leonard and Jack enlisted, 4th Brigade moved to Thetford, Norfolk, taking over several country houses which had space for the men together with their guns, equipment and horses. Whilst the war in France and Belgium was being fought by men of the regular army serving in the BEF, the Territorials of 4th Brigade trained in the Thetford area. In January 1915, Leonard Mapley was granted leave to travel to London where, at St Mark's, Old Street, he married Mabel Overbury, a domestic servant.

The following April, Harry, Leonard and Jack's unit was redesignated 1/4th East Anglian Brigade and shortly afterwards moved to a practice camp on Salisbury Plain. They returned to Thetford the following month soon after the redesignation of the division to 54th (East Anglian) Division before moving to the St Albans area, with 1/4th Brigade being billeted in Hemel Hempstead.

On 8th July 1915, 54th Division received orders to prepare to move to the Dardanelles. In the event, due to overcrowding at the landing beaches at Gallipoli, only a part of 54th Division was able to be sent there, the artillery batteries having to remain in England, although Jack Hales, being part of the division's ammunition column, sailed from Devonport with the infantry on 29th July. He arrived on 16th August and was attached to the 1st, 2nd and 3rd Norfolk Batteries.

The remaining gunners and units of 54th Division returned to Thetford, unsure when they would see any action. It was to be four long months of waiting. To keep the men like Harry and Leonard occupied, in addition to the usual training, a series of competitions between the individual batteries were organised, whilst the 1st/1st Northants Battery spent some time in the Northamptonshire area on a recruiting drive.

The long period of waiting finally ended in November 1915 when orders came to move to the Western Front. Just before they left Thetford, all the battery's guns were replaced with new 18-pdrs. Entraining at Thetford on 16th November, Harry, Leonard and the remaining members of 54th Division sailed from Southampton the following day and landed at Le Havre and moved to the Béthune area. Even then, apart from 1st/1st Brigade, the Division's batteries were not used in anger against the German forces. It soon became evident that the Western Front was not their destination, another theatre of war was beckoning.

With casualties rising, and no prospect of defeating the Turks on the Gallipoli peninsula, the British Government decided to evacuate their troops. Under conditions of great secrecy, the evacuation started in December 1915 with Jack Hale's unit leaving on 12th. Sailing for Alexandria in Egypt, they arrived a week later and moved to Mena Camp near Cairo. Meanwhile the remainder of 54th Division, including Harry Carter and Leonard Mapley, left Marseilles on 3rd February 1916 on board three transport ships, HMTs *Andania*, *Rhesus* and *Missouri*. Crossing the Mediterranean at that time was still risky as U-boats operating from enemy bases in the Adriatic posed a constant threat to shipping. On one occasion during the journey, the 18-pdrs of one of the batteries were rolled onto the deck of HMT *Rhesus* to provide an additional deterrent to any submarine captain trying his luck. The three ships arrived safely at Alexandria on 8th February with the men, guns and equipment moving to Mena Camp where they were reunited with the remainder of the division. Their new role was to help defend the strategic Suez Canal from attack by the Turks. In March 1916, whilst waiting to move to the canal area, Jack Hales was confined to barracks for 14 days and fined 7 days' pay for 'insolence to a non-commissioned officer'.

Advance parties from the division moved out to the bases along the Suez Canal at the end of March, with the remainder of the division following in early April. Conditions in the desert were dire, with men spending most of the day under cover in their bivouacs to avoid the sunlight and sweating profusely. In May 1916, 1/4th East Anglian Brigade was renumbered using Roman numerals, becoming CCLXXIII Brigade, otherwise known as 273 Brigade. The batteries in which Harry and Leonard were serving were also renumbered with 1st/1st Herts Battery becoming 'A' Battery, 1st/2nd Herts Battery 'B' Battery and 1st/1st Northants Battery becoming 'C' Battery. Soon after this, 54th Division moved north to Serapeum, on the Suez Canal due east of Cairo. Here the heat was even greater, with temperatures frequently only just below 50 degrees Celsius in the shade. Harry, Leonard and Jack were to remain here for the next six months awaiting a Turkish attack that never came.

In December 1916, 273 Brigade's batteries were re-organised again with the guns of 'B' Battery being split between 'A' and 'C' Batteries which now had six 18-pdrs each. At the same time, the brigade was once more renumbered following the acquisition of a new howitzer battery from 3rd East Anglian (Howitzer) Brigade, becoming CCLXX Brigade, otherwise known as 270 Brigade. The names of the new larger batteries also changed to A/27 (Herts), B/270 (Northants) and C/270 (How.) (Suffolk). The Brigade would remain in this formation until the end of the war. A further change, but this time to the men's service numbers, took place around the same time with men recruited from Hertfordshire given numbers in the range 890001 to 891000 and men in the Ammunition Column beginning with 895001. Leonard became 890736, Harry, 890737 and Jack 895995.

January 1917 saw the end of Harry and Leonard's two-year wait to see some action following success on the Egyptian/Palestine border against the Turks, who had withdrawn northwards towards the city of Gaza. There followed a series of long, hard battles against the Turks, during which 270 Brigade provided artillery support, that eventually led to the capture of Gaza the following November. In December, 270 Brigade's artillery provided covering fire during an infantry crossing of the Yarkon river as part of the Battle of Jaffa.

After the Turkish defeat at Jaffa, no further progress north was possible as the rainy season had started. Consequently, 54th Division spent their time organising defences in case of an attack once the rains had ended. On 1st March 1918, Jack Hales received a good conduct badge.

Throughout the next few months, the Turks were pushed back further, but in June 270 Brigade were withdrawn from the front line and told to await further orders. The German Spring Offensives had made a severe dent in the British forces on the Western Front and reinforcements were urgently required. The following month, however, with the situation in France stabilised, it was decided that 54th Division should remain in Palestine after all.

A few days before the Turkish Armistice was signed in October 1918, Jack Hales was appointed an Acting Lance Bombardier. A promotion to Acting Corporal followed shortly afterwards, but was annulled within days, due to Jack being 'found in a private house'. Following the Armistice, 54th Division trekked north to Beirut. On 9th and 10th December 1918 the division left Beirut by sea bound for Egypt and took part in a Victory Parade in Cairo on their arrival. Christmas 1918 saw the brigade at camp outside of Cairo with all 48 guns of its batteries, fully clean and sparkling in the bright sunlight and lined up side by side.

Demobilisation started in March 1919, and by the middle of the month one third of the brigade had left for England. Serious civil unrest suddenly broke out among the Egyptian population with widespread vandalism and the murder of several Europeans. As a result, the demobilisation process was suspended and British troops took on additional police duties until the unrest subsided. Jack Hales's demobilisation was one of those delayed by the events in Egypt and it was not until June that he started his voyage home. By this time, he had been appointed Acting Bombardier. It is not known when Harry Carter and Leonard Mapley were demobilised.

After his demobilisation, Jack returned to his parents in Northchurch who were now living in Willow Cottage in the High Street. In 1921, he married Florence Wilbourn in St Albans and later joined the Hertfordshire Constabulary. By 1939, he had risen to the rank of Police Inspector and was based at the police station in St Albans Road, Watford. He would later become a Police Superintendent. He died in 1966, aged 70.

Upon his demobilisation, Harry Carter returned to Northchurch and in 1920 he was living in a cottage on Northchurch High Street. Three years later he married Annie Clark. By now, he was working as a gardener at Barncroft, just off Shootersway, which was one of the houses that served as a hospital and was also used by the Inns of Court Regiment during the war. Harry spent the next few years working there, but by 1939 he and Annie had moved to Newbury, Berkshire. Details of his life after that are unknown. Harry Carter died in the late winter of 1971, aged 79.

After his demobilisation, Leonard Mapley moved back to north London, the 1920 Electors Roll showing that he was registered in Holloway with his wife, Mabel. Sadly, a few months later, after moving to Shrublands Avenue in Berkhamsted, Mabel died, aged just 26. Leonard remarried two years later. In 1939 he was still living in Shrublands Avenue and working as a butcher. Leonard Mapley died in 1964, aged 69.

Ernest Frederick Delderfield (1894 – 1976)
Gunner 357252, Hampshire (Southampton) Fortress, RGA(T)

Ernest Frederick Delderfield, known as Fred, was born into the Wigginton branch of the Delderfield family in May 1894. One of nine children, he was the son of farmworker, James Delderfield, and his wife, Mary. Sometime in the early 1900s James moved with his family into a cottage in Northchurch High Street and started worshipping at the nearby newly-built Baptist Chapel. By 1911, Fred was working as a stable groom and he and his older brother, James, together with their younger sister were the only siblings still living at home.

On 9th September 1914, shortly before Harry Carter, Leonard Mapley and Jack Hales enlisted, Fred travelled to Hertford to join 4th East Anglian Brigade, RFA as a driver with the service number 871.

Fred travelled to France with Harry Carter, Leonard Mapley and the remainder of 54th Division in November 1915 before being transported across the country to the Mediterranean coast a few weeks later en route to Egypt. He was still serving with 54th Division in Egypt in early 1917 when new service numbers were allocated to all soldiers serving in the Territorial Force, Fred being renumbered 890666.

Private Fred Delderfield
Courtesy of Linda
Pottinger

Shortly afterwards, probably just before the advance into Palestine, Fred left 54th Division and was transferred to 266th Brigade RFA, 53rd Division as a gunner. He subsequently saw action during the Second and Third Battles of Gaza which opened up the chance to capture the highly-prized, but strategically unimportant, walled-city of Jerusalem.

On 7th December the British launched their attack on the Turkish troops defending the area. Highly demoralised, having suffered a series of major defeats, the Turks quickly evacuated Jerusalem, leaving a residual force on the Mount of Olives as a rear-guard. On 9th December Fred's battery was in action against the Turks still holding out on the Mount and it was only when infantrymen subsequently stormed their positions in a bayonette charge that they finally surrendered.

Following the surrender of Jerusalem, the 18-pdr guns of Fred's battery were hauled up the Mount of Olives where they were positioned among the trees to protect the city from an expected Turkish counter-attack. Over the next few days Fred, like many of his fellow soldiers, were allowed some sight-seeing in Jerusalem, albeit access to many of the religious sites was strictly controlled, and it was from here that he sent a number of postcards home wishing his family a merry Christmas. The Turkish counter-attack took place on 26th December, but with strong defences being put in place over the previous days, including Fred's battery on the Mount of Olives, the Turkish attack was easily repelled.

It would appear that for some time Fred had been suffering with an ongoing problem with his stomach, and a postcard back to his mother around the start of 1918 stated that he was in hospital and inferred that this was not the first time he had been treated. Telling her not to worry, Fred said that he would write a letter to her as soon as he could.

As a result of his medical condition he was probably sent home shortly afterwards as he next appears with a new service number serving as a gunner with the Hampshire (Southampton) Fortress, RGA, which had its base at the Drill Hall in St Mary's Road, Southampton. Around this time some of the Hampshire gunners were posted to Coventry and Birmingham to provide anti-aircraft defence against the growing threat of air raids by German Zeppelin airships and Gotha bombers, but it is not known whether Fred was among them. In August 1918, Fred's older brother, James, who was serving with the Labour Corps in France, was killed[21].

On 20th April 1919, Fred, now aged 24, was discharged from the RGA and awarded a Silver War Badge having been deemed no longer fit for military service and surplus to military requirements. The following year, he married Edith Kate Welling at St Peter's, Berkhamsted. Edith was a domestic servant working at Falkland House in Kings Road, and upon her marriage moved into a cottage in Gossoms End where she and Fred would later raise four children.

Fred would go on to have several jobs in Berkhamsted, including working as a milkman at the Castle Street dairy and a gardener at Berkhamsted School. In 1939, he and Edith were living in Dell Road, Northchurch, Fred describing himself as a 'Public Works Skilled Worker'. He died in 1976, aged 82.

---

[21] James Delderfield's story is told in *For Them's Sake*

Horace Edward Lewis (1898 – 1972)
Gunner 891920, 34th Brigade, RFA(T)

Horace Lewis, sometimes known as Edward Lewis, was born in April 1898 in Gossoms End to Walter Lewis, a sawyer, and his wife, Mary Ann. Walter came from Redbourn and probably worked at the nearby East & Son timberyard. Horace grew up in Gossoms End with his two elder sisters and three younger brothers and later worked alongside his father as a sawyer.

His service record has not survived, but his service number indicates that he joined 4th East Anglian Brigade, RFA. In 1917, Horace was sent to France to join 50th Battery, 34th Brigade, RFA whose 18-pdr guns and 4.5-inch howitzers were supplied with ammunition by the divisional ammunition column in which Robert Haynes was serving.

After his demobilisation in 1919, Horace returned home and resumed his job as a sawyer. He married Edith Snoxell, the daughter of a dairyman from Boxmoor, in the late summer of 1923 and the following year he became a father. In 1927, the family were living in Eddy Street, Gossoms End, a few yards from where Horace grew up. They later moved to Bell Lane, Northchurch. In 1939, he was still working as a wood sawyer and living at Overdene, a bungalow on Northchurch Common. Horace Lewis died in 1972, aged 74.

Alfred James Rickard (1891 – 1985)
Driver 884582, 311th Brigade, RFA(T)

Alfred Rickard was born in Aldbury in February 1891. Both his parents, William and Ruth, came from Aldbury, where William worked as a farm labourer. Ruth would later give birth to seven more children. Christened at the local parish church three months after his birth, Alfred grew up in the village and later at nearby Frithsden. In 1911, aged 20, Alfred was working as a groom and gardener, possibly for the Redding family who owned the nearby nursery.

With Alfred's service record no longer in existence, it is uncertain when he joined 4th East Anglian Brigade, RFA, but his medal record shows that he was not sent abroad before 1916. The 1918 Absent Voters List shows Alfred serving with the Ammunition Column of 311th Brigade, 62nd Division.

During the 1918 German Spring Offensive the speed of the enemy advance mean that 311th Brigade lost several guns and associated equipment before they were able to evacuate. New positions had to be quickly established to the rear, with the division's ammunition column battling to keep the remaining guns supplied. Following the allied advances after the Battle of Amiens, 311th Brigade advanced northwards to Vimy Ridge which dominated the landscape to the north of Arras and provided clear views across France to the Belgian border. By the end of the war they were located at Valenciennes, west of Mons.

Early in 1919, some members of 311th Brigade were transferred to the newly created Army of the Rhine, but all the brigade's stores and vehicles were sent to Calais to await transfer back to England. There is no evidence that Alfred was one of those sent to Germany and it is likely that he was demobilised in the summer of 1919. Returning to his parent's home in Frithsden, Alfred resumed his job as a gardener. In 1934, Alfred married Emily Jones and five years later they were living at Nursery Cottage in Frithsden where Alfred was working as a market gardener. He died in 1985, aged 93.

9 – The Colonials

The British Empire reached its peak at the end of the nineteenth century. Developments in transport and technology and the integration of former colonies had opened up vast amounts of territory, particularly in Australia and Canada. Elsewhere, the continuing demand for tea and coffee led to the growth of plantations in places like India and Ceylon (now Sri Lanka). Between 1890 and 1914 members of the Thelwall family and Jack Harman, who all had connections with Northchurch, emigrated to India and Ceylon, with the aim of becoming tea planters. Another Northchurch man, Frank Alcock, emigrated to Rhodesia (now Zimbabwe) in 1911 to become a farmer. Hubert Thelwall, Jack Harman and Frank Alcock would all lose their lives during the war[22].

Australia became an independent nation on 1st January 1901, with the British monarch remaining as Head of State. One of the priorities for the new Australian government was the need to increase the population of the country. A falling birth rate, combined with the potential threat of an expansionist Japan, were seen as risks to the country's defence and led to the government encouraging immigration to the country, but not just from anywhere. The policy defined by the Australian government was that the country should remain predominantly British and white. Consequently, two highly restrictive immigration acts came into force in 1901, similar to those introduced in South Africa, and prohibited most non-European immigration into the country. Additionally, the selection policy for immigrants from Great Britain and other European countries was focused on economic and political needs, with the emphasis being placed on the need to settle in rural rather than urban areas.

Between 1906 and 1912 the Australian state governments introduced assistance schemes offering not only reduced fares, but also grants of land and other concessions. A new High Commissioner was also appointed to promote Australia abroad, specifically directed at the 'preferred' type of immigrant e.g. British farmers and labourers. Among the men from Northchurch who decided to start a new life in Australia during the immigration boom between 1910 and 1913, were Albert Pickthorn, Charlie Sutton, Horace Neville and Maurice Phillips.

When Great Britain declared war on Germany in 1914, Australia automatically followed. The Australian Government additionally offered some 20,000 men to fight. This offer was gladly received by the British Government, which asked for them to be sent as quickly as possible. With

---

[22] Their stories are told in *For Them's Sake*

no standing army to speak of, the Australian recruitment campaign started immediately and, as in Great Britain, queues soon started forming at the recruiting centres.

Horace Neville (1894 – 1951)
Private 3885, 6th Battalion, Australian Imperial Force

Horace Neville, the youngest of Charles and Matilda Neville's eleven children, was born in Northchurch in July 1894. His father worked in the local watercress beds between the canal and the High Street that were fed by the River Bulborne. At the time of his birth, the family were living in Northchurch High Street and later moved to Bankside Cottages in Northchurch.

Horace grew up in the village and later started work on a nearby farm. Like many young people at the time, he longed to start a new life abroad, and in June 1913 he left London on board the SS *Norseman* bound for Melbourne, Australia. Arriving there in mid-August, he quickly sought work as a farm labourer and moved to Cudgewa, 267 miles north-east of Melbourne.

On 10th August 1915, a few days after the holding of the first Australia Day, which had been created to raise funds for Australian troops wounded at Gallipoli, Horace travelled to Melbourne where he enlisted with the Australian Imperial Force (AIF). After three months of training, on 23rd November he left Melbourne on board HMAT *Cerarnic* as part of the AIF's 12th Reinforcement Draft bound for Egypt. His eventual destination was neither the Middle East nor Gallipoli, however, and on 26th March 1916 he and his draft left Alexandria and sailed for Marseilles en route to the Western Front. There, he would join the AIF's 6th Battalion.

Within a month of landing in France whilst serving in the Somme sector, Horace was shot in the arm. Initially treated at 7th Casualty Clearing Station near Merville-au-Bois, he was sent to 26th General Hospital, one of many military hospitals in the vast military complex at Étaples on the French coast. Here his wound was treated and he returned to duty on 4th August 1916. Three weeks later, Horace was part of a detachment of men temporarily transferred to 1st Canadian Tunnelling Company.

The age-old technique of undermining enemy positions meant that skilled tunnellers were always in great demand during wartime. In September 1915 the British Government specifically asked their dominions to raise dedicated tunnelling companies for deployment on the Western Front and this resulted in the creation of 1st Canadian Tunnelling Company early the following year. In May 1916 the Tunnelling Company was sent to the area known as 'The Bluff', a large mound of earth and rock spoil near St Eloi, which had been created during the construction of the Ypres-Comines Canal. The previous February the area had seen heavy fighting as the Germans attempted to capture the area, but they had been repulsed. Not giving up, the Germans started tunnelling deep below the mound with the aim of blowing up the troops defending it. Forewarned by the Canadian tunnellers, who had heard their German counterparts digging, the allied troops were able to evacuate their positions before the Germans detonated their large mine below them. Quickly advancing into the newly created crater, the allied troops were able to prevent its capture by the waiting German troops. Further mining and counter-mining activity continued in the area and so a constant stream of new troops like Horace was required to keep the allied operations going. By October 1916, things were quieter and he was able to return to his battalion.

Within three weeks he was back in the trenches near Albert, which were now in a deplorable state and thigh-deep in mud. The abysmal weather in the area prevented any maintenance work being done to the trenches and effectively brought the fighting during the Somme Offensive to an end. He spent Christmas 1916 back in billets at Mametz.

Over the next three months, Horace's battalion alternated their time in reserve doing salvage work with spells in the front line, where they were able to frustrate several German raiding parties. On 4th April 1917, he was found to be absent without leave between the hours of 09.00 and 11.00 whilst the battalion were training at Buire-sur-l'Ancre. His absence was considered serious enough for him to be held in custody and eventually fined 27 days' pay.

After spending several months in the Somme sector, in July 1917, 6th Battalion moved north to the area near Cassel. The following month Horace was granted two weeks' leave and travelled to England and presumably took the opportunity to visit his parents back in Northchurch. Ten days after his return, Horace took part in the Battle of Menin Road, which, although successful, resulted in the battalion losing 10 officers, one of whom was posthumously awarded the Victoria Cross, and 247 other ranks. Later that year his battalion took part in the Third Battle of Ypres.

Horace returned to England again on two weeks' leave in February 1918. At this time the battalion were still near Ypres and, although put on warning of a possible enemy attack, it was too far north to be affected by the launch of the first German Spring Offensive. The battalion remained in the same area until August, when it returned to the Somme sector prior to the Battle of Amiens.

The battalion's attack on the opening day of the battle proceeded as scheduled, but they soon started to incur heavy casualties. Despite this, several German trench systems were captured. Two days later, the Germans launched a vicious artillery attack using 'Blue Cross' shells, combined with gas shells, on their former positions. 'Blue Cross' shells were glass canisters of Diphenylchlorarsine contained in high explosive shells. Their purpose was to act as an irritant forcing soldiers to remove their gas masks after which the gas from shells fired at the same time would take effect. The attack was made worse by the hot dry conditions in the area which caused the chemical elements to last considerably longer.

Horace was injured during the attack and rushed to 61 Casualty Clearing Station and then to 16th General Hospital at Le Trefort. His condition was deemed serious enough to invalid him back to England and on 2nd September he left on board the hospital ship *Essequibo*. Taken by train to the Southern General Hospital in Birmingham, he made a slow recovery and on 6th November, a few days before the Armistice was signed, he was granted 14 days' leave.

During his time in Birmingham, Horace met and fell in love with Ethel Mary Fielding from the village of Amington, near Tamworth. They were married at St Editha's, Amington in January the following year. That July, Horace returned to Australia with his new wife on board the HT *Zealandie*. Two months later Horace was demobilised from the Australian army.

Horace and Ethel settled in Corryong, a small town in Victoria, near the upper reaches of the Murray River close to the New South Wales border and he became a successful dairy farmer. Horace died there in 1951, aged 57.

Maurice Phillips (1895 – 1981)
Private 5091, 58th Battalion, Australian Imperial Force

Maurice Phillips, the son of a jobbing domestic gardener from Great Kingshill, Buckinghamshire, was born in Dudswell in February 1895. His father, Peter Phillips, regularly travelled around the country looking for work and taking his wife, Hannah, and family with him. Maurice's younger brother and sister were born three years later in Westbourne, Warwickshire, and by 1901 the family were living in Alconbury, in what was then South Huntingdonshire.

On 25th September 1913, Maurice, now 18 years old, left Liverpool on board the *Irishman*, bound for Melbourne, Australia. About the time of his 19th birthday, he attested with the Australian Army, but it was not until July 1917, whilst living in Terang, Victoria, 132 miles south-west of Melbourne, that he was mobilised.

Maurice's service papers describe him as 5ft 8½ins tall and weighing 146lbs and his religion is described as Salvationist. Having completed his basic training, Maurice was posted to the 14th Draft of 29th Battalion, AIF. This draft of new recruits left Melbourne on 22nd December 1917 on what was to be a lengthy two-and-a-half-month journey to Great Britain via Egypt and France, changing ships several times. The recruits arrived at Southampton on 15th February 1918 and entrained for the Australian training camp at Codford on Salisbury Plain.

Maurice finally arrived in France on 6th October 1918 and four days later he was taken onto the strength of the 58th Battalion, AIF. Within a month however, the war was over without him being in action. He remained in France until the end of February 1919 when he was granted three-weeks' leave, which he probably used to visit his parents. At the end of his leave, he went back to his battalion in France before returning to England for the final time, ready for the long journey back to Australia.

He sailed for Melbourne on board SS *Bakara* in July 1919. On his return, his girlfriend, Ada Bertha Kate Hallett, was waiting eagerly to see him arrive on the *Bakara*, writing to the Depot Commander for permission to be at the docks. Soon after his arrival he was demobilised.

Maurice and Ada later married and moved to Colac on the southern shore of Lake Colac, 93 miles south-west of Melbourne, where Ada later gave birth to a boy. They lived there for the rest of their lives, Maurice becoming a farmer. He died in 1981 aged 86.

Overall 416,809 men from Australia enlisted during the war, many of them originated from Great Britain and spoke with British accents. More than 60,000 of them were killed, including Albert Pickthorn and Charlie Sutton from Northchurch[23]. A further 156,000 were wounded, gassed, or taken prisoner.

---oOo---

New Zealand was not as successful as Australia in encouraging immigrants from Europe. Assisted passages began to be offered from the early 1870s, but economic problems in the 1880s and 1890s made New Zealand less attractive compared with Australia and Canada. Consequently, the assisted passage schemes ended in the late 1880s and even after that many immigrants to New Zealand later moved on to Australia. It was not until the early 1900s that European immigration to New Zealand resumed in significant numbers.

Frederick Reuben Bedford (1865 – 1944)
Private 24/2151, 3rd Light Trench Mortar Battery, New Zealand Defence Force

The second oldest Northchurch man to serve during the war left the village in the late 1880s and later emigrated to New Zealand. His name was Frederick Reuben Bedford and he was born in Gossoms End during the summer of 1865, the son of Reuben Bedford and his wife, Rebecca. When he was three years old, he was christened at St Mary's, Northchurch, along with his younger sisters Annie and Sarah.

---

[23] Their stories are told in *For Them's Sake*

Frederick's father, was involved in starting the watercress industry in Berkhamsted. In the early 1880s, with support from Lord Brownlow, he widened part of the river Bulbourne that flowed through Northchurch and Berkhamsted to construct a series of watercress beds near St John's Well, and in 1881 he was farming ninety-five acres and employing twenty-six men and five boys. By then his son, seems to have left home.

Frederick next appears some 11,000 miles away in New Zealand and consequently may have been one of the last people to benefit from its assisted passage scheme. In 1888, aged 23, he married Caroline Godbaz, a New Zealander. The following year she gave birth to a son, also called Frederick, but not in New Zealand, as would be expected, but in Australia. It appears that, initially at least, life in New Zealand was not what Frederick had anticipated.

By 1891, he had returned home and was working as a gardener and living with his family in Berkhamsted High Street, close to *The Lamb* public house. Frederick and Caroline would not stay in Berkhamsted for long, however, as their remaining children were all born in Dorset. By 1901, the family had moved once again, this time to Damerham, Hampshire, with Frederick growing watercress in the local beds there, and he was later joined by his two sons.

Sometime between 1911 and 1914, Frederick decided to leave Damerham and return with his family to New Zealand. On their return, the family moved to North Island, settling a few miles inland from the town of Hastings at Mangawhero, where once again he became a gardener.

In December 1915, Frederick, now 50 years old and still working as a gardener, presented himself at the recruiting office at Hastings. Knocking six years off his actual age, he managed to persuade the Recruiting Officer that he could still be of service to the British Empire for the duration of the war. His medical examination showed him as being 5ft 3ins tall and having good vision and teeth, weighing 148lbs and with a dark complexion, blue eyes and not surprisingly, grey hair. His religion was shown as Methodist. With the medical passed, Frederick was posted to the New Zealand Rifle Brigade (NZRB). Four months later, following the completion of his training, Frederick left Wellington, bound for Egypt.

Frederick arrived at Suez on 2nd May 1916, but Egypt was not to be his destination. Two weeks later, he left

Private Frederick Bedford
Courtesy of Martin King

Alexandria bound for Marseilles. On arrival in France, he travelled north to the New Zealand base depot at Étaples and soon afterwards became a member of 'B' Coy, 2nd Battalion, New Zealand Defence Force. After a short period of familiarisation, Frederick became Batman to an officer in 3rd Light Trench Mortar Battery, NZRB.

The role of Officer's Batman was made famous in 1989 by the actor, Tony Robinson, playing 'Baldrick' in the final Blackadder comedy series, *Blackadder Goes Forth,* written by Richard Curtis and Ben Elton. In effect, the batman was at the beck and call of the officer doing a variety of tasks which ranged from the menial, like making tea, to delivering urgent messages, often in extreme situations.

New Zealand troops entered the Somme Offensive in September 1916, as part of the 'big push' that was designed to break the German defences once and for all. In the event, some 6,000 New Zealand soldiers were to be wounded and more than 2,100 lost their lives before the offensive ended two months later. Frederick remained in the Somme sector until January 1917, when he reported sick and spent nearly three weeks under treatment in hospital at Rouen. He was with back with 3rd Light Trench Mortar Battery during the Battle of Messines the following June when, following the massive explosion of mines under the German lines, the New Zealanders quickly captured the newly created landscape, together with the surviving dazed and demoralised German defenders.

At the end of 1917, Frederick was granted two weeks' leave and returned to England where he may have visited his brother, William, who was now living in Dorset. Returning to France, Frederick was to retain his role as batman until just before the end of the war when he was declared 'unfit for military service', given a 'C' medical classification, and sent back to England. He left for New Zealand a few days before the Armistice was signed, on board the SS *Ulimaroa*. The following year, Frederick was registered at the Provincial Hotel in Napier, close to his pre-war home.

Frederick continued working as a gardener until he retired. He died in New Zealand in 1944, aged 79.

---oOo---

The Dominion of Canada came into being in 1867 consisting of the provinces of Quebec, Ontario, New Brunswick and Nova Scotia. Within a few years they had been joined by two additional provinces - Manitoba and British Columbia. In 1905, the area between Manitoba and British Columbia became the provinces of Alberta and Saskatchewan. Closely linked to this expansion was the development of the Canadian railway network. In fact, one of the conditions of British Columbia joining the Canadian Federation was the building of a trans-continental railway, linking the east and west coasts. The Canadian Pacific Railway Company was founded in 1881 and in 1886 the first train made the long journey from Montreal to Port Moody, a short distance from the port of Granville, which would later become the city of Vancouver.

With these vast territories opening inland, the need for settlers to transform the prairie flatland into flourishing farms and settlements increased exponentially. Unlike the Australian Government, the Canadian Government encouraged people from all cultures and backgrounds from across the world to migrate to Canada. In 1903, an emigration office was established at Trafalgar House in Trafalgar Square, London, where banners promoting 'Healthy Climate, Light Taxes, Free Schools' and '160-acre Free Farms' encouraged visitors to start a new life in the country. Emigration to Canada reached its peak in 1913 when 158,398 people from Great Britain emigrated, 39% of the overall immigrants to Canada in that year.

As with Australia, the relationship between Great Britain and Canada meant that when the British government declared war on Germany in August 1914 so did the Canadian government. In a speech, former Canadian Prime Minister, Sir Wilfrid Laurier, stated that *"It is our duty to let Great Britain know, and to let the friends and foes of Great Britain know, that there is in Canada but one mind, and one heart, and that all Canadians are behind the Mother Country."* Following the offer of assistance, work commenced on the mobilisation of an Expeditionary Force.

Among the men from Northchurch who were enticed to start new lives in Canada prior to the war, and would later return to take part in it, were George Beddall, Frank Bunn, James Dell, Harry Delderfield and Henry Marchant.

George Beddall (1876 – 1948)
Sapper 2714007, 4th Canadian Railway Troops

George Beddall was born in Northchurch in November 1876, the son of George Beddall (snr), a farm worker, and his wife, Lydia. After leaving school George started working as a groom, but on reaching the age of 18 he decided to join the army. Instead of joining one of the local regiments, he chose to enlist with 1st Hampshire Regiment for the standard period of 12 years. During most of the time he spent with the regiment he was on garrison duty in India and returned to England in 1904.

It is unclear when George decided to emigrate to Canada. He does not appear in the 1911 England census, and the first record of him being in Canada is the 1916 Census of Regina, Saskatchewan. This shows him working as a caretaker and living with his English-born wife, Ada Mary, and both having Canadian citizenship.

It was not until 23rd May 1918 that George, now aged 42, decided to attest. Why he decided to join up at this late stage of the war is unclear, but by then, following the entry of the United States into the conflict, the eventual outcome was certain. His Attestation Papers show him as standing 5ft 5ins tall with a 38inch chest, brown hair, blue eyes and with a fair complexion. Declared fit, he was posted to the 94th Draft, Army and Navy Veterans Construction Corps.

Following his training, George left Montreal on 13th July 1918 en route to Liverpool. He then travelled by train to Purfleet, Essex where he was posted to 4th Battalion, Canadian Railway Troops. He left for France at the end of October, just two weeks before the war ended.

Canadian troops had been responsible for the construction of most of the new railway lines in France during the war. They had the necessary expertise, as more railway track had been laid in the Canada in recent years, than anywhere else in the British Empire. The first 500 Canadian railway builders had arrived in France in 1915, with a further 1,000 arriving the following year. In 1917, they were reorganised into ten Canadian Railway Troop Battalions and played a major part in building the railway infrastructure that enabled troops, supplies and ammunition to be brought close to the front line. This was especially useful during the capture of Vimy Ridge by Canadian troops. By the end of the war nearly 15,000 Canadians were working in the Railway Troop Battalions.

George returned to England in January 1919 and was posted to the Canadian Railway Troop depot at Witley Camp, Surrey ready to be demobilised. He was struck off the strength of the unit the following month and sent to Kinmel Park, Rhyl to await his return to Canada.

Embarking from Liverpool in March 1919 on board HMT *Celtic* George returned to his caretaking job in Regina, Saskatchewan. He died in 1948, aged 71.

Frank Bunn (1882 -?)
Private 174213, 1st Canadian Machine Gun Battalion, Canadian Expeditionary Force

Frank Bunn was born in Northchurch in January 1882, the son of William Bunn, the Sexton at St Mary's Church who also ran his own rag and bone business, and his wife Mary. After leaving school he became a carpenter, but in 1903, aged 21, he decided to start a new life in Canada and settled in Hamilton, a large port on the tip of Lake Ontario.

It was not until the end of August 1915 that Frank, now aged 32 and still living in Hamilton, decided to enlist. His medical examination followed shortly afterwards and he was described as 5ft 5ins tall, weighing 152lbs, with grey eyes and brown hair. Under occupation he was described as a painter.

Frank was posted to 86th Machine Gun Battalion, which recruited almost exclusively from the Hamilton area, and left Canada with the battalion on board the SS *Adriatic*, bound for Liverpool on 19th May 1916. Following the battalion's arrival in England, the men moved to the Shorncliffe Army Camp, near Cheriton, Kent for further training. The main machine gun used by Canadian forces at the time was the American-built Colt. Weighing 35lbs, plus a tripod of 56lbs, the Colt machine gun was very cumbersome to use on the battlefield and was gradually replaced by the standard British Vickers machine gun. On 8th October 1916, having completed his training in England, Frank was transferred to 3rd Canadian Machine Gun Company and sent to France.

His new unit was attached to the 3rd Infantry Brigade, 1st Canadian Infantry Division which was then based near Warloy in the Somme sector. Within days of his arrival, the troops moved north to Arras where they remained during the winter of 1916.

In April 1917, Frank's unit took part in the successful assault on Vimy Ridge. The following month, he received a groin injury and was hospitalised for a month. His unit remained in northern France for several months until, on 1st November, it moved to Ypres, taking part in the closing days of the Third Battle of Ypres, including the capture of the strategic Passchendaele Ridge.

Unfortunately, Frank's groin suffered a relapse whilst he was lifting machine-gun ammunition off a pack-horse shortly afterwards and he was taken to a nearby Casualty Clearing Station. Here it was discovered that his injury was serious enough for him to be invalided back to England and Frank subsequently underwent surgery at the Royal Victoria Military Hospital at Netley, near Southampton. The operation was a success and afterwards he spent several months recovering at Epsom Convalescent Hospital.

By the middle of May 1918, Frank was fit enough to be sent to the Central Machine Gun Pool at Seaford, West Sussex, to retrain and await a new posting. He returned to France at the end of September, joining 1st Canadian Machine Gun Battalion. By now, the Germans were in full retreat and the war was in its last few weeks. Frank ended his war near the small town of Somain, near the French/Belgian border.

On Armistice Day, after the award of several Military Medals, new orders came stating that the Canadian Corps would become part of the Second Army, and that it was to proceed to the Rhine to form part of the army of occupation. Preparations for the long march began immediately, and on 15th November they set off.

On 4th December 1918, the first detachment of Canadian troops crossed the German border and continued to their destination east of Cologne. Frank remained in Germany until the beginning of March 1919 when the long return journey to Canada began, travelling first to the French coast by train. His unit left for England on 25th March on board the SS *Mona's Queen*, an iron-built paddle steamer that used to belong to the Isle of Man Steam Packet Company. Being a paddle steamer, it was painfully slow, and the troops on board suggested marching across a hypothetical bridge over the English Channel would have been faster.

Frank and his mates disembarked at Weymouth, and proceeded to Bramshott Camp, Hampshire, which had served as the home for thousands of Canadian troops in transit during the war. Here, medical examinations and the long demobilisation process commenced. No doubt Frank took the opportunity over the following few weeks to visit friends and family in Northchurch before his return to Canada. On 31st March 1919, he left England on board the SS *Mauritania* and on arrival at Montreal he was demobilised.

Frank returned to Hamilton and on 14th June 1921, aged 39, he married 36-year-old Isabel Stevenson. He is last recorded in 1933 as working as a painter and being a passenger in transit between Canada and England.

James Dell (1878 – 1946)
Sapper 506055, Canadian Royal Engineers

James Dell, known as Jim, was born in Northchurch in March 1878, the son of general labourer, Joseph Dell, and his first wife, Mary Ann. In the late 1890s, Jim, now working as a carpenter, left Northchurch and in 1901 he was lodging in the village of Mountnessing near Billericay, Essex. Whilst working in the Mountnessing area, Jim became friends with George Denny and his wife, Alice Clara. George Denny was a fellow carpenter and it is likely that he and Jim worked together. Two years later however, Jim decided to leave England to start a new life in Canada. Shortly after his departure, George Denny died, leaving his widow, Alice, with a young son to raise.

Two years on, Jim was living in Winnipeg in Manitoba Province, but was finding the extremely cold Canadian winters difficult to handle and at one point considered returning to England. In a letter to an uncle and aunt in Berkhamsted in December 1905, Jim mentioned that he had noticed that in Canada, poverty was still a problem for some, especially when trying to earn enough to heat their homes during the harsh winters.

By 1916, Jim was still single and working as a carpenter in the small town of Kelwood, some 145 miles to the west of Winnipeg. That September, aged 38, he decided to enlist as a Sapper with the Canadian Royal Engineers, his service papers describing him of being 5ft 6ins tall, with a dark complexion, blue eyes and brown hair. He gave his brother, William Dell, who was still living in Northchurch, as his next of kin.

Jim arrived back in England just after Christmas 1916 and was sent to Crowborough, Sussex where the Canadian Training School was based. Having completed his basic training, he was posted to 5th Division Engineers at Witley Camp, Surrey, which, like its sister camp at Bramshott Common in Hampshire, was a major training base for Canadian troops. The following month, he was transferred to 13th Field Company, Canadian Royal Engineers.

It was not until March 1918 that Jim finally left England for France, having been posted to the Canadian Engineer Pool. On his arrival he spent two months on 'general duties' before being posted to 4th Battalion Canadian Engineers, which had been in France since the autumn of 1915 and had provided support during the attack in Vimy Ridge in April 1917. More recently, they had returned to the easier task of road and bridge repairs.

As the Germans retreated east, the Canadian Sappers were called in to repair shell-damaged roads and bridges, water mains, and dugouts, as well as building light tramways to allow ammunition to be brought quickly to the newly-built gun emplacements. Armistice Day saw the battalion making repairs to the roads near Elouges, just south of Mons.

Sapper Jim Dell
Courtesy of Clive Blofield

Over the coming weeks, Jim and his fellow Sappers moved into the Rhineland as part of the army of occupation, but by the end of January 1919, plans for their return to Canada were well advanced, and the long journey home commenced.

Jim returned to England much faster than many of his mates; on 8th March 1919, he was given 14-days special leave to get married. Having crossed the Channel, he made his way to St Briavels, Gloucestershire, where on 5th April 1919, he married his old friend, Alice Clara Denny, who he had first met nearly 20 years earlier whilst working in Mountnessing, Essex. Now a 48-year-old widow with an 18-year-old son, Alice was the housekeeper at St Briavels Castle. After the wedding, Jim reported back to the Canadian Depot at Seaford, Sussex to await his return to Canada.

On 14th June 1919, Jim arrived back in Canada where he was formally discharged from the Canadian army. He did not stay there for long however, and returned to England to be reunited with his new wife and stepson. He later found work as a carpenter and never returned to Canada. By 1939, he had retired and was living in Luton but later moved to a cottage in Northchurch High Street where in 1946, he died, aged 68, two years after his wife.

Harry Delderfield (1886 – 1965)
Gunner 45941, 434th Siege Battery, RGA

Harry Delderfield was born in Northchurch in 1886, the first of four sons of Samuel Delderfield, a hay binder from Aldbury, and his wife, Emma. Harry later moved to Sparkbrook, Birmingham, where he found work as a tram driver. Soon after his arrival there Harry started to date Nellie Fiddian, who worked in a shoe shop and lived near his lodgings. In 1913, Harry decided to emigrate to Canada and that April he crossed the Atlantic on board *The Empress of Ireland*, landing at St Johns, Newfoundland. His destination was the city of Saskatoon, the largest city in the province of Saskatchewan where, soon after his arrival, Harry acquired a plot of land. Events back in Europe were however about to forestall his plans.

Wanting to volunteer in the war effort, Harry returned to England. In October 1914, he enlisted with the Royal Garrison Artillery at an old Victorian fort in Gosport, called Fort Rowner, which was being used as an army recruitment centre. His training as a gunner started immediately, initially with 44th Siege Company, and later with 16th Siege Company. Shortly before being sent to France, he returned to Sparkbrook where he married his girlfriend, Nellie Fiddian.

On 20th July 1915, Harry landed in France ready to join his new unit, 19th Siege Battery, which was equipped with four Mark V 8-inch howitzers. The guns were effectively old naval canons salvaged from obsolete warships, whose

Gunner Harry Delderfield
Courtesy of Paul Burke

barrels had been cut down and rebored to take an 8-inch shell and mounted on a heavy trailer. At the time Harry joined the battery, it was operating in northern France near Loos, but moved to the Somme area in the spring of 1916 to take part in the massive bombardment of the German lines prior to the launch of the Somme Offensive. On 25th June his battery alone fired 542 rounds at the enemy lines.

On 14th June 1917, Harry was transferred to the newly-established 351st Siege Battery which was based near Ypres and equipped with four 6-inch howitzers. By now, the British forces were building up to what would become known as the Third Battle of Ypres. Even before the British had launched their offensive, however, Harry's battery came under sustained enemy fire consisting of a mixture of high explosive and gas shells. As a result, the battery had to be moved several times to new, better protected positions. He stayed with the battery until October 1917 when he was transferred to 434th Siege Battery with which he remained till the end of the war.

Harry was demobilised in June 1919 and returned to Birmingham. He initially considered returning to Canada and even asked the Army Repatriation Office to cover the cost. After a lengthy wait Harry's request was eventually approved, but by then Harry had changed his mind, stating that it was now too late for him to undertake the journey. Presumably, he had wanted to build a house on the plot of land he had purchased in Saskatchewan before the harsh Canadian winter set in.

Harry never did return to Canada, but remained in Birmingham, working as a builder's labourer. Sadly, in 1929 his wife, Nellie, died. He remarried two years later and lived for the rest of his life in the city where he died in 1965, aged 78.

10 – The Royal Engineers

The men serving in Royal Engineers (RE) played a vital role in the war effort supporting the front line infantrymen. They were responsible for a multitude of tasks ranging from the building and upkeep of the military infrastructure including the railways, communications, fortifications and tunnels to anything mechanical, covering the maintenance of bicycles, motorcycles, lorries, tanks and railway locomotives. The soldiers serving in the Royal Engineers were normally called sappers, with many of them putting their previous civilian employment skills, such as bricklaying and carpentry, to good use for the war effort.

Harry Herbert Barker (1897 - 1963)
Sapper 63999, 38th Field Company, RE

At the outbreak of war, all infantry Divisions included two Field Companies, which increased to three in 1915. Consisting of over two hundred men, each Field Company was responsible for supporting the troops in the field, offering various roles such as shoesmiths, builders, bricklayers, carpenters, painters and plumbers. As the war progressed, their role expanded to include the construction of huts and the laying of barbed wire, and they often supervised infantrymen performing this role when out of the front line.

One of the Northchurch men serving in the Field Companies was Harry Barker. Born at New Lodge Cottages in the easternmost part of Northchurch Parish in the autumn of 1897, he was the fourth child of Frederick and Amelia Barker. Frederick Barker was employed as a domestic coachman at The Hall in Berkhamsted. Harry's service record has not survived so it is not known what he did after leaving school nor why he chose to join the Royal Engineers in early 1915.

Having completed his army training, he arrived in France on 2nd August 1915 where he joined 38th Field Company. In October 1915, Harry and 38th Field Company left Marseilles, as part of 28th Division, bound for Egypt. Shortly after their arrival there, however, they were transferred to Salonika where they would remain until the end of the war.

After his demobilisation in May 1919, he returned home to New Lodge Cottage, and in 1923 he married Lois Beulah Moore, the daughter of William Moore, a blacksmith from Gossoms End. They later moved to Hemel Hempstead and in 1939 he was working at a local printing works. Harry Barker died in 1963, aged 65.

Walter Edward Bryant (1881 – 1953)
Sapper 525906, 366th Forestry Company, RE

Walter Bryant was born in the small village of Hawridge, just across the county boundary with Buckinghamshire, in the late autumn of 1881. His mother, 21-year-old Annie Bryant, worked at *The Stag* public house in Northchurch High Street. Three years after Walter's birth, Annie married Joseph Aldridge, a blacksmith's labourer from Northchurch and over the coming years she would give birth to seven more children, four of whom would die in infancy. Walter grew up with his step-siblings in a cottage in Gossoms End until July 1901, when, at the age of 19, he married Eliza Ann Dwight in St Mary's, Northchurch.

In May 1908, Walter was living with his wife and young daughter in Eddy Street, Gossoms End, and was employed as a sawyer at the East & Son timberyard. That year, he decided to join the local Territorial Force unit, 2nd Herts Volunteer Battalion, Bedfordshire Regiment, signing up for a period of one year, which he renewed every year at their annual camp.

At the outbreak of war, Walter was embodied, but had to wait for two years to be mobilised, by which time he had been promoted to the rank of Sergeant. Now 35, he arrived in Boulogne on 12th August 1916 and was immediately sent to the huge Base Depot at Étaples, where he was posted to 1st Battalion, Hertfordshire Regiment, joining them at the start of September in the Somme sector. Soon after his arrival, the Hertshires faced a ferocious German attack on their trenches including a mixture of gas and high explosive shells. Consequently, he and his comrades spent most of their time repairing the trenches as best they could whilst having to wear unwieldly gas helmets. Two weeks after joining his unit, Walter was sent back to Étaples classed as 'unfit', but returned in the middle of November during the Hertshires move to the Ypres salient. For some reason Walter was unhappy with retaining his rank of Sergeant and soon after re-joining his unit he requested to revert to the rank of Private.

In July 1917, Walter's skills as a sawyer were recognised and he was transferred to No6 Forestry Company, 2nd East Anglian Division, RE, becoming a sapper. His new unit would later become 366th Forestry Company, 69th (2nd East Anglian) Division.

The need for vast amounts of wood for use in the construction of defences, tunnels, trench duckboards etc. had been recognised early in the war. Initially, the British supplies of wood came from Scandinavia, but as these began to decrease the army started to look at local areas behind the front lines to fulfil their requirements. At first, the acquisition of 'local' wood was somewhat uncontrolled, and led the French to request that their British allies set up a forestry directorate to control the felling of trees. Several new Forestry Companies were subsequently established with No6 Forestry Company being formed in June 1917 to operate in the Forest of

Brotonne, to the east of Rouen. Initially made up of three officers and thirty other ranks, over the coming months additional men like Walter would join the unit in various roles, and by the end of November 1917 numbers had increased to over 110 servicemen. Many of those serving in the British Forestry companies were either older men, who were deemed no longer fit for front line service, or, as in Walter's case, had been skilled workers in the timber industry.

British Forestry Company in France
Author's collection

In January 1919 Walter returned home on leave, and after this was extended several times he was discharged from the army and returned to his old job at East's timberyard. Unfortunately, his wife, Eliza, died the following year, aged just 39, possibly during the influenza outbreak. He remarried in 1929 and later moved to Granville Road, Northchurch with his new wife, Elsie. He was still working at East's timberyard ten years later. Walter Bryant died in 1953, aged 72.

The work of the allied Forestry companies in northern France, combined with the effect of artillery shells over four years of warfare, decimated many of the forests in the country. By March 1918, 119,000 tons of wood were being felled, more than seven times the quantity felled two years earlier. In the last year of the war alone, the British used some two million tons of French timber for construction purposes. It would take several generations for the French forests to recover, and even today unexploded ordinance prevents access to many forested areas.

William Bryant (1885 – 1970)
Sapper WR289126, 115th Railway Company, RE

William Bryant was born in Gossoms End in October 1885, the son of John Bryant, a platelayer with the London & North Western Railway, and his wife, Ellen. Having left school, he helped his elder brother, Walter, as a milk carrier, but later followed into his father's trade and became a platelayer. In August 1913, he married Lottie Wootton.

Following the outbreak of war, William and many of his railway workmates volunteered to join the army. He became a core member of the 115th Railway Company at the RE camp at Longmoor, Hampshire, which, like many of the other railway companies formed around the same time, operated very much like the 'Pals Battalions', being made up of local groups of skilled railwaymen.

At the start of September 1915, William and his mates were sent to France, but within weeks they found themselves travelling across France to Marseilles, where they set sail for Egypt.

Following the evacuation of allied troops from Gallipoli at the end of 1915, the Turkish army was able to redeploy thousands of troops that had been tied up fighting on the peninsular. The obvious place for the Turks to focus their attention was on the strategic Suez Canal, which was the vital lifeline bringing troops to Europe from India, Australia and New Zealand. Before the war, the Turks, with German support, had built a new railway from Constantinople to the port of Basra in southern Mesopotamia, which included a junction heading south towards Damascus and Beirut. Using this route Turkish troops would be able to reach the Egyptian border quickly, and thus threaten the Suez Canal.

In anticipation of this happening, the British decided to capture the territory in the mountainous area to the north of the Sinai Peninsular in southern Palestine, thus creating a buffer zone to protect the canal. The only way to move the Egyptian Expeditionary Force (EEF) and its equipment to the area in enough numbers however, was to build a new railway heading north. Several Railway Construction Companies, including 115th, were consequently transferred from France to start work. The new railway began at the village of Kantara, located between Port Said and Ismailia, and soon became a huge depot complete with railway sidings and dumps for ordinance and supplies. Building a new railway under the constant glaring sun and heat was particularly difficult, but speed was vital. As the EEF advanced north across the desert, William and his mates extended the railway lines to keep them supplied.

In February 1917, following a short battle, the EEF captured the town of Khan Yunus in Palestine, midway between the Egyptian border and the town of Deir el Belah. This resulted in the Turkish army withdrawing north to Gaza and Beersheba and enabled the railway to be extended to Deir el Belah. Two months later it became the new railhead enabling vast amounts of supplies to be brought up whilst the EEF attempted to dislodge the Turks from Gaza.

The initial attempts to capture Gaza failed and the new commander of the EEF, General Sir Edmund Allenby, decided to change the focus of the attack and make Beersheba the principle objective. This meant extending the railway eastwards across formidable territory. Back at the Deir el Belah railhead, engineers started to lay a new pipeline that would later bring water directly from the River Nile. The building of the new railway towards Beersheba by the railway engineers enabled the EEF to launch their successful attack on the city at the end of October 1917. With the fall of Beersheba, the EEF resumed its attack on Gaza, which fell the following month. With both towns now in British hands, the road to Jerusalem was open and it fell to the EEF in December 1917.

Poor weather at the end of 1917 prevented any further offensives by the EEF, but work on the railway continued with the new line to Jerusalem being opened at the end of January 1918. Work continued during the spring of 1918 as the EEF pressed on towards Jericho and the Jordan valley with the Railway Companies kept busy converting much of the existing Turkish-built narrow-gauge tracks to standard gauge and linking them with the line from Kantara.

By January 1919, William and his fellow railwaymen had laid over 600 miles of track in Palestine in extremely hazardous conditions. The construction of the new railway had proved vital in helping in the defeat of the Turkish army.

He left Egypt with 115th Railway Company in March 1919 and was demobilised on his return to England. Back in Gossoms End, he returned to his job as a platelayer with the London & North Western Railway and remained with the company for the rest of his working life. William Bryant died in 1970, aged 84.

Cecil Stanley Burney (1884 – 1964)
Lieutenant, Signal Corps, RE
Edward Alexander Burney (1886 – 1971)
Captain, ASC

Cecil Stanley Burney and Edward Alexander (Alick) Burney, were among the first men from Northchurch to enlist at the outbreak of war. They were both pioneering motor-cycle engineers, but engineering was not a family trade. In 1832, their paternal grandfather, Henry Charles Burney LLD, opened a school in Gosport, Hampshire, called the Royal Academy, which advertised places *"Under sanction and patronage of his most gracious majesty, ... where young gentlemen are boarded and educated for the navy, army and learned professions and public offices ... Young gentlemen are expeditiously prepared for admission to the Royal Navy and Military Colleges and go with many advantages from this establishment."* A key feature of this school was the use of an observatory, from which he used to send regular readings and reports to the local newspaper in Portsmouth.

In 1861, Henry Burney, along with his young family, which now included Cecil and Alick's father, James Edward Burney, moved to the United Service College, Little Green, Richmond, Surrey, where he set up a new school and used similar advertising. Tragically, he died the following year, aged 62, following an accident when he fell out of a window whilst trying to adjust an outside bell wire.

Little is known about James Edward Burney after he left school. He was born in Bruges, Belgium in 1857 and in later years described himself as living 'on own means', or simply 'a gentleman'. He was living in Stoke Hammond, Buckinghamshire in 1882, when he married Gertrude Mary Finlay, at St James's, Westminster. Not long afterwards, they moved to Cookham Dean, Berkshire, where James purchased the house where Cecil was born in June 1884. However, Alick was born two years later in the village of Newton Longueville, Buckinghamshire, a few miles from his father's former home in Stoke Hammond. By 1888, the family had moved again to a large property called Ashleigh in the small village of Bridstow, close to Ross-on-Wye, Herefordshire. Here they employed a governess and two servants. James Burney joined the local Masonic Lodge in 1888, but died four years later, aged just 35.

In the late 1890s, Gertrude Burney moved her family to Durrants Farm in Northchurch and Cecil and Alick were sent to boarding schools – Cecil to Burlington House, a small school on the Hounslow Road in Hampton, Middlesex, and Alick to Bradfield College, Berkshire. In January 1900, whilst Alick was at Bradfield College, the school introduced a new engineering class which was described in the college history as "...*intended as a means of prolonging the Public School discipline of those who are entering an engineering life, so postponing to an older growth the date at which it is inevitable that such boys should encounter the roughness and dangers to their moral welfare of public workshops...*". It was the spark that ignited Alick's life-long interest in engineering and which he quickly passed on to his older brother. Neither Cecil nor Alick progressed to university, choosing instead to follow engineering careers.

In 1903, Cecil and Alick started work as apprentices with Messrs Willians & Robinson in Rugby, Warwickshire. The company had been founded 23 years earlier at Thames Ditton, Surrey and initially manufactured steam engines for river launches. A successful engine design subsequently led to the expansion of the company, and in 1897 it moved to Rugby, which at that time was one of the main centres for engineering and manufacturing in the country, benefitting from a central location in the country with excellent railway links in all directions.

One of Cecil and Alick's fellow apprentices at Willians & Robinson was Geoffrey de Havilland. Before becoming an apprentice, he had studied at the Crystal Palace Engineering School where he had built his own motorcycle, which established his name in engineering circles. Whilst at Willians & Robinson, de Havilland built another motorcycle using his own design, which he later gave to his brother, Hereward. Things might have turned out differently for the Burneys had not de Havilland found himself short of money just before leaving Willians & Robinson, and sold them his motorcycle drawings and patterns for the sum of £5, the equivalent of about a month's wages at the time. De Havilland moved on to the Wolseley Tool

& Motor Car Company in 1905 and would later enter the aircraft industry and create one of the biggest aircraft manufacturing businesses in the world.

The Burneys and de Havilland remained friends and in 1912 de Havilland became the first and only person to land an aircraft in Northchurch, whilst visiting the brothers at Durrants Farm.

Shortly after de Havilland left Willians & Robinson, the Burney brothers also left the company, having completed their apprenticeship, to join the Daimler Company in nearby Coventry. Meanwhile, they continued to work on improving de Havilland's motorcycle design, changing the metals used and redesigning key parts. Cecil subsequently entered the new motorcycle in the Coventry MC 100 Mile Trial in August 1907 and won the Schulte Cup for best performance in the open class.

Geoffrey de Havilland landing his aeroplane at the Burney's home at Durrants Farm, Northchurch in 1912
Courtesy of BLH&MS

Cecil continued to develop the motorcycle's engine, whilst in 1908, Alick spent some time working in Laboulaye, Argentina. In 1910, Cecil left Daimlers and moved to the Rudge Whitworth factory in Coventry as head of their experimental department, spending many hours in the motorcycle saddle and becoming a well-known trials and hill-climb rider. The ground-breaking 'Multi' motorcycle was introduced in 1912, and with its variable gear ratios it quickly became a sought-after machine, breaking many records.

Following his return from Argentina, Alick started work at Godfrey and Nash, at their Elms Motor Works in Hendon, north London. Henry Ronald Godfrey and Archibald Goodman Frazer-Nash had been fellow students at the City and Guilds in Finsbury and later became apprentices at Willians & Robinson, where they met the Burneys. In 1910, they built their first car at the Frazer-Nash family home, and the following year, moved production to the Elms Motor Works. The resulting car, using a new 1,100cc engine, could reach a top speed of 60mph.

In 1912, the Burney brothers decided to form their own motorcycle manufacturing business. Following a discussion with the aviator, Harold Blackburn, whom Alick had met whilst working at Godfrey and Nash, the Burneys decided to develop their own motorcycle in a small workshop at their mother's home at Durrants Farm with Blackburn providing the initial set-up costs. The motorcycles themselves were assembled by the local cycle firm of Charles Southey in Berkhamsted High Street.

The workshop at Durrants Farm soon proved unsuitable for long-term use, so Burney & Blackburn, as the partnership was then known, moved to bigger premises at Tongham, near Aldershot. Harold Blackburn's main interest lay in aviation however, and his initial investment in the partnership was subsequently repaid. The Burneys then formed a limited company, Burney & Blackburne Ltd, and were soon joined by two fellow young motorcycle enthusiasts, Cecil Quinlan Roberts and his brother, Allan. They exhibited their latest models at the 1913 London Motor-Cycle Show and that September one of their motorcycles won the Gold Medal at a Six Day Trial.

The outbreak of the war in 1914 had a profound impact on the company. Two days after the declaration of war, Cecil and Alick both enlisted at Chatham with the Motor Cyclist Section, Royal Engineers. Cecil's service record shows him as being 5ft 10¼ ins tall with a fresh complexion, blue eyes and dark brown hair. Initially given the rank of Privates, both Cecil and Alick were immediately promoted to Corporals in recognition of their new role of artificers, i.e. skilled mechanics, and posted to 5th Signal Company, RE.

Forming part of 5th Division, 5th Signal Company was then based at Carlow, the county town of County Carlow, Ireland. As a result, Cecil and Alick travelled by train together with their own Burney & Blackburne motor-cycles to Holyhead, where they boarded a ferry and arrived at Carlow on 8th August and then waited for the arrival of the rest of the unit. Their reputation as motor-cycle experts led one newly-arrived despatch rider to later write "... *We realised that what they did not know about motor-cycles was not worth knowing, and we had suspected at Chatham what we found afterwards to be true, that no one could have chosen for us pleasanter comrades or more reliable workers*".[24]

On 15th August, Cecil and Alick (now christened "Grimmers" by his new mates), together with the remainder of No1 Section, 5th Signal Company, entrained for Dublin. Two days later, they sailed for Le Havre on board the severely overcrowded SS *Archimedes*. Arriving in France later that day, they spent their first night in a large warehouse full of wool (and fleas) and the following day they entrained for the village of Landrecies, where the unit set up a temporary headquarters with their horses and wagons housed overnight in the market square.

As the German troops advanced swiftly across Belgium and into France, the BEF started to withdraw south and 5th Signal Company found themselves dangerously exposed at the small town of Dour, just south of Mons. With the BEF in a fluid state, the only way to communicate quickly was by using motorcycle despatch riders, but finding army units in the dark

---

[24] WHL Watson – *Adventures of a Despatch Rider*

proved extremely difficult. On one occasion, Alick was sent out with messages for 15th Division, but failed to find them. Another despatch rider, sent out later, never returned. Such was the speed of the unit's retreat that the company's field kitchen, which was the last wagon in the unit, overturned and it was some time before it was missed. Fortunately, the advancing Germans were not as close as feared, and some troops returned the way they had come and were able to recover it.

The retreat south continued and soon they passed the small town of Le Cateau, stopping just south of the town where 15th Infantry Brigade set up its headquarters. The following morning, the British II Corps, under the Command of Horace Smith-Dorrien, made a stand at Le Cateau. Despite overwhelming odds, the British were able to hold up the advancing German forces and give the BEF valuable time to withdraw further south in safety. Again, motorcycle despatch riders were key in enabling the various units to communicate effectively with each other, and at one point, Alick even carried a knapsack full of fuses for a heavy artillery unit.

With the German advance slowed, 5th Signal Company, along with the remainder of II Corps, continued south. Repairs and maintenance to the motorcycles were done whenever possible, but with limited spare parts available Cecil and Alick's ingenuity in keeping the machines running was severely tested.

By 5th September 5th Signal Company had reached Combreux, due east of Orléans. The 'Retreat from Mons' as it later became known was over, and the BEF were about to turn and fight the Battle of the Marne. There was still considerable confusion among the troops however, and on one occasion Alick was accidentally shot at by an over-enthusiastic sentry. He was lucky - the bullet only caused a slight graze to the back of his neck.

The BEF and French army's advance north commenced on 6th September. Over the coming days, the exhausted German army, which had been further weakened by the withdrawal of some troops to the Russian Front, fell back until they dug in on the north bank of the River Marne. Even though the retreat was over, the war was still in a very fluid state and the role of the motorcycle despatch rider continued to be highly dangerous; frequently the exact locations of units was unknown, and it was up to the despatch rider to seek them out. Similarly, areas which were once free of enemy troops could suddenly change hands without warning. Added to this were the constant threat of snipers and enemy reconnaissance patrols.

One night, soon after the end of the Battle of The Marne, which dislodged the Germans and caused them to fall back to the river Aisne, Cecil and Alick, along with some fellow despatch riders, were on duty patrolling a forest. In the dark, all the tracks looked identical and the riders expected to be fired on by German troops at any time. Alick's night-sight was not particularly good, and he always rode with a loaded revolver in one hand. On one occasion, Cecil reported a smell of dead horses in the air, which turned out to be the bodies of eight German soldiers that had been piled up at the side of the road and had begun to decay in the heat.

Whilst providing communication support during the Battle of the Aisne, 5th Signal Company spent three weeks based at the small village of Serches, mid-way between Rheims and Compiègne. At the start of October, orders arrived to move north to Beuvy, just outside Béthune, to help prevent the German army making a final dash to capture the Channel Ports and cut off the BEF's supply line. Cecil and Alick, together with their fellow motorcycle despatch riders, left Serches at dusk the following day. Crossing territory which, until a few days before, had been in German hands, the despatch riders were always the first to receive the grateful thanks of the local inhabitants. On 7th October, Cecil and Alick and their mates entrained at Pont-Sainte-Maxence, the riders making themselves comfortable with plenty of straw in one of the French railway wagons labelled *8 Chevaux, 40-5 Hommes*. This luxury was not to last however, as they were soon forced to take in extra troops due to the other carriages being overcrowded.

The fierce fighting at La Bassée, and the subsequent First Battle of Ypres, severely tested the despatch rider's abilities. It was not just the fighting and the constant threat of artillery shells and snipers that caused problems, heavy rain, together with the constant movement of troops, had turned roads into muddy tracks, and driving a motorcycle at speed along them became extremely perilous.

Following the failure of the German offensive at Ypres the Western Front became quieter and there was a chance of some leave. Cecil and Alick were among the first to return to England at the start of December. They returned to France in time for Christmas, with Alick producing a hand-printed menu for the despatch rider's Christmas meal. They did not want for food as the menu shows:

CHRISTMAS, 1914.
DINNER
OF THE
TEN SURVIVING MOTOR-CYCLISTS OF THE
FAMOUS FIFTH DIVISION.

Sardins très Moutard.
Pottage
Dindon Rôti-Saucisses. Oise Rôti.
Petits Choux de Bruxelles.
Pommes de Terre.
Pouding de Noël Rhum.
Dessert. Café. Liqueurs.
Vins – Champagne. Moselle. Port.
Benedictine. Whisky.

On the reverse of the menu were written the unit's battle-honours – Mons, Le Cateau, Crêpy-en-Valois, the Marne, the Aisne, La Bassée, the Defence of Ypres.

During his time back in England Cecil applied for a temporary commission and a few weeks after his return to France he left 5th Signal Company to join the Southern Section Signal Corps, RE, as a motorcyclist officer responsible for training new despatch riders. The following month, Alick also left to become an officer with the Motorised Transport Section of the Army Service Corps.

By now, the strain of the war had begun to tell on Cecil. In March 1915, he was examined by a doctor in London and found to be suffering from exhaustion and at least six weeks' leave was recommended. He returned to Northchurch to rest and two months later he was passed as fit for service by a Medical Board at Aylesbury.

Cecil returned to France to rejoin his unit where he spent the next three years, but by July 1918 the exhaustion had returned. Returning to his mother's home at Durrants Farm on two weeks' ordinary leave Cecil visited an army doctor, who extended his leave by a further two weeks. A further request for an extension received an unsympathetic hearing from the Medical Board at

2nd Lieutenant Cecil Burney circa 1916, sitting on a Triumph motorcycle
Author's collection

Aylesbury in August, and he was ordered to report to the Signal Service Training Centre in Bedford. He was later transferred to the Signals base at Wellingborough. On 7th December 1918, Cecil was promoted to acting Captain but three months later, he was demobilised and returned to Northchurch.

Less is known about Alick's time in the Army Service Corps, but, considering his experience, he is likely to have overseen a maintenance section. He, too, ended the war with the rank of Captain and was demobilised in 1919, and returned to Northchurch.

In *The Times* of 26th August 1919, the engagement was announced of Edward Alexander Burney, late Captain, RASC, to Eileen Mary Gates, third daughter of Mr and Mrs Howard Gates of Hove, but the engagement was called off some time later.

Neither brother returned to Burney & Blackburne Ltd, nor did Allan Roberts, who also survived the war. Alick joined Powell Brothers and Whitaker in Wrexham, who manufactured engines and later experimented with motorcycles. Unfortunately, they were not successful, and Powell Brothers eventually went into liquidation in 1927. Alick returned south in 1923, going into business with Captain Oliver M Baldwin, who raced at Brooklands. They jointly developed a new motorcycle, but this also proved not to be commercially successful.

After his demobilisation, Cecil went back to work for Godfrey and Nash, which had moved to a factory in Wandsworth, south London, and trading as GN Limited. Here he enjoyed some success as a work's driver, competing in several events in 1921 and 1922. Whilst there, he designed and built a motorcycle sidecar combination powered by a Blackburne engine, but again it was not commercially successful. In 1923, now aged 39, Cecil moved to FE Baker Ltd in Kings Norton, Birmingham. Whilst there, he continued to look for other suitable jobs, applying for registration on the Institute of Automobile Engineers Appointments Bureau. Preferring to stay in the Birmingham area with a salary of not less than £400 per annum, Cecil described himself in his registration as an all-rounder of the trade.

In 1924, he moved to Wonersh near Guildford with his mother. Alick was to join them there two years later. By this time, Cecil had started his own business, dealing in early motorcars and motorcycles and the brothers started collaborating on their last motorcycle venture under the name of Burney, but once again their design proved commercially unsuccessful. Gertrude Burney died in 1927, and having wound up their mother's estate, Cecil and Alick took a holiday together in Algiers. Cecil still looked for a challenge, however, and in July 1929 he learnt to fly a Moth 80hp Cirrus II at the Brooklands School of Flying.

In 1930, the two brothers were living at the same address in Addlestone, Surrey and around this time Cecil became involved in the Pioneer Run for veteran motorcycles. The brothers were still living in the same house in 1943 when Alick decided to marry the recently-widowed Esme Davie. The marriage was not to last however, possibly because Cecil continued to live in the same house, and by 1946, Esme had moved out and was living elsewhere in Chertsey. That year Cecil became the first secretary of the Vintage Motorcycle Club and spent a happy retirement in that role. By 1953 he was living in Hazelmere and Alick was living in a house in nearby Farnham. Within two years, however, they were both back living together. Cecil Burney died in 1964 aged 80. Alick Burney died in 1971 aged 85.

William Henry Collin (1877 – 1947)
Lieutenant, Royal Engineer Services

William Collin was born in June 1877 in the village of Calderdale, two miles south of Carlisle, where his father, George Collin, was a successful local businessman. Not much is known about his early life except that he trained as a civil engineer after leaving school.

On 18th June 1904, he married Mary Adelaide Smith at Farnworth parish church. By this time William was working as an inspector with the Local Government Board in London, which had been set up by the government in the early 1870s and brought together a variety of responsibilities such as public health, local government, town improvements, housing and the registration of births, marriages and deaths.

In order to be in easy reach of London, William and Mary settled in Loughton, Essex, where their first two children were born. By 1909 however, the family had moved to Highlands, a large house on Shootersway, where William employed a nursery governess and a general domestic servant. A second daughter was later born there. William's work as a local government inspector took him to towns across the country where he held formal planning inquiries, including those in Dover and Portsmouth, which considered the construction of new social accommodation for working men.

With the onset of war, William applied for a temporary commission with the Royal Engineers, becoming an Inspector of Works with the Royal Engineer Services with the rank of Honorary Lieutenant. This little-known unit was responsible for the design and construction of new military barracks, hospitals and associated buildings and so enabled William to put his civilian skills as a planning inspector to good use. There is no evidence that he travelled overseas during his time with the unit, and he probably oversaw the construction of many of the military camps in Great Britain that were established during the war. At the end of the hostilities he did not receive any war medals in recognition of his war service.

The war over, William resumed his work with the Local Government Board and when it was later abolished he transferred to what would eventually become the Ministry of Health. He and his family remained at Highlands for several years before moving to Bovingdon, and later to Hempstead Lane in Potten End. He died in 1947, aged 69.

Thomas William Dancer (1889 – 1965)
Sapper 251501, 114th Railway Company, RE

Like William Bryant, Thomas Dancer, worked for the London & North Western Railway before the war. Born in July 1889, he was the son of Thomas William Dancer (snr), a watercress grower, and his wife, Martha and lived in Bourne End Lane. Thomas was their first child and the eldest of seven children. On leaving school, he started work on a farm, but in 1913 he changed jobs, becoming a platelayer with the railway and joined the National Union of Railwaymen. The previous year he had married Kathleen Charge from nearby Boxmoor.

When war broke out in August 1914 Thomas was already the father of one child and his wife was about to give birth to a second. Despite this, he readily signed up with the Royal Engineers and was posted to 114th Railway Company at Cheltenham. Soon afterwards he joined an army boxing team.

On 1st May 1915 Thomas and his unit arrived in France and were based at Audruicq, near Calais, where work had already started on the construction of a major store and ammunition dump, together with locomotive, carriage and wagon repair shops. Despite working some distance from the front line, the war was never far away. In July 1916, several German aircraft approached Audruicq from the east and dropped bombs on the construction site, setting one of the ammunition sheds alight. The fire quickly spread and it took until the following day to bring it under control.

Over the next two years 114th Railway Construction Company helped build several of the new military depots in France, the one at 'International Corner' near Poperinghe, being key to supplying of troops during the Third Battle of Ypres. The construction of the depots, and their connection to the growing rail network enabled ammunition, supplies and men to be brought directly to the front line, and was a key part of the strategy that eventually led to the defeat of the German army.

Thomas was demobilised in the spring of 1919 and returned home. Kathleen had recently given birth to another son and a further three children would be born over the coming seven years. He went back to work as a platelayer for the London & North Western Railway and was based at Boxmoor (now Hemel Hempstead) station. He was still working for them in 1939. Thomas Dancer died in 1965, aged 76.

Arthur Thomas Davis (1887 – 1949)
Driver 611760, 207th Field Company, RE

Arthur Davis was born in Eddy Street, Gossoms End, in November 1887, one of seven surviving children (of eleven) born to Sarah Ann Davis and her husband, Thomas Arthur Davis. Like many of the men living in Eddy Street at the time, Thomas Davis worked as a sawyer at the East & Son timberyard. After leaving school Arthur found work as a warehouseman. In the spring of 1912, he married Edith Rose Burgess from Harpenden, and their first child was born later that year.

Upon the outbreak of war, Arthur, unlike his younger brother, George, did not volunteer and it was only at the end of 1915, with the introduction of the Derby Scheme and the prospect of conscription, that he attested. By then, he was working as a coal carter for the Berkhamsted Co-operative Society and had a second child to support.

His mobilisation came in 1916 and he was posted to one of the Suffolk Regiment's battalions. With his service record no longer in existence, it is unclear why Arthur was subsequently transferred to the Royal Engineers and posted to 207th Field Company. However, an entry in the unit's War Diary of 9th October 1917 makes mention of 30 men from 11th Battalion, Suffolk Regiment, being among 100 men compulsorily transferred from infantry units to form a new sapping company.

The previous month, Arthur's younger brother, George, was killed whilst serving with 16th Battalion, Sherwood Foresters at Ypres[25]. At the time of his death, 207th Field Company was employed further south in the Somme sector strengthening the British defences in the area.

March 1918, saw Arthur and his unit acting as emergency infantry at the start of the German Spring Offensive, but they were withdrawn as soon as practicable to help construct new defensive lines to the rear. The following month 207th Field Company moved north to Armentières, but soon after their arrival they again came under heavy attack from the Germans, who had launched their second offensive of the spring. Once again, the unit was employed as emergency infantry, but the extensive use of Yellow Cross gas by the attacking Germans inflicted heavy casualties. Fortunately, Arthur was not among them. With the arrival of fresh infantrymen, he and his mates were withdrawn to start building yet more defensive positions in the area around Poperinghe. By the middle of July, the German offensives had petered out and the men of 207th Field Company spent much of their time repairing military camps and emplacements and salvaging as much reusable material as they could find.

After the war had ended, 207th Field Company was sent to Bonn in the Rhineland to construct new facilities for the Army of the Rhine. Demobilisation commenced in April 1919 and by July Arthur had returned home to Eddy Street. The following year Edith gave birth to their third child with their last child being born in 1927. It is currently not known whether he returned to his old job with the Berkhamsted Co-operative Society, but in 1939 he was living at Dropshort Cottage, Northchurch and working as a general labourer for Hertfordshire County Council. Arthur Davis died in the late winter of 1949, aged 61.

Sidney Reginald Dwight (1891 – 1961)
Lance Corporal 206981, Signals Service, RE

Born in August 1891, Sidney Dwight was the youngest child of pheasant breeder William Dwight and his wife, Jane. Like his older brother, Percy,

---

[25] His story is told in *For Them's Sake*

Sidney was educated at Berkhamsted School and later started working for his father on his pheasant farm.

Although the brothers enlisted together with 19th (Public Schools) Battalion, Royal Fusiliers, which later became an Officer Training Corps in France, Sidney decided not to apply for a commission in 1915. By then he had become an acting Corporal, and had applied for a transfer to the Royal Engineers' Signals Service. With his considerable experience in raising and looking after gamebirds, it was no surprise that Sidney would be posted to a unit where his knowledge would be put to good use – the Signal Service's Carrier Pigeon Section.

The need for clear communication between military units during any engagement is vital and can make the difference between victory and defeat. Both sides used numerous methods of communication during the war, but one type was used more by the British army than any other participating country - the carrier pigeon. The use of homing pigeons was a well-established sport in

Mobile Carrier Pigeon Loft
Author's collection

parts of Great Britain before the war and converting it to wartime use was relatively straightforward and simply involved attaching a suitable light container to the pigeon's leg into which a coded message could be inserted. The pigeon would then fly back with the message to its home loft where it would be decoded and read.

The Royal Engineers' Carrier Pigeon Section was formed in 1915, with the introduction of the first 15 mobile lofts, each one holding four pigeons and having a dedicated handler. The initial mobile lofts were converted from standard horse-drawn army waggons and fitted with a new superstructure resembling a hut, complete with windows. Sometime later, former London Transport 'Old Bill' 'B-Type' omnibuses, which had been used to transport thousands of British troops to the front line earlier in the war, were converted to motorised pigeon lofts. Later in the war, tanks, due to the cramped space inside them, together with the constant noise and vibration from their engines, used pigeons to communicate back to their headquarters. By 1918, some 200,000 carrier pigeons had joined the British armed forces and the number of mobile lofts had increased to 150.

Sidney was demobilised in March 1919 and returned home. His father had died two years earlier and he helped keep the family business running. In the spring of 1928, he married Sarah Elizabeth Birks at Leighton Buzzard. Sidney and his family were still living at The Pheasantries in 1939, and the following year he followed his father in becoming a Churchwarden at St Michael and All Angels, Sunnyside, a post he retained until a year before his death in 1961, aged 70.

Harry Geary (1883 – 1953)
Sapper 262677, 260th Railway Company, RE

In December 1883, Annie Geary, the wife of William Geary, a labourer living in Northchurch High Street, gave birth to twin boys. They were named Harry and Thomas and on 3rd February the following year they were christened together at St Mary's, Northchurch. William and Annie would raise a total of eight children, including Walter and Frederick, who would both be killed within weeks of each other during the Gallipoli campaign in 1915[26].

Thomas, married Emily Davis in 1907 and moved to a cottage in Gossoms End, whilst Harry became a general labourer and in 1911 was still living with his parents, younger brother and three sisters at the family home in Bank Cottages in Northchurch High Street. His other brothers, Walter and Frederick, were by that time serving in the army with the Border Regiment.

By 1914 Harry had changed jobs, and was now working as a platelayer with the London & North Western Railway and living in Leavesden Road, Watford. In November 1915, he attested at Watford under the Derby Scheme, but it would be a year before he was mobilised and sent for training to Longmoor Camp, Hampshire. Here he was posted to 260th (Railway) Company.

Harry's unit left Longmoor on 3rd February 1917 and arrived at Le Havre the following day. The unit then travelled by train to Varennes, where work began on the construction of a new stores yard, and remained there for four months before moving to Saigneville, near Abbeville, to help construct a new ammunition depot and associated railway sidings. By the end of September, the major work had been completed and Harry and his fellow sappers were sent north to install new railway track at another large ammunition base being built at Zeneghem a few miles from the coast, midway between Calais and Dunkirk. Not long after their arrival, German aircraft bombed the construction site several times, killing several of his workmates and damaging or destroying several railway wagons.

By the end of November 1917, the construction work at Zeneghem had been completed and Harry and his mates set off for St Jean, near Ypres. By

---

[26] Their story is told in *For Them's Sake*

165

then the Third Battle of Ypres had ended, but that did not stop German artillery firing regular salvoes at the British lines close to the construction site where the company was working and once again caused several casualties.

In January 1918 260th Railway Company were transferred to the Somme Sector to take over from American engineers who had been maintaining the railway track in the area. On 20th March, the Company's War Diary reported an increase in artillery fire to the north. What they did not know was that this was the prelude to the launch by the Germans of their Spring Offensive.

The speed of the German advance was so rapid that there was little time to withdraw some of the heavy artillery pieces in the area, and a detachment from Harry's company was sent to help in their recovery. These men were also given orders to destroy five bridges and all the railway stock in the sector to help delay the German advance. While most of the company loaded their equipment onto the railway wagons and headed west towards Amiens, a small demolition party was assembled. At 21:00 on 21st March, the party set out with two days' rations to lay the charges on the five bridges and await orders. Coming under increasing machine-gun fire, the demolition squad just managed to complete the laying of the charges before the Germans arrived. Igniting the fuses, the resulting explosion destroyed the bridges and the squad made its way safely back to the British lines. Additional groups of men were later sent out to destroy other key railway tracks and road bridges to delay further the German advance. In the following days, with the German offensive petering out, Harry and his unit started laying new railway tracks at the large ammunition dumps and new gun emplacements near Amiens.

Influenza broke out in the company in the middle of May, with twenty-seven men reporting sick on the first day, fifty-two on the second, sixty-seven on the third and seventy-four on the fifth. Fortunately, this was not the more serious strain of influenza that was to strike Europe later in the year, and only a small proportion of men were sent to hospital. With no sign of the epidemic easing, however, all men in 260th Railway Company who were not infected were isolated from the rest of the unit. By the end of May, the epidemic had died out and those men who had been sent to hospital returned to their duties.

Harry and his mates remained at Saint-Léger-lès-Domart until the end of August when they started to extend the railway tracks eastwards so that supplies and ammunition could be sent to the advancing allied troops following the Battle of Amiens.

Railway reconstruction work did not end with the signing of the Armistice in November 1918 and 260th Railway Company continued working in the former German occupied areas of France repairing the lines that had been damaged over the recent months. In January 1919 their demobilisation began.

On 17th March, Harry had a medical examination in France and was sent to the Dispersal Unit at Purfleet, Essex. He then returned to Northchurch, where later that year he married Annie Davis. He rejoined the London & North Western Railway as a labourer and later moved to Watford. He died there in September 1953, aged 69.

William Bonner Hopkins (1868 – 1958)
Lieutenant, Royal Engineer Services, RE

William Bonner Hopkins was born in July 1868, in the small village of Great Limber, Lincolnshire. His father, Thomas Hopkins, was a wealthy local farmer who employed a workforce of twenty-five people on his 860-acre farm. Unsurprisingly, William had a private education, boarding at a school in Harrogate. In September 1888, Thomas Hopkins died and his widow, Mary, later sold the farm and moved south with her family to settle at Fairhill on Berkhamsted Common, where Walter Samuel Cohen would later live. By 1891, William was training to become an architect at Watts & Co, the offices owned by George Frederick Bodley, a member of the 'Gothic Revival' movement and a former pupil of Sir George Gilbert Scott, who had designed the chapel of ease at Bourne End for the then Rector of Northchurch, Revd. Sir John Hobart Culme-Seymour. In 1893, he formed a partnership with fellow architect, Ernest Robert Walker.

In 1902, William married Constance Maud Ashton, the daughter of a clergyman from Uggeshall, Suffolk and the newlyweds set up home at Mainland Cottage, Harpenden. The following year, Constance gave birth to a boy at his mother's home, Fairhill.

After five years in partnership with Ernest Walker, William decided to set up his own offices at 97 High Street, Berkhamsted, and became a member of the local Masonic Lodge. By 1911, the business was doing very well and he was employing two domestic servants at his home. Three years later, the family moved to Rosemary Cottage in Northchurch High Street, opposite Northchurch Hall.

Wanting to put his skills as an architect to good use in the war effort, like William Collin, he applied for a temporary commission with the Royal Engineers, becoming an Inspector of Works. He was given the honorary rank of Lieutenant and remained in Great Britain throughout the war and by 1918 he was based in Norwich.

At the end of the war he returned to his architect business, and later moved to Coldbrook in Dudswell. By 1939, William had retired and he and Constance were living at Hapton House, a 16th century timber-framed house in the village of Depwade in Norfolk. He died there in 1958, aged 89.

Joseph Albert Hosier (1890 – 1951)
Sapper 188132, 70th Field Company, RE

Joseph Hosier's war service was somewhat unconventional. Born at the family home in Berkhamsted High Street in February 1890, he was Charles and Esther Hosier's third child. Charles Hosier came from Boxmoor and worked in a brickyard, whilst his wife, Esther, came from Little Stanmore, near Edgware, Middlesex.

By 1901, Esther had given birth to four more children and the family were living in a cramped four-roomed terraced cottage in Bell Lane, Northchurch. Not surprisingly, Charles later moved to a larger property in Orchard End, but by 1911, only the youngest children were still living at home.

After leaving school, Joseph probably started work alongside his father as a brickmaker, but in late summer of 1908 he enlisted with the Bedfordshire Regiment, joining their 4th (Special Reserve) Battalion for a six-year term. Special Reservists agreed to be called up in the event of a general mobilisation and had to complete an initial six months of full-time training, during which they received the same pay as a regular soldier. This was then followed by annual refreshers lasting three to four weeks. With his initial six months' training completed, Joseph returned to brickmaking.

In March 1911 and now 21, Joseph and several of his similarly-aged Northchurch mates, James Bunn,

Private Joseph Hosier (centre)
Courtesy of Bert Hosier

Charles Bignall, James Meager, Thomas Howlett and Walter Welling, found themselves up in front of the local magistrate charged with 'hooting and yelling' and failing to stop when directed by the local village policeman, PC Mead. Joseph was found guilty, along with two others and fined eight shillings. The following month and in a more controlled environment, he was at Hertford barracks and taking part in his annual training with the reserves whilst billeted at the *Black Swan* public house.

At the outbreak of war, Joseph was mobilised and he reported to the Regimental Depot in Bedford. He was posted to the Bedford's 2nd Battalion which was on its way back from South Africa, having been recalled from garrison duty there. After a short period of further training, he was assigned to the battalion's 'B' Coy and arrived in France on 11th November 1914, joining the battalion at Bailleul. By this time northern France was experiencing frequent snow showers and the cold would make life in the newly-dug trenches particularly miserable over the coming weeks.

On Christmas Eve 1914, Joseph and his battalion were in the trenches near the small town of Fleurbaix, due west of the German-held city of Lille. The subsequent events, recorded in the battalion's War Diary, stated that at about 20:00 lights appeared along the German parapets a few yards in front of the Bedford's trenches, hanging from what appeared to be Christmas trees. Soon, the German soldiers started singing *'Stille Nacht'* – 'Silent Night', followed by *'O Tannenbaum'* – 'O Christmas Tree'. After the singing had finished, a German officer called out in English, *'I want to arrange to bury the dead - will someone come out and meet me?'* Cautiously, one of the Bedford's officers went out into 'no-man's land', accompanied by three men. Here they met five Westphalians of the 15th Regiment, whose leader apparently spoke excellent English, having lived in both Brighton and Canada before the war. The German officer wanted to bury about twenty-four of their dead, who were lying close by, but could not do so fearing British rifle or artillery fire. Uncertain what to do next, both sides returned to their trenches.

At 10:00 on Christmas Day, with the thick snow still crusted by overnight frost, another German officer and two unarmed men left their trenches holding a white flag and spoke to one of the battalion's captains. The German officer formally requested to bury their dead and both sides agreed an informal cease-fire until 11:30 to complete the task. The War Diary goes on to describe the large garrison of soldiers lining the German parapets as, *'a young lot from 19-25 years well turned out & clean'*. The Bedford's Commanding Officer had previously given strict instructions that none of his men should approach the German lines without definite orders, and that only men on duty were to show themselves. Additionally, no Germans were to be allowed to come near to the Bedford's trenches, but British officers could inspect the German wire. Having buried their dead, the German and British troops returned to their trenches and the war resumed.

The next two months in the trenches were relatively quiet, and it was not until March 1915, and the arrival of slightly warmer weather, that Joseph saw action during the Battle of Neuve Chapelle. The next major fighting took place on 16th May with the Battle of Festubert, during which 'B' Company suffered several casualties from artillery fire and poison gas. On 31st May 1915, Joseph was admitted to 18th General Hospital at Camiers, suffering from what was initially recorded in the hospital's medical log as influenza and was subsequently changed to bronchitis. It highly likely however, that Joseph was suffering from the effects of poison gas and the following month he was invalided home to England on board a hospital ship.

On 11th October 1915, Joseph was officially discharged from the army, not because of his sickness, but simply because his six-year term of service with the army for which he had signed up in 1908, and which had immediately been extended by a year following the outbreak of war, had expired. The army regulations at that time, which only applied to pre-war soldiers, still allowed 'time expired' servicemen to be discharged and return to civilian life, even during war time. Joseph returned to Northchurch and became a labourer at Lagley, a large house which stood on the south side of the road between Northchurch and Gossoms End. His discharge papers describe Joseph as standing 5ft 7ins tall and with a fresh complexion, grey eyes and light brown hair. His general character during his time as a soldier was described as 'good'.

The Military Service Act came into force early in 1916 and made a special exemption of 'time expired' men like Joseph, meaning that he was not obliged to rejoin the army, although those who were willing to rejoin were offered a monetary incentive. After a few months, however, rumours started to circulate that the numbers of new recruits were still insufficient to meet the army's needs and consequently conscription would be extended to include married men and former soldiers. Faced with little choice, Joseph decided to re-enlist.

His service record from this time has not survived, so how the subsequent events developed are somewhat unclear. Joseph next appears in Chatham, where, instead of returning to the infantry, he enlisted with the Royal Engineers. The family story is that he either did not disclose his previous service with the Bedfordshire Regiment, or it was missed in an administrative error. It appears however, that when the error or non-disclosure was subsequently discovered, Joseph was charged with 'impersonating a new recruit' and placed for a period in the cells at Chatham Barracks. Joseph's 'Certificate of Employment during the War', which was given to all servicemen on being demobilised after 1918, states that he served in France from April 1916, initially with the Infantry, and then 70th Field Company, Royal Engineers. His discharge papers, issued in 1919, however, state that he enlisted with the Royal Engineers on 10th July 1916. What the infantry unit was, or how he came to be released from the cells at Chatham, is not known.

Formed in May 1915, 70th Field Company, RE, like most field companies, spent most of their time digging trenches and dugouts in France. Another more dangerous role was the clearing of captured enemy positions, which Joseph called 'suicide missions', because they were frequently booby-trapped. During one of these missions, he 'liberated' a large German cuckoo clock from one dugout which he eventually brought back home to Northchurch.

The 1918 Northchurch Absent Voters List shows Joseph as still serving with 70th Field Company, but at some point, he was transferred to 12th Field

Company and sent to Ireland where he remained until his demobilisation in November 1919. The citation on Joseph's Certificate of Employment, written by a Major of 12th Field Company, reads '*Sapper Hosier is a diligent and conscientious workman. I can safely recommend him to fill any position of trust*'. Following the medical taken on his demobilisation, Joseph was categorised as B2 which allowed him to receive a small war pension.

Returning to his home in Orchard End, Joseph found work at the brickworks in Aldbury. In 1925, he married Lizzie Hill, a domestic servant responsible for looking after the poultry at Lagley, where Joseph had briefly worked following his discharge from the army in 1915. The newly-weds set up home in a cottage in near Aldbury close to the brickworks where Joseph now worked. He and Lizzie would later have three children together. In the mid-1930s, Joseph moved his family to Northchurch, initially to a house on the newly-built Home Farm estate, on the site of the now demolished Northchurch Hall, and later to a cottage in New Road. At that time Joseph was working at a brickyard near Shootersway. Joseph Hosier died in November 1951, aged 60.

Frederick Hosier (1887 – 1957)
Driver 92170, 7th Horse Pontoon Park, RE

Frederick Hosier was the first of Charles and Esther Hosier's children. Born in July 1887, in the family home in Berkhamsted High Street, Frederick grew up in Northchurch and, like his father, became a brickmaker. Sadly by 1911, a fierce family argument had resulted in Frederick leaving home and moving to the hamlet of Hyde Heath near Chesham.

In September 1915, Frederick enlisted with the Royal Engineers and was posted to Aldershot as a driver with the recently-formed 7th Horse Pontoon Park. A few weeks before being sent to France with his unit, 28-year-old Frederick married Kate Wright, the daughter of a woodman who worked on an estate near Hyde Heath.

Frederick left Aldershot with his unit for France on 18th May 1916. 7th Horse Pontoon Park consisted of 238 men as well as 64 heavy draft horses and 60 motor vehicles capable of pulling specially-designed two-axled pontoon wagons. Each wagon carried a pontoon which could be used either as a boat or, when linked to other pontoons, form the basis of a temporary bridge. The wagons were normally drawn by six heavy draft horses and Frederick was one of 57 riders in the unit.

It was not long before defects in the standard pontoon wagon's design became apparent to men like Frederick, and over the coming months changes were made to make them more resilient, especially when being pulled over rough countryside. When not being used to transport pontoons, the wagons were easily modified to carry boxes capable of holding other equipment for the Royal Engineers. During the spring of 1917, the unit worked closely with 1st ANZAC Corps on general carting work in the Somme sector. Later that year, at the start of the Third Battle of Ypres, the unit was used to bring water pipes up to the front line as part of the effort to supply the British troops with fresh water. By necessity most of this work had to be done under cover of darkness, but Frederick's unit still suffered several casualties of both men and horses through artillery fire.

It was not until the October 1918, with the German army now in full retreat, that 7th Horse Pontoon Park was put to its proper purpose when British troops crossed the river Lys west of Ypres, using the unit's pontoons. Within days, Ostend, Lille and Douai had fallen and the following month the Armistice was signed.

Frederick was demobilised in March 1919. On his Employment Certificate, a Captain in the Royal Engineers wrote: '*Character – exemplary. An exceptionally good man, hardworking, painstaking and reliable. Always ready and willing to give a helping hand to others. Has done exceedingly well throughout his service and set a fine example to all, even under the worst conditions*'. Returning home to Hyde Heath, Frederick resumed his work as a brickmaker. He remained there until his death on 1957, aged 70.

Leonard David King (1880 – 1968)
Sapper 213057, 2nd Provisional Company, RE

Born in the family home in New Road, Northchurch, in June 1880, Leonard King was one of seven children born to Nash King, a carpenter, and his wife, Carrie. The King family had a long non-conformist tradition going back some generations, and at the time of his birth both his parents were members of the Baptist Chapel in Bell Lane, Northchurch. Sadly, when Leonard was just four years old, his mother died of cerebral apoplexy and was buried in the chapel graveyard. Five years later, Leonard's father was admitted to St Luke's Lunatic Asylum in Hoxton, London, where he later died. Their children were subsequently raised by various members of their extended family, with Leonard being brought up by John Richbell and his wife, who ran a grocer's shop in Northchurch High Street. John Richbell died in 1898 and Leonard, who was now eighteen and working as a carpenter, moved into lodgings in Gossoms End.

In 1905, he married Louisa Bolt from Cheddington, and moved to Bay Cottage in Northchurch High Street. Over the next five years, Louisa would give birth to two children. Continuing the family connection, Leonard and Louisa worshipped at the new Baptist Chapel on the High Street which had opened in 1900, and where one of Leonard's uncles, William King, was a leading member. By 1911, Leonard had become a skilled carpenter and joiner and had obtained several government contracts for the army and navy. Around this time, he also became a member of Northchurch Parish Council, along with his uncle William, and was the Northchurch representative on Berkhamsted's Joint Fire Engine Committee.

A man with strong Christian convictions, Leonard abhorred warfare, but was prepared to continue with his government contracts for the army and navy. Following the extension of the Military Service Act to married men in the summer of 1916, he was conscripted and ordered to report to the army recruitment centre in Watford. Leonard appealed to the Berkhamsted Military Tribunal, using the exemption from military service on the grounds of conscientious objection on religious grounds, but his appeal was rejected. However, he was allowed to appeal to the County Tribunal at Hertford. In October 1916, the Hertford Tribunal dismissed Leonard's case and with no other options available, he reluctantly reported to the Watford recruiting office, stating that he wished to be posted to the Royal Engineers to use his skills as a joiner.

He was fortunate as his request was granted, probably due to his age and proven skill in carpentry. Sent to the Royal Engineers' base at Chatham, Leonard started his military training and was officially classified a skilled carpenter and joiner. He was to remain there until early September 1917 when he left England for France. Two months later, he returned home for treatment at the Military Heart Hospital in Colchester.

This hospital was established in buildings at the Sobraon Barracks in Colchester in August 1917. Although the understanding of stress experienced by soldiers during wartime was in in its infancy, the growing numbers of men reporting sick from heart problems led to the creation of several specialist centres across the country, the one at Colchester being the first. Men diagnosed by doctors in the field as suffering from heart issues were classified as either 'Disorderly Action of the Heart' (DAH), sometimes known as 'soldiers' heart', for which a genuine abnormality could not be found, or 'Valvular Disease of the Heart' (VDH), for which there was a genuine physical abnormality. The doctors at Colchester introduced a strict exercise programme aimed at weeding out those diagnosed with DAH who in fact had no genuine heart problem.

Leonard would remain at Colchester undergoing treatment until February 1918, after which he was granted two weeks' home leave and told that on his return he would be posted to 17th Battalion, Northumberland Fusiliers (Pioneers). At the end of his leave, Leonard returned to France to join his new unit, which was based on the French/Belgian border.

Although ostensibly a railway construction battalion, Leonard found that most of the work undertaken by his new unit related to digging trenches and improving roads, tracks and bridges. As the British forces advanced slowly north-eastwards, the pioneers and other engineer battalions advanced alongside them ensuring that physical obstacles did not hold up the advance. By the time the Armistice was signed, Leonard and his unit had reached the village of Sirault to the west of Mons. The following month, he was granted special Christmas leave and returned home.

Despite the war being over, work needed to continue with the repair of four years of war damage, and consequently Leonard was posted back to the Royal Engineers. He finally returned to England in March 1919 and was demobilised. He was subsequently awarded a military pension, boosted slightly by an allowance to reflect his heart issues.

Back in Northchurch, he resumed his job as a carpenter and joiner and took responsibility for the upkeep of the Baptist chapel graveyard in Bell Lane, a role he performed until resigning in 1939. He also took on a new job as an undertaker, whilst doing various other duties at the Baptist Chapel. Leonard King died in 1968, aged 87.

Herbert John William Manners (1896 – 1967)
Sapper 209828, Railway Operating Department, RE

Herbert Manners was born in south-east London in August 1896, the only child of Herbert Arnold Manners, a railway clerk, and his wife, Amelia. Throughout his childhood, his parents lived in the same four-roomed property in a tree-lined avenue in Walworth, not far from the Elephant and Castle. After leaving school, Herbert became a solicitor's clerk, but later changed employers and followed his father to become a railway clerk for the South Eastern & Chatham Railway, based at London Bridge station.

Herbert received his conscription papers in 1916, but appealed on the grounds of ill health. Despite presenting the local Military Tribunal with a detailed medical report, Herbert's request was rejected, albeit that it was noted that he would not be fit enough to serve as a front line soldier.

On 6th November 1916, Herbert reported to the Recruiting Office at Southwark and was sent to the Royal Engineers base at Longmoor Camp, Hampshire. Here he was posted to the Railway Operating Department, where his experience as a railway clerk could be put to good use.

The Railway Operating Department consisted of several companies, the first of which was deployed to France in 1915. Their orders were simple – keep the trains running. Most of the men who worked in the new operating companies had been former railway company clerical employees before the war and, just as in their roles in civilian life, they were responsible for the management of traffic on the standard gauge railway lines, the provision of drivers and firemen, and overseeing the repair of the locomotives. With the expansion of the railway network in France and Belgium and the construction of new track to supply the troops on the front line, the scheduling of trains to and from the supply depots on the coast became more and more difficult.

It appears that Herbert adapted to his new role with some enthusiasm, and in September 1917 he was upgraded to become a 'superior'. In January the following year he returned to England on two weeks' leave for the first time. By now, his parents had moved to a house on Berkhamsted High Street, with Herbert being registered in Eddy Street, Gossoms End.

In January 1919, he returned to England where, following a medical check at 4th London General Hospital in Denmark Hill, he was diagnosed with dermatitis. As this was partially attributed to his war service, his war pension was increased accordingly. Herbert was discharged from the army in April 1919 and awarded a Silver War Badge. He moved back to London soon after returning to England and resumed his job as a railway clerk. In 1926, he married Alice McPherson, the marriage being registered in Southwark. Later, the couple later moved to a house in Lewisham. By 1953, he had changed jobs and had started working for the Post Office. Herbert Manners died in South Norwood in 1967, aged 70.

Harry Meager (1881 – 1969)
Sapper 143779, Unknown Unit, RE

Henry (Harry) Meager was born in Northchurch in October 1881, the second child and first son of bricklayer, Frederick Meager and his wife, Lucy, who would have a total of eight children together, although one would die in infancy. Having finished his schooling, Harry became a bricklayer and later left his parents' home in the High Street to work in Watford. In 1902, now living back in Northchurch and aged 20, he married 26-year-old Alice Winter in St Mary's, the wedding certificate describing Harry's occupation as 'mason'. Alice worked as a private music tutor and was the daughter of James Winter, a piano tuner who lived in Charles Street, Berkhamsted. Their first child was born in 1903 with two more being born over the next seven years. By 1911, Harry and his family were living in a small four-roomed cottage in Bell Lane, Northchurch.

Along with his younger brother, Fred, in 1913 Harry was instrumental in setting up the Berkhamsted branch of the Operative Bricklayers' Society, a trades union that dated back to 1818. He acted as one of its banking stewards alongside William Fantham and William Skidmore, whilst Fred Meager served as the society's branch secretary.

By the summer of 1914, Harry was a father of five children, which may account for his not volunteering to join the army at the outbreak of the war. Unfortunately, his service record has not survived, so it is unclear whether he later volunteered, or was conscripted into the army. Joining the Royal Engineers, where his bricklaying skills would be put to good use, he became a sapper.

Little is known about Harry's wartime service. Meager family tradition has it that he was gassed on one occasion, and that in the spring of 1918 he received either a leg wound or other injury. Neither event was to cut short his military service, however, and towards the end of 1918 he was posted to one of the busy Royal Engineer base depots close to the English Channel.

He was demobilised in 1919 and upon returning home to Northchurch he resumed his job as a bricklayer. Harry and his family remained in their Bell Lane home until the 1930s and it is thought that he was one of the bricklayers responsible for building the row of houses in nearby Duncombe Road. By 1939, he and Alice had moved into one of them and he was working as a builder's foreman. Harry Meager died in 1969, aged 87.

Fred Meager (1884 – 1953)
Sapper WR/315061, Inland Water Transport Section, RE

Fred Meager was one of Harry Meager's younger brothers and also became a bricklayer after leaving school. In 1909, he married Ada Maria Mapley, a domestic servant in one of the larger houses in the area and they set up home in Orchard End, Northchurch.

With his elder brother, Harry, Fred set up the Berkhamsted branch of the Operative Bricklayers' Society in 1913 and became its first branch Secretary. The meetings were held in *The Goat* public house in Berkhamsted and by October that year it had 13 members, but by 1916, with only six members remaining, due to war service, the branch was closed and merged with the larger Watford branch.

When war broke out in 1914, Ada Meager was expecting her first child and Fred decided not to volunteer for military service. She gave birth to a boy the following November. Fred was conscripted in the summer of 1916 and reported to the Recruiting Office at Watford. It was not until the following September, however, that he had his medical examination and was given a B1 medical category and sent home to await his mobilisation. The medical record from that time shows him as being 5ft 7½ins tall and weighing 141lbs. Four months later, Fred reported back to Watford, where he was posted to the Inland Water Transport Section (IWT) of the Royal Engineers.

Fred joined No60 Traffic Company IWT, based at Richborough in Kent. The IWT had been set up to run and maintain the transport links on the canals and navigable rivers in the various war zones. Expansion of the base at Richborough started in 1916, with the dredging and partial diversion of the River Stour, together with the laying of new railway track, to allow larger cross-channel vessels to operate from there. Fred's bricklaying skills were essential as the base expanded further in 1917 with the addition of new barge construction facilities and locomotive repair shops. By the end of 1917 a regular cross-channel railway ferry was also in operation from Richborough, transporting locomotives and wagons from the English coast from where they were driven onto the French railway system. Soon, Richborough covered some 2,200 acres and employed over 20,000 men in various roles. When he joined the IWT in 1917, Fred's bricklaying skills were described as 'superior', but by June 1918 he had been reassessed as 'V superior'. Despite this, in October 1918 he and other sappers, were compulsorily transferred to the Machine Gun Corps to train as machine-gunners to replace those lost on the Western Front. He was given a new service number and allocated to 'B' MGC Training Battalion, based in Rugeley Camp, Staffordshire.

The war ended before Fred had completed his training, and he spent the next few months in Rugeley awaiting demobilisation. As he had not served overseas in a war zone he was not awarded any war medals by the British Government.

Fred Meager returned to Northchurch and resumed work as a bricklayer, later becoming a foreman. He died at his home in Duncombe Road, a few doors away from his brother, Harry, in 1953, aged 69.

James Henry Thomas Moore (1880 – 1943)
Sapper 161615, 1st Indian Army Signal Corps, RE

James Moore was born in Aldershot in April 1880, the son of James Moore (snr), a Corporal in the Royal Engineers with an Irish linage, and his wife, Ann, from Little Gaddesden. Not long after his birth, his father left the army and moved his family to his father-in-law's small cottage in Little Gaddesden whilst he looked for work in the area. The arrival of a family with a young baby must have made the conditions in the cottage particularly cramped. James's younger brother was born in Tamworth, Staffordshire, the following year, so it is probable that his father later found work there. Two years later however, the family were back in Hertfordshire, first at Nettleden, where Ann gave birth to a daughter, and later on in George Street, Berkhamsted, then part of Northchurch Parish, where a second daughter was born. By 1891, his father was working as a general labourer and his 81-year-old paternal Irish grandfather had moved into the family home.

James's father died in 1899, and to make ends meet his mother, along with his elder sister, started taking in washing. James was also bringing in money as a general labourer and in 1911 he was working at the nearby factory of William Cooper & Nephews.

At the outbreak of war, James was still the main breadwinner in the house, and consequently did not volunteer for active service. His mother died in 1915 and the following year James was conscripted. By then, he had changed jobs and was working for the stationery manufacturer, Dickinson & Sons Ltd, at Apsley. His employers submitted two appeals to the Berkhamsted Military Tribunal, but both were rejected, so in May 1916, James reported to the Royal Engineers Depot at Fenny Stratford.

Staple Hall in Fenny Stratford, Buckinghamshire, had been requisitioned by the army a few days after the start of the war. Initially, it was used as the headquarters for the local Territorial battalions who were billeted in the area, but by February 1915, the Royal Engineers' Signals Section had taken it over as a training school. Soon wooden huts were built in the grounds to accommodate the trainees like James, as well as providing classrooms where the new recruits could learn

Staple Hall, Fenny Stratford
Author's collection

new skills. It was during his time at Staple Hall that James became proficient in laying telephone cables.

His training over, James left England in October 1916 to join the Indian Expeditionary Force in Mesopotamia. There he joined 30 Signal Company, which formed part of the 12th Indian Division. It is not clear how long he remained in Mesopotamia, as he was later transferred to Poona, India.

In September 1918, James arrived back in England for treatment for bradycardia (a slow heart rate) at 2nd Western General Hospital, Manchester. He was discharged the following month but given a medical category of B3. A note on his service record, however, states that he was still fit for home service. He was demobilised the following March.

He returned to his home in George Street, but it is currently uncertain whether he returned to his old job at Dickinson & Sons Ltd. He remained in Berkhamsted until the late 1920s when he moved to Broadstairs, Kent, where he met and married Mabel Harriet Lawrence. At the time of his marriage he had become a gardener. James Moore died in Broadstairs in 1943, a few days before his 63rd birthday.

Cyril Mosley Wagstaff DSO (1878 – 1934)
Major-General, Royal Engineers

Cyril Wagstaff was born in Calcutta (now known as Kolkata), India, in March 1878. The Wagstaff family came from the south Midlands and had a long tradition of becoming surgeons. Cyril's father, Phillip Wagstaff, broke with this tradition however, and travelled to India to become the Secretary to the East India Railway Company, based in Calcutta. Formed in 1845, the East India Railway Company was at the forefront of the expansion of the British Empire across the Indian subcontinent, opening it up to trade as well as enabling the transportation of British troops to their garrison posts. The first twenty miles of track opened in 1853 and within ten years it had expanded to some 600 miles. In 1879, the British Indian Government effectively nationalised the company, but leased it back to its management to run.

Cyril Wagstaff spent his formative years in India, but by 1891 his mother, Ada, had returned to England with him and his younger siblings and was living at Blendworth, a 11-roomed house in Kitsbury Terrace, Berkhamsted, leaving his father to continue his work in India. Educated at the United Services College at Westward Ho, he was commissioned into the Royal Engineers in 1897 and his first posting abroad was in 1903, aptly to the Northwest Frontier of India.

It was during one of his periods on leave back in Berkhamsted that Wagstaff met Rosabell Thelwall, a governess and daughter of retired artillery officer, Lieutenant Colonel Eubule Thelwall. The Thelwall family lived in nearby Shrublands Road and were regular worshippers at St Mary's, Northchurch. Rosabell also had strong family connections with India. All her four brothers had been tea planters at Dooars in the eastern Himalayas, but only one, Ernest, was still working there. Wagstaff, now a Captain in the Royal Engineers, and Rosabell were married in Calcutta in 1906, with Ernest acting as one of the witnesses. By 1911, Rosabell had given birth to three children, but one died in infancy. A fourth child was born in 1913.

Returning to England at the outbreak of the war in 1914, Wagstaff was appointed a General Staff Officer, and later was promoted to Major. The following year, in recognition of his services with the Indian Army, he was made a Companion of the Most Eminent Order of the Indian Empire (CIE) as part of the King's Birthday Honours.

In the spring of 1915 Wagstaff was posted to Cairo to join the Mediterranean Expeditionary Force and the staff of Lieutenant-General William Birdwood, the commander of the recently-arrived troops from Australia and New Zealand. Birdwood, like Wagstaff, had been an officer in the Indian Army and was a protégé of Lord Kitchener. It was during his time working for Birchwood that Wagstaff is credited with suggesting to him the acronym by which the troops from Australia and New Zealand were later to become world famous. It came about after he was given the task of devising a codeword for Birchwood's troops. One of his clerical staff suggested the term ANZAC, derived from the wording 'A and NZ Army Corps' painted on crates that were stored in a corridor at their headquarters. Wagstaff proposed the acronym to Birchwood, who authorised its official use.

In April 1915, ANZAC troops, along with Wagstaff and the remainder of General Birdwood's staff, landed at a small cove on the Gallipoli peninsula. They were to remain there, restricted to short strips of land along the coast, for eight long, agonising months until they were evacuated at the end of the year. By the end of the Gallipoli campaign, 8,709 men from Australia and 2,721 men from New Zealand had been killed, along with over 27,000 men from Great Britain, Canada and India. Far more had been wounded, or had become incapacitated due to sickness, the overall casualties thought to be over half a million men. Most of the allied troops returned to Egypt, where they spent the next few months recovering from their ordeal. For his services during the Gallipoli Campaign Wagstaff was later awarded the DSO.

Wagstaff remained with the ANZAC troops in Egypt, building them into a new fighting force, which became 5th Australian Division. Delays in assembling the division's artillery, however, forced them to remain in Egypt until June 1916, when they finally sailed to France.

The ANZACS arrived too late to take part in the first day of the Somme Offensive, but they did participate in a diversionary attack at Fromelles in late July with Wagstaff, now with the rank of temporary Lieutenant Colonel, continuing to serve under Birchwood as a Staff Officer. The following year, ANZAC troops fought during the German retreat to the Hindenburg Line, the Battle of Arras and the Third Battle of Ypres.

Major Cyril Wagstaff circa 1915
Courtesy of Anthony Wagstaff,
Annie Jermain & Simon Thelwell

In the summer of 1917, Wagstaff was appointed to a new senior role reporting directly to Field Marshal Sir Douglas Haig, Commander of the BEF. His new role was unique, and would involve setting up and overseeing the day-to-day relationship between the British and United States armies on the Western Front and the ongoing liaison between the two General Staffs.

When war broke out in Europe in August 1914, the US President, Woodrow Wilson, pledged that the United States would remain neutral. However, the USA was a key trading partner with Great Britain and soon several US ships were damaged or sunk by German-laid mines whilst crossing the Atlantic. In February 1915, the German government announced that any ship entering the 'war zone' around Great Britain risked sinking by German vessels. On 7th May 1915 the liner *Lusitania* was torpedoed without warning just off the coast of Ireland, killing 1,201 passengers including 128 Americans. Further attacks at sea led to the loss of more American lives and in February 1917 the US government broke off diplomatic relations with Germany. Two months later, on 6th April, the US Congress voted in favour of a declaration of war.

On 8th June 1917, Major General John J Pershing, the recently-appointed head of the American Expeditionary Force (AEF), arrived at Liverpool onboard the SS *Baltic* accompanied by several senior army officers and a small contingent of troops. They were the first of over a million American soldiers that would serve in Europe during the First World War. By coincidence, also on board the *Baltic* were several senior British army officers who were returning to England from America and they spent much of their time crossing the Atlantic answering questions on their experiences of fighting in France. Pershing and his staff were consequently able to learn first-hand about British army training, tactics, strategy and logistics, as well as identifying many differences between the two armies in terms of customs and culture.

The day after arriving in Liverpool, Pershing and his entourage travelled to London on board the royal train for an audience with King George V at Buckingham Palace. Over the next four days he met Prime Minister David Lloyd George and members of the Imperial General Staff in the first stage of what would sometimes prove to be a difficult relationship between the two allies.

Assigned as Chief of the newly-established British Mission, at the AEF Headquarters at Chaumont, 170 miles west of Paris, Wagstaff set to work, quickly establishing a strong working relationship with the American officers. His American counterpart, Lieutenant Colonel Robert H Bacon, performed a similar role at Sir Douglas Haig's headquarters located in an old chateau near St Omer. With Haig and Pershing only

Lieutenant Colonel Cyril Wagstaff (right) with Major General John J Pershing
Author's collection

meeting infrequently, Wagstaff and Bacon were responsible for resolving any day-to-day issues, relaying messages between their commanders, smoothing out disagreements and ensuring good communication between the two armies.

The most contentious issue concerned the timing of the arrival of large numbers of American troops in Europe and their subsequent training and integration into the war effort. The American government were determined that their troops in France would fight as an independent army, and not be mere reinforcements to be used under the direction of either the British or French army commanders. For this to happen however, a massive recruitment and training programme would be required, and it was estimated that this would take some eighteen months before a fully-trained American army, together with their associated equipment, could be sent to France. The British and the French, in contrast, proposed that the simplest solution would be to provide training facilities for the American troops in England and France where they would train alongside their 'allies' and thus learn from their experiences gained over three years of warfare. The American troops would then fight alongside the British at battalion level until enough American troops were available to form their own division. The British would also provide the ships to transport the troops, minus their heavy equipment, which the British would provide, and thus free up space for more troops to be sent across the Atlantic.

Pershing was reluctant to agree to this proposal as he foresaw problems with the British and French commanders being unwilling to release the American troops once they had been trained and equipped. It was also anticipated that many American 'doughboys', particularly those of Irish origin, would be reluctant to fight alongside British troops, especially following the suppression of the 'Easter Rebellion' in Dublin in 1916. On a day-to-day level among the troops there were also differences in culture, terminology and communication to overcome, particularly the understanding of the strong regional dialects used by both sides, but time to resolve these differences was running out.

In December 1917, the Russian and German armies signed an Armistice, which was later ratified by the Treaty of Brest-Litovsk. The German High Command saw this as a perfect opportunity to transfer vast numbers of German troops to the Western Front ready for a major offensive before a significant number of trained American troops would become available and so launched their Spring Offensive in the early hours of 21st March 1918. Two days later, the War Office sent an urgent message to Wagstaff, now promoted to temporary Brigadier General, stating that he should stress to the Americans that the British and French troops were now engaged in what might prove to be the decisive battle of the war, and ask them to send over more troops as fast as possible. Reluctantly, Pershing agreed to speed up the despatch of American troops to France on board British ships, with priority being given to the infantry and machine-gun units. In a second memorandum on 2nd April, Wagstaff was asked to convey the War Office's 'appreciation and gratitude' to General Pershing for the manner in which he had agreed to the British request. The same day, the British Prime Minister wrote to the King and War Cabinet explaining the key role that the American troops would have in stabilising the Western Front.

By the end of March 1918 there were 284,000 American troops in Europe, compared to 175,000 the previous December. By July, that had increased to one million men. That month, nine American divisions under French command faced the German First, Third, Seventh and Ninth Armies at the River Marne. The ensuing battle, which ended in the allies' favour, saw the end of the series of German offensives on the Western Front.

On 8th August 1918 the allies, including troops from the American 33rd Division, launched their own major offensive at Amiens. It was to be the defining point of the war and resulted in the German army being pushed out of France and the signing of the Armistice the following November. By then the number of American troops in France had reached 1.8 million men.

With the war over, the awards commenced. Wagstaff became a Companion, Order of St Michael and St George (CMG) and was awarded the *Croix de Guerre* by both France and Belgium, together with the French *Commandeur Ordre de la Couronne* and the Order of the Crown of Italy, whilst his role in liaising with the American army resulted in the award of the American Distinguished Service Medal. Wagstaff remained as Liaison Officer to the American Expeditionary Force until April 1919, after which he returned to the War office. He later returned to India on secondment to the Indian Army and in October 1920 he was promoted to Brigadier General.

In 1925, Wagstaff returned to England to became a member of the General Staff at the War Office, and moved to Uxbridge. Sadly, the following year his wife, Rosabell, died from a brain haemorrhage. He remarried a year later, his new wife being the widow of a fellow army officer. In 1928, he returned to India again as commander of the Nowshera Brigade in the Northwest Frontier, an area which he knew well. Coming back to England after two years, he became a Companion of the Order of the Bath and was appointed Commandant of the Royal Military Academy at Woolwich. His last promotion, to the rank of, Major-General, took place in 1931.

Major-General Cyril Mosley Wagstaff CB CMG CIE DSO, died suddenly of a stroke in February 1934, aged 55. His funeral was held at St Mary's, Northchurch, where his body was laid to rest in the churchyard, close to the area when his first wife and other members of the Thelwall family were buried.

Stanley Reginald Waite (1897 – 1960)
Sapper 347609, 277th Railway Co, RE

Born in July 1897 at the family home in Thorn's Yard, Northchurch, Stanley Waite was Benjamin and Harriet Waite's fourth child. Stanley's father was a cowman from Garsington, Oxfordshire, whilst his mother came from Peckham Rye, south London. Although details of Stanley's life between the time he left school and when he joined the army are unknown, it is likely that he became a gardener, following his three older brothers into that profession. It appears that he did not stay long in Northchurch once he had completed his education, as he next appears in Scotland.

On 21st June 1915, two weeks before his 18th birthday, Stanley enlisted with 10th Battalion, Cameronians (Scottish Rifles) in Hamilton, a town 11 miles south-east of Glasgow. With his service record no longer in existence, the details of his subsequent time with the Scottish Rifles is unclear, but it is likely that he joined them in France sometime during the Somme Offensive and later participated in the fighting around Arras and Ypres in 1917. Stanley was probably wounded or had become sick, as that November he was back in Scotland and one of five soldiers transferred from the Scottish Rifles' 3rd (Reserve Battalion), based at Nigg, to the Royal Engineers railway depot at Longmoor. Only a few months earlier, his oldest brother, William, had been killed in Belgium[27].

By the spring of 1918, Stanley was serving with 277th Railway Company, near Steenwerck in Flanders. That April the Germans launched an offensive in the area where Stanley and his comrades were working and forced them to withdraw, loading up what equipment they could whilst destroying railway lines and bridges to hinder the enemy's advance. Later in the year, they built new railway infrastructure to support the British troops as the Germans were pushed back.

In April 1919, 277th Railway Company moved to Calais to build additional transit camps to hold soldiers awaiting their return to the UK and demobilisation. The Company's war diary ends in September 1919, so it is likely that Stanley returned to Great Britain at that point.

On 4th August 1920 and back in Scotland Stanley married Mary McFarland at Greenock. The following year, having spent six years 'in the colours', he joined the Reserves and in 1927, after serving twelve years as a soldier, he left the army, his discharge certificate describing him as '*Has been very good. He is sober, honest and hardworking*'.

Returning to Northchurch, Stanley and Mary moved to Rosemead in South Bank Road. They were to remain there for many years and Stanley became a local postman. Just before the outbreak of the Second World War he also took on the role of an ARP Warden in Berkhamsted. Stanley Waite died in 1960, aged 62.

William John Weedon (1883 – 1957)
Sapper 89897, 174th Tunnelling Company, RE

William Weedon was born in Berkhamsted in October 1883. At the time of his birth William's mother, Lizzie Weedon, was already an unmarried mother with one child and living with her parents at the *Kings Head* public house in Berkhamsted. William's apparent father was William Duncombe, whom Lizzie married in 1885. Sadly, Lizzie died in 1890 and William was subsequently brought up by his maternal aunt, Lucy, and her husband, Edward Jenks, a professional cricketer who lived in Walthamstow, north London.

By 1901 William and the Jenks family had moved south to Epsom, where Edward Jenks was a groundsman on a local golf course and eighteen-year-

---

[27] William Waite's story is told in *For Them's Sake*

old William had become an apprentice bricklayer. Five years later, William had left home and was back in Berkhamsted and still working as a bricklayer. Here he met Nellie Meager, the sister of Northchurch bricklayers Harry and Fred Meager, and they were married in St Mary's, Northchurch in the summer of 1906. The couple later moved to a cottage in Northchurch High Street where, over the next few years, Nellie gave birth to four children, although one died in infancy.

William's service record has not survived, but from his medal record it is known that he enlisted with the Royal Engineers in early 1915 and arrived in France on 18th October that year, leaving a pregnant wife awaiting the birth of another child.

In 1918, William was serving with 174th Tunnelling Company, Royal Engineers. Members of tunnelling companies were often moved between units and no doubt he had been a member of one or more during his time in France, where his bricklaying skills would have been put to good use.

The first tunnelling companies had already been formed by the time William arrived in France in October 1915 and by the middle of 1916, some 25,000 men were employed in various aspects of the work. William would not have been digging the tunnels as such, but would have been kept busy using his skills securing entrances, shafts and other key parts with bricks.

It was not long before a new front opened underground, where opposing teams of tunnellers suddenly came face to face when breaking into each other's tunnels. The effectiveness of tunnelling was proven in June 1917, when some 958,000lbs of high explosive were detonated in 22 tunnels under the German defences on Messines Ridge. The resulting blast was said to have been heard in London, and was recorded on a seismograph in Switzerland. Some 10,000 Germans were subsequently listed as missing or killed with a further 7,000 surrendering soon after the blast. The territory formerly occupied by the Germans now consisted of a series of deep craters and was occupied by British troops in less than three hours.

It is likely that William was serving with 174th Tunnelling Company in March 1918 when the Germans launched their Spring Offensive. At the time his company was working on machine-gun emplacements at Bullecourt and suffered severe casualties during the onslaught whilst fighting as emergency infantry. Fortunately, William appears to have escaped uninjured.

He was demobilised in May 1919 and returned home to Northchurch. He resumed his work as a bricklayer and in 1939 was living in Granville Road, Northchurch. The following year, his son, Harold, enlisted with the army and later saw service in North Africa, Sicily and Normandy. He was tragically killed during an attack on German positions in Normandy on 9th August 1944[28]. William remained at Granville Road for the rest of his life. He died in 1957, aged 74.

---

[28] Harold Weedon's story is told in *For Them's Sake*

11 – The Army Ordinance Corps

The Army Ordnance Corps dates to the time of King Henry V, who in 1414, a year before the Battle of Agincourt, authorised the creation of the Office of Master of Ordnance, based at the Tower of London. The Master of Ordnance was the King's military treasurer and paymaster and was also responsible for the supply of gunpowder and other weapons to the English Army. Over the next five hundred years it underwent numerous reorganisations and name changes, before becoming the Army Ordnance Corps (AOC) in 1896.

By 1914 the AOC was responsible for the procurement, storage and issue of items to the army, ranging from personal equipment, armaments, small arms ammunition and artillery shells through to the provision of armoured vehicles.

Those serving in the AOC were mainly at the upper end of the age limit for servicemen, or deemed unsuitable for frontline duties due to being given a low medical classification. Additionally, the AOC also needed men with good administrative and financial skills such as bank clerks, and those with specialist skills needed to maintain military equipment in the field, such as wheelwrights, engineers and carpenters.

Frederick William Foskett (1880 - 1974)
Lance Corporal 21811, 20th Company, AOC

Frederick Foskett was nearly 36 years old when he was conscripted in the summer of 1916. A father of two children, he had followed his father, Alfred's, profession after leaving school and became a carpenter. In 1896 Alfred Foskett died and Frederick's mother, Catherine, moved from their home in Potten End, where he was born, to a four-roomed cottage in Eddy Street, Gossoms End. To bring in money to raise her family Catherine began taking in washing.

By 1901, Frederick had enhanced his skills as a carpenter and was working locally as a shaft maker. Later he became a coachbuilder's mate and by 1913 he had joined the local branch of the Amalgamated Society of Carpenters & Joiners. The previous December, he had married Lily Elizabeth Hoare at St Mary's, Northchurch. She came from Hounslow and worked as a parlour maid for a Mr Stephenson at one of the large houses off Gravel Path, Berkhamsted, and by February 1916, they were the proud parents of two children.

Frederick's service record has not survived, but in the 1918 Berkhamsted Absent Voters List he is recorded as serving with 20th Company, AOC. By the time of his demobilisation towards the end of 1919 he had been appointed Lance Corporal.

On his return home, Frederick resumed his civilian job as a carpenter. Just before the outbreak of the Second World War he was working as a wheelwright and still living in Gossoms End. He died in 1955, aged 74.

Richard John Grace (1887 – 1969)
Private 18779, Army Ordnance Corps

Richard Grace was born in June 1887 in George Street, Berkhamsted, in what was then in the eastern part of Northchurch Parish. His father, William, worked at the William Cooper & Nephew chemical factory in nearby Manor Street. Christened the following October, the record of the event is recorded at both St Mary's, Northchurch, and its daughter church, St Michael's and All Angels, Sunnyside, which was much closer to Richard's home. One of eleven children, by 1901 Richard and his family had moved to larger accommodation in nearby Ellesmere Road.

In January 1908, aged 21, Richard married Laura Bignell, the daughter of one of his father's workmates at Coopers. Laura would give birth to a girl later that year and two more children would follow over the next three years. The 1911 Census shows Richard as living by himself in Harrow Weald and working as a golf caddy on a local golf course. It is not clear where Laura and the children were living at this time.

During the war Richard served overseas with the AOC, but no further details are currently known, except that he was not demobilised until 1920. By then, Laura and the three children had moved to a terraced house in Alma Road, Northchurch, close to her parents, and this remained the family home for at least the next ten years. In 1939, with all their children now married and moved away, Richard and Laura were living in nearby Seymour Road and he was working as a gardener. Richard Grace died in 1969, aged 82.

Frederick John Howard (1891 – 1960)
Private 19297, Ordnance Officer Docks, AOC

Frederick Howard was serving with the AOC in France in 1918. Little is known about his early life, except that his mother was Alice Howard, an unmarried mother, and that he was born in the St Pancras Workhouse in June 1891. Later becoming a gardener, by 1914 he had moved to Northchurch and was probably working at one of the large houses in the area. Two days after the outbreak of war, Frederick married Margaret Halsey at St Mary's, Northchurch. She was a local parlour maid, whose family lived opposite the church in Northchurch Terrace on the High Street.

Unfortunately, Frederick's service record has not survived, so it is unclear when he joined the AOC. In the 1918 Northchurch Absent Voters List, he is shown as serving in France in a section called Ordnance Officer, Docks. As such he would have been working at one or more of the ordnance base depots which operated from Boulogne, Calais, Le Havre and Rouen. At these ports, goods arriving in bulk from Great Britain were broken down into smaller units and then either put into store for later allocation to the troops, or immediately shipped inland by road or rail. The base depots were also the place where damaged equipment was returned, either for repair at the local workshops, or prepared for shipment back to Great Britain. When repair was not practicable, any salvageable items were removed and put in store for later use.

Following his demobilisation, Frederick returned home and resumed his job as a gardener. Initially living in Norris's Terrace in Gossoms End, he and Margaret later moved into the Halsey family home in Northchurch Terrace. By 1939, they had moved to one of the recently-built semi-detached houses at the Northchurch end of Bridgewater Road. Frederick Howard died in 1960, aged 69.

12 – The Army Service Corps

The Army Service Corps (ASC) dates to 1794 with the formation of the Corps of Wagoners. In August 1914 the Corps consisted of 498 officers and 5,900 other ranks and was made up of three main sections – the Horse Transport Division, the Military Transport Division and the Supply Division. All were responsible for getting supplies to the troops in the field except for ammunition, which fell under the remit of the Army Ordnance Corps. The ASC also provided drivers of both horse-drawn and motorised transport to other parts of the army, ranging from field ambulances to heavy artillery tractors.

George Bedford (1889 – 1960)
Private 133679, 151st Brigade, ASC

Although not a member of the Royal Garrison Artillery, George Bedford served with 151st Brigade in their Motor Transport Section responsible for hauling the heavy guns.

He was born in Berkhamsted in September 1889. His father, also named George, was a gardener, but later became a successful coal merchant in the area. His mother, Louisa, originally came from Lakenham, Norfolk, and later ran a grocer's shop at Dudswell Wharf and it is here that George started his working life.

It is not known when he volunteered to join the army as his service record has not survived, but his medal record shows that he arrived in France as an artillery driver in November 1915. By then, alternatives to using horses and steam-driven tractors to haul heavy artillery over rough and muddy ground were being investigated. Steam-driven traction engines had the major disadvantage that the steam coming from their funnel could be clearly seen from enemy observation positions and were consequently prone to frequent artillery attacks. Looking for less identifiable alternatives, the War Office purchased an American-built Holt tractor for evaluation. It proved a success, hauling heavy artillery at a speed of 2mph over difficult terrain. Popularly known as 'cats', after their caterpillar tracks,

Holt Artillery Tractor
Author's collection

numerous Holt tractors were later purchased from the Americans by the War Office. George Bedford was the driver of one of the Holt tractors used by 151st Siege Battery to haul their 8ins guns.

In 1917, whilst on a few days' home leave back in Dudswell, he married Rose Hewlett, a domestic servant working for a family in Cowper Road, Berkhamsted. After his demobilisation in 1919, he went back to work at his mother's greengrocery store, and later became a market gardener.

George's wife gave birth to their only child in 1921 and they named him Donald George. Just after the start of the Second World War they were all living is a cottage in Dudswell.

Tragedy struck the Bedford family in 1946, a few days after Donald Bedford had returned from the war. He had served with the Royal Air Force during the war as a radio and radar mechanic and was a keen motorcycle enthusiast. To celebrate his return, George had bought Donald a new motorcycle, but a few weeks later he was tragically killed whilst riding it near the village of Ivinghoe[29]. George Bedford died in 1960, aged 70.

John Belshaw (1892 – 1960)
Private 08900, 615 Motor Transport Division, ASC
Robert Belshaw (1893 – 1961)
Private 09383, Unknown Motor Transport Unit, ASC

John Belshaw, the first son of John Belshaw and his wife, Grace, was born in Dublin in January 1892. The family moved to Carlow, County Carlow soon after John's birth, and after his father's early death he helped bring in money to support his mother. By 1911, John was the main breadwinner for the family, earning his living as a bicycle mechanic.

John's service record has not survived, but like his younger brothers, Thomas, Robert and Gilbert, it is likely that he was still living in Carlow in August 1914. His medal card however, shows that John arrived in France on 4th October 1914, which may indicate that either he was already a member of the reserves when war broke out, or that his engineering skills made him a natural recruit for the ASC. Little is known about his subsequent war service except that he is shown in the 1918 Northchurch Absent Voters List as serving with 615 Motor Transport Division in Dublin.

By the spring of 1918, John's mother had left Carlow and moved to a cottage in New Road, Northchurch, and this is where he and his brothers later returned after demobilisation. John did not stay in Northchurch long however, as by 1921 he had moved to West Ham, London where here he later married Sophia Margaret Maslen. They would go on to raise two children together.

---

[29] Donald Bedford's story is told in *For Them's Sake*

In 1939, John was still living in West Ham with his family and working as a motorcycle engineer. He died in 1960, aged 67.

John's younger brother, Robert, was born in Dublin exactly eighteen months after him. By 1911, he was also working as a bicycle mechanic, probably alongside John. Robert also joined the ASC soon after the outbreak of the war and was sent to France on 14th November 1914. His service record has also not survived, but the 1918 Absent Voters List shows him as serving with a Motor Transport Division in London. After being demobilised, Robert resumed his occupation as an engineer and in 1920 he married Annie James in Southwark. Robert Belshaw died in Barnet in 1961, aged 67.

Oswald Blount (1879 – 1971)
Captain, ASC

Oswald Blount was the first of George Bouverie Blount's sons not to be given the first name of George, nor did he pursue a military career on leaving school. Born in October 1879 at the family home in Belvedere, Kent, Oswald was educated at the Grange Preparatory School in Eastbourne and later at Malvern College.

On leaving Malvern in 1897, Oswald started work in the City of London, and in 1902, in partnership with three other people who had set up an office in Old Broad Street, he applied to join the London Stock Exchange as a stockbroker. Whilst working in London Oswald continued to live at the Northchurch Rectory, where his ageing mother and other family members were now living, and travelling to London each day from Berkhamsted by train. It appears that Oswald was also a keen follower of the Berkhamsted and Lord Rothschild's staghounds, riding with them regularly until 1914.

Oswald did not join the rush to enlist in August 1914 and continued working as a stockbroker in the City. It was not until July 1915, aged 35, that he decided apply for a temporary commission with the ASC. Among the personal references on his application form was that of Rossway owner, Major-General Sir Charles Frederick Hadden. His commission confirmed, Oswald arrived at Aldershot to start his training and was later posted to 33rd Divisional Train based at Bulford Camp on Salisbury Plain. Each Division of the army had its own transport, which was normally horse-drawn, and called a Divisional Train. Its usual complement was 26 officers and 402 other ranks who were responsible for 378 horses, 17 carts, 125 wagons and 30 bicycles.

In November 1915, 33rd Divisional Train was reorganised and all its horses were replaced by mules. Three months later they were told to prepare to move to France and left Southampton for Le Havre on 20th March 1916 on board two ships, the SS *Inventor* and HMS *Bellerophon,* being renamed 29th Divisional Train on their arrival.

Two months later, the Divisional Train's mules were replaced by horses and preparations began in building up substantial stores ready for the Somme Offensive. On the first day of the offensive however, the Divisional Train was forced to take on a new, unexpected, role; instead of bringing up supplies, the high casualty rate among the attacking British troops meant that their wagons were used as emergency ambulances to evacuate the wounded soldiers away from the battlefield.

The constant strain put on the Divisional Train's horses at the start of the Offensive soon became apparent; within three weeks they were totally exhausted and the unit was transferred north to Poperinghe for a period of recovery. They returned to the Somme sector three months later, but the arrival of early winter weather turned the ground to mud, making it hazardous for the horses to bring up supplies. After a further two months in appalling conditions, the Divisional Train was once again moved to a rest area and, with temperatures regularly falling below zero, this led to many soldiers serving in the front line facing delays in receiving their supplies.

April 1917 saw Oswald and the Divisional Train move north again to Arras. As with the Somme Offensive, supplying the troops in the field during a major offensive was a tortuous process, with the troops and horses of the Divisional Train frequently coming under fire. Even when out of the front line, shelling by long-range German artillery caused havoc, especially when shells landed close to the vicinity where horses were being stabled.

In June 1917, Oswald was appointed acting Captain and took temporary command of No3 Company and in the process acquired a staff car, but not for long, as within days a transfer to No1 Company was approved. Moving to 'International Corner', north-east of Ypres, and close to the junction of the British and Belgium Army lines, No1 Company prepared to supply the troops during the opening days of what was to become the Third Battle of Ypres.

In February 1918, Oswald took command of No4 Company. Over the coming months the Divisional Train would be responsible for the supply and feeding of up to 20,000 men. In September 1918 he became an acting supply officer and transferred to 3rd Cavalry Reserve Park, a series of supply units at the disposal of the BEF's General Headquarters, as opposed to specific divisions. A month later he was granted leave and was still in England when the Armistice was signed. He rejoined his unit in France on 20th November.

Returning to England in January 1919 following his demobilisation, Oswald was given the honorary rank of Captain. With the death of his mother in 1916, the remaining members of the Blount family had now moved from Northchurch Rectory and were living at The Wolds, a large detached property close to Tring Station. In 1920, having taken some time off, Oswald renewed his membership of the London Stock Exchange and resumed his job as a stockbroker. Being so close to the railway station at Tring made commuting to his office in the City of London particularly easy.

In 1937, by now retired, and no doubt using much of the monies earned from stockbroking, Oswald, purchased Woughton House, a large, early Victorian mansion with over sixty acres of land at Woughton on the Green, near Bletchley, Buckinghamshire. Here, he started to breed and show horses. Oswald's younger brother, Major-General Harold Blount, joined him there after his retirement from the Royal Marines the following year. Oswald never married and continued to live at Woughton House until his death in 1971, aged 91.

William Broyd (1885 – 1939)
Private R/390956, Remounts Service, ASC

William Broyd was born during the early winter of 1885 in the village of Finchingfield on the Essex/Hertfordshire border where his father, John, worked on a local farm as a blacksmith. He grew up in Essex and later became a groom. In due course he found work in the Northchurch area, probably at one of the large houses, and in 1910 he married Emily Parsley in St Mary's, Northchurch. They later set up home in a cottage in Orchard End, where Emily would subsequently give birth to two children.

William's service record has not survived, but it is known that on 30th August 1915 he enlisted with the ASC, which, making use of his occupation as a groom, posted him to the ASC's Remounts Service at Swaythling, just north of Southampton.

The Remounts Service was responsible for the supply of horses and mules to all units of the British Army. Initially four remount depots were set up at Woolwich, Dublin, Melton Mowbray in Leicestershire and Arborfield in Berkshire. As the war progressed the demand for horses and mules continued to grow and they were compulsorily purchased from owners across the country, or purchased from countries like Spain, Portugal and even as far away as the Americas, India and China. With the never-ending demand for horses, new remount depots began to be set up close to the major ports. The new depot at Shirehampton trained horses arriving at Avonmouth, the depot at Romsey trained those arriving at Southampton, and the depot at Ormskirk trained those arriving at Liverpool. Prior to being shipped overseas however, the trained animals were sent to the main collection centre at Swaythling, where William was posted. An edition of *The Times* in April 1919 stated that since being set up this depot had received 342,020 horses and mules, many of them having come from the United States.

William remained at Swaythling until he was demobilised and returned to his home in Northchurch, resuming his job as a groom. He died in 1939, aged 55.

Horace William Bruton (1893 – 1967)
Driver T4/038041, 25th Divisional Train, ASC

Horace Bruton was born in George Street, Berkhamsted in July 1893, the son of William Bruton, a carter working on a local farm, and his wife, Mary Ann. By 1905, the family were living in a cottage on Northchurch High Street. Horace's father later started working for the Barnett family who owned Northchurch Hall, a job which came with a rent-free home at Dropshort Cottage on Tring Road, Northchurch, together with free wood, coal and milk. Dropshort Cottage dated from the 18th century, and was so-named as it was built by Thomas Smart, the then owner of the local Norcott Court estate, as a private waiting room for the stagecoach that travelled through Northchurch. After leaving school Horace also started working for the Barnett family as one of the gardeners and later, as their chauffeur.

Horace, now aged 21, was not one of the men who immediately volunteered on the outbreak of war, waiting a few weeks before travelling to Watford to enlist. The morning that he enlisted there was a call for horse drivers, and he and seven others immediately signed up with the ASC. Horace was sent to Woolwich where he had his medical examination, which recorded him as being 5ft 6ins tall, weighing 137lbs and in good physical condition. He remained there until the end of September 1915 when he travelled to Bournemouth to join 25th Division, distinguished by the red horseshoe in the centre of its badge, which was preparing to depart for France. He

Private Horace Bruton
Courtesy of Sylvia Odell

landed at Le Havre on 26th September 1915 as part of 4 Coy, 25th Divisional Train, 25th Division, in charge of two horses.

Horace's first impressions of France were not great. In a talk he gave about his wartime experiences some 25 years later, he explained that it was pouring with rain when 25th Division landed, and everybody and everything seemed miserable as the men made their way to their tented camp where they would stay before moving inland. At 03:00 the following morning he and his mates were up and happy to leave their tents, which were now surrounded by mud. Driving the horses of the Divisional Train down the cobbled streets, Horace was surprised to find that, even then, the French drove on the opposite side of the streets to England. Added to this, when in convoy formation there was the constant need to keep five yards' distance from the wagon in front. Constant unplanned stops, especially in the dark, often resulted in the wagon pole between the front set of horses hitting the rear of the wagon in front and incurring the wrath of the unit's sergeant major.

The unit then travelled inland via railway to Hazebrouck. Loaded into carriages labelled *8 Chevaux, 40-5 Hommes* Horace discovered that four horses were placed at each end of the carriage facing each other, which was different from the English system, where all the horses were placed side by side. The four drivers, together with the horses' harnesses and other kit, had to fit in the middle of the carriage between the two rows of horses, which Horace found particularly cramped. One of his mates was accidentally knocked out during the journey, when a horse's hoof hit his head.

On his arrival at Hazebrouck, some ten miles from the front line, Horace could immediately hear the guns firing and see flashes in the sky caused by the exploding shells. The unit moved on to Ploegsteert, close to Armentières, where it remained over a very uncomfortable winter living under canvas, whilst the horses were left out in the open standing in mud up to their hocks.

The two horses for which Horace was initially responsible were called 'Sandy' and 'Mary' and he described them as a hard-working pair, often coming to the rescue of other wagons that needed recovery. Unfortunately, some two years after arriving in France one, of 'Mary's' legs was hit by a piece of shrapnel and she had to be shot. 'Sandy' survived for longer, but eventually fell ill.

25th Division first saw major action at Vimy Ridge in May 1916 and later supplied the troops throughout the Somme Offensive. Horace simply described this period in his talk as "*It was in the Somme that we had the most shell fire and there were some exciting moments*". He was awarded the Good Conduct Medal at the end of 1916 and on 24th January 1917, he was appointed an Acting Lance Corporal. During 1917, his Divisional Train supplied the troops during the Battle of Messines and later during the Third Battle of Ypres.

By the spring of 1918 Horace had become a Lance Corporal. His Divisional Train had been in the Bapaume area since the previous November and now faced the full force of the German Spring Offensive. Supplying the troops during the ensuing chaos proved particularly difficult, especially when horses and their drivers were frequently split up, so both horses and drivers had to get used to working in new teams. It was not until the early autumn that his unit was in a fit state to rejoin the line.

At the end of October 1918 Horace fell ill with influenza and was admitted to hospital at Rouen. Invalided back to England early the following month, he found himself lying on a stretcher on a railway platform along with dozens of wounded soldiers. He was then put on a train, purportedly to be sent to a convalescence hospital located close to his home. After a lengthy journey, he arrived in Sunderland and was taken to one of the Voluntary Aid Detachment hospitals in the town, where he remained until early January 1919, when he was discharged and took a train south to Berkhamsted station.

He then made his way to his parents' cottage. He was one of the first Northchurchmen to return home.

Horace went back to his old job as gardener and chauffeur for the Barnett family at Northchurch Hall, living in one of the six tied cottages on the opposite side of the High Street from the Hall. Early the following year he married Alice Roff and set up home in a cottage in Northchurch High Street, where Alice gave birth to a boy in 1922. Horace later became the head gardener at Northchurch Hall and by 1939 he was living with his family in Darrs Lane, Northchurch. He died in 1967 aged 74.

Bertie Bryant (1892 – 1954)
Private T4/107973, 52nd Division Military Transport Company, ASC

Bertie Bryant, a coal carter, was born in Gossoms End in April 1892, the third son of John Bryant, a platelayer with the London & North Western Railway, and his wife Ellen.

Soon after the outbreak of war, he enlisted with the ASC as a driver, putting his skills in driving horse-drawn coal carts to good use. Unfortunately, Bertie's service record has not survived, but it is known that the unit in which he served arrived in France in June 1915. In the 1918 Northchurch Absent Voters List, Bertie is shown as serving in 52nd Division Military Transport Company, a unit based at Aldershot. How long he had been allocated to this unit, and why he had returned from France, is however, not known. He was demobilised in August 1919 and returned to Gossoms End.

Three years later, he married Alice Williams, and the newlyweds set up home in Queens Road, Berkhamsted. By now he had followed his father's profession and joined the London & North Western Railway as a lengthsman, responsible for maintaining a section of railway track in the local area. Shortly after the birth of a daughter, they moved to a house in Cross Oak Road. Bertie Bryant died in 1954, aged 62.

Frank Honor (1891 – 1952)
Private M/379992, Unknown Mechanical Transport Unit, ASC

Like Fred Carter, Frank Honor decided to join the Norfolk Regiment soon after the outbreak of war. Frank was born in December 1891, and was the son of bricklayer, and later roadman, Frederick Honor and his wife Ann. He grew up in the family home in Orchard End, and was one of eight children. After finishing his schooling, Frank became a general labourer and remained so until enlisting with the Norfolk Regiment in 1914.

Frank's medal card shows that he joined the Norfolk's 7th Battalion, the same as Fred Carter, and left England for France in 1915 on board the SS

Invicta. Although his service record no longer exists, Frank's time with the Norfolk's would have followed that of Fred Carter up to the end of 1917 and the Battle of Cambrai. Thereafter their paths diverged as, in February 1918, Frank is recorded as being one of numerous infantrymen from various regiments being transferred to the ASC. Although the rationale for these transfers has not been identified, it is possible that the men involved may have been deemed unable to continue in a fighting role and transferred to support units. His new service number indicates that Frank joined a mechanical transport unit, although unfortunately no further information can be found.

He was demobilised in April 1919 and returned to the family home in Northchurch. The following year, however, he had moved to Watford, where he remained for the rest of his life, becoming an engineer with the London, Midland & Scottish Railway. Frank never married and died in 1952, aged 60.

William Culshaw (1884 – 1956)
Private M2/183371, 776th Mechanical Transport Company, ASC

As was the case for many other young men living in and around Northchurch in 1914, it was work that brought Lancashire-born William Culshaw to the area. He was born in early 1884 in the village of Haskayne in the parish of Downholland, twelve miles north of Liverpool. Both his father, James, a farm labourer, and his mother, Margaret, came from Downholland. James died in 1890, aged just 32, leaving his widow to bring up her three children with the help of William's grandmother.

On leaving school, William started work as a stable boy, and by 1901 and aged 17, he was working for the Revd. Thomas Blundell at the Rectory at nearby Halsall. Sometime later, he left Lancashire and moved south in search of work. By 1911, he was lodging in Ellesmere Road, Berkhamsted and working as a domestic groom.

Around that time, William met Elsie May Daniels, who was born in Chelsea and after leaving school had entered service. In 1911, she was employed as a housemaid for a wealthy family living in Bournemouth, and presumably later moved to Berkhamsted to work for a new employer. They were married at St Michael's, Sunnyside, on Christmas Day 1914.

William attested under the Derby Scheme in November 1915, by which time Elsie was pregnant with their first child. Details of his military service are unclear, but it is known that in 1918 he is shown in the Absent Voters List as serving with 776th Mechanical Transport Company. This was a unit based in the Chatham area, and it appears that he did not serve overseas. This is borne out by Elsie giving birth to a second child in the late spring of 1918, by which time she had moved to a cottage in River Terrace, Gossoms End.

William was demobilised in June 1919 and returned home. He and Elsie were to have two more children over the coming years and by 1939, the family had moved to a larger house in Granville Road, Northchurch. By then he was working as a motor driver and salesman. William Culshaw died in 1956, aged 72.

Bert Davis (1887 – 1975)
Private M2/181142, Motor Transport Unit, ASC

Bert Davis was born in May 1887 in Little Heath, in the eastern part of Northchurch Parish, where his father, Joseph, worked as a farm labourer. By 1911, the Davis family had moved to a house in George Street, Berkhamsted and in the Census taken that year, his occupation is described as 'gentleman's servant and gardener', possibly for Charles Dealtry Locock. Charles Locock owned one of the large houses in Kings Road, Berkhamsted and was a famous literary scholar and writer on the games of chess and billiards and the editor of the croquet magazine *The Handicapper*. Later in 1911, Bert married Alice Hicks, who worked as a parlour maid for the Locock family.

Although Bert's service record has not survived, the fact that he joined the ASC as a driver would indicate that his duties as a 'gentleman's servant' may have included that of chauffeur. In 1918, Bert was serving with 51st Auxiliary Bus Company in France. This unit was formed in England in April 1915 as 339 Company ASC, which was part of 22nd Division. When 22nd Division's infantry was later sent to Salonika, Bert's unit was renamed 51st Auxiliary Bus Company and sent to France.

During the war over 1,000 London buses were requisitioned by the army and sent to France to transport British troops over long distances. Most of these buses were AEC 'B-Type' vehicles and gained the nickname of 'Old Bill' after Bruce Bairnsfather's cartoon character. Originally still in their red livery, the buses were soon repainted in British khaki green and their glass windows replaced by wooden boards. The upper deck, reached by semi-circular steps, remained open to the elements. As such, the vehicles could carry 24 fully-equipped infantrymen, but this number

B-Type Buses in army service
Author's collection

was often exceeded. Normally travelling in convoys at night to avoid detection, the buses transported fresh troops to the front and returned with sick, wounded and weary soldiers.

In January 1917, whilst Bert was serving with the unit, 51st Auxiliary Bus Company had at least 40 'B-type' buses in regular use transporting troops of the British 3rd Army in the area to the north of Amiens. According to the unit's War Diary that month, their vehicles covered a total of 39,555 miles alone and carried 25,991 troops, using 11,876 gallons of petrol in the process. The following month, some of 51st Company's 'B-type' buses were replaced by multi-purpose 3-ton Daimler lorries and 4 charabancs.

May 1917 saw the unit move north to the west of Ypres, ready to transport troops about to take part in the Third Battle of Ypres. Returning to the Somme Sector the following autumn, 51st Company ferried soldiers westwards during the chaotic fall-back of the troops during the German Spring Offensive the following year. As a result of their swift action, their commanding officer received a letter stating that *"The General Staff, GHQ wishes to express to all Ranks of the Bus Park their admiration and thanks for the work done during the past 10 days. It has been of vital importance"*. Several of Bert's comrades were later awarded the Military Medal for their efforts. A further congratulatory letter was received the following May, this time from Field Marshal Haig, the Commander in Chief of the British Army, thanking the unit for their efforts since March 1918.

After the success of the Battle of Amiens in August 1918, 51st Company's vehicles began ferrying British troops eastwards across France as they started to drive the Germans back, travelling over 86,400 miles that month alone. The following month, with the German army now in full retreat, this increased to over 99,400 miles.

With the war over, the unit continued to ferry troops across France, but this time in a westerly direction, bringing them back to the transit camps on the Channel coast to await demobilisation and their return home.

After his own demobilisation, Bert and Alice moved to Potten End and Bert soon found work as a chauffeur in the area. He died in 1975, aged 88.

Albert Stanley Dealey (1890 – 1961)
Private M2/202962, MT Unit, ASC

Albert Dealey was born in November 1890 in Northchurch, where his father, also called Albert, worked as a house painter. The family lived in a cottage on the High Street, next door to his grandfather, George Dealey, a farm worker.

By 1911, Albert had started work as a boot repairer and postman. The following year, he married Amy Saunders and settled in a cottage in Gossoms End. Within three years they were proud parents of two children with Albert now running a small motor-cycle and cycle agency in Gossoms End.

In the summer of 1916, when Amy was pregnant once again, Albert was conscripted and reported to the Recruiting Centre at Aylesbury. Declared unfit to serve in the infantry, Arthur, wanting to use his experience working with motor-cycles, expressed a wish to join the Motor Transport section of the ASC.

After his initial army training, he was posted to 67th Auxiliary (Steam) Company, ASC, whose unit badge was a kettle boiling over a camp fire. Formed in November 1916, 67th Auxiliary (Steam) Company, despite its name, did not solely use steam-driven vehicles, and while it was based at Bulford Camp on Salisbury Plain its fleet consisted of thirty Foden steam wagons with tipper body, three 3-ton American Peerless lorries used as support vehicles, a Vauxhall motor car and a Douglas motorcycle. According to his service record Albert was a petrol lorry driver, who required significantly different skills from those of a steam wagon driver. About 12,000 of the American-built Peerless lorries were purchased by the British Army in 1915 to supplement the limited number of home-built lorries, and used them for a variety of purposes. The three belonging to 67th Steam Auxiliary Company were a workshop lorry, a general service lorry and a field kitchen. When not driving one of the Peerless lorries, Albert also acted as the despatch rider for his unit using the Douglas motorcycle.

His unit left Bulford Camp on 8th June 1917 for Portsmouth, where it boarded the SS *Hunsgate*. Upon arrival at Rouen, they were attached to 2nd Army. Six days later, the unit left for Mont St Eloi, near Arras, their route there being primarily dictated by the availability of rivers or streams to refill the water tanks of the Foden steam wagons. Its role in the area was to supply material and equipment to the soldiers responsible for keeping the roads in a decent state of repair.

The following month, Albert and his company moved north to Poperinghe, ready to supply the troops preparing to take part in the Third Battle of Ypres, but with the Foden's giveaway plumes of steam and smoke it was not surprising that on 29th August a German air attack resulted in the loss of several vehicles, though, fortunately, without any casualties. Around this time several Sentinel and Garrett steam wagons were also acquired by the unit to supplement the Fodens.

Albert was to remain with his unit in the Ypres area for the rest of the war. The signing of the Armistice in November 1918 made little difference to their daily work as the material to repair the roads still needed to be brought up from the depots.

In January 1919, whilst he was on home leave in Gossoms End, Albert's demobilisation came through. He quickly restarted his motorcycle business, and in 1923 he purchased a larger showroom at 61 Gossoms End. On the adjacent land he built a new garage, where repairs were undertaken. The business thrived, and after his retirement it continued to be run by his two sons. Albert Dealey died in December 1961, aged 71. The motor repair business he founded finally closed in 1986.

William Fay (1881 – 1956)
Private M2/184254, 739th Motor Transport Company, ASC

William Fay was born in Paddington, London in August 1881, four years before Karl Benz built his first motor vehicle in Germany. His first job after leaving school appears to be that of copper machinist, but, excited by the growing number of motor vehicles appearing on the roads, he decided to learn to drive. By 1911 he had obtained work as a chauffeur for the George family who owned Lagley, located between Gossoms End and Northchurch, and was living with his wife, Susan, whom he had married in 1908, above the garages there. Three years later, having become parents, they moved to larger accommodation in Shrublands Avenue, Berkhamsted.

William's military service record has not survived, but the 1918 Absent Voters List shows him as serving with 739th Motor Transport Company, ASC. This unit was formed in July 1916 specifically to provide motorised transport for 127th Siege Battery RGA, which served in Salonika. William would therefore have been one of the military truck drivers supplying the siege battery's four 6-inch howitzers and driving for hours across the difficult terrain in the area.

After his demobilisation in the summer of 1919, William returned to Berkhamsted, but by then his employer at Lagley had died. It appears that he soon found another employer and 20 years later he was still working as a chauffeur in the area, supplementing his income with occasional gardening work. The Fay family continued to live in Shrublands Avenue until 1929 before moving to nearby Charles Street. William died in 1956. Aged 75.

Thomas Graham (1876 – 1927)
Private T/440683, Horse Transport, ASC

Thomas Graham, a roadman working for Hertfordshire County Council, attested under the Derby Scheme in December 1915, giving his age as 39 years and 9 months. This may have had a bearing on the fact that it was not until 17th September 1918, with the war nearing its end, that he was finally mobilised. He was born in the spring of 1876 in the small Hertfordshire village of Sarratt, and his parents, George and Jane Graham, moved to Northchurch whilst Thomas was still an infant. In July 1881, five-year-old Thomas was christened at St Mary's, Northchurch, along with his four brothers and sisters.

In 1901, the extended Graham family occupied three four-roomed cottages on New Road, Northchurch. Thomas's elder brother, George, lived at No25 with his wife and young son, whilst another brother, Harry, lived at No26 with his wife. Thomas, now working as a carter, lived with his parents and five remaining siblings, including younger brother, Charles, at No27.

On 18th June 1910, he married 23-year-old Alice Maud Mary Spragg, and the couple set up home at No26 New Road, his brother and family having by then moved to nearby Alma Road. In 1911, Alice gave birth to a daughter with another daughter being born two years later. Their final child, another daughter, was born a few days after the Armistice was signed.

Thomas's medical, conducted at Watford in December 1915, stated that he stood 5ft 5½ins tall and weighed 128lbs and had brown hair. He was given the medical classification of 'B1', which was probably influenced by his age. In September 1918, following his mobilisation, Thomas reported to the Recruiting Officer at Hertford and was posted to 666 Coy ASC, a horse transport unit based at Park Royal, Willesden, West London. He remained there until January 1919, when he transferred to 407 Coy ASC at St Albans. Three months later, he was demobilised.

He returned to Northchurch, but it is currently not known what he subsequently did for a living. Thomas Graham died in 1927, aged just 51.

Alfred George Halsey (1890 – 1958)
Private M2/117142, Motor Transport Unit, ASC

Alfred Halsey was born in Northchurch in June 1890 and was the fourth child of George Halsey, a sawyer, and his wife, Elizabeth, both worshippers at the Baptist Chapel in Bell Lane. By 1901, George Halsey had changed occupations and now ran the small grocer's shop, known as Bell Lane Stores, on the corner of Bell Lane and Northchurch High Street with his family living in the rooms above the shop. His life as a grocer was not to last however, as by 1911 he was back in his old job as a sawyer and had moved to Northchurch Terrace, directly opposite St Mary's school. Alfred was still living at home and working as an apprentice motor mechanic.

He decided not to enlist when war broke out and it would be another twelve months before he decided to attest as a driver with the ASC at Grove Park, Lewisham. Alfred's service record indicates that he was initially posted to the Mediterranean Expeditionary Force, but it is unclear whether he joined them, as on 3rd February 1916, he arrived in France as a motor-cycle rider with the recently-formed 3rd Field Survey Company. The role of a field survey company was to survey and provide up-to-date, detailed, accurate maps for military use, especially as the Western Front had become an everchanging network of trench systems and fortified bunkers. Alfred's role was to transport the survey staff between locations as they recorded their readings, which would eventually lead to the production of detailed maps. His driving was not limited to motorcycles, however, and during this time with the unit he also drove their motor cars and 3-ton lorries. His driving skills were highly commended by one of the Field Survey Company's officers who wrote that he was *"... an excellent driver and keeps his car and engine in excellent condition"*.

In July 1918, Alfred became a lorry driver with 16th Division, which had suffered badly during the German Spring Offensive and was to remain with them until April 1919. A final transfer to 24th Coy, ASC took place that month before Alfred was demobilised.

Alfred returned home and, unsurprisingly, continued as a civilian lorry driver. In 1939 he was living in Berkhamsted High Street. He died in 1958, aged 67.

Edward James Mustill (1899 – 1994)
Private M/296074, Motor Transport Unit, ASC
Henry Herbert Mustill (1896 – 1938)
Private 4327, Expenses Store, ASC

Edward Mustill was 17 years and nine months old when he walked into the Recruiting Office in Queen's Road, Watford on 18th September 1916. As he was underage, Edward's details were recorded and he was told to return home. Born in January 1899, he was the last child of George and Florence Mustill. George was the lockkeeper at Lock 46 on the Grand Junction Canal at Cow Roast, just to the west of Northchurch. He died the year after Edward's birth, leaving his widow to bring up their children. To help make ends meet she started work as a water checker for a local mill owner. By 1911, Florence was working as a clerk at the mill and Edward and his older brother, Henry, were the only boys still living at home; another of her sons, George, was now serving in the army. Soon after leaving school Edward had become a printer's apprentice at the *Bucks Herald* in Aylesbury.

Three months after attempting to sign-up, Edward's conscription papers arrived and he was posted to the ASC depot at Isleworth in West London to train as a lorry driver. His training completed, he was attached to 52nd Anti-aircraft Company at Craigend Farm, Renfrew, Scotland. This was one of several anti-aircraft units located to the west of Glasgow to protect the city and the Clyde shipyards from aerial attack by German Zeppelin airships and Gotha bombers. In June 1918, he left Glasgow and was posted to 614 Mechanised Transport Company in Edinburgh.

Only six weeks later he was compulsorily transferred to the Royal West Kent Regiment as the army urgently needed replacements for the men lost during the German Spring Offensive. In the event Edward never was sent to France, as in December 1918 he contracted influenza and spent three weeks in a military hospital in Edmonton. Fortunately, he made a full recovery and in April 1919 he was demobilised and returned home.

By 1925, Edward had moved to Dunstable and in 1926 he married Fanny Elizabeth Poulton. It is uncertain whether he returned to printing after the war, for in 1939 he was working as a Furnishers Agent & Collector in

Dunstable and was one of the local ARP Wardens in the town. He died in 1994 aged 95.

Very little is known about Edward Mustill's older brother, Henry, who was also born at Cow Roast Lock in the autumn of 1896. By 1914 he had left home and moved to Southall, where he worked as a fishmonger for a Mr Smith in Clarence Street. On 8th September 1914 he volunteered at the Southall Recruiting Office and was posted to 8th Reserve Battalion, Middlesex Regiment. Oddly, Henry gave his age as 21 years and 10 months, when he was only just 18 years old. Described as being 5ft 6½ ins tall with fair vision it was the latter that prevented Henry from receiving an 'A' medical category.

No further information on his military service has been found, except that, as no medals were awarded to him, he did not serve overseas. In the 1918 Northchurch Absent Voters List, Henry is recorded as serving at the Expenses Store at Pitt Corner Camp on the outskirts of Winchester, which was the base of various branches of the army, including the Royal Garrison Artillery and the Army Veterinary Corps. That same year he married Phoebe Victoria Kathleen Jenvey, the daughter of a stone cutter, in Winchester.

He was demobilised early in 1919. Remaining in Winchester, over the next fifteen years Henry and Phoebe would raise six children together. Later becoming a school caretaker, Henry died in Winchester in September 1938, aged only 42.

William George Penn (1881 – 1941)
Temporary Squadron Sergeant Major, S/15062, ASC

The saying 'an army marches on its stomach' was particularly true in William Penn's case. For some 21 years he served in the ASC as a baker, feeding the troops, frequently under difficult, and often life-threatening, conditions. He was born in August 1881 in Shenley, Hertfordshire, where his father, also called William, worked as a groom. By 1891 the Penn family had moved to Berkhamsted, where William (snr) had obtained work as a coachman at Haresfoot, the home of the Smith Dorrien family, and William and his family were living in a cottage on the Haresfoot estate. At that time only the eldest child, Charles, was working, the other three siblings were still attending school.

William Jnr initially worked for Samuel Dickens, a baker and grocer in the village of Aldbury. After working there for several years, and in search of adventure, he decided to join the ACS. Consequently, in June 1899, aged eighteen and armed with a glowing reference from his employer, William enlisted in London for a period of eight years. His service record from that time shows him as being 5ft 4¾ins tall, weighing 116lbs and with a fair complexion, brown eyes and dark brown hair. Within six months of enlisting, he found himself posted abroad and baking bread for the British troops fighting in the Boer War in South Africa.

William and his unit returned to England following the defeat of the Boers and he no doubt took the opportunity to visit his parents, who had now moved to a small cottage in Bell Lane, Northchurch. His stay in England was to be short-lived, as within months of his return he was promoted to Lance Corporal and transferred to Gibraltar to help supply fresh bread to the garrison there. In July 1908 he became a Corporal and decided to extend his length of service by a further four years.

Following his return to England, William was promoted to Lance Sergeant and then Sergeant and it appears that he was enjoying his army life so much that in 1909 he decided to extend his length of service once again, this time to bring it to a total of 21 years. In 1910 he was transferred to Peking (now Beijing) as part of the guard at the British Legation in the city.

Great Britain was one of eleven countries represented in a three-acre site just outside the Chinese Imperial City, close to what is today's Tiananmen Square. Ten years before William's arrival it had been the site of the 'Boxer Rebellion', during which many of the buildings in the Legation Quarter had been destroyed. Following the failure of the rebellion, the Chinese were banned from living in the area and new fortified foreign embassies like the British Legation, each guarded by their own troops, were built to prevent any further uprisings. William was to remain in Peking until February 1915, rising to the rank of Squadron Quartermaster Sergeant.

On his return to England, he married Amy Riley at St John's, Potters Bar, and Amy moved to Northchurch to be closer to her new in-laws. William's stay in England was once again to be short-lived as three months later he found himself in the hellhole that was the Gallipoli Campaign. Still making bread to feed the troops, and under the direst of conditions, William was later 'Mentioned in Despatches' *"For consistent good work on the Gallipoli Peninsula from May to September 1915 when the depots and bakeries were repeatedly under shell fire"*. Evacuated to Egypt at the end of the campaign, he returned to England once more and he stayed there for the remainder of the war. Around this time, William's older brother, Charles, was wounded and captured by the Germans in France.

William was promoted to Warrant Officer in 1918. That same year, he became a father for the first time when Amy gave birth to a son. A second son was born the following year.

The running of the stores at Aldershot Barracks was to be his last role in the army. In July 1920 he was discharged, having served his desired 21 years of service for King and Country. A citation on his discharge papers described William as *"Exemplary. An efficient and capable Warrant Officer, tactful & discreet and with good control of men. He is thoroughly honest and trustworthy and has always given satisfaction"*.

In 1925, Amy gave birth to their last child, another boy. By this time the family had moved to nearby Guildford, with William still retaining his links with the army and working as a civilian storekeeper. William Penn died in 1941, aged 59.

Albert (Bertie) Pratt (1883 – 1976)
Private M2/184269, 1023rd Coy, Motor Transport Unit, ASC

Albert Pratt, known as Bertie, was born in Mortlake, Surrey, in September 1883 and was the eldest of eight children of Joseph Pratt, a cowman, and his wife, Sophia. Having completed his schooling, Bertie became a groom and when the Pratt family moved to Aston Clinton around 1900 he found work as a stable helper at Northchurch Hall. In 1911 he was living in a small two-roomed cottage on Northchurch High Street, which he shared with Herbert Waters, the Barnett family chauffeur at Northchurch Hall.

Bertie's service record has not survived, but according to the 1918 Northchurch Absent Voters List he served with 1023rd Coy ASC MT which was one of two units created in the autumn of 1917 to operate a supply column using versatile Ford 'Model T' vans in Mesopotamia. He would have sailed from Southampton in January 1918 on board the SS *Lydia* bound for Egypt, where the two ASC units transferred to HT *Aronda* which took them on to Basra.

Bertie and his colleagues spent the rest of the war in Mesopotamia working alongside Burmese troops who were performing a similar role. The dire state of the roads in the area meant that breakdowns of the unit's 'Model T' vans were commonplace, and the local repair workshops were constantly kept busy getting them back into service.

Following his demobilisation in January 1920, Bertie returned to Northchurch but whether he resumed his job at Northchurch Hall is currently unknown. By 1930 he had moved to Bovingdon, where he worked as a jobbing gardener. He died in 1976, aged 92.

Sidney A Redding (1885 – 1946)
Private S4/109506, Supply Depot, ASC

Sidney Redding was born in Berkhamsted in June 1885 to an unmarried mother, Selina Redding, from Ashley Green. Details of his early years are unclear, but on the night of the 1891 Census, aged 5, he was staying with his aunt and uncle in Northampton, but later returned to Berkhamsted. In 1888 his mother married Francis Draper and moved to a cottage in George Street. Sidney subsequently became a baker's assistant and within ten years he had become a qualified baker, working for the Berkhamsted Co-operative Society. In 1911 he was lodging in Gossoms End and the following year he married Mary Messenger, a domestic cook working for a family in Kitsbury Road, Berkhamsted.

Although Sidney's service record has not survived, it appears that he enlisted with the Bedfordshire Regiment following the outbreak of war and later transferred to the supply branch of the ASC. In July 1915 Sidney's unit was sent to Gallipoli, where it remained until being evacuated five long months later, and it is quite possible that he worked as a baker alongside William Penn. The conditions at Gallipoli meant that Sidney spent most of his time on the beaches, where the food supplies were stored in conditions ranging from extreme heat to extreme cold, and under the constant threat of Turkish artillery fire and disease. Subsequent to his evacuation at the end of 1915, Sidney and his unit were posted to the Egyptian Expeditionary Force Supply Depot, which was probably the large supply base at Samalut in the Nile Valley.

Sidney was demobilised at the end of March 1919 and returned home to Gossoms End. It is currently unclear whether he returned to baking, as in 1939 he was working as a general labourer, and still living in Gossoms End with his wife and children. Sidney died in 1946, aged 61.

Albert James Sear (1887 – 1962)
Driver T4/037855, Horse Transport, ASC

Albert Sear was born in October 1887 in Marsworth, the son of Henry Sear, a farm worker, who a few years later would become the Lockkeeper at No 51 Lock on the Grand Junction Canal near East and Son's timberyard in Gossoms End. Having left school, he started work on a local farm and in March 1909 he married Lucy Ann Baker, the daughter of a carter from Wigginton, at St Mary's, Northchurch. He later became a stableman for his wife's uncle, Ernest Baker, at Shootersway Farm and he and Lucy moved into one of the farm cottages. In 1911, she gave birth to their first son, with another following three years later. By then they had moved to a cottage in River Terrace, Gossoms End, although Albert was still working at Shootersway Farm.

Despite having two young boys and a wife to support, Albert decided to volunteer soon after the war started, and enlisted with the ASC at Watford. His medical records show him as being 5ft 8ins tall, weighing 142lbs and with good vision. Having passed his medical, he was sent to Woolwich for training and was later posted to 151st Coy ASC, one of four Horse Transport Companies that formed part of the Divisional Train for 18th (Eastern) Division.

On 24th July 1915, Albert and 151st Coy left Southampton on board the SS *Archimedes* bound for Le Havre. In early May 1916 he was granted nine days' home leave and returned to France during the final build-up leading to the Somme Offensive. For his services during the offensive, Albert was later awarded a good conduct badge and proudly wore the inverted chevron on his lower left sleeve.

In 1917, Albert's Divisional Train supported 18th (Eastern) Division during the fighting that ensued after the German retreat to the Hindenburg Line, the Battle of Arras and the Third Battle of Ypres. In September that year, he returned home on ten days' home leave before returning to France and the atrocious muddy conditions that existed during the final stages of the fighting around Ypres. Nine months later, Albert's wife, Lucy, gave birth to a third son and he came home again in October 1918 to see his young son for the first time, returning to France a week before the Armistice was signed.

Albert was demobilised in April 1919. Sadly, Lucy died in 1931 aged only 43 and leaving Albert to bring up their three children. By 1939, he had moved to Norris's Terrace, Berkhamsted and was working as a foreman and APR Warden for the local gas company in Billet Lane. Albert Sear died in 1962, aged 76.

Albert Victor Skinner (1883 – 1941)
Private 189114, Motor Transport Unit, ASC

Albert Skinner was born in May 1883 in Kemsing, near Sevenoaks, Kent, where his father, William, worked as a gardener. William Skinner died when Albert was just four years old, leaving his widow, Julia, to bring up the family. Albert subsequently followed his father's profession and started work as a gardener in the local area. In January 1911 he married Julia Mary Elizabeth Alice Jewsbury, the daughter of a London docker, at St James's, Hatcham, south-east London. Shortly afterwards, Albert starting looking for a new gardening job and the couple took rooms in Castle Street, Berkhamsted. It was not long before he found work as a gardener for Walter Cohen, who at that time lived at Fairhill on Berkhamsted Common and had just commissioned the building of Amersfort, with its Gertrude Jekyll-designed garden. Following the completion of Amersfort, Albert and his wife moved into the newly-built lodge on the estate.

The new garden at Amersfort was specifically designed to complement the house; there were raised grass walks with short borders either side and views over the surrounding countryside. Elsewhere, azaleas, heathers, lilies and other shrubs featured. There was also a rose garden and a kitchen garden providing colour during all the seasons, which kept William and his fellow gardeners busy throughout the year.

Tragically, in 1912 Albert's wife died shortly after giving birth to a daughter. Albert remarried the following year, his new wife, Annie Elizabeth Smith, coming from Essex. She gave birth to a daughter in 1915.

Following the outbreak of war, Albert's employer, Walter Cohen, applied for a Commission but, with a family to support, Albert decided not to volunteer and it is likely that he was conscripted in the summer of 1916 when Annie was pregnant with their second child. According to the 1918 Northchurch Absent Voters List, Albert was then serving as a driver with an ASC Mechanised Transport unit in Great Britain.

After his demobilisation, Albert returned home, but within two years his second wife also died, possibly during the influenza pandemic. In the autumn of 1922, he married, Rose Brooker, who came from Playden, Sussex and was the daughter of a local head gardener. Albert later became the head gardener at Amersfort and remained there until his death in 1941, aged 58.

Herbert Waters (1888 – 1977)
Private, Unknown Unit, ASC

Although it is known that Herbert Waters was one of the early volunteers to join up in 1914, it is unclear in which unit of the ASC he served. Using a process of elimination, together with the circumstantial use of the records that have survived, it can be deduced that he served in a motorised transport unit of the ASC.

Herbert was born in February 1888 in Cheddington, Buckinghamshire, and was the first child of William Waters, a farm worker from nearby Ivinghoe, and his wife, Estelle. After leaving school he started working as a butcher's boy and in 1901 he was living with his maternal aunt who worked for a butcher in Fulham, London.

How long Herbert remained there is unclear, as in 1905 his father was killed in a freak accident involving a horse on the Model Farm on the Mentmore estate where he worked, close to his home in Cheddington. Six years later Herbert was working as the chauffeur for the Barnett family at Northchurch Hall and lodging with Bertie Pratt in one of the Hall's cottages in the High Street.

One of the first to enlist at the outbreak of the war in 1914, Herbert's name was included on the list of volunteers published in *West Herts and Watford Observer* on 19th September. Thereafter there is no record to uniquely identify in which unit he served, there being multiple 'Herbert Waters' being awarded medals at the end of the war. The most likely unit, considering that he had the rare skill at that time of driving motor vehicles, is a motorised transport unit of the ASC. There are two 'Herbert Waters' who meet this criterion, both were Privates - M2/019490 and M2/021330, who both arrived in France in December 1914 and survived the war, being demobilised within weeks of each other.

Following his demobilisation, Herbert Waters became the family chauffeur for the Smith-Dorrien family at New Lodge, Berkhamsted. In 1921, he married one of the Smith-Dorrien domestic staff who worked at the family's Scilly Isles home. Herbert spent the rest of his working life employed by the Smith-Dorrien family and living in one of the New Lodge cottages and died in 1977, aged 89.

James Thomas Hope Whent (1876 – 1962)
Private M2/192127, 43rd Auxiliary Petrol Company, ASC

James Whent was born in June 1876 in the small village of Raydon, some ten miles south-east of Ipswich, where his parents, Thomas and Eliza Whent, ran a small 10-acre farm. By 1891, Thomas Whent had moved his family to the village of Higham and was now working as a domestic gardener and this is where James started work.

In 1894, eighteen-year-old James, using the surname 'Hope', decided to join 4th Queen's Own Hussars, but soon transferred to 13th Hussars. His regiment was one of the first cavalry units to be sent to South Africa during the Anglo-Boer War and was to remain there until October 1902, when it returned to its base at Aldershot. Here, James met and fell in love with Dorothy Louisa Williams, and they were married on 1st March 1905. Following his departure from the Hussars, they moved to Saffron Walden in Essex, where he had found work as a coachman. Here, Dorothy would give birth to two sons.

Sometime later James became the chauffeur for William Favill Tuke, a wealthy Saffron Walden banker, and when, in 1915, the Tuke family moved to Norcott Court near Northchurch, James and his family came with them, moving into one of the cottages in the grounds.

On 11th December 1915 and now aged nearly forty, he decided to attest under the Derby Scheme. Six months later he was mobilised and after passing his medical examination he was posted to the ASC Depot at Grove Park in Lewisham and later joined 731st Motor Transport Company, 57th (2nd West Lancashire) Division Supply Column at Aldershot. His unit left Southampton in February 1917 bound for France on board the SS *Duchess of Argyll* and on their arrival, he was posted to 'Y' Supply Column as a lorry driver.

Later in 1917, James was posted to two other units in France driving lorries supplying the troops. He returned to England in January 1918 on two weeks' home leave for the first time since he attested. Just before the war ended he was transferred to 43rd Auxiliary Petrol Company.

Following his demobilisation in June 1919, James returned to Norcott Court and his role as the Tuke family chauffeur. When the Tukes left Norcott Court for a new home in Andover, James moved with them and remained their chauffeur until he retired. James Whent died in 1962, aged 85.

George Henry Wright (1887 – 1966)
Private DM2/190889, Unknown Motor Transport Unit, ASC

Little is known about George Wright's time in the army during the war. He was born in September 1887 to tinsmith and iron worker, George Wright, and his wife Matilda at their home in George Street, Berkhamsted, then in the eastern part of Northchurch parish. By 1901 the family had moved to Norris's Terrace in Gossoms End. George's first job after leaving school was to work alongside his elder brother, Frederick, as a stationery labeller, probably at Loosley's premises in Berkhamsted High Street. Within ten years, however, he had changed occupations and like many of his age in the Northchurch area was working as a domestic gardener, whilst still living with his parents in their new home in Shrublands Avenue.

Around this time George met and fell in love with Annie Rickett, a cook from the tiny hamlet of Battlesden, close to the village of Hockcliffe, Bedfordshire, who worked for a family in Shootersway. On Christmas Day 1912 they were married at the local parish church of St Peter and All Saints. Their first child was born the month before war broke out two years later.

George's service record has not survived, but it is likely that he was conscripted when the Military Service Act was extended to married men in May 1916. By then Annie was pregnant with their second child, who was born the following month. George was posted to the Army Service Corps and learnt to drive motor vehicles. It would appear that Annie and her two children returned to her parents' home at this time as this is where George was later registered as an absent voter in 1918.

Following his demobilisation in 1919 George and his family returned to Northchurch setting up home in what was then called Orchard End and later became Seymour Road. Annie would later give birth to two more children. The family were still living in the same house in 1939 with George working full time as a gardener and transport driver and also as one of the local ARP Wardens. He died in 1966, aged 79.

Ernest William Young (1886 – 1971)
Private M/282602, Motor Transport Unit, ASC

Like George Bedford, Ernest Young served alongside the gunners of the Royal Garrison Artillery, driving a Holt artillery tractor. He was born in Wing, Buckinghamshire in November 1886 where his father, Frederick, worked as a groom. The Young family later moved to Tring, where Ernest started working as a grocer's assistant, but later changed occupation to become a cycle engineer in Berkhamsted. In 1909, he married Ethel Chennells at St Peter's, Berkhamsted, and they set up home in a cottage in Gossoms End. The following year Ethel gave birth to a boy.

Ernest was conscripted in 1916 and was posted to the ASC where he learnt to drive the newly-introduced Holt artillery tractor. He left England in the following year with 269th Siege Battery, RGA, bound for Mesopotamia. He was to serve alongside the gunners for the remainder of the war, hauling the battery's 6-inch howitzers. Two months before the war ended Ernest's younger brother, Leonard, who had emigrated to Canada in 1913, was killed in action whilst serving with the 87th Canadian Infantry (Quebec Regiment) in France.

After his demobilisation in late 1919, Ernest returned to Gossoms End. By 1930, he and his family had moved to 294 High Street, Berkhamsted and he later became a garage proprietor in the town. Ernest Young died in 1971, aged 85.

13 – The Labour Corps

Prior to the formation of the Labour Corps in 1917, the British Army's demand for manual labour was met by soldiers serving in special battalions in each infantry division. These men were also trained to fight as standard infantrymen in emergency situations. Given the name 'Pioneers', the men serving in these special battalions were often skilled labourers in their civilian lives, such as miners, bricklayers, carpenters and smiths. Other army units, such as the Royal Engineers and the Army Service Corps, also formed their own Labour Battalions.

As the war progressed, more and more men were required to perform basic labouring tasks, especially the digging and maintenance of trenches and as an expedient the British sought additional workers from as far away as China. By 1917, the running of individual labour units throughout the British Army was seen as inefficient and a new, dedicated Labour Corps was created, amalgamating the existing infantry labour battalions and companies into one overall organisation. Men no longer deemed fit for front line service through age, sickness or injury, but still fit enough to perform labouring tasks, were also transferred into the new Corps and given a new service number. The Labour Corps was divided into various groups, including Area Employment Companies, Divisional Employment Companies and Agricultural Companies.

The Area Employment Companies were created specifically to deal with salvage work, and absorbed the army's existing Divisional Salvage Companies. Normally consisting of two officers and 270 men, those serving in these units often worked unarmed and under hazardous conditions close to the battlefield. Each man serving in the employment companies also faced the prospect of a monthly medical examination to see whether he was considered fit enough to serve in the front line. During the German Spring Offensive in 1918 several Labour Corps units regularly fought as emergency infantry.

In addition to those men serving abroad, some 100,000 men of the Labour Corps served at military bases, hospitals and key factories in Great Britain. A further 75,000 men served in the Agricultural Companies working on farms and were key to providing food for the country, especially at harvest time. The men working in the Agricultural Companies either lived at home, if their work was located close by, or were billeted near the farm or smallholding at which they were employed.

Following the end of the war, the work of the Labour Corps continued without a break as the debris created in France and Belgium during four years of warfare needed clearing. Men from the Labour Corps also helped in the gruesome recovery and reburial of the bodies of dead soldiers in the newly created cemeteries as part of the Graves Exhumation team.

John Butler (1885 -?)
Private 197300, 377th (Home Service) Battalion, Labour Corps

Very little is known about John Butler's early life. He was born in Arklow, County Wicklow, Ireland in May 1885. Sometime in the early 1900s, no doubt in search of work, John left Ireland and moved to Middlesbrough, Yorkshire, where he eventually became a steel plate worker at one of the local steelworks.

One of the early volunteers at the start of the war, John enlisted with the newly-formed 12th Battalion, Northumberland Fusiliers and later travelled south with them to Hertfordshire and Buckinghamshire where their training began. He was probably billeted in either Berkhamsted or Northchurch when he met Edith Gurney from Orchard End, who worked as a parlour maid at one of local large houses and it was not long before they became engaged to be married. In May 1915, John's battalion left the area and moved into newly-built huts at Halton Park near Wendover, Buckinghamshire, where they remained until leaving for France.

The battalion arrived in France on 9th September 1915 and was soon involved in the heavy fighting around the town of Loos. By December the winter weather had forced an end to fighting in the area and John returned to England to marry his fiancée at the Roman Catholic Church in Berkhamsted. By the start of 1916, he was back in the trenches leaving his new wife back in Northchurch.

It would appear that John fell ill in the late spring of 1916 and was invalided back to England. Now deemed unfit for front line service, John, like many other former infantrymen, was transferred to one of the home-based Labour Corps battalions. In the 1918 Absent Voters List, he is recorded as serving with 377th (Home Service) Battalion, Labour Corps.

In December 1918, Edith gave birth to a daughter at the family home in Gossoms End. John was demobilised in March 1919 and he and his family remained in Gossoms End until 1927. It is currently not known what John did for a living on his return to civilian life, but by 1939, he was back in Middlesbrough and once again working as a steelworker. His date of death is unknown.

Charles Cripps (1894 – 1972)
Private 584007, 597th (Home Service) Employment Company, Labour Corps

Charles Cripps was born in the small hamlet of Piccotts End in October 1894. At that time, Piccotts End did not have a church, and consequently Charles was christened at the nearby church of St Mary's, Hemel

Hempstead. His father, John Cripps, was an assistant gamekeeper on one of the local estates, later becoming a gamekeeper in his own right. Charles grew up in Piccotts End along with his eight siblings, including his older brother, John, and on leaving school began work as a carter. The Cripps family later moved to a larger house in nearby Potten End where his mother, Elizabeth, gave birth to two more children.

At the start of the war, Charles, then aged 19, enlisted in the Bedfordshire Regiment and was posted to their 7th Battalion, otherwise known as 'The Shiny Seventh'. His army training took place at Codford on Salisbury Plain and he sailed with his battalion for Boulogne onboard the SS *Onward* in July 1915.

'The Shiny Seventh' saw service throughout the Somme Offensive in the summer and autumn of 1916 and it is probable that Charles was either wounded or injured around this time. He was sent back to England to recover and was later transferred to the Suffolk Regiment. It is unclear whether he returned to France, as by the spring of 1918 he was serving with 597th (Home Service) Employment Company, which formed part of the Eastern Command and operated in the Colchester area.

Charles was demobilised in March 1919. By then, the Cripps family had moved to the hamlet of Frithsden and this is where he lived until the summer of 1921, when he married Jennie Hawes from Piccotts End. Moving to a cottage in Piccotts End, they would later have three children together. In 1939, Charles and his family were living at Boxted Farm, near Piccotts End, where he worked as a farm labourer. Charles Cripps died in 1972, aged 77.

Robert Davis (1873 – 1939)
Sergeant 372498, 280th Area Employment Company, Labour Corps

Robert Davis, christened William Robert Davis, was born in Northchurch in the early spring of 1873. He was the last of ten children born to John Davis, a labourer from Tring, and his wife, Marta, from Aston Abbots, Buckinghamshire. Starting work as a general labourer after leaving school, Robert later decided to join the army and signed up for 12 years' service with 2nd Battalion, Bedfordshire Regiment. It is likely that he served with the 2nd Bedfords during the Boer War, returning to England in 1903 and would have ended his term with the regiment by 1914.

In August 1914, Robert, was now 40 years old and working as a nurseryman, probably for Lanes Nurseries, in Berkhamsted. Despite his age, within days of war being declared he decided to play his part in the war effort and travelled to Hertford, where he enlisted with his old regiment. His medical examination described him as being 5ft 7½ ins tall, weighing 145lbs with grey eyes and brown hair. The following day, he was posted to 4th Battalion, Bedfordshire Regiment which served as a collecting battalion for newly joined men as well as providing a home defence force at Harwich.

Although he was far older than many of the other recruits, it was obviously thought that Robert's previous experience with 2nd Bedfords could be put to good use in the field, as on 11th November 1914, he was transferred to his old battalion and sent to France as part of a draft of 119 men.

By the end of 1914 there were at least four other Northchurch men serving alongside Robert in 2nd Bedfords – Joseph Hosier, Edwin Morgan, George Curl and James Delderfield, the last three of whom would be killed before the war ended. Robert served with 2nd Bedfords during the next three years including the heavy fighting at Neuve Chapelle, Givenchy, Loos, the Somme Offensive, the German withdrawal to the Hindenburg Line and the Third Battle of Ypres.

In November 1917, with the Third Battle of Ypres still underway, Robert was posted to 280th Area Employment Company, part of the newly-formed Labour Corps. By then, he had turned forty-four and was no longer deemed fit for front line service, but he was still strong enough to undertake physical labour. He remained in France working in various Area Employment Companies until the end of the war, rising to the rank of Sergeant.

Soon after his return to England in 1920, Robert married Susan Dean, the daughter of a local carpenter, and the couple set up home in Clarence Road, Berkhamsted, before moving to a cottage in New Road, Northchurch. It is currently not clear what his occupation was after his demobilisation. He died in early 1939, aged 65.

Frank Dwight (1878 – 1967)
Private 158403, 587th (Home Service) Employment Company, Labour Corps

Frank Dwight was born in the family home in Eddy Street, Gossoms End, in November 1878, and was the third son of William and Mary Dwight. He started his working life as a wood turner for East & Son, where his father, and many other men living in Eddy Street, also worked.

On 23rd December 1901, he married Alice Batchelor, the daughter of a local gardener, and the couple moved into a cottage in Gossoms End, which would remain the family home for many years.

It is likely that Frank was conscripted in the summer of 1916 and his age at the time (he was 38), may well have influenced the decision to post him to 587th (Home Service) Employment Company, which operated in the military bases and hospitals in the Bedford area.

He was demobilised soon after the end of the war and returned home and restarted he job at East's timber yard. Frank died in 1967, aged 88.

James William Eggleton (1880 – 1935)
Private 239780, 396th Agricultural Company, Labour Corps
Frank Hearn (1888 - 1974)
Private 428849, 396th Agricultural Company, Labour Corps

Very little is known about James Eggleton's military service during the war. He was born in 1880 in the hamlet of Buckland Wharf, close to the Wendover Arm of the Grand Junction Canal, some seven miles north-west of Northchurch and was the first of four sons born to Thomas Eggleton, a labourer from Wigginton and his wife, Annie. After leaving school, he started work on a local farm.

On 22nd December 1900, James married 20-year-old Elizabeth Redding at St Mary's, Northchurch. She had grown up in Northchurch and worked at the Mantle Factory in Lower Kings Road, Berkhamsted.

By 1911, James and Elizabeth were living in a four-roomed cottage in New Road Northchurch with their three children. With a young family to bring up, James did not volunteer when the war started and was probably conscripted in the summer of 1916. His younger brother, Arthur, had joined the army before the war and was sadly killed during the opening days of the Somme Offensive whilst serving with the Northamptonshire Regiment. James however appears to not to have been sent abroad after being conscripted as he was not awarded any medals and it is assumed that his age, together with a low medical classification, meant that he was deemed unsuitable for front line service and consequently was posted to the Labour Corps. The 1918 Absent Voters List shows James serving in 396th Agricultural Company which operated in the area around Henley-on-Thames, Berkshire.

He was demobilised soon after the end of the war and returned to his home in Northchurch. It is currently unknown what he did on his return. James Eggleton died in 1935, aged 55.

Frank Hearn was born in June 1888 in the hamlet of Lee Common, near Great Missenden, Buckinghamshire, one of nine children. His father, Thomas, worked on a nearby farm where Frank joined him after leaving school. By 1901, the Hearn family had moved into a four-roomed cottage in nearby Chartridge.

On 11th November 1911, a date no doubt chosen for its numerical significance, Frank married Gertrude Annie White at St Peter's, Berkhamsted. She worked as a domestic servant for Sir Samuel Augustus Mason Satow, a master in the Chancery Division of the High Court in London, who lived at Northcote in Kings Road, Berkhamsted. Just under three years later Frank and Gertrude became parents for the first time and the couple moved to a house in Chesham, by which time Frank had become a timber hauler. A second child would be born two years later.

Frank's military service record has fortunately survived, and it appears that he volunteered to join the Royal Engineers sometime before 1916, but after serving just sixteen days he was discharged, presumably as he did not meet the required medical standard. This did not exclude him from future military service, however, and in the summer of 1916, he was conscripted. Mobilised in April 1917, Frank's subsequent medical record shows him as standing 5ft 5¾ins tall, weighing 124lbs and with good physical development. Frank's eyesight however was recorded as poor, and he suffered from partial loss of hearing. As a result, he was given a B1 medical classification, which would probably account for his earlier rejection by the Royal Engineers.

Frank was posted to the Labour Corps and spent the remainder of the war working in four different Agricultural Companies on farms located in the Thames Valley area. His last posting was to 396th Agricultural Company, where he worked alongside James Eggleton.

By the time the war had ended his wife had moved back to Berkhamsted with their two children and was living in a cottage in Gossoms End. Frank rejoined her there in February 1919 following his demobilisation and later that year, Gertrude gave birth to a daughter. He became a builder's labourer and in 1939 was also serving as a local APR Warden. Frank Hearn died in 1974, aged 86.

Thomas Delderfield (1874 – 1926)
Company Quartermaster Sergeant 476554, 736th Area Employment Company, Labour Corps

Thomas Delderfield, the second son of Joseph Delderfield, a general labourer from Aldbury, and his wife, Frances, was born in New Road, Northchurch in the late summer of 1874 and later started working locally as general labourer for a Mr Jones.

In February 1893, aged eighteen, Thomas decided to join the army and enlisted with the Bedfordshire Regiment. Posted to their 4th Battalion, his medical record shows him as being 5ft 8¾ins tall, weighing 136lbs with a fresh complexion, blue/grey eyes and brown hair. He initially signed up for six years in the army but, as he does not appear in the 1901 Census, it can be assumed that he later extended his period of service and it is therefore likely that he was still serving with 4th Battalion in South Africa during the Boer War.

After leaving the army, Thomas returned to Northchurch and started working alongside his father as a hay and straw binder. In October 1910, he married Fanny Howlett at St Mary's, Northchurch. She came from Orchard End and was some nine years younger than him and worked at the Mantle

Factory in Lower Kings Road. The newlyweds set up home in a four-roomed cottage in Orchard End, close to her family.

By August 1914, Thomas was forty years old, but that did not prevent him enlisting for a second time with the Bedfordshire Regiment. Posted to the Bedfords 3rd (Reserve) Battalion, he was later transferred to their 6th Battalion which was initially made up of some 200 experienced former soldiers like himself. Within weeks the battalion had reached its capacity, with the newly-raised 7th (Service) Battalion taking the remainder of the volunteers.

His reintroduction to army life initially took place at Aldershot and then, when his battalion became part of 112th Brigade, at Andover, with training taking place on Salisbury Plain. By early June 1915, Thomas and his comrades realised that they would soon be off to fight, and in mid-July they left Southampton onboard the *Empress Queen*, bound for Le Havre. Around this time, Thomas was appointed Corporal.

The details of his subsequent service with 6th Battalion are unknown. It is likely that he fought with them during the Somme Offensive, but by now he was 41-years-old. Whether due to his age, or some other reason, by 1918 Thomas had been transferred to the Labour Corps and was working in 736th Area Employment Company. Probably due to his previous experience in the army, Thomas was later appointed the company quartermaster sergeant (CQMS), a non-commissioned officer role overseeing supplies, and also acting as the deputy to the company sergeant major.

He was demobilised in February 1919 and returned home. By now his wife, Fanny, had moved to Thorn's Yard, Northchurch. Thomas started work as a general labourer but died in 1926 of pleurisy and pneumonia, aged just 51. Whether this was partially attributable to his time serving on the Western Front is not known.

Charles Ginger (1898 – 1973)
Private 651666, 225th Divisional Employment Company, Labour Corps

Charles Ginger was born in February 1898 in Gossoms End. Both his parents, William and Ada Ginger, originally came from Buckinghamshire, and William worked as a cutter on one of the local watercress farms. After leaving school, he initially started working with horses, but later became a van driver.

Charles was conscripted in February 1916 and mobilised the following November. His medical examination took place at Bedford and showed that he was 5ft 2ins tall, weighed 130lbs and had blue eyes and dark hair. He was then posted to 69th Provisional Battalion, which consisted of men like him, who had not yet reached the age of nineteen.

Following the completion of his military training, Charles embarked for France and arrived there in July 1917 and was sent to the large military base at Étaples, where 69th Provisional Battalion was renamed 19th Battalion, Royal West Surrey Regiment. Two weeks later, he was reassigned, and on 8th August he joined 2nd Battalion Royal West Surrey as part of a draft of 56 men.

Putting his skills as a van driver to good use, Charles became a transport driver for the battalion, normally well away from the front line. In October 1917, Charles was admitted to 21st Field Ambulance suffering from a problem with his foot. After being treated he returned to duty, but a month later he was admitted to 30th General Hospital in Calais. Found to be unfit for further front line service, he was given a B1 medical classification and sent back to Étaples for reassignment. After spending the next two months working at the depots at Étaples and Cayeux Charles was again admitted to hospital for treatment of an infection. On his discharge from hospital, he became one of the cooks in his battalion. Another infection ensued two months later, however, and he was sent back to England for further treatment. He returned to France in late April 1918 and was posted to 225th Divisional Employment Company, Labour Corps, resuming his role as an army cook. Despite the end of the war, the troops still needed feeding, so it was not until March 1919 that he was demobilised and returned to Northchurch.

On 25th July 1920, Charles married Blanche Beales, at St Peter's, Berkhamsted and they set up home back in Gossoms End. Three years later Charles joined the Territorial Army for a period of four years, becoming a Private with No2 Company, 1st Battalion, Hertfordshire Regiment. The following year, he transferred to 86th Brigade, Royal Field Artillery as a driver. He remained with them until 1927. In 1939, Charles was living in Berkhamsted and working as a labourer, probably for the local council. He died in the spring of 1973, aged 75.

Arthur Gladman (1882 – 1930)
Private 209380, 574th Agricultural Company, Labour Corps

Arthur Gladman was born in 1882 in the village of Studham, on the edge of the Chiltern Hills, some seven miles north-east of Northchurch, and was the son of carpenter, Alfred Gladman, and his wife, Sarah. On leaving school Arthur started work as a horse keeper on a local farm. In 1905, aged 23, whilst working on the farm, he suffered a hernia injury and was treated in hospital. Two years later, he married Fanny Whitman at St Peter and St Paul's, Little Gaddesden. Annie gave birth to a daughter in the early summer of 1909 and shortly afterwards the family moved to Frithsden.

In August 1914, Arthur was working as a carman at nearby Nettleden Farm and decided not to volunteer when war broke out. A week before

Christmas, however, he changed his mind and travelled to St Albans to enlist with the ASC. Passing his medical examination with an A1 classification, Arthur was described as 5ft 4ins tall and weighing 128lbs. His training took place at the ASC headquarters depot at Woolwich. On 24th July 1915, he left Southampton onboard the SS *Archimedes* bound for Le Havre and he was now a fully qualified driver in 2nd Coy (151 Coy), 18th Divisional Train.

In February 1916 tragedy hit the Gladwell family when Fanny died of sarcoma and exhaustion aged just 33. He was granted compassionate leave and returned to England and was able to be present at her death. Soon afterwards, he was permanently transferred back to England and posted to the Base Horse Transport Department in the Bedford area. Meanwhile, his young daughter was looked after by his mother in Studham.

The following October, Alfred was posted to 433rd Agricultural Company, which operated in the Bedford area. Within weeks however, Arthur had suffered another hernia injury, possibly a recurrence of the injury he had suffered back in 1905, and was treated in a hospital in Reading. On his discharge he was posted to 112th Training Reserve Battalion and given a new medical classification of C2. He was subsequently posted to 692nd (Home Service) Employment Company, Labour Corps.

In August 1917, Arthur rejoined 433rd Agricultural Company before moving to 428th Agricultural Company, which also operated in the Bedford area. Then, in May 1918, he was posted to the Oxfordshire-based 574th Agricultural Company, by which time his medical grade had been reassessed as B1. He remained in the Oxford area until April 1919 when he was finally demobilised and returned to his parents' and daughter's home in Studham.

In 1924, he married Jesse Carter, and two years later became a father once again. Sadly, in 1930 Arthur Gladwell died, aged just 48.

Joseph Kempster (1893 – 1967)
Private 270379, 693rd Agricultural Company, Labour Corps

Joseph Kempster was born in Hog Lane, Northchurch, in November 1893 and was one of William and Emma Kempster's ten children. Like his younger brothers, Arthur and Robert, he went to school at nearby Ashley Green and later started work as a farm labourer. In the autumn of 1914 he enlisted with 10th Battalion Gloucestershire Regiment and was sent to France with his battalion in August 1915.

Details of Joseph's military career are somewhat uncertain, as his service record has not survived. Soon after landing his battalion took part in the Battle of Loos, and in 1916 it was involved in the Somme Offensive and later the German retreat to the Hindenburg Line. At some point during this period, Joseph was either wounded or injured and sent back to England for treatment. After recovering, but being unfit to return to frontline service, Joseph was transferred to the Labour Corps.

The 1918 Northchurch Absent Voters List shows Joseph serving with 693rd Agricultural Company, which worked on farms in the counties of Bedfordshire and Hertfordshire.

Joseph was demobilised at the end of March 1919 and returned to the family home at Hog Lane. Later that year, he married Florence Winifred Lacey from nearby Chesham. In 1939, he and his family were living in a cottage on the Rossway estate in Northchurch where he presumably had obtained work. Joseph Kempster died in 1967, aged 73.

Ernest Mapley (1887 – 1968)
Lance Corporal 543854, Unknown Agricultural Company, Labour Corps

Ernest Mapley's service history during the war is not entirely clear, as his service record has not survived. Born in Orchard End, Northchurch, in October 1887 to George Albert Mapley and his wife, Esther, Ernest was their seventh child. Both of his parents came from Wigginton and around 1884 moved to Northchurch, where George worked as a labourer. By 1901, the family had moved to a cottage in New Road, and this was to remain the family home for several years. In due course Ernest found work as a bricklayer's labourer, as did his younger brother, David.

In September 1914 Ernest enlisted with 1st Battalion, Hertfordshire Regiment and landed in France on 23rd January 1915 as part of a draft of 195 new recruits, joining his battalion a week later. In subsequent months the Hertshires took part in the battles of Festubert and Loos and, later, the Somme Offensive. Ernest was either wounded or injured during his time in the front line, which resulted in him being transferred to the Labour Corps. In the 1918 Absent Voters List, Ernest is shown as serving as a Lance Corporal 'at Mrs Leggatt, East Marden, Chichester'. No further information as to a unit within the Labour Corps is given, but the Leggatts were a local family of farmers, so his unit was likely to have been an agricultural company.

Ernest was demobilised in February 1919 and returned home to Northchurch. He remained at the family home in New Road until 1925, when he married Annie Mason. They moved to a cottage on Northchurch High Street and two years later Annie gave birth to a daughter. By 1939, they had moved to nearby Granville Road and Ernest was working as a labourer. He died in 1968, aged 80.

William Henry Pocock (1883 – 1954)
Private 274371, 433rd Agricultural Company, Labour Corps

Extremely little is known about William Pocock's time in the Labour Corps. Born in Dudswell in October 1883 to George Pocock, a blacksmith, and his wife Jane, he later became a gardener.

The Northchurch Absent Voter Lists show William assigned to 433rd Agricultural Company which operated in the Bedford area and was the same unit in which Arthur Gladman had served. There is no evidence of William being awarded any military medal, which would indicate that he did not serve overseas in another army unit prior to joining the Labour Corps. His name appears in the Autumn 1919 Northchurch Absent Voters List so he was not demobilised until the end of that year or in early 1920. In 1939, he was still living in Dudswell with his sister, Gertrude, and working as a butcher. In the autumn of 1946 William married Agnes Draper. He died in 1954, aged 70.

George Reynolds (dates unknown)
Private 500115, 693rd Agricultural Company, Labour Corps

George Reynolds is registered at Bottom Farm Lane in the 1918 Northchurch Absent Voters List, and working in the same unit, 693rd Agricultural Company, Labour Corps, as Joseph Kempster. George was not a local man, and consequently nothing is known of his background. He first appears in the list of men who attested under the Derby Scheme towards the end of 1915, during the time he was working for the Honourable AD Ryder, at his home at Ashlyns Hall on the southern edge of Berkhamsted, and may have been a gardener. He was mobilised the following year. The lack of a military medal record would indicate that he only served in the Labour Corps in England. There is currently no evidence to suggest that George Reynolds returned to the local area after the war.

Frederick George Scott (1878 – 1952)
Private 152195, 753rd Area Employment Company, Labour Corps

Frederick Scott was born in Orchard End, Northchurch, in October 1878 and was the first child born to bricklayer, James Scott, and his wife, Emma. Later the Scott family would move to a cottage in Northchurch High Street where the remainder of James and Emma Scott's children, Harry, Charles, Albert and Florence, were born. After leaving school, Frederick started work as a builder's labourer, possibly helping his father, and later became a bricklayer in his own right. On 24th October 1912, Frederick married Margaret May Bonham in St Peter's, Berkhamsted. She worked as a domestic servant in one of the large houses and came from Wingrave, near Aylesbury, where her father was the postmaster.

Frederick was 36 when the war broke out and consequently decided not to volunteer. It is therefore likely that he was conscripted in 1916 and his age and skill as a bricklayer resulted in him being assigned to a labour unit. In 1917 he became part of the Labour Corps and by 1918 he was serving with 753rd Area Employment Company.

He was demobilised at the start of 1919 and at that time he was registered as living in a cottage in Northchurch High Street. It is currently not known whether he continued as a bricklayer on his return to civilian life as, by 1939, he had changed occupation and was now working as a painter. Frederick Scott died in 1952, aged 73.

Alfred Toothill (1886 – 1979)
Sergeant 399715, 794th Area Employment Company (Labour Corps)

It was his work as a groom that led 28-year-old Alfred Toothill to Northchurch. He was born in St Pancras, London in December 1886, the second son of an iron worker and tinsmith called Joseph Toothill. After leaving school, he started work as a carter for a John Evans, who owned a company near Euston Square making churns, buckets and other items for dairy farmers. Looking for more excitement than just carting dairy equipment around, in December 1904, aged 17, Alfred joined the Militia unit of the East Surrey Regiment, obtaining the permission of his father and a reference from his employer to do so. Two months later, now aged 18 and having liked what he has seen of army life, Alfred decided to enlist with 1st Battalion, East Surrey Regiment at their base at Kingston-upon-Thames for a 12-year term. His medical record describes him as in excellent health, being 5ft 3ins tall, weighing 117lbs, and with a fresh complexion, grey eyes and fair hair.

Alfred remained in England with the battalion until January 1907, when he was transferred to the East Surrey's 2nd Battalion and sailed for India. He spent the next three years based at Mhow, a small town in Madhya Pradesh, or central state, which had been founded by the British in 1818 at a strategic position near the Chambal and Narmada river basins and had been used by many of the British army regiments that had visited India. A few months after their arrival Alfred contracted an ear infection, which resulted in an 8-day hospital stay. The following year he was back in hospital suffering from malaria. During his time in Mhow, Alfred became proficient in using Maxim machine-guns, in transport duties and as a mounted infantryman and in October 1908 he was appointed Lance Corporal. All was not well however, as on three occasions over a period of eight months in 1909, Alfred was severely reprimanded for his behaviour.

In September 1910, Alfred's battalion left Mhow for Thyetmyo, a port on the right bank of the Irrawaddy River in Burma. Four months later, he received a fourth and final serious reprimand for 'making an improper reply to a senior NCO' and lost his Lance Corporal stripe. Alfred remained in Burma until 1913 when he transferred to the Reserves.

In his service record Alfred expressed the desire to become a groom, and on his return to England in April 1913 he started work at one of the large houses in the Berkhamsted area. In June 1914, he married Alice Chennells, a brush maker, at St Mary's, Northchurch and moved into a cottage in Northchurch High Street. Two months later, following the outbreak of war, Alfred was recalled to his unit, and Alice was pregnant with their first child.

In August 1914, 2nd Battalion, East Surrey Regiment, was still in Burma and was immediately recalled to England. Alfred was ordered to Dover along with other reservists from the battalion to await the battalion's return. Whilst there Alfred regained his Lance Corporal's stripe and was later appointed Corporal. On 3rd December 1914, he arrived in France with his battalion. Three weeks later Alice gave birth to a boy.

Alfred's first experience of fierce fighting took place during the Second Battle of Ypres, during which he suffered a head injury. Initially treated at 14th Field Ambulance, he was transferred to 8th General Hospital in Place de l'Église, Rouen. Ten days later, still suffering from hearing problems, Alfred was discharged from hospital and sent back to England to recover. During his time in hospital Alfred became a Sergeant.

On his return to duty in November 1915, Alfred found himself posted to 3rd Battalion, Border Regiment, a holding unit for soldiers returning to front line service after serious injury or illness. Within days, he had been transferred again to 1st Battalion, Border Regiment and told that he was sailing imminently for Gallipoli.

1st Battalion, Border Regiment had been on the Gallipoli peninsula since April 1915 and had suffered heavy casualties during the subsequent seven months, including the deaths of two Northchurch men, Walter and Frederick Geary. By now, the weather had changed, and it was becoming cold and wet, and with the front at stalemate the British and French Governments were secretly considering withdrawing their troops at the end of the year. Alfred's stay on the Gallipoli peninsula was fortunately relatively short before he was evacuated to Egypt.

March 1916 saw 1st Battalion leave Egypt for the Western Front as part of the preparations for the Somme Offensive. On 1st July 1916, the opening day of the Offensive, Alfred and his colleagues were in the trenches just south of Beaumont Hamel. Their objective was the heavily defended Behucourt Redoubt, with the Borderers following 2nd Battalion, South Wales Borderers in the second wave of the attack. During the first wave most of the Welshmen were wiped out by German machine-gun fire within seconds of leaving their trenches, many not even getting past the British barbed wire defences. Alfred and his fellow Borderers followed and managed to make more progress, but by 08:00 the attack had stalled. At the start of their attack, Alfred's unit comprised 832 officers and men, but by the time the attack was called off, they had suffered 639 casualties. Alfred was fortunate; although he had been hit in his left leg by a bullet, he was able to make his way back to the British line. Taken to 87th Field Ambulance, he was later transferred to 6th General Hospital in Rouen.

The following December, Alfred contracted bronchitis and spent several days at 1st General Hospital on the coast at Étretat. After being discharged and given a B2 medical classification, he was sent to No3 Rest Camp just up the coast at Boulogne and later started work as sergeant mess caterer with 6th Labour Group. He remained at Boulogne for several months before being posted to 794th Area Employment Company, Labour Corps in November 1917. A month later, he returned to Northchurch on the first of two periods of short home leave.

Alfred was demobilised at the end of February 1919 and a month later Alice gave birth to a second boy, with a daughter following in the autumn of 1920. It is not currently known whether Alfred returned to working as a groom on returning to civilian life. In 1922 he became a father for the last time. In 1939, he and his family were still living in the same cottage in Northchurch High Street and he was working as a painter. Alfred Toothill died in 1979, aged 93.

William Welling (1864 – 1945)
Private 29666, 16th Battalion, Yorks & Lancaster Regiment

William Welling was the oldest Northchurchman to enlist in the army during the war. Born in September 1864, he was the son of farm worker, William Welling, and his wife, Elizabeth. William's father died in 1880, but by then all but one of William and Elizabeth's children had left school and were working. To help make ends meet, Elizabeth started work as a straw plaiter.

William started working as a labourer, but in 1885, aged 20, he decided to join the army and travelled to Bedford to enlist with the Bedfordshire Regiment for the normal twelve years of service, the last five being in the reserves. His medical examination at the time described William as being 5ft 8ins tall, weighing 138lbs and with a pale fresh complexion, hazel-brown eyes and brown hair. Having passed his medical and completed his training, William was posted to the Bedford's 1st Battalion. He spent the next few years based at the Bedford Depot until 12th February 1890 when he left England with his battalion for a nine-month spell of garrison duty on the island of Malta, followed by three years on garrison duty in India.

William returned home in February 1894 and entered the reserves, once again becoming a general labourer. In May that year he married Selina Warrall at St Mary's, Northchurch, and the couple moved into a small cottage in Thorn's Yard (now Duncombe Road) adjacent to the George & Dragon public house in Northchurch High Street. William's time in the Reserves ended in October 1897, but he immediately signed up as a volunteer reservist with 'D Coy', the Bedford's 3rd Volunteer Battalion which had its headquarters at Dunstable. The same year Selina gave birth to their first child, William Jnr, followed by two daughters in 1898 and 1900 respectively.

In January 1900, following the outbreak of the 2nd Boer War in South Africa, William joined the Bedfords 2nd Battalion and sailed with them to Cape Town. Initially the battalion was used to contain the Boers in the Orange Free State area, whilst other units slowly recaptured the territory that the Boers had taken since the outbreak of fighting the previous year. William returned home in 1902 with a fractured jaw and having earned medals relating to the fighting in Cape Colony, the Orange Free State and the Transvaal. He was discharged from the army on 18th August 1902. By now he was 38 years old, but over the next ten years Selina would give birth to four more children in their Thorn's Yard cottage.

The outbreak of the First World War in August 1914 gave 50-year-old William the opportunity to serve his country for the last time. That October, William travelled to Hertford to enlist, knocking two years off his actual age. Too old to serve as a frontline soldier, William was added to the list of men in the reserves and told to go home.

It was not until July 1916 that William was called up and posted to 16th Battalion, Yorks & Lancaster Regiment which had its headquarters at Colsterdale, Yorkshire. The unit had been formed a few months earlier and was made up of men too old for frontline service overseas, but capable of performing labouring tasks on the home front. Consisting of eight Companies, William was allocated to the Tyne Dock detachment which helped keep the docks on the south side of the River Tyne running.

Private William Welling
Courtesy of Roger Welling

William was demobbed for the last time in March 1919 and returned to Northchurch where he became a well-known figure in the village as one of the road sweepers, gaining the nickname 'Brave Un' which originated from an apparent link he had with a fellow Bedfordshire soldier who had gained a Victoria Cross during the Boer War. The 1939 Register shows William still living in the same cottage, but described as disabled. He died six years later, aged 80.

Frederick Wells (1876 – 1957)
Private 350453, 763rd Area Employment Company

Frederick Wells was 39 years old when he attested at Watford under the Derby Scheme in December 1915. Born in Chesham in February 1876 to William and Eliza Wells, he grew up in Chesham and nearby Ashley Green before becoming a shoemaker's apprentice at one of the local boot and shoe factories. At the age of twenty, Frederick married Minnie Newton and they had three children together. By 1901 he was no longer working as a bootmaker, but as a coal carter, and had moved to Watford with his family.

Over the next ten years Frederick's life would change substantially following the sudden death of his wife. Having found work as a coal carter for the Berkhamsted Co-operative Society, Frederick left Watford with his children and moved into to a cottage in New Road, Northchurch. He later met and married Ethel Coleman, who originally came from Norfolk and who worked as a domestic servant at one of the houses in Charles Street, Berkhamsted. Between 1913 and 1915 Frederick became the father to two more children.

When he attested at Watford in December 1915, Frederick was described as just over 5ft 7ins tall, weighing 146lbs and with good physical development and eyesight. His age however, probably resulted in him being allocated a B2 medical classification. Frederick was mobilised eight months later and told to report to Bedford. There he was posted to 32nd Reserve Labour Company in Thetford, where he received his basic training and he was subsequently posted to 257th Area Employment Company, which was working near St Omer in northern France. Four months later he was transferred to 763rd Area Employment Company working near Poperinghe.

By the time of Frederick's demobilisation in March 1919, his wife and family had moved to a cottage in Gossoms End. Their oldest son, George, had recently been conscripted and was then under training at a military base in England.

It is currently uncertain whether Frederick returned to his job with the Berkhamsted Co-op, as in 1939, whilst the family was still living in Gossoms End, he was working as a boot repairer and gardener. He died in 1957, aged 81.

14 – The Royal Navy

Being some 70 miles inland from the nearest naval base, there was never a strong seafaring tradition in the Northchurch area. In the years before 1914 however, several Northchurch boys, no doubt in search of action and adventure, did enlist in the Royal Navy soon after leaving school.

At the turn of the twentieth century the British Navy was the largest and most powerful navy in the world, its primary role being to protect the Empire and trade routes across the globe. With key bases in the Far East, the Mediterranean and the Pacific, as well as in Great Britain itself, the Royal Navy offered plenty of opportunities to the young men that joined it.

The minimum enlistment age for the Royal Navy was fifteen, and those signing up at that age had to obtain the permission of their parents or guardian. The new recruits, provided they passed the obligatory medical examination and were of 'good character', would be classified as 'Boy 2nd Class' and sent for training at one of the major bases, such as HMS *Ganges* at Shotley Gate, near Ipswich. On reaching the age of eighteen, the recruits were expected to sign up for twelve years' service with the Royal Navy and given the rank of Ordinary Seaman.

Charles William Avery (1895 -?)
Able Seaman J13736, Royal Navy

Charles Avery was born in October 1895, the son of Joseph Avery, a brewer's drayman from Berkhamsted, and his wife, Margaret, from Penn, Buckinghamshire. The Avery family lived in a four-roomed cottage in River Terrace, Gossoms End. Before he was married, Charles's father had served with 1st Battalion, Bedfordshire Regiment, having previously spent nearly two years in the local militia. In 1894, having completed nine years in 'the colours', Joseph Avery transferred to the reserves and was married the following year. Within two years, Margaret Avery had given birth to two children, Charles, and his younger sister, Maud. With his time serving in the reserves coming to an end, Joseph decided to take the option to extend his army service by a further four years and consequently in 1900, following the outbreak of the Boer War, he went with 2nd Battalion, Bedfordshire Regiment to fight in South Africa. Margaret, was left at home to raise her young family in Gossoms End with the help of Joseph's elderly mother, Martha. He returned home in 1902, and he and Margaret would later have two more children.

In 1911, fifteen-year-old Charles Avery decided to leave home and, with the permission of his parents, joined the Royal Navy. His initial training took place on board the training ship TS *Arethusa*, a former warship that had seen action during the Crimean war against Russia over fifty years before, and was moored in the Thames estuary just off Greenhithe. It was not long before Charles had passed the navy test for sounding the 50 or more bugle calls and was rated as a Bugler. By the time he became an Ordinary Seaman at the age of eighteen, he had already served aboard two ships, HMS *Talbot*, an Eclipse-class light-cruiser, and HMS *Cadmus*, one of the last Royal Navy vessels built with a full rig of sails as well as a steam engine. He was still serving in the Far East on board HMS *Cadmus* in August 1914 when war broke out. Promoted to Able Seaman the following year, he remained on *Cadmus* in the Far East until May 1916.

Charles transferred to the powerful brand-new 22,960-ton battle cruiser, HMS *Courageous* the following November. *Courageous* had been launched nine months earlier and was armed with four 15-inch guns, eighteen 4-inch guns, two 3-inch guns and two 21-inch torpedo tube arrays and was manned by a crew of 842 men. After her commission, *Courageous* was assigned to the Grand Fleet's 3rd Light Cruiser Squadron and later became the flagship of 1st Cruiser Squadron. Charles remained as part of the crew of *Courageous* until October 1917.

In January 1918, he was posted to HMS *Rowan*, a 1,495-ton Armed Boarding Steamer, launched in 1909 and which served in the eastern Mediterranean, enforcing the naval blockades of the Turkish and Austrian ports. His next posting was to HMS *Hannibal*, a former Majestic-class pre-dreadnought battleship, now used as a depot ship in Alexandria. Charles was serving on *Hannibal* when the war ended and returned with her to Chatham in January 1919. Until then, his character had been recorded on his service record as 'VG' (Very Good), yet on 30th September 1919 he deserted.

The first official notification of Charles Avery's desertion appeared in the *Police Gazette* on 21st October 1919 in which he was described as 24-years-old, born in Northchurch, and being 5ft 5½ins tall, with a fresh complexion, light hair and blue eyes. He had tattoos on both forearms and a scar over his right eye. Known as a 'straggler' or a 'runner', terms used for someone who has deserted, he faced immediate court martial on his capture and the forfeiture of the three military medals he had earned during the war.

It appears that Charles managed to evade the authorities and returned to Berkhamsted. In October 1920, using the address of his parent's home in Bridge Street, he married Ivy Roads, described on their wedding certificate as a 'Lady's Companion', at Berkhamsted Registry Office. At the time of the wedding, Ivy was three-months pregnant, and she gave birth to a son the following year. Her address, according to the 1921 Electoral Roll, was in George Street, Berkhamsted. There is, however, no mention of Charles Avery living at the same address and Ivy appears to have moved away a few months later. In the 1939 Register, taken just after the start of the Second

World War, Ivy is shown as having remarried and living in Oxford with her new husband and Charles Avery's son.

What made Charles desert is not known, nor has any information as to his fate so far come to light. Being a deserter, he could not openly live with his wife for fear of imminent arrest, court martial and probable imprisonment. It is likely therefore, that he left Ivy to bring up their son and moved away, probably changing his name in the process as so many other deserters from the armed forces did at that time.

George Ronald Beddard Blount, DSO (1877 – 1964)
Captain, RN

George Ronald Beddard Blount, known in the family as Ronald, was the only member of George Blount's family not to live for a period of time at the Northchurch Rectory, although he would have been a frequent visitor there during his shore postings. He was born in October 1877 at Belvedere, Kent and later educated at Felsted Endowed Grammar School, Essex. Continuing the Blount family's naval tradition, and having finished his schooling in 1892, he joined the Royal Navy as a cadet at HMS *Britannia*, the Royal Navy's training ship moored at Dartmouth. His first posting was to the newly-commissioned HMS *Centurion*, a 10,500-ton lightly-armed battleship which was about to become the Royal Navy's China Station's flagship. Blount returned to England in early 1897, and after joining the crew of the battleship HMS *Majestic* he was promoted to Sub-Lieutenant.

After serving on two more warships, in 1900, Blount, now a Lieutenant, was sent to the naval gunnery school, HMS *Excellent,* in Portsmouth Harbour to qualify in gunnery and later trained other Royal navy men in gunnery, in a similar role to that performed by his older brother, Percy, at the army gunnery school at Shoeburyness.

In 1906, Blount was serving as the gunnery officer on board HMS *Montagu*, a newly-commissioned *Duncan*-class battleship, when it ran at full speed into Shutter Rock on the south-west corner of Lundy Island. The severe damage included several holes in her hull, the worst being a 91-foot long gash in her starboard side. Fortunately, there was no loss of life but the Montagu's Captain and another officer were later court-martialled. Blount's next postings as gunnery officer back on board HMS *Majestic* and later on HMS *Albion* were less fraught.

In 1909, after requalifying in gunnery at HMS *Excellent*, Blount became Gunnery and First Officer on-board HMS *Leander* and then HMS *Sapphire*, a *Topaze*-class cruiser, where he remained until May 1912. During his time on *Sapphire*, he was commended for his high standard as Gunnery Officer and the high scores his gunners achieved. He was promoted to Commander in June 1912, and later that year he married Cecilia Frances Hove in East

Farleigh Parish Church, Kent. A two-year shore posting as the Assistant to the Director of Naval Ordnance at the Admiralty followed.

In October 1914, with the war with Germany now into its second month, it was decided to put Blount's gunnery experience to good use against the enemy forces now employed on the Belgian coast following their capture of the ports of Zeebrugge, Ostend and Nieuwpoort. Although there had been time to make these ports unusable by the Germans before they were captured, a dispute arose between the Royal Navy and the BEF, with the BEF insisting that they could retake the three ports and bring them into use to supplement the French Channel ports further south. As a result, the Royal Navy took no further action. Following the BEF's resources being concentrated north-east of Paris however, the Germans quickly started fortifying the coastal area and brought U-boats into Zeebrugge. In October 1914, the Royal Navy brought the obsolete HMS *Revenge* back into service and fitted it out as a floating gun platform. On 26th October, Blount joined its crew as Gunnery Officer and a week later it was ready for service as the flagship of the newly created Channel Fleet's 6th Battle Squadron.

Unfortunately, bad weather prevented the Battle Squadron's first planned attack on the Belgian coast, but ten days later they bombarded the German troops at Nieuwpoort. The following month, Blount led a long-range naval bombardment of the German heavy guns which were firing at the British forces in Belgium. During the bombardment *Revenge* was hit twice and, with one hit below the waterline, she was forced to retire for repairs.

In April 1915, during the refit of *Revenge* at Chatham, Blount was posted to the Dover Patrol, and played a key part in planning the ongoing bombardment of German forces on the Belgian coast. A year later, his services were formally acknowledged by the Admiralty and this was to be the first of several formal notes of wartime recognition that he received.

On 20th June 1917, Blount was awarded the DSO by King George V at Buckingham Palace. Ten days later, he was promoted to Captain, retaining his planning role in the bombardment of the German positions on the Belgian coast.

In April 1918, Blount took part in the raids on Zeebrugge and Ostend and commanded the monitor, HMS *Marshal Soult,* which, along with six other vessels, launched a diversionary bombardment of the German forces at Ostend, whilst the main naval force attacked Zeebrugge. The aim was to block the Bruges ship canal and the German U-boat base with three obsolete cruisers filled with concrete. In order to prevent German troops counterattacking during the raid, a key bridge leading to the port was destroyed by explosives contained in an old submarine used as a floating bomb. Although the port of Zeebrugge was not completely blocked, the overall operation was deemed a success and Blount was later Mentioned in Despatches.

A few days before the end of the war, he took command of HMS *Commonwealth*, a *King Edward VII*-class battleship, which in July 1919 became a gunnery training ship. With the end of the war came a succession of medals, with Blount being awarded the Belgian Order of Leopold and the French *Croix de Guerre with Palm*.

Blount remained in command of HMS *Commonwealth* until August 1920 and subsequently became the Head of the Gunnery School in Devonport, a role he retained until May 1923. A series of executive posts at Portsmouth associated with ordinance and gunnery followed. His last commands were on HMS *Ramillies* and HMS *Barham* in the Mediterranean Fleet. He later became Naval *Aide-de-Camp* to King George V, a largely honorary position.

In 1927, Blount was awarded the Greek order of Redeemer (Commander), and the following year he was promoted to Rear-Admiral. Rear-Admiral George Ronald Beddard Blount, DSO, retired from the Royal Navy in 1928. Six years later, he became an honourary Vice-Admiral. Blount was to spend his last years in retirement at his home in Tenterden, Kent and died there in 1964 aged 86.

Harold Blount DSO (1881 – 1967)
Major, Royal Marine Artillery

The last of George Bouverie Blount's sons, Harold, was born at Woodside in October 1881. Like his older brother, Oswald, Harold was educated at the Grange Preparatory School in Eastbourne and then at Malvern College, where he was a House Prefect and a keen footballer. Harold left Malvern in 1897, a term after Oswald, and applied to join the Royal Marines. Within a year, he had graduated from the Royal Naval College as a Second Lieutenant, Royal Marine Artillery (RMA), and became the third of George Bouverie Blount's boys to be associated with big guns. In July 1899, he was promoted to Lieutenant and was posted to the RMA headquarters at Eastney Barracks, Portsmouth. Men of the RMA were responsible for the operation of one main gun turret on all ships above destroyer size, the other gun turrets being operated by Royal Navy gunners.

On 24th December 1901, Blount was posted to HMS *Repulse*, a *Royal Sovereign*-class battleship built in 1892, which formed part of the Channel Fleet and later was sent to Malta to join the Mediterranean Fleet. Having served for sixteen months on *Repulse*, he returned to Eastney. His next ship posting was in 1904, when he joined the officers on board HMS *Crescent*, an *Edgar*-class cruiser built in 1892 and based at the Cape of Good Hope Station in South Africa. Following *Crescent's* return to Portsmouth in 1907 for a refit, Blount was posted to the Royal Naval College at Dartmouth where he spent the next two years as an assistant professor in charge of cadets. On returning to Eastney Barracks, he was promoted to Captain.

November 1912 saw Blount taking command of the RMA crew and serving as the Intelligence Officer on board the newly-commissioned HMS *New Zealand*. This would prove to be one of his most important postings. Built by Fairfield Shipbuilding and Engineering Co at the Govan Shipyards in Glasgow, *New Zealand* was entirely financed by the New Zealand government. In 1909, with the growing threat of German naval power in the South Pacific, the New Zealand government offered to pay for the building of a new battleship. A battlecruiser of the *Indefatigable* class, *New Zealand* displaced 18,800 tons and was armed with eight 12-inch guns and had a top speed of 26 knots. Although never under the command of the New Zealand Navy, the ship contained several of the dominion's features, including a carving of its Coat of Arms and a silver bell from a previous ship of the same name. Among the original crew were three New Zealanders. *New Zealand*'s first captain was Lionel Halsey, who would some years later unveil the Northchurch War Memorial in St Mary's churchyard.

In February 1913, *New Zealand* embarked on a world tour, with the ship visiting some forty-seven ports including St Vincent, Ascension Island, St Helena, Capetown, Durban and Melbourne. During its ten-week stay in New Zealand, the battleship visited eighteen ports and over 350,000 people, about half of the country's population, came to see it. Whilst

HMS New Zealand
Author's collection

there, Captain Halsey was given a Māori *piupiu* (a warrior's skirt) and a greenstone *hei-tiki* (a type of pendant) with instructions to wear them when the vessel was engaged in battle; both items were meant to ward off evil spirits. Although based in New Zealand, *New Zealand* was intended to be the China Station's flagship, but the growing tension in Europe changed these plans and in November 1913 she returned to Great Britain to become part of the Royal Navy's First Battle Cruiser Squadron.

Blount and the RMA crew of *New Zealand's* 'Q' gun turret, first saw action off Heligoland Bight on 28th August 1914. On that day, two British light cruisers and thirty-one destroyers, under the command of Commodore Reginald Tyrwhitt, attacked German shipping near the port of Heligoland on Germany's north-western coast. Having sunk two German torpedo boats, the British force came under fire from several German ships and, finding his own ships now outgunned, Tyrwhitt called for assistance. The call was answered by Vice Admiral David Beatty, whose First Battle Cruiser Squadron, consisting of the battleships, HMS *New Zealand*, HMS *Invincible* and three battlecruisers, engaged the German vessels and sank three cruisers resulting in the loss of over 1,000 men. The remaining German ships escaped into the mist.

Just over three months later, on the morning of Wednesday 16th December 1914, ships of the German High Seas Fleet under Admiral Franz von Hipper sailed from their naval base. After evading British mines, they attacked the North Sea towns of Hartlepool, Scarborough and Whitby, opening fire on the largely civilian populations and causing considerable damage and leaving over 25 civilians dead. The Germans considered the attack such a success that a commemorative medal was later struck. Meanwhile in Great Britain, questions were asked in Parliament as to why such an attack had been allowed to happen.

The Royal Navy was determined not to allow a repeat of this incident and when tipped off by the Admiralty's codebreakers in London that another attack was about to be launched, the flotilla of German ships was intercepted by Beatty's Battle Squadron. Realising their attack on the coastal towns could not continue, the German ships quickly turned about and headed for home at high speed. A race to catch them ensued, and within an hour the Battle Squadron, including the guns in Blount's 'Q' gun turret on *New Zealand*, had opened fire. The leading German ship, the *Seidlitz* was set ablaze and lost 192 crew members, but managed to return to Germany, whilst the oldest of the German ships, the *Blucher*, was sunk with the loss of 782 men. Fearing the presence of German submarines as they got closer to the German coast however, Beatty broke off the engagement, allowing the remaining enemy ships to return to port.

Following the thwarting of their attack, the Germans devised a new, risker strategy. Hipper's battlecruisers would now start attacking British merchant shipping in the area between Denmark and Norway, which the Germans called Skagerrak and the British called Jutland. German submarines would be posted near the main British naval bases to attack any vessel going to the aid of the merchantmen. Once again, the British codebreakers came to the Royal Navy's assistance, and at the end of May 1916 they deciphered another German signal that told of the German Fleet's imminent departure from port. This enabled the British Grand Fleet to leave their bases under cover of darkness and thus avoid the enemy submarines lying in wait. The main battle fleet, under Sir John Jellicoe, and Beattie's battlecruisers, including *New Zealand*, now under the command of Captain John Green, headed eastwards across the North Sea. Meanwhile, the German fleet headed north, unaware that the British Fleet was at sea.

New Zealand was the fifth in line of Beatty's battlecruisers. Once again, Blount was in command of 'Q' turret and when in range, he opened fire on the approaching German warships. Minutes later, HMS *Indefatigable*, which was astern of *New Zealand*, was hit several times in quick succession causing her magazines to blow up and she quickly sank. Twenty minutes later, another battlecruiser, HMS *Queen Mary*, was hit and sunk. Later in the battle, the Third Battlecruiser Squadron lost HMS *Invincible*, on which Northchurchman, Surgeon George Shorland, was serving[30]. Despite the British losses, the Germans sensed defeat and turned for home.

By the time the battle had ended, the Germans had lost one battlecruiser, one elderly battleship, four light cruisers and five destroyers. The British had lost three battlecruisers, four armoured cruisers and eight destroyers. During the battle *New Zealand's*, Captain Green wore the Māori *piupiu* and *hei-tiki* given to his predecessor, Captain Lionel Halsey, a few years earlier. The charms apparently worked as *New Zealand* was hit only once during the battle and suffered no casualties.

Although the Battle of Jutland, as the engagement later became known, was not a definitive defeat for the German Imperial Fleet, it was enough to keep its surface ships in port for the remainder of the war. For his part in the battle whilst in charge of *New Zealand's* 'Q' turret, Blount was promoted to Major, awarded the DSO and the Imperial Russian Order of St Stanislas. Soon afterwards, Blount was officially posted to HMAS *Australia*, but remained on *New Zealand* serving as the Senior Royal Marine Officer. *New Zealand* saw further action in the North Sea in November 1917 during the inconclusive Second Battle of Heligoland Bight, and in 1918 she served on convoy escort duty.

Following the signing of the Armistice in November 1918, the fate of the German High Seas Fleet was left undecided. It was finally agreed that the fleet should be interned at Scapa Flow in the Orkney Islands whilst the politicians resolved the issue. The German submarine fleet would surrender to Rear-Admiral Tyrwhitt at Harwich, while the surface ships would sail to the Firth of Forth in Scotland and surrender to Admiral Beatty. They would then be escorted to Scapa Flow.

The surrender of the 70 serviceable ships of the High Seas Fleet on 21st November 1918 was a spectacular affair. They were led to the rendezvous point by the British cruiser HMS *Cardiff* where they were met by the imposing sight of 250 ships of the British Grand Fleet including *New Zealand*, their guns at the ready, should the Germans decide to make a final stand. The German ships were then escorted to Scapa Flow where they dropped anchor and Beatty gave orders for the German Flags to be hauled down and not hoisted again without permission.

In 1919, *New Zealand* returned to port for a refit and Blount was again posted to the Royal Marine Headquarters at Eastney. On 17th June 1919, whilst he was at Eastney, the German High Seas Fleet was scuttled at Scapa Flow.

---

[30] George Shorland's story is told in *For Them's Sake*

September 1922 saw Blount posted to the Royal Naval base at Malta for two years serving as the Royal Marine Officer for the Mediterranean Fleet. He returned to Portsmouth in 1924 as Brigadier-Major. In 1928, he returned to Malta as Fleet Royal Marines Officer, Mediterranean and two years later, he returned to England with the rank of Colonel, taking up a new post as Second Commandant at Chatham Dockyards. In 1934 he became Depot Commandant, Royal Marines, at Deal.

Blount was appointed an *Aide-de-Camp* to King George V in 1935, repeating the honour bestowed some years before on his brother, Ronald. He was also a recipient of the King's Silver Jubilee medal. In 1937, and approaching retirement, he was promoted to Major-General.

Blount retired from the Royal Navy in 1939 and moved to his brother Oswald's home at Woughton House, near Bletchley. Following the outbreak of the Second World War in September 1939, Blount put his military training to good use, becoming the commander of the Bletchley Home Guard, which had its base at the local police station. He remained in this role until 1944. Between 1940 and 1946 Blount also held the post of Honorary Secretary of the local Whaddon Chase Hunt and became a member of Newport Pagnell Rural District Council in 1941.

Harold Blount spent his remaining years at Woughton House with his brother Oswald. He died there in August 1967, aged 85.

Frederick George Burton (1880 – 1959)
Chief Yeoman of Signals 185114, RN

Frederick Burton did not come to live in Northchurch Parish until after he had completed 25 years serving in the Royal Navy, although he had married his wife, Evelyn, at St Peter's, Berkhamsted in 1913. Born in Symondsbury, a small, picturesque village in southwest Dorset in March 1880, he was the youngest son of the innkeeper of *The London Inn* in the village and grew up there. On reaching the age of fifteen, he persuaded his father to agree to him travelling to Portsmouth to join the Royal Navy. His training took place on HMS *Impregnable*, a training ship at Devonport, where he was later promoted to Boy 1st Class. Further training took place on HMS *Victory 1* at Portsmouth and his first sea posting was to HMS *Majestic*, on which Sub-Lieutenant Ronald Blount was then serving.

In March 1898, Frederick signed up for the standard 12 years' service with the Royal Navy and decided to become a signaller, and the following year he reached the grade of 2nd Class Signaller whilst serving on HMS *Hannibal*. Three and a half years later he was posted to HMS *Pallas* in Nova Scotia and became a Leading Signaller. Leaving HMS *Pallas* in February 1904, he spent the next eight years serving on a variety of ships and during this time he extended his period of service for a further ten years and rose to the rank of Yeoman of Signals.

In June 1912, Frederick joined the 778-strong crew of HMS *Hercules*, a heavily-armed *Colossus*-class dreadnaught battleship which had been commissioned the previous year. Six months after he joined the crew, *Hercules* became the flagship of the Home Fleet's newly-formed Second Battle Squadron based at Scapa Flow under Vice-Admiral Sir John Jellicoe.

Around this time Frederick met, and fell in love with, Evelyn Mary Kent, who worked as the cook for retired army officer, Lieutenant Colonel Eubule Daysh Thelwall at Oak Vale in Shrublands Road, Berkhamsted. How the couple came to meet each other is not known, but they were duly married at St Peter's, Berkhamsted in December 1913. The same month HMS *Hercules* was transferred to the Royal Navy's 1st Battle Squadron.

Frederick served as Yeoman of Signals on board HMS *Hercules* until June 1916 and took part in the Battle of Jutland, during which his ship engaged several German vessels, scoring two direct hits on the battlecruiser, SMS *Seydlitz*. *Hercules* returned to base having not suffered any damage during the engagement.

Frederick's final wartime posting was to HMS *Benbow*, an *Iron Duke*-class battleship commissioned in October 1914, which served as the flagship for 4th Battle Squadron. HMS *Benbow* saw limited action during his time on board, and at the end of 1918 she was reassigned to the Mediterranean Fleet. In July 1919 Frederick joined the crew of HMS *Dido*, an *Eclipse*-class cruiser which served as a depot ship and here, Frederick became Chief Yeoman of Signals, a rank he held until he was discharged from the Royal Navy in 1920, having served for 25 years.

By now, his wife had left the service of the Thelwall family[31] and was living in Gossoms End. Later that year, she gave birth to a daughter, the first of three children that she and Frederick would have together. He, meanwhile, had started working at one of the local timberyards, a significant contrast to his role as a Royal Navy signaller. In 1927, the family moved to larger accommodation in Swing Gate Lane, Berkhamsted and later to nearby Curtis Way. Frederick Burton died in 1959, aged 79.

Sydney Dell (1897 – 1980)
Engine Room Artificer M21181, RN

Sydney Dell was born at his grandfather, Joseph Dell's, cottage in Tring in April 1897. His unmarried mother, Henrietta Dell, was in service and had given birth to Sydney's older brother, Cyril, two years earlier. Family legend has it that both boys were fathered by the same man, a highly respected and internationally known inventor and engineer. By 1911 Henrietta was working as a domestic servant in Fulham, leaving her elder son to be looked after by her parents. The Census taken the same year shows Sydney being

---

[31] Lieutenant Colonel Eubule Daysh Thelwall died in September 1914

the adopted son of Henry Baker, a labourer at Shootersway Farm, Northchurch and his wife, Mary. After leaving school, Sydney became an apprentice fitter and turner at William Cooper & Nephews factory in Berkhamsted.

In April 1916, shortly after his 19th birthday, Sydney travelled to Portsmouth and joined the Royal Navy Volunteer Reserve (RNVR) and was posted to the shore establishment HMS *Victory*. His service record from this time describes him as being 5ft 2½ins tall, with blue eyes and brown hair. A month later, he joined HMS *Excellent* as a member of the armourers' crew. HMS *Excellent* was the Royal Navy's gunnery school based on the man-made Whale Island in Portsmouth harbour. It was here that Lieutenant George Ronald Beddard Blount had developed his gunnery skills some years earlier.

Three months after joining the Royal Navy, Sydney married his girlfriend, Dorothy Bedford, at St Mark's, Portsmouth. They had met in Berkhamsted, and their first child, a daughter, was born the following year.

Sydney remained on HMS *Excellent* until the end of 1916, having qualified as a gunner, and he was then posted to HMS *Centurion*, a *King George V*-class dreadnought battleship, which formed part of the Second Battle Squadron and had taken part in the Battle of Jutland in 1917. With the German High Seas Fleet now largely confined to Wilhelmshaven, *Centurion* spent the remainder of the war on patrol. It was during this time that he gained a formal qualification as a fitter and turner.

In February 1919, the ship returned to Portsmouth and Sydney was demobilised. He returned to Northchurch and later moved to Berkhamsted, where he started work as an engineer. Sydney Dell died in 1980, aged 83.

Frederick John Freeman (1900 – 1974)
Ordinary Seaman J74871, RN

Frederick Freeman was one of the youngest Northchurchmen to serve in the war. Born in April 1900, the son of Frederick John Freeman (snr), a bootmaker, and his wife, Louisa, the family lived in a cottage in Northchurch High Street.

Having finished school, he became a plumber's mate and attended the Northchurch Technical Institute, where, in 1916, he was awarded a prize for forge work. The following year, wanting to join the war effort and being below the age for conscription, Frederick obtained his parents' permission to apply to join the Royal Navy. His initial training took place on HMS *Powerful*, a former battleship which, with its guns removed, had served as a troopship earlier in the war and was now moored at Devonport and being used as a training ship for boy stokers. After three months Frederick moved to HMS *Pembroke*, the Naval Barracks at Chatham, to continue his training. In January 1918, Frederick joined the crew of HMS *Royal Oak*, a *Revenge-*

class battleship which formed part of the First Battle Squadron. On 21st November 1918, whilst serving on HMS *Royal Oak,* he witnessed the surrender of the German Grand Fleet at Scarpa Flow.

Demobilised three months later, Frederick returned to his parents' home in Northchurch and found work as a plumber. He married in the late 1920s and by 1939, he had moved to Tring and was serving as a reserve fireman with the local fire brigade. He died in 1974, aged 74.

Edward George Gadbury (1894 – 1926)
Leading Seaman J14308, RN

Edward Gadbury was born in village of Nettleden in December 1894 to unmarried mother Maria Gadbury and was brought up by his mother at his grandfather's four-roomed cottage in Nettleden and later started work at a nearby market garden.

At the age of seventeen, with his mother's permission, Edward joined the Royal Navy as a Boy 2nd Class. His service records describe him as being 5ft 5¼ins tall, with brown hair, blue eyes and a fresh complexion. His initial training took place at HMS *Ganges* before he was posted for short spells of duty on board HMS *Africa*, HMS *Revenge* and HMS *Venerable*. A year after he joined the Royal Navy he became an Ordinary Seaman and a six-month spell of duty followed at the navy's torpedo school, HMS *Vernon*, in Portchester Creek, near Portsmouth.

In October 1913, Edward joined the crew of the newly-commissioned *King George V*-class battleship, HMS *Audacious*. Launched in 1912, this ship displaced 23,400 tons of water and was armed with 10 13.2-inch guns, 16 4-inch guns and 3 21-inch torpedo tubes. Her armour, made by the German firm of Krupp, was up to 12-inches thick in places. Crewed by 900 men, she was one of the most powerful battleships in the British fleet and formed part of the Royal Navy's Second Battle Squadron.

Early in the morning of 27th October 1914, with Edward, recently promoted to Able Seaman, on board and under the command of Captain Cecil Dampier, *Audacious* left her base at Lough Swilly in Ireland with other ships of the Second Battle Squadron for gunnery exercises. A few days earlier, the SS *Berlin*, a German passenger liner converted to a minelayer, had laid a

HMS Audacious
Author's collection

240

minefield across the strategic shipping lane between Ireland and Britain which was used by ships crossing the Atlantic[32]. Two merchant ships struck the mines soon afterwards, but news had not reached the Admiralty by the time the Second Battle Squadron set sail.

At 08:45, *Audacious* struck one of the mines. Fearing a submarine attack, the rest of the Battle Squadron sailed away, whilst *Audacious*, with water seeping into her hull, attempted to sail towards the nearest Irish port. Some six hours later, his ship unable to make much headway and slowly sinking, Captain Dampier ordered all non-essential crew to leave the ship. The passenger ship, RMS *Olympic,* which was close by, attempted to take *Audacious* under tow, but was not powerful enough to make any headway, and at 19:15 Captain Dampier ordered 'abandon ship'. Ninety minutes later, *Audacious* capsized and soon afterwards the ammunition on board exploded, the blast sending shrapnel thousands of yards away.

Fortunately, the sinking of *Audacious* only resulted in the loss of one man, a petty officer who was watching the ship sink from some 800 yards away onboard HMS *Liverpool* and who was hit by shrapnel from the explosion. Fearing public unease about the loss of one of the most powerful ships in the British Fleet so early in the war, the Admiralty put restrictions on the reporting of the loss, albeit that passengers on the *Olympic* had witnessed the event and several photographs of the incident had been taken. It was not until four years later that the Admiralty formally announced the loss of the ship.

The day after the loss of *Audacious*, Edward, transferred to HMS *Excellent,* the gunnery and diving training school at Portsmouth, where he remained until May 1915, becoming a proficient diver. His next posting was to HMS *Venus,* an *Eclipse*-class cruiser which was about to set sail for Egypt for seven months of patrolling the Red Sea. The following year *Venus* sailed to Aden en route to Colombo, the capital of Ceylon (now Sri Lanka), where she would remain for the next three months.

Now promoted to Leading Seaman, Edward remained on *Venus* whilst she made numerous journeys between the British naval bases at Columbo, Singapore and Hong Kong, before returning to Portsmouth in April 1918, where he went back to HMS *Excellent* for more diving training. He was still there when the Armistice was signed the following November.

With the war over, Edward took the opportunity to travel back to Hertfordshire and marry Daisy Muriel Wilson, a domestic nurse who lived

---

[32] The captain of the *Berlin* had initially planned to lay mines outside all the major ports on the west side of Britain and Scotland, but was unable to get close enough to achieve his task. He laid a single minefield in the shipping lanes but, running out of fuel, was forced to sail for Trondheim in Norway where the ship was interned for the rest of the war.

in Frithsden, close to where he grew up. After a period based on shore, Edward transferred to the Royal Yacht, HMY *Victoria and Albert*.

Sadly, in 1923 Edward contracted tuberculosis and left the Royal Yacht. He spent the next three years in various hospitals in Portsmouth before succumbing to the disease. His widow moved to Berkhamsted and lived there for the rest of her life.

Cecil Herbert Gibbs (1888 – 1957)
Ordinary Seaman LZ8243, RNVR

Son of Master Butcher, Herbert Gibbs, Cecil Gibbs was born in Kennington, south London, in the closing days of 1888. Soon after his birth, Herbert moved his family north of the river to Upper Holloway and lived there for several years before leaving London and moving to Moss House in Gossoms End. Here, he set up a successful dairy business, earning enough income to enable the family to employ a servant.

After leaving school, Cecil did not follow his father into either of his trades, but instead started work as a clerk for the London & North Western Railway at their goods depot at Broad Street Station, located on the eastern edge of the City of London. It was a job he was to retain for the rest of his life, apart from a short interval serving in the Royal Naval Volunteer Reserve (RNVR).

In July 1915, 26-year-old Cecil married Jessie Caroline Codgbrook, the daughter of a shoemaker from Rushden, Northamptonshire, at St Peter's, Berkhamsted. Jessie's brother, Charles, was a manager at the Berkhamsted Gas Works in Gossoms End, and she and her parents were now living at his house in Berkhamsted High Street.

It is not clear how Cecil managed to avoid conscription, but it is possible that his job working for the railway was considered a 'reserved occupation' under the Military Service Act and consequently he was exempt. However, by the end of November 1917, he had decided to join the London division of the RNVR and was under training at HMS *Victory II*, their base at Crystal Palace, south London. His training complete, he became an Ordinary Seaman.

For the remainder of the war, and for a few months afterwards until his demobilisation, Cecil, like many other RNVR sailors, served aboard former fishing vessels like HMS *Onyx* and HMS *Daisy 2*. Both vessels had been requisitioned by the Royal Navy and lightly armed to become mine layers and anti-submarine net layers operating in coastal waters.

Demobilised in June 1919, he returned home to Gossoms End and resumed his job as a railway clerk in London. Cecil lived in the same house in Gossoms End until his death in 1957, aged 68.

Walter John Grover (1884 – 1973)
Able Seaman J206846, RN

Walter John Grover was born in January 1884 in Berkhamsted, where his father, William Grover, worked as a labourer. Walter grew up in Bourne End Lane and, before joining the Royal Navy, worked as an errand boy.

On his eighteenth birthday, Walter signed up at Chatham for the standard 12-year term with Royal Navy. His service record describes him as being 5ft 2½ins tall, with dark brown hair, brown eyes and a dark complexion. He spent the next twelve years serving on various ships and shore establishments, including three years on HMS *Minotaur* in the Far East, during which time he rose to the rank of Able Seaman.

In early 1914, having completed his twelve years' service in the Royal Navy, Walter returned home proudly displaying a tattoo of two snakes around his neck. It was not long, before he was back in naval uniform however, as in September 1914 he returned to Chatham to sign-up for the duration of the war. His first posting was to HMS *Diana*, an *Eclipse*-class cruiser, part of the Twelfth Cruiser Squadron.

In May 1915, he transferred to the recently-commissioned HMS *Calliope* and served as part of her crew for the remainder of the war. *Calliope*, alongside her sister ship HMS *Champion*, was under construction in Chatham at the outbreak of war and was a C-class light cruiser. With a crew of 368, and armed with two 6-inch guns, eight 4-inch guns and two 21-inch torpedo tubes, *Calliope* was commissioned in June 1915 and assigned as the flagship of the Fourth Light Cruiser Squadron.

In August 1915, *Calliope* took part in the hunt for the German minelayer, SMS *Meteor*, which had been laying mines in the Moray Firth, one of which had just sunk HMS *Ramsey*. SOS signals from the *Ramsey* were received by *Calliope* and together with other cruisers they chased after the German ship. Facing certain defeat, the captain of the *Meteor* decided to scuttle his ship to avoid capture.

A boiler room fire badly damaged *Calliope* in March 1916 and she returned to her base for repairs. Two months later, the repairs completed, she rejoined her Light Cruiser Squadron and shortly afterwards took part in the Battle of Jutland. Whilst the main capital ships of both navies exchanged fire, Fourth Light Cruiser Squadron engaged the smaller German vessels until the German Fleet withdrew. *Calliope* was one of the last vessels to maintain contact with the retreating German ships, firing a torpedo at them from 6,500 yards. In retaliation, she came under fire from the German battleships *Kaiser* and *Markgraf*, being hit by four shells which killed ten of Walter's comrades and wounded a further nine.

Later that year, Walter received the sad news that his younger brother, George, who was serving with the 6th Battalion, Bedfordshire Regiment, had been killed on 17th July during the Battle of Bazentine Ridge, part of the Somme Offensive.

In September 1917, *Calliope* helped to sink four German trawler minesweepers in the same area. That same month, Walter married Ethel Maria Vandyke who worked at a south London hospital. After the wedding, he returned to *Calliope*, and spent the remainder of the war on patrol protecting convoys in the North Sea.

He was demobilised in February 1919. By now Ethel was living in Deptford, Kent and would later give birth to two daughters. It is currently not known what Walter did on his return to civilian life after the war. He died in 1973, aged 89.

Fred Mashford (1900 – 1982)
Able Seaman J80354, RN

Fred Mashford was born, in George Street, Berkhamsted, then part of the eastern portion of Northchurch Parish, in July 1900. He was the second of George and Sarah Ann Mashford's children. George, who worked as a pit sawyer at one of the local timberyards, sadly died in the late summer of 1901, leaving Sarah Ann to bring up her two young children alone. Fred went to Berkhamsted and Northchurch National School, leaving there in 1914.

After leaving school, Fred became a bricklayer's labourer, but in 1917 he joined the Royal Navy as a Boy 2nd Class and began his training aboard HMS *Powerful* in Devonport. Fred's service record shows that he had fair hair, blue eyes and stood 5ft 4½ins tall. In February 1918, he joined the crew of the depot ship, HMS *Dido,* which provided maintenance and accommodation for reserve crewmen for the Tenth Destroyer Flotilla based at Harwich. Fred later transferred to HMS *Thisbe*, an 'R' Class destroyer. On his eighteenth birthday, he became an Ordinary Seaman.

Following the end of the war, *Thisbe* was redeployed to the Medway and Fred went with her, transferring to her new depot ship, HMS *Prince George*, based at Sheerness. At that time the Royal Navy was being reorganised and in March 1919, Fred was sent to HMS *Pembroke 1* at Chatham to await a new posting. The following month, he joined HMS *Sandhurst*, a depot ship for one of the new Grand Fleet Flotillas, and was assigned to a 'V' Class Destroyer, HMS *Vimiera* and promoted to Able Seaman.

On 24th November 1919, Fred was "Discharged to Shore" at Chatham and officially joined the Royal Fleet Reserve list the following day. Throughout his service Fred's character was described as "VG" (Very Good) and his ability was mostly assessed as "Sat" (satisfactory), but "Sup" (superior) at his discharge.

He returned to his home in George Street and started working for his uncle Fred as a cabinet maker. In August 1925, he married Alice May

Osborn at St Peter's, Berkhamsted and the newlyweds would later have two children together. Fred Mashford died in 1982, aged 81.

John Lewis Mellor (1893 – 1949)
Artificer M1087, RN

John Mellor was the son of Edgar Mellor, the Headmaster at Northchurch Village School. He was born in the London Borough of Harrow in June 1893, where his father worked as a teacher at a local elementary school. John's mother, Elizabeth, was also a teacher. In 1909, with his father's permission, John, then aged 16, entered the Royal Navy as a Boy Artificer.

Artificers were the mechanics in the armed forces and John was posted to HMS *Tenedos*, a training establishment for boy artificers at Chatham, where he started to learn a trade. The Royal Navy prided itself on the quality of its artificers and their training took four years to complete. In 1910, artificer training was moved to HMS *Indus,* which operated at both Portsmouth and Devonport, with John being posted to Portsmouth. The following year, now eighteen years old, he signed up for the standard 12 years' service. Completing his training in July 1913, John became an Engine Room Artificer (ERA) 5th Class.

August 1913 saw John, now promoted to ERA 4th Class, joining the crew of the battleship, HMS *King Edward VII*. Built in 1905, *King Edward VII* was by then considered obsolete in terms of firepower following the introduction of the more modern *Dreadnought* battleships and formed part of the Home Fleet's Third Battle Squadron. After the outbreak of war Third Battle Squadron transferred to the Grand Fleet and was assigned to the naval blockade of Germany, becoming part of Northern Patrol. On 6th January 1916, *King*

HMS King Edward VII
Author's Collection

Edward VII left her base at Scapa Flow bound for Belfast, where a scheduled refit was planned. Sailing off Cape Wrath, it struck a mine laid earlier by the German cruiser, SMS *Möwe*. There were no initial injuries, but immediately the ship started to list to starboard. Attempts by the ship's captain to steer it closer to the coast, and beach her if necessary, failed and other ships were requested to help. With nightfall approaching, and *Edward VII* slowly sinking further into the water, the decision was taken to abandon her and all bar one of the crew were safely transferred to the other ships. One man was lost when he fell between *Edward VII* and one of the rescuing ships. HMS *Edward VII* sank later that night.

On his return, John was posted to HMS *Dolphin*, the submarine base at Gosport. In August 1914, the Royal Navy had 80 submarines in service but, unlike the German navy, the Admiralty saw them as being inferior to surface vessels and as a result, no major submarine development had taken place in recent years. The appointment of Admiral Fisher as Head of the Admiralty in 1914 changed this perception, and new submarines began to be built. To keep them supplied at sea, dedicated depot ships were assigned to each submarine. In March 1916, John joined the crew of HMS *Arrogant,* a former cruiser, which had been converted to a depot ship to support the elderly submarine *C35* which, along with other 'C -class' submarines, served in the Baltic.

Four months later, he transferred to HMS *Maidstone*, a submarine depot and repair ship commissioned in 1912, which serviced the submarines of the Eighth Submarine Flotilla based at Harwich. John was assigned to submarine *E19,* an 'E-class' vessel built in 1914 at Barrow-in-Furness, which like *C35*, served in the Baltic. In January 1918, he returned to HMS *Dolphin* at Gosport and was promoted to ERA[33] 3rd Class. The following October, he was posted to the depot ship HMS *Vulcan.*

In the Autumn of 1919, John married Helen Uglow, the daughter of a hardware store manager, in Hertford. Returning to *Vulcan*, which was then based at Blyth, Northumberland, John witnessed the accident at the dockyard when *Vulcan's* engines were being repaired. Moored alongside *Vulcan* during the repair work was the submarine *H41*. When *Vulcan's* engines were restarted, H41 was drawn towards it by the suction caused by the revolving propellers. Despite attempts by both crews to keep the two vessels apart the propellers struck the stern of *H41* and cut through her outer casing breaching her pressure hull. *H41* sank within minutes, but fortunately all her crew were saved. John remained with *Vulcan* until September 1922, being promoted to ERA 2nd Class.

In June 1923, John started experiencing problems with one of his eyes and he was admitted to the Royal Navy's Hospital at Gosport for treatment. In view of his imminent retirement from the navy, it was decided to award John a disability pension and he was subsequently discharged.

In 1939, John was living with his wife and family at Stowey Park, near Long Ashton in Somerset and working as an aero engine research engineer for the Bristol Aeroplane Company at Filton, Gloucestershire. By then, the Bristol Aeroplane Company were playing a vital part in the war effort, supplying Beaufighter, Blenheim and Beaufort aircraft to the RAF. He died in the autumn of 1949, aged 54.

---

[33] Engine Room Artificer

Robert Neville (1882 – 1958)
Stoker 194976, RN

Born in New Road, Northchurch in March 1882, Robert Neville was one of eleven children of watercress worker, Charles Neville, and his wife, Mathilda. In 1897 when he was fifteen, Robert decided that he wanted to join the Royal Navy and, with the support of his father, travelled to Devonport to start his training as a Boy 2nd Class. His service record from this time shows him as being 5ft 4½ins tall, with light brown hair, blue-grey eyes and a fresh complexion. In 1901, he was promoted to Able Seaman.

In August 1902, Robert, who was then based at Gillingham, Kent, married 17-year-old Ada Louisa Davis at St Mary's, Northchurch. She was the daughter of Thomas Davis from Gossoms End and worked at the timberyard of East and Son. Three months later, Robert joined the Royal Naval Reserves and became a painter and decorator, moving to Clarence Road, Berkhamsted. Ada would later give birth to three children, although one would not survive infancy. After five years in the Royal Naval Reserves, he was formerly discharged from the Royal Navy in November 1907.

In 1914, Robert and his family were living at his father-in-law's house in Gossoms End, but it was not until November 1916 that he decided to re-enlist and returned to Devonport for training. In March 1917, he was posted as a stoker to the engine room of the *Iron Duke*-class battleship HMS *Marlborough*. Commissioned two years earlier, *Marlborough* was based at Scapa Flow and was powered by eighteen coal-fired Yarrow boilers and could hold up to 3,250 tons of coal, giving her a range of some 7,780 miles travelling at 10 knots. Robert's role, along with his fellow stokers, was to feed *Marlborough's* hungry furnaces with coal to keep the boilers working. Throughout his time serving on board *Marlborough*, she did not take part in any major action against German shipping.

A month after he was discharged from the Royal Navy in March 1919, *Marlborough* took part in the rescue of the surviving members of the Russian Imperial Royal family from the Crimea.

Returning to civilian life, Robert found work as a painter and decorator in north-west London and in 1939 was living in Willesden. He died in 1958, aged 75.

Leonard Francis Thomas Saunders (1883 – 1963)
Chief Writer 345853, RN

In the 1860s, the Admiralty introduced a new class of sailor, the Writer, to handle all administration matters aboard ship. This role had previously been done by clerks located at the naval bases across the British Empire. As such, Writers became responsible for keeping numerous records up to date, including recording the pay received by the ship's officers and men, recording the money spent by the ship's captain, logging all incoming mail to the officers and maintaining records of the regular inspections and updating the ship's log and diaries. After enlisting with the Royal Navy, and having chosen the trade of a writer, the recruit would go through the standard naval training programme, and on completion would be given the rank of Writer 3rd Class.

One of the writers serving with the Royal Navy in August 1914 was Leonard Saunders. Born in a cottage in Northchurch High Street in March 1883, he was the son of Job Saunders, a coachman, and his wife, Elizabeth. By 1901, the Saunders family was living in a cottage in Gossoms End with Leonard working as a solicitor's clerk. The following year however, he signed up for twelve years' service as a Writer with the Royal Navy.

Leonard stood a good 5ft 11ins tall and had grey eyes and brown hair when he was posted to HMS *Pembroke* to start his training. Having become a Writer 3rd Class, Leonard was posted to HMS *Dido*, which had recently returned from service in the Far East. Over the next three years, Leonard served on three differing classes of ship, together with a shore base, whilst he trained as a ship's writer. Four years after joining the Royal Navy and whilst serving on HMS *Topaze*, Leonard was promoted to Writer 2nd Class.

After a short period back at HMS *Pembroke* in 1906, Leonard spent two years serving on the depot ship, HMS *Blenheim,* before being transferred to the battleship HMS *Albion*. Whilst serving on *Albion* he became a Writer 1st Class and just before he left the ship in 1910, he married Clara Nichols at a church in East London. She moved to a property in Gillingham, not far from where his new base ship, HMS *Goliath* was moored. In the summer of 1913, Leonard was back at HMS *Pembroke.* Having been based in home waters since joining the Royal Navy, Leonard's final pre-war posting was to HMS *Weymouth*, a *Town*-class light cruiser serving in the Mediterranean and he was serving on *Weymouth* when war broke out.

Soon afterwards *Weymouth* was ordered to the Indian Ocean to hunt for the German raider SMS *Emden*. Before the war, *Emden* had been based at the German-run port of Tsingtao, China. Anticipating the outbreak of war during the summer of 1914, *Emden's* seasoned captain, Karl von Müller, took his ship out to sea just before an Anglo-Japanese force captured Tsingtao. Over the coming weeks *Emden* effectively became a 20th century pirate ship, attacking allied shipping across the Indian Ocean and occasionally disguising herself as a Royal Navy vessel to lure ships closer. On one occasion, von Müller sailed *Emden* into Madras harbour and opened fire on the port's fuel depot, setting it ablaze. By the middle of September 1914, the disruption to allied shipping caused by *Emden* was substantial and risked delaying the transport of significant numbers of Empire troops from India, Australia and New Zealand to France.

With the desperate need to bring these troops into the war as quickly as possible, the Admiralty gathered together a task force of warships to find and sink the *Emden*. Among the ships in this force was HMS *Weymouth* with the recently-promoted Chief Writer, Leonard Saunders, on board. He had just completed his twelve-years' service with the Royal Navy and had re-enlisted for the duration of the war.

On reaching the Indian Ocean, the task force set about searching for the *Emden*, but it was like looking for a needle in a haystack, with thousands of square miles of ocean to cover. Fortunately, two months later, von Müller's luck ran out when sailors from the *Emden* attacked a British telegraph station on a remote island in the Cocos Islands. Before being captured, the radio operator had been able to send off an SOS signal, which was picked up by the Australian cruiser, HMAS *Sydney* which happened to be nearby. Changing course for the islands, *Sydney* was able to open fire on the *Emden* before it made its escape, scoring several direct hits and forcing von Müller to head for a nearby sandbar to stop his ship from sinking.

Following the removal of the threat from the *Emden*, HMS *Weymouth* remained in the Indian Ocean during the search for the German cruiser SMS *Königsberg*. Recently based at Dar-es-Salaam in the colony of German East Africa, *Königsberg* had also proved a threat to allied shipping in the area, although her range was limited by the supply of coal to heat her boilers. With the increase in British warships in the area and needing repairs and refuelling, *Königsberg*'s captain took his ship into the Rufiji River estuary on the East African coast which was surrounded by dense foliage. Here, he could hide his ship and venture out on surprise attacks when it was safe. One such attack in the Indian Ocean on 19th September left two allied

SMS Königsberg
Author's collection

vessels, including an old British cruiser, ablaze, but engine problems forced *Königsberg* back to her lair. Repairs to her engines could only be done by engineers at Dar-es-Salaam some 140 miles away, however, so a route was cut through the jungle to enable thousands of Africans to pull the damaged engine parts, mounted on sleds, to the repair shops. Amazingly, ten days later, the repaired or replaced parts had been returned and their installation had started.

Before the repairs could be completed however, the British discovered *Köenigsberg*'s hiding place, and three warships, including *Weymouth*, arrived off the coast to ensure that the cruiser was unable to escape from the estuary. There followed a heavy naval bombardment, which, combined with the deliberate sinking of an old freighter in the estuary, effectively prevented *Köenigsberg's* escape. Two attacks by small shallow-draft gunboats, combined with air attacks, sealed her fate. However, the ship's crew were able to remove some of her heavy guns, which were later mounted on carriages and used by the local German *Schutztruppe*, led by its commander, Colonel Paul von Lettow-Vorbeck, in the subsequent fighting in East Africa. Most of the surviving crew of *Köenigsberg* also joined von Lettow-Vorbeck's force and so, with the guns removed, she was finally blown up.

In May 1916, Leonard left *Weymouth* and returned to HMS *President* where he served until April 1918. He then transferred to the newly-formed Royal Air Force, doing a similar role as a writer. Details of his subsequent life are somewhat vague. At the start of the Second World War he was a Warrant Officer in the RAF Volunteer Reserve and after the war became a clerk. He died in Berkhamsted in 1963, aged 79.

Archibald William Seabrook (1896 – 1938)
Petty Officer J23540, RN

Archibald Seabrook was born in August 1896 and was the second son of Joseph Seabrook, who ran Beeton Wood Farm in Ruislip, Middlesex. By 1911, the Seabrook family had left Ruislip and moved to Gossoms End, where Joseph changed occupations, becoming an off-licence keeper. After leaving school, Archibald started work running errands for his father and later, no doubt because of his father's contacts, worked as a labourer at Locke & Smith's brewery in Berkhamsted. It was not long before he decided that he wanted to join the Royal Navy, however, and in March 1913 aged 16, he entered the Royal Naval training establishment of HMS *Ganges* at Shotley Gate, near Ipswich as a Boy 2nd Class. He remained there until January 1914 when he transferred to the training ship HMS *Impregnable*. In August 1914, four days after the outbreak of war, he became an Ordinary Seaman.

The following month, Archibald joined the crew of HMS *Duncan*, which was under refit at Chatham dockyard. Following the completion of the refit, *Duncan* joined the Third Battle Squadron at Scapa Flow, becoming part of the Royal Navy's Northern Patrol. Not long after, *Duncan* and her fellow *Duncan*-class battleships were transferred to the Channel Fleet in response to the German Navy's activity in the English Channel.

Archibald left *Duncan* in January 1915 and on his return to Chatham he was posted to HMS *Tyne,* a troop and shore ship based at Queensferry on the Forth estuary near Edinburgh. He was to remain a crewmember on board the *Tyne* for the rest of the war.

In the spring of 1919, Archibald returned to Berkhamsted where he married Dorothy Newton at St Peter's church. The following year she gave birth to a girl. With the remainder of his service with the Royal Navy still to complete, Archibald later served on several other ships including HMS *Prince George*, HMS *Blenheim*, HMS *Vulcan* and HMS *Cyclops*. By the time his twelve-year term of service in the Royal Navy came to an end in 1926, he had qualified as a gunner. Deciding to continue serving with the Royal Navy, Archibald later passed the necessary examinations to become an officer and became a Lieutenant. Around that time his wife and daughter moved from their home in Kitsbury Road, Berkhamsted, to a house in nearby Shrublands Road.

Sadly, Archibald died of heart failure in 1938 whilst serving with the Royal Navy at their base at Esquimalt in British Columbia. The 1939 Register shows his widow and their daughter still living in Shrublands Road.

Francis Joseph Seabrook (1895 – 1970)
Petty Officer M7790, RN

Francis Seabrook was born in Ruislip in January 1895. In 1911, sixteen-year-old Francis was continuing with his education before becoming a clerk. Possibly influenced by his younger brother, Archibald, in June 1914 Francis decided to change career and join the Royal Navy for the standard 12 years' service. One inch taller than his brother, Francis stood 5ft 6ins tall and had brown hair and grey eyes.

Following the completion of his initial training at HMS *Pembroke I*, Francis was assigned to HMS *Sutlej*, a *Cressy*-class armoured cruiser, built in 1899 and which had recently joined the Royal Navy's Ninth Cruiser Squadron. In May 1915, he was transferred to HMS *Baralong*, one of the Royal Navy's most secret vessels.

Baralong had been built in 1901 as a merchant ship for the Bucknall Steamship Lines Ltd, and was requisitioned by the Royal Navy in August 1914. With the growing threat of German submarines operating against allied shipping bringing valuable supplies across the Atlantic, the Admiralty authorised the conversion of ships of all sizes, including *Baralong*, into what became known as 'Q-ships' named after the identification code given to the first of the converted vessels. The task of the 'Q-ships', which were disguised as unarmed merchant vessels, was to act as decoys, diverting German U-boats away from the real merchant ships before opening fire on them from strategically concealed guns. *Baralong* was armed with three 12-pdr guns, enough to destroy any U-boat on the surface, and operated under the false name of *Wyandra* and flew the American flag. The Navy crew on board were given 30 shillings to purchase second-hand clothing to wear on board and on any shore leave.

On 7th May 1915, the Cunard liner *Lusitania* was sunk off the Irish coast by the German submarine *U-20* with the loss of 1,198 lives. Public outrage on both sides of the Atlantic led to the Admiralty sending an order to the *Baralong's* captain, Lieutenant Godfrey Herbert, that, should he come across any enemy submarine, it was 'most undesirable' for him to take any prisoners. That August, *U-24* sunk the White Star liner *Arabic* with the loss of 44 lives and *Baralong* was ordered to track down and sink the U-boat.

Later the same day an SOS message was received from the Leyland liner *Nicosian* which was being shelled by *U-27*. Racing to her aid and flying 'The Stars and Stripes' *Baralong* signalled 'am saving life' and came up on the starboard beam of the *Nicosian*, thus blocking the U-27's view of her. Whilst hidden, *Baralong* raised her White Ensign and when *U-27* came back into view as the ship passed the *Nicosian* the submarine presented a perfect target. Opening fire, the *Baralong's* gunners scored a direct hit below the submarine's waterline and it began to sink. They continued to fire on the doomed submarine until it disappeared below the water for the final time. Several of the U-boat's crew managed to escape before it sank, however, but most were shot in the water by the Royal Marines on board the *Baralong*, whilst others, including the U-boat's Commander, managed to get aboard the *Nicosian*. When Lieutenant Herbert discovered this, he ordered the Marines aboard the *Nicosian* to shoot them as well. A total of 37 German submariners were killed during the incident. In contrast to subsequent protests from the German government, which demanded that Lieutenant Herbert and his crew be put on trial, Herbert was awarded the DSO for his actions.

The following month, *Baralong* sank *U-41* in the Western Approaches. There were two survivors who managed to get into a lifeboat. *Baralong* returned to the area a few hours later, and when Lieutenant Herbert spotted the lifeboat he ordered it to be deliberately run down, killing the survivors in the process. Following another set of protests by the German government, the Admiralty, realising that the usefulness of *Baralong* as a 'Q-ship' had ended, recalled it back to base with all the crew being either transferred to other ships or shore establishments. All references to *Baralong* were also removed from Lloyd's Register and other official records, and the vessel was later transferred to the Mediterranean under the new name of *Manica*.

Having left *Baralong,* for most of the next twelve months Francis was based at several shore establishments before being posted to another 'Q-ship', *Q24* otherwise known as *Laggan*. Originally built in 1907 as a cargo ship, *Laggan* was commissioned as a 'Q-ship' in January 1917 and was armed with one 4inch and two 12-pdr guns. He remained on *Laggan* until the end of the war, when he returned to England.

In the spring of 1919, Francis married Dorothy Mary Alice Kempster at St Mary's, Northchurch. After a short honeymoon, he returned to the Royal Navy in which he remained until after the end of the Second World War, serving on several warships, including HMS *Royal Oak,* HMS *Royal Sovereign* and HMS *Marlborough,* and rose to the rank of Lieutenant Commander. In 1949, he received the Royal Navy Long Service and Good Conduct medal. Francis Seabrook died in 1970, aged 75.

15 – The Airmen

In 1914 the concept of powered flight was still relatively new. It was only eleven years earlier that the Wright brothers had made the first ever successful powered flight, which even then only lasted for just under a minute. This was followed six years later by Louis Blériot, who became the first pilot to fly an aircraft across the English Channel.

As with the motor car and the motorcycle, the invention of the aeroplane was the spark that lit the enthusiasm of many skilled engineers, like Geoffrey de Havilland, who saw their future in aircraft design. Others however, saw the potential for the aeroplane as a military asset, the Italians being the first to use aircraft in a military capacity during their conquest of what is now Libya in 1911-12. In Great Britain, the army also started to look at the aeroplane as a weapon of war, but as the early aircraft were only just powerful enough to carry a pilot and an observer, let alone any form of armament, they were initially used only for observation and reconnaissance purposes. As aircraft design evolved, however, so came the capacity for them to carry guns and bombs and to be used in an offensive role.

The Royal Flying Corps (RFC) came into being in April 1912 and consisted of a Military Wing and a Naval Wing. A training school at Upavon, Wiltshire, was created the following June to train the pilots of both wings, although the Naval Wing also established a separate flying school at Eastchurch, Hampshire. A month before the outbreak of war the Naval Wing moved under the control of the Admiralty and the following year it became a totally separate unit, being renamed the Royal Naval Air Service (RNAS). The RFC remained under army control until on 1st April 1918, when it and the RNAS were brought together again under the control of the new Air Ministry and given the new title of the Royal Air Force (RAF).

John Forster Alcock (1896 – 1977)
2nd Lieutenant, RAF

John Forster Alcock, the second son of John Forster Alcock (snr) and his third wife, Augusta, was born in Northchurch in March 1896. The Alcock family lived at Exhims, a large house with outbuildings, on the corner of Darrs Lane and Northchurch High Street.

In 1896 John Forster Alcock (snr) was serving as Chairman of the Northchurch Parish Council and was a fervent orchid breeder, winning numerous prizes, with one orchid, the heavily-blotched *Cypripedium bellatulum, Exhim's var.* being named after his Northchurch home. In their earlier years, he and his younger brother, Charles, had been keen footballers and founder members of the Football Association, but business pressures had forced him to concentrate on his shipping and ice merchant business, John F Alcock and Co., based at 21 Great St Helens in the City of London.

He died in 1910, and the family business was wound up. His eldest son, Frank Alcock, who had joined the family firm in 1903, subsequently decided to emigrate to Rhodesia (current day Zimbabwe) to begin a new life as a farmer. Shortly after her husband's death Augusta Alcock decided to sell Exhims and move to Box Cottage a few hundred yards further down Northchurch High Street.

John Alcock (jnr) was educated at Kelly College, Tavistock, and later at Bradfield College, Berkshire, before gaining a National Science Scholarship to Clare College, Cambridge, where he studied Mechanical Engineering. He had just started his studies and was living in lodgings in Sidney Street, Cambridge, when war broke out.

Deciding to defer his studies, Alcock applied for a commission with the army in September 1914, stating that his preference was to serve in the Royal Engineers, and being under 21 years of age at the time, he had to get his mother to countersign his application. He was given a medical examination at Bedford and, being 5ft 9ins tall, weighing 154lbs with good hearing, teeth and vision, he was found to be fit for service.

On 19th November 1914, Alcock was granted a temporary Commission with 6th Battalion, Bedfordshire Regiment, but it was not long before he started looking for a new challenge and, like many other newly-commissioned officers, he wanted to fly. Consequently, in April 1915, he applied for a transfer to the RFC. On his application, he highlighted his recent signals training with the Bedfordshire Regiment, together with the use of field telephones and wireless telegraphy and his general scientific training during his short time at Clare College. His transfer to the RFC was subsequently approved and

2nd Lieutenant John Alcock
Courtesy of Richard Hicks

on 15th August 1915 he arrived at Castle Bromwich, Warwickshire, to begin his flying training.

The piece of grassland called Castle Bromwich playing fields had become a private aerodrome in 1909 and the base of the recently-formed Midland Aero Club. Following the outbreak of the war, it soon became evident that the RFC would have to enlarge its training facilities if it were to serve the army in France. Its Farnborough-based Central Flying School did not have the capacity to expand, so new training units were opened and existing civilian flying clubs, like the Midland Aero Club at Castle Bromwich, were commandeered. Within weeks, new aircraft hangars and access roads began to appear on the Castle Bromwich site.

The standard practice at the time was for RFC pilots to be trained at several bases before joining their squadron, and Alcock's training was no exception. Having completing his basic training at Castle Bromwich in September 1915, flying Maurice Farman aircraft and gaining the all-important Royal Aero Club Certificate, he transferred to the Netheravon aerodrome on Salisbury Plain, where he spent the next two months training as a military pilot.

Unfortunately, his training did not go well, particularly when trying to land his aircraft on a designated spot. Wanting to continue with the RFC, however, Alcock formerly asked to be transferred to a two-week aerial observer course. His request approved, Alcock awaited his formal transfer to the observer course at No7 Wing, RFC, based at Fort Grange near Gosport. During this period, he persevered with his flying practice and finally mastered his landing technique. On 29th December 1915 he wrote to the Officer Commanding No7 Wing asking to be reconsidered as a pilot, but his request was rejected, and he joined the aerial observer course as originally planned.

Alcock remained at Gosport until the middle of January 1916 when he left Devonport, bound for Egypt, on board the *Llandovery Castle*. Disembarking at Alexandria fifteen days later, he reported for duty at Cairo and travelled to 17 Squadron's headquarters at Heliopolis, just outside the city. The airbase there was also shared with 14 Squadron, as part of No5 Wing, RFC. Reconnaissance flights with de Havilland BE2c biplanes over the Turkish lines in the Sinai desert followed his arrival and Alcock was later attached as an Observer to No1 Squadron, Australian Flying Corps, in Heliopolis.

The first squadron of the Australian Flying Corps was formed at Point Cook in Victoria in January 1916. The following March, it sailed from Melbourne, and arrived in Egypt four weeks later, moving to Heliopolis where it was renamed 67(A) Squadron. Many of the less experienced Australian pilots were immediately sent to England to continue their training, whilst more experienced RFC men, like Alcock, were placed on temporary attachment to make it an operational unit. During his time serving with the Australians, he became a Qualified Observer. As with 14 Squadron, the Australian unit's role was to provide aerial reconnaissance flights over the Sinai desert looking for, and occasionally attacking, any Turkish forces in the area.

In late October 1916, Alcock, now an Appointed Flying Officer, started his last Egyptian posting, becoming an instructor with 23 Reserve Squadron, based at the large RFC Training School at Abukir. He spent three weeks the following month in hospital in Cairo suffering from eczema, no doubt exacerbated by the hot, dry conditions in Egypt, and two days after leaving hospital he boarded the HT *Katyan* bound for Marseilles. Alcock was on his way home.

On his return to England at the start of 1917, Alcock transferred to 50 (HD) Squadron RFC, which was a Home Defence unit based at Dover and equipped with a variety of aircraft spread across several airfields in Kent. The need for military aircraft to be based in England had dramatically increased in recent months with both German Zeppelin airships and Gotha bombers causing an increasing loss of life as a result of their bombing raids.

Alcock's technical skills, particularly with compasses, was recognised the following May with his next move and promotion to Equipment Officer 2, working at the Admiralty's Compass Department at Ditton Park, Buckinghamshire. It was not long before Alcock met and married Marian Winifred Pulman, the marriage taking place on 1st December 1917 at nearby Eton. She gave birth to their first child the following year.

September 1917 brought the sad news of the death from dysentery of his elder brother, Frank, whilst fighting the German troops in East Africa. The following month, Alcock became an Assistant Instructor at No5 School of Aeronautics, and two months later passed a course in Aerial Navigation. Following the creation of the RAF in April 1918, he became a 2nd Lieutenant and transferred to the Aerial Research Detachment. He had recently qualified as a military pilot, flying de Havilland DH9s, a two-man strategic bi-plane bomber, and it likely that these were used to test new ground observation devices.

Alcock spent his last few months in the RAF at two Training Depot Stations in south-west England before being demobilised on 20th January 1919. Returning to his studies at Clare College, Cambridge he graduated in 1920 with a 1st Class Honours Degree in Mechanical Engineering. The same year, he joined the engine manufacturer, Ricardo & Co Ltd, in Old Shoreham, Sussex, where he worked as a research engineer specialising in the development of air-cooled aero engines. Alcock became a father for the third time in 1921.

By 1927, he had become Ricardo & Co's chief scientist and over the coming years he would be responsible for the creation of several British and international patents. He remained with Ricardo & Co until he retired. In the 1951 King's Birthday Honours, John Forster Alcock was awarded an OBE. Outside of work, he was very keen on sailing, and apparently spent much of his retirement pottering about in a small dinghy on the south coast. He died at Shoreham-by-Sea in 1977, aged 81.

William Erith Baines (1892 – 1975)
Air Mechanic 18937, RAF

William Baines was born on the Channel Island of Jersey in 1892, the son of George Henry Baines and his wife, Freda. George Baines came from Tring, but was working as a schoolmaster in Jersey at the time of William's birth. By 1901 he had been appointed schoolmaster at Northchurch Village School and was living at the schoolmaster's house in the High Street. On completion of his schooling, William left home and by 1911 he was working as an assistant chemist for a Mr Robinson who ran a chemist's shop in Clapham, south London.

On 17th January 1916, a week before he enlisted with the RFC, William married Nellie Millicent Liddington at St Stephen's Church, Paddington. Nellie came from Tring and was the daughter of a local brewer. On joining the RFC, William became an Air Mechanic 2nd Class and was promoted to Air Mechanic 1st Class six months later when he joined the newly-formed No15 Wing, RFC, as a motorcyclist. No15 Wing, which consisted of 4 and 15 Squadrons, both flying de Havilland BE2 aircraft, moved to France on 1st July 1916 and first saw service as an aerial unit during the Somme Offensive, working closely with the gun batteries of the Royal Field Artillery. William served as a despatch rider with the RFC and as such he would have been responsible for rushing messages between the airmen and the artillery batteries and other units.

Like many servicemen, William went down with influenza at the end of 1916. This was not the strain that was to cause millions of deaths just over twelve months later, but a much milder form. However, it was serious enough for him to be admitted to No16 Military Hospital at Tréport, where he remained for a week.

William was promoted to Corporal in April 1917 and remained with No15 Wing in France until February 1919. Returning to England, he was posted to RAF Halton, near Wendover, Buckinghamshire, where he was to remain awaiting his transfer to the reserves. He was awarded the Meritorious Service Medal in June 1919.

William and Nellie later moved to Edmonton, north London, where he worked as a pharmacist. After his retirement, William went to live in Tring where he died in 1975, aged 83.

Frederick Charles Lewis Barker (1889 – 1985)
Chief Mechanic 4774, RAF

Frederick Charles Lewis Barker, commonly known as Lewis, was born in Berkhamsted in October 1889, the son of coachman, Frederick Barker, and his wife Amelia. After leaving school, Lewis joined 1st (Hertfordshire)

Volunteer Battalion, The Bedfordshire Regiment, which later became the local Territorial Force. He left in 1910, having served with them for six years, and joined the City of London police, based at Snow Hill Police Station.

Lewis seems to have not enjoyed police life, however, as he later moved back to Berkhamsted to become a carpenter. In April 1915, he enlisted with the RFC as an Air Mechanic 2nd Class and was sent to Farnborough, becoming an Air Mechanic 1st Class three months later. In the summer of 1915, Lewis returned to Hertfordshire and married Nelly Hales at St Mary's, Northchurch. His service record shows that during this time he was working as a rigger. Riggers, many of whom were trained carpenters, were used extensively within the RFC to repair or replace damaged wooden parts of an aircraft. Lewis would later become a sailmaker, responsible for repairing the fabric that covered an aircraft's wooden structure.

His movements until April 1917 are somewhat unclear, but he was promoted to Corporal on 1st November 1915 and a few weeks later to Acting Sergeant. His next promotion came in March 1916, when he became a Sergeant. Then, in April 1917, Lewis was transferred to Canada as part of the newly-formed 86th Training Squadron.

In 1917, the RFC was facing another crisis. It was losing pilots in air accidents or to enemy action at a faster rate than they could be replaced. Training facilities in England were limited, so new ones were created in Egypt and Canada. In Southern Ontario, Canada, the site of the former Rathbun logging company at the town of Deserono was deemed suitable. Rathbun's office buildings were still in place and the adjacent flat land was ideally suited to turn it into an airfield. Rented sheds to the north of the town were also acquired, which was where Lewis and his team of riggers and sailmakers worked to keep the squadron's training aircraft serviceable. In August 1917, Lewis became a Flight Sergeant.

During the winter of 1917/18 the harsh Canadian climate proved unsuitable for training to continue at Camp Rathbun, as it was now known, and with the United States having entered the war, advantage was taken of their offer to use the facilities at Fort Worth, Texas. The winter over, 86th Training Squadron returned to Camp Rathbun, where training resumed and following the creation of the RAF on 1st April 1918 Lewis was reclassified as Chief Mechanic. By the end of the war Camp Rathbun had trained over 1,300 pilots and provided work for many of the local people. Unfortunately, 30 trainee airmen also lost their lives in air accidents.

Lewis returned to England in January 1919, and was placed in the reserves and discharged from the RAF in April the following year. His wife, Nellie, had been living with her parents in Northchurch High Street during his time in Canada. Lewis and Nellie would eventually move away from the Northchurch area and in 1939 they were living in Malden, Surrey, and he was working as a day watchman at the Bank of England in the City of London. Lewis Barker died in 1985, aged 95.

John Chappin (1888 -?)
Air Mechanic 244393, RAF

John Chappin, was born at Dudswell Lock in May 1888. His father, Job Chappin, came from Long Marston, Hertfordshire and worked as a navvy on the Grand Junction Canal. His mother, Margaret, came from nearby Wilstone.

Sometime between 1901 and 1906, the Chappin family left Dudswell and moved to Bierton, near Aylesbury, where John found work at a local printing company. In 1906, John joined the local Volunteer Force, 1st Buckinghamshire Rifle Volunteers, and by the time he left in 1913 he had risen to the rank of Corporal.

Moving to Fulham the same year, John became an engine fitter and married Lizzie Hicks St Dionis Church, Parson's Green. She was a domestic servant from Aylesbury who worked at a house in Fulham, which probably accounts for his move to London.

There is no record of John being conscripted in 1916, so it is presumed that his job fell under one of the exemptions. However, on Christmas Day 1917, he enlisted with the Royal Naval Air Service (RNAS) at Crystal Palace, south London, becoming a mechanic. His service record shows him as being 5ft 8¾ins tall with blue eyes and brown hair.

John remained there until March 1918, when he was posted to the RNAS depot at Wormwood Scrubs in west London. The RNAS had taken over a huge hangar on Wormwood Scrubs at the start of the war. Constructed in 1909 to house the *Clement-Bayard II* airship, some 1,000 tons of steel had been used in its construction. Until the RNAS took it over, it had lain unused for several years, apart from storage by the army. It proved an excellent base for the RNAS; in addition to being a base for its airships, the RNAS Armoured Car Squadron was based there. Other RNAS facilities were located nearby at the former Clement-Talbot Motor Works in Barlby Road.

A few days after his arrival at Wormwood Scrubs, the RAF came into being and John was reclassified as an Air Mechanic 1st Class. The end of the war made little difference to him, as he decided to remain with the RAF and on June 1919, he was transferred to the military base at Chingford, north London, which had been a naval flying school and base for three aircraft squadrons during the war. After three months he returned to Wormwood Scrubs and then moved to the RAF's flying boat base at Felixstowe.

John ended his military career at RAF Halton, seven miles from where he was born at Dudswell Lock. He was discharged in March 1923 and six months later, having decided to start a new life in Australia, he and Lizzie, boarded the SS *Beltana* in the Port of London. They settled in Sydney where he soon found work as an engineer. By 1937, he had become a storekeeper at Gosford, some 47 miles north of Sydney. It is not known when John Chappin died.

Lancelot Desmond Fellows (1879 – 1961)
Sergeant Mechanic 401668, RAF

Lancelot Fellows was born in Harleston, Norfolk in December 1879, the third son of Spenser Fellows, the Rector of nearby Pulham St Mary the Virgin, and his wife, Amelia. Little is known about his early life, other than that he grew up in Pulham St Mary and in 1901, at the age of 21, he was described in the Census as a studying electrical engineering. Within a few years however, Lancelot had changed career, and in 1908 became a clerk at the Principle Probate Registry in Somerset House, London and on at least one occasion, he represented the Probate Registry as a witness at the Old Bailey. In March 1909, he joined the Territorial Force, becoming a Private in 28th (County of London) Battalion, The London Regiment (Artists Rifles) and by 1914 he had risen to the rank of Corporal.

May 1911 saw his marriage to Audrey Katherine Plummer, the daughter of a clergyman, in Bideford, Devon. The couple initially set up home in Wood Green, London, before settling in a house in nearby Muswell Hill.

On the outbreak of war, Lancelot reported to the Artist's Rifles London headquarters in Dukes Road, opposite Euston Station. The next few weeks were spent training, much of which involved lengthy route marches in the Home Counties, before being despatched to France in October 1914. One of Lancelot's fellow members in the Artist's Rifles was the trainee solicitor, Nigel Keith Farrar Porter, but unlike him, he did not later seek a commission. He remained with the Artist's Rifles until 1st August 1917 when, on becoming a Sergeant, he requested to be transferred to the RFC.

Lancelot was posted to No2 Auxiliary School of Aerial Gunnery at Turnberry, Scotland, where he became an Instructor. By 1901 the golf links at Turnberry had opened, becoming an immediate success and attracting all the key golfers of the time, the Ladies' British Open Amateur Championship being held there in 1912. Soon after war broke out, the golf course and buildings were acquired by the RFC and the pristine greens, fairways and sand dunes were flattened to make way for airstrips, hangers and huts. The adjacent luxurious Turnberry Hotel was turned into a convalescent hospital and Officer's Mess, whilst the other ranks were accommodated in 25 huts built nearby. Turnberry's location on the west coast of Scotland was not ideal in terms of providing flying weather, and trainee pilots often had to make do serving in the role of observer / gunner in the two-seater aircraft piloted by experienced airmen. Consequently, it was not unknown for pilots to pass their training course without having accumulated the necessary number of flying hours.

With the creation of the RAF in April 1918 Lancelot was reclassified as Sergeant Mechanic and became Chief Mechanic the following August. He was demobilised in June 1919, the same year that the RAF returned Turnberry to the golf club.

In the 1918 Northchurch Absent Voters List Lancelot is registered at the Old Cottage, but it is not clear when his wife and daughters moved there. Following his demobilisation, he returned to his job with the Probate Registry in London and the family remained in Northchurch until 1927. By the time of his death in 1961, aged 74, he and Audrey were living in Great Missenden, Buckinghamshire.

Samuel Halsey (1887 – 1952)
Petty Officer Mechanic, 15571 RAF

Samuel Halsey was born in Northchurch in March 1887 and was one of seven children of William Halsey, a platelayer with the London & North Western Railway, and his wife Mary. After leaving school Samuel started work at one of the local timberyards as a sawyer's labourer but in August 1906, a few months after his father had died, Samuel decided to travel to London to enlist with the Royal Marine Light Infantry (RMLI), for some reason declaring to be exactly one year younger than he actually was.

Having passed his medical examination, which described him as being 5ft 6ins tall with a fresh complexion, dark brown hair and brown eyes, Samuel was sent to the RMLI base at Chatham to begin his training. The RMLI at that time had the dual role of ensuring the security of a Royal Navy vessel's officers and crew and taking part in battles, either firing from their own ship or in boarding actions and small-scale landings.

Samuel's first posting to a naval vessel was HMS *Jason*, a torpedo boat built in 1892 and from March 1910 he spent two years serving on HMS *Shannon*, a Minotaur-class armoured cruiser which served as the Flagship of the Royal Navy's 2nd Cruiser Squadron. In October 1913, he was posted to HMS *Hermes*, a move that would change his career path

Launched in 1898, *Hermes* was a Highflyer-class cruiser built by Fairfield Shipbuilding & Engineering at their shipyard on the River Clyde. She formed part of the Channel Fleet until 1905, when she was put in reserve until given a reprieve to serve a further seven years in the West Indies. Returning home in 1913, *Hermes* was given a major overhaul, converting her into a seaplane carrier to test the viability of launching aircraft from a seaborne vessel. This involved removing much of her existing forecastle and gun-deck to make way for an elongated flight deck. Up to three seaplanes could be carried, which would return to the ship by landing on the water and then being hoisted onboard by a derrick lifting system.

Seeing the capability of using aircraft fired Samuel's imagination and in December 1913, after serving seven years as a Marine, he transferred to the Naval Wing of the Royal Flying Corps as a mechanic. Following the formation of the RNAS he became an Air Mechanic.

Samuel's training took place at the RNAS base at Crystal Palace, South London. The site of the 1851 Great Exhibition, the vast area occupied by the Crystal Palace and its grounds had been taken over by the Royal Navy a few weeks after the start of the war, turning it into a major training base for all its branches, including military observation balloons and airships.

Unlike the German Army, which had invested heavily in the development of airships before the war, both the British Army and the Admiralty had only experimented with the concept. In 1913 the army airship *Gamma* had landed in the grounds of Berkhamsted Castle whilst on trials, its short visit being recorded by author Graham Greene in his autobiography *A Sort of Life*.

Following the outbreak of the war the Admiralty saw the potential for airships to reduce the threat to British shipping by spotting submarine and other naval vessel activity from the air. The opening months of the war soon proved the submarine threat to be real after the sinking of several Royal Navy warships and it was quickly realised that a rapid stop-gap solution was required before the situation became critical.

Development of the new Submarine Scout class airship started in early 1915, with testing taking place in early March. Some 140ft in length and with a size of 70,000 cubic feet, the 'SS' airships consisted of a large elongated envelope containing hydrogen gas under which the fuselage of a BE2c aircraft, minus its wings, was connected by cables. On each side of the fuselage a 160lb bomb was strapped for use against any enemy submarine within range. Following the successful completion of its trials, the first 'SS' airship entered service in March 1915 and production commenced at several factories. Shortly afterwards Samuel was promoted to Leading Mechanic working with the 'SS' airships. Other versions of the 'SS' airship used the adapted fuselage of a Maurice Farman aircraft, but unfortunately the two types were not interchangeable due to the location of their fixing cables.

A promotion to Petty Officer Mechanic came at the end of 1916, by which time Samuel was teaching other mechanics. Practical experience of the use of airships in a frontline role came in March 1917, when he joined the crew of an 'SS' airship operating from the airship base at Kassandra at Salonika and which was used in a reconnaissance role against enemy submarines operating in the Adriatic. For Samuel this was probably a combined operational and training role, and he remained there until November 1917, when he returned to Crystal Palace.

April 1ˢᵗ 1918 was a memorable day for Samuel; on that day the RNAS and RFC merged to become the Royal Air Force and he married his sister-in-law, Jane Styles, at St Stephen's Church, Walthamstow.

Little is known about his subsequent service with the RAF. He appears to have remained with them after the war and later moved to the Air Ministry. In 1939 Samuel and his wife were living in Gosport, Hampshire. He died in February 1952, aged 64.

William Stewart Jones (1887 – 1955)
Air Mechanic 38875, RAF

William Jones was born in Berkhamsted in November 1887 into a family with a long tradition of carpentry. He was one of twelve children born to Edward and Louisa Jones and the family lived in a five-roomed terraced house at the bottom of Cross Oak Road. Next door lived William's grandfather, Richard Jones, a master carpenter, who ran the family carpentry business, employing his father, and in due course William, and at least one of his younger brothers.

In 1903, William joined the local militia, becoming a Private in 2ⁿᵈ (Herts) Volunteer Battalion, Bedfordshire Regiment. Following the creation of the Territorial Force in 1908, William became a Private in 1ˢᵗ Hertfordshire Regiment (TF) and attended all their annual camps until the outbreak of war.

William married Kate Vane in Berkhamsted in 1911. She came from the village of Wye in Kent and probably came to Berkhamsted to work as a domestic servant in one of the large houses. Setting up home in Clarence Road, Berkhamsted, they would later have three children before moving to a cottage in Gossoms End.

On 5ᵗʰ August 1914, William, along with many of his fellow Hertshires, was embodied and sailed to France three months later. Unfortunately, in January 1915, whilst serving in northern France, William sustained a serious injury to one of his feet and returned to England for treatment at a Voluntary Aid Detachment Hospital in Hertfordshire. It took him several months to recover, by which time he may no longer have been fit to return to front line service. This may account for his decision to seek a transfer that would put his carpentry skills to good use and in April 1916 William joined the RFC as an Air Mechanic. Interestingly, when he underwent a medical examination he was found to be 5ft 2½inches tall, just under the minimum height for a soldier at the start of the war.

William was posted to No44 Squadron, based at Hainault Farm, Essex. This was one of several airfields set up towards the end of 1915 to protect London from the increasing threat of German air raids. By 1918, No44 Squadron was equipped with formidable Sopwith Camel fighter aircraft. Introduced the previous year, the Camel had a wingspan of 28ft and a top speed of 117mph. Armed with two forward-firing machine guns, two Camels from No44 Squadron were the first to shoot down a German Gotha bomber during an air raid on London at the end of January 1918.

In February 1919, William was transferred to the RAF Reserve and formerly discharged the following year. Back in Gossoms End, he returned to his job as a carpenter. In the build-up to the Second World War, William, now working as a general jobbing builder, again volunteered to serve as an air mechanic at RAF Halton and it is believed that he remained there during the war. He died in 1955, aged 67.

Gerald Herbert Loxley (1885 – 1950)
Major, RAF

During the nineteenth and twentieth centuries, members of the Loxley family played a significant part in Northchurch village life. The connection with Northchurch started in June 1812, when John Loxley, a landowner from the village of West Ham in Essex, married Elizabeth Smart, the daughter of William Smart, the owner of the Norcott Court estate north of Dudswell, the marriage taking place at St Mary's, Northchurch. With no male heirs to inherit the estate, William Smart left Norcott Court to his daughter, Elizabeth, and on her death, it passed into the Loxley family. It was John Loxley, Elizabeth and John Loxley's grandson, that contributed most to the village, among other actions founding the village school in 1864 in conjunction with the local Lord of the Manor, Lord Brownlow. John Loxley's son, Arthur Smart Loxley, became a clergyman and in the 1870s, during the time of the Rector, Revd. Sir John Hobart Culme-Seymour, he was one of the curates at St Mary's, Northchurch.

In 1873, Revd. Arthur Smart Loxley married Alice Mary Duncombe, a member of the Duncombe family who owned Lagley House situated between Northchurch and Gossoms End. Soon after their marriage, Arthur Smart Loxley was appointed the vicar of Lamport, Northamptonshire, where his first son, Arthur Noel Loxley (known as Noel) was born. The Loxley family later moved to Fairford, Gloucestershire where Arthur and Alice's four remaining children, Vere Duncombe, Gladys Marjorie, Gerald Herbert, and Reginald Victor Byron, (known as Roy), were born. All four boys would later serve in various capacities during the war, but tragically only Gerald Loxley would survive[34]. A plaque in the south transept of St Mary's, Northchurch, commemorates the deaths of his three brothers.

Gerald Herbert Loxley, the fourth of Arthur and Alice's children, was born in January 1885 and later christened by his father at Fairford parish church. Sadly, three years later, Revd. Arthur Smart Loxley died having been in ill health for some time, and his body was laid to rest in the

---

[34] Their stories are told in *For Them's Sake*

churchyard of St Mary's Northchurch. His widow and family subsequently moved to a cottage in Little Cloisters, adjacent to Gloucester Cathedral.

Educated at Malvern College, Gerald Loxley became a house prefect there, and later went up to Oriel College, Oxford to read French, German and Spanish. Meanwhile, his two older brothers, Noel and Vere, entered the armed services, Noel in the Royal Navy and Vere in the Royal Marines. After graduating in 1908, Gerald, decided to become a schoolmaster and taught at Church Stretton School in Shropshire.

Unlike his brothers, Gerald Loxley's heath had never been particularly strong, and consequently, when the war broke out in 1914, he did not look for a temporary commission with a fighting unit. The following year, however, he gained one with the Royal Naval Volunteer Reserve (RNVR) and was subsequently posted to the RNAS, in which his younger brother, Roy, was now serving. Being fluent in French, Gerald moved to Paris where he joined the Department of Aircraft Production, which formed part of the Ministry of Munitions.

Located in the Paris suburb of Neuilly-sur-Seine, conveniently close to several aircraft manufacturers, the Department of Aircraft Production procured military aircraft, spare parts and other supplies, and then issued them to the RFC, RNAS and from April 1918, the RAF. To keep this operation running

Lieutenant Gerald Loxley
Courtesy of Patrick James
Coleridge Sumner

smoothly, hundreds of clerks spent their day manually updating massive spreadsheets and tracking the building of each aircraft through to its testing and finally its allocation to a squadron. The department was also responsible for evaluating captured German aircraft, co-ordinating the testing of new aircraft, and even developing camouflage for both aircraft and buildings on airbases.

In October 1918, Gerald Loxley's younger, and by then his only surviving brother, Roy, who had become an Adjutant at the Department of Aircraft Production earlier in the year, fell ill with influenza and died. Gerald was the only family member to attend his funeral in Paris. The following month, not only he was promoted to the rank of Major, but in recognition of his work at the Department of Aircraft Production, he became a *Chevalier de la Légion d'honneur*, the highest decoration awarded by the French Government.

Gerald remained in Paris until being demobilised in January 1920 when he returned to Gloucester. Deciding not to return to teaching after the war, he became a translator with the Allied Reparations Commission, which had recently been created following the signing of the Treaty of Versailles in 1919 to determine how much Germany and her allies should pay in war reparations. He continued at the Commission until the late 1920s, when he moved to Warrington, Lancashire, and became a civil servant working for the National Savings Scheme.

In September 1930, aged 45, Gerald married Alice Blundell Booth, the daughter of a local farmer, at St Peter's, Altrincham. One of the witnesses at their wedding was his nephew, Peter Noel Loxley, the son of his older brother, Noel, who would later become a high-ranking British diplomat but would die in an air accident in 1945[35].

By the time he retired to a house in Ledbury, Herefordshire, Gerald had become the Commissioner for National Savings in Lancashire. He died in 1950, aged 65.

---

[35] Peter Loxley's story is told in *For Them's Sake*

16 – The Sick, Wounded and their Medics

The First World War was the first war conducted on an industrial scale and saw the mass use for the first time of weapons like tanks, artillery, bomber and fighter aircraft, machine guns and poison gas of varying types. As a result, the constant risk of injury or death no longer applied just to front line servicemen, but also to those serving far back from the fighting in support roles and who now found themselves within the range of more powerful artillery and air attacks.

Depending on when and where they served, each serviceman also faced the additional risks of frostbite, trench foot, sunstroke, malaria, dysentery and later, influenza. Added to these were the little-understood effects of being on the battlefield for long periods of time and the mental scars that this caused. The concept of shellshock was hardly understood by the medical authorities of the period and many sufferers were considered malingerers, or in extreme cases, cowards, and shot at dawn by firing squad.

Within the British army, the Royal Army Medical Corps (RAMC) was formed in 1898 through a merger of the Medical Staff and Medical Staff Corps, and provided a single unit responsible for the medical care of soldiers of all ranks, albeit that 'Officers' and 'Other Ranks' were frequently kept apart during their treatment.

The key to a wounded or sick soldier's survival and recovery was to get him as quickly as possible to a medical post where he could be assessed. The 1914 Field Service Pocket Book, issued by the War Office to every British officer, outlined the basic procedure to evacuate a wounded soldier from the front line. Firstly, where possible, the wounded soldier would be examined by his unit's medical officer and, if requiring treatment, would walk, or be carried by trained stretcher bearers, to an aid post. Here, initial medical treatment, such as the basic cleaning of wounds and the application of bandages, would be performed, with more serious cases being passed down the line by stretcher bearers to the next stage in the process. This would either be an Advanced Dressing Station or a Field Ambulance.

Each army division had three field ambulances which were mobile medical units that travelled with them and were responsible for setting up medical posts in the field. Each unit was run by ten officers and 224 men, who would evaluate the soldier's wounds or injuries, with minor ones being treated on the spot and the soldier returning to his unit. More serious cases would be transferred by horse-drawn or motor ambulance to a Casualty Clearing Station located some way away from the front line. Many of the wounded arriving at the field ambulances or advanced dressing stations during battles were, unfortunately, beyond help, and the administration of morphia and/or other pain killing drugs was the only possible treatment.

Unlike the mobile field ambulances, casualty clearing stations were in permanent locations, and normally consisted of tented camps or occasionally wooden huts, or a mixture of both, and designed to accommodate up to 1,000 patients at a time. Frequently, the casualty clearing stations were located close together. For example, Hazebrouck in northern France, some 20 miles from the front line near Ypres, had seven such stations based there in 1915. Serious wounds requiring surgery, such as amputations and major stitches, were normally dealt with at the casualty clearing stations. As the war developed some of these units started to specialise in treating specific diseases or types of injury.

The final stage in the evacuation process was the military hospital. At the start of the war, several military hospitals were set up in schools and chateaux in northern France. The Lyceé Buffon in Paris was one of these, where soldiers like Private Walter Dell, the first man from Northchurch to be killed, was sent[36]. Later, new military hospitals were established at the main military bases on the English Channel, like Le Havre and Étaples, which allowed for the easy evacuation of soldiers to a hospital in England if needed. These units were known as Stationary Hospitals, or General Hospitals, depending on their size. Initially, stationary hospitals could accommodate 400 casualties whilst the larger general hospitals could accommodate over 1,000 patients.

Even after treatment, there was always the risk of infection. At that time there were no antibiotics, such as penicillin, available, and frequent use was made of carbolic lotion to keep wounds clean. Walter Dell died when his headwound became infected, simply because of the lack of an effective treatment at the time.

Soldiers needing longer term treatment and convalescence were evacuated to hospitals in Great Britain. These were frequently set up in stately homes, like Ashridge House, that had been made available by their owners, or large houses or asylums requisitioned by the War Office. In Northampton, the Berrywood Asylum became Northampton War Hospital, and was later to specialise in the treatment of poison gas-related injuries.

During the soldier's recovery, he would be subject to regular medical reviews and assessed using the same classifications as those used when signing up (see Appendix 3). Those given an 'A' grading were considered fit to return to front line duties; those with a 'B' grading were considered suitable for non-fighting roles abroad; those with a 'C' grading were considered suitable for garrison work at home, and those with a 'D' grading were classed as unfit and unsuitable for redeployment for at least six months.

---

[36] Walter Dell's story is told in *For Them's Sake*

Those considered no longer physically fit to serve in the armed forces were discharged under the King's Regulations Paragraph 392 (xvi). From 1916, these men were awarded a 'War Badge', designed to be worn on civilian clothing, to show that the wearer had served during the war. It was later retrospectively awarded to men and women discharged from the start of the war. The badge was introduced to prevent men of military age, and with no apparent disability, being thought of as shirkers and being given 'white feathers' by over-zealous people to indicate their cowardice. Commonly known as the 'Silver War Badge', the badge was 1¼ inches in diameter and on its front were the words *'For King and Empire. Services Rendered'*. On the reverse was stamped a unique badge number.

Servicemen under treatment in hospital or convalescing normally wore a hospital blue uniform, that was sometimes called convalescent blue, instead of an army uniform. These uniforms were made from a type of flannel material and had a white lining and were worn with a white shirt and red tie.

Edwin Dell (front right) and other wounded servicemen wearing hospital blue uniforms. Courtesy of Clive Blofield

As the war progressed, so did the treatment of the wounded and injured, with great advances being made in the fields of medicine, surgery and the use of prosthetics. New techniques were also developed, and early plastic surgery evolved from the pioneering work of Frenchman, Hippolyte Morestin, and New Zealander, Howard Gillies. By the time the war ended in November 1918, the chances of a soldier's survival from a severe wound was far greater than was the case in August 1914.

Percy Walter Allum (1889 – 1955)
Private 534621, RAMC

Percy Allum was born in February 1889 at Albion Terrace, Hemel Hempstead, the son of Frederick Allum, a fitter at the nearby Boxmoor Iron Works, and his wife, Martha. He went to school at Bury Mill End School, gaining 1st prize in 1898 for 425 consecutive school attendances. Leaving there at the age of fourteen, he became a brush maker at the newly-opened factory of GB Kent & Sons in Apsley.

Percy did not volunteer when war broke out and only decided to do so in September 1915. After enlisting, he was posted to 3/9th Battalion, Middlesex

Regiment, a training battalion that had been raised in Willesden a few months earlier and was now based at Cambridge. Shortly before his training ended in April 1916, Percy married Edith Bloomfield, the daughter of a local carpenter, at St Peter's, Berkhamsted. Returning to his unit, he was later posted to 20th Battalion, Rifle Brigade.

Percy's new unit was a territorial battalion formed in 1915 from men of the Northumberland Fusiliers, Durham Light Infantry and the East and West Yorkshire Regiments. This was not a frontline unit and fell under the control of the City of London Territorial Association, as opposed to the Rifle Brigade. At the start of 1916, 20th Battalion, Rifle Brigade was sent to Egypt for garrison duties and Percy joined them there during the summer. From the scant information that exists, it appears that the unit spent much of its time in Egypt guarding Turkish prisoners of war.

How long Percy spent with 20th Battalion is unclear, as by 1918 he had been transferred to the RAMC, presumably as an orderly, and was working at No17 General Hospital in Alexandria. The hospital had been opened in Alexandria's Victoria College in April 1915 and, with 2,460 beds, it was one of the largest in the Middle East and was used extensively to treat the sick and wounded during the Gallipoli Campaign. He was still serving at the hospital at the end of the war.

In the 1918 Absent Voters List, Percy is registered at Exhims on the corner of Northchurch High Street and Darrs Lane, then owned by the Brockman family. It is therefore likely that Percy's wife, Edith, was working and living there as a domestic servant.

In 1919, before he was demobilised, Percy became ill and was discharged from the army and awarded a Silver War Badge. In 1920 he and Edith were living at his parent's home in Hemel Hempstead. Three years later, Edith gave birth to a son. 1939 saw Percy and his family still living in the same house and he was now working as a storekeeper at the Apsley Paper Mills, alongside many of his relatives. Percy Allum died in Hemel Hempstead in 1955, aged 66.

Frank Ashby (1889 – 1974)
Private 55473, Machine Gun Corps

In November 1889, Elizabeth Ashby, the wife of local farmer, John Ashby, gave birth to her fourth son whom they named Frank. John Ashby, was a well-known figure in Northchurch, farming fifty acres of land at Norcott Hill farm, running the local butcher's shop in the High Street and later becoming a Parish Councillor and a Churchwarden at St Mary's, Northchurch.

By 1911, Frank was working at the butcher's shop, which was now being run by his elder brother, Thomas, and he later moved to Hemel Hempstead, becoming a butcher in his own right. On 26th October 1915, now aged 26, he married Dorothy Grange at St Bartholomew's, Wigginton. She was the daughter of the farmer who ran Park Farm in Wigginton. After their marriage the couple set up home with Frank's parents at Norcott Hill Farm.

Two months later, with the prospect of conscription increasing, Frank decided to attest under the Derby Scheme, and on being mobilised he was posted to the Machine Gun Corp's depot at Belton Park for training. Later posted to the newly-formed 197 Machine Gun Coy, he arrived at Le Havre in December 1916 and moved south to the Somme Sector, where his unit became part of 9th (Scottish Division).

On 25th April 1917, by which time his unit had suffered numerous casualties during the Battle of Arras, Frank was taken sick whilst in billets at Averdoingt. Initially sent to 42 Casualty Clearing Station at nearby Aubigny-en-Artois, Frank was then transferred to 18th General Hospital at Camiers before being repatriated to England. The nature of his sickness is not clear, the hospital record only describing him as 'permanently unfit' and no details have been found as to where he was subsequently treated in England. He never returned to frontline duties and in November 1918 he was formally discharged from the army and awarded a Silver War Badge.

In due course Frank returned home to Northchurch where he and Dorothy continued to live with his parents at Norcott Hill Farm before later moving to Dropshort Cottage on the outskirts of Northchurch. By 1927 they were the parents of two children.

In 1939, the were living in Oxford where Frank was running a butcher's shop in the city centre. He died in 1974, aged 84.

Frederick George Batchelor (1897 – 1983)
Private 72733, RAMC,
later Private 55124, 1/6th Battalion, Essex Regiment

Frederick Batchelor was born in May 1897 at Heath End, Wigginton. His father, James, was a domestic gardener from Hawridge, whilst his mother, Charlotte, came from Wigginton. He initially worked as a farm labourer and later became one of the many gardeners on the Rossway estate.

In October 1915, 19-year-old Frederick enlisted at Watford, and joined the RAMC the following month. His service papers show him as being 5ft 5ins tall and weighing 126lbs. He remained in England until the September 1916, when he was sent to France to join 17th Field Ambulance, which, along with 16th and 18th Field Ambulances, formed part of 6th Division, joining them at Sandpits Camp, near Mametz, during the closing weeks of the Somme Offensive. At this time heavy fighting was taking place at Delville Wood, a few miles to the north, and the men of RAMC were under tremendous pressure, not only dealing with the casualties as they came in, but also with the atrocious conditions under which they were working. Recent heavy rain and shelling had turned the ground and roads to mud, not only making the life of stretcher bearers intolerable, but making the use of horse-drawn ambulances almost impossible. The evacuation of wounded soldiers consequently became a long, slow, arduous process with the resulting high risk of fatalities due simply to the length of time it took to get them treated.

In November 1916, 17th Field Ambulance moved to the area south of Béthune, where it set up a new headquarters and a hospital at Nœux-les-Mines. Here preparations were made for the next major allied offensive at Arras. During March 1917, before the offensive started, German artillery attacked the area, with several shells landing on the hospital. Fortunately, there were no casualties, but the shelling forced the hospital to be evacuated until the attack had ceased.

The following month, Canadian forces captured the strategic Vimy Ridge north of Arras and 6th Division entered the battle a few days later, with 17th Field Ambulance standing ready to handle the inevitable casualties. 100 beds were made available in the Town Hall, 150 in the nearby YMCA and a further 100 in huts built in the grounds of the local state school. An evacuation route was set up, and staff allocated to the 'walking wounded post' and the advanced dressing stations between Nœux-les-Mines and the front line.

At 08:00 on 22nd April, 6th Division attacked the German strongpoints on Hill 70. Within the first 24 hours 17th Field Ambulance had handled 100 casualties. The following day the defending Germans deployed gas shells and ten soldiers suffering from the effects of gas were treated. German shells did not differentiate between combatant and non-combatant soldiers, and one 17th Field Ambulance officer and two other staff were killed on 23rd April, and a further three men wounded. The evacuation of wounded men proceeded as planned, but on 26th April an advanced dressing station was hit by two German shells, which injured two RAMC staff, one of whom later died.

The Battle of Arras ended on 16th May. The procedures set up prior to the battle by 17th Field Ambulance had worked efficiently and the most serious casualties had been transferred to hospitals in towns well out of range of the German artillery. The following day, Frederick became a patient of 17th Field Ambulance himself, having contracted trench fever.

Since the start of the war, soldiers in the trenches, together with those who had contact with them, had started to suffer from a mysterious illness. The symptoms included a sudden fever, loss of energy, headache, dizziness, skin rash and lower leg pain. The fever was particularly characteristic, in that it would last for five or six days and then subside, only to reappear several days later, repeating the cycle up to eight times. Recovery was therefore slow and difficult to treat, especially as the root cause was initially unknown. After the war, it was discovered that trench fever was caused by body lice living in soldiers' uniforms, particularly in the seams where they would hide. The trenches were ideal breeding grounds for lice as the soldiers were living in very close proximity to each other. Even RAMC staff were not immune to the disease, as they were in constant contact with wounded front line troops, and in the middle of a battle there was little opportunity for thorough washing of uniforms.

Having reported sick, Frederick was sent to No1 Casualty Clearing Station at nearby Chocques. From here, he was transferred to No14 General Hospital at Wimereaux, just north of Boulogne. His condition was deemed serious enough for him to be shipped back to England to recover.

After spending fifteen days in hospital, Frederick was discharged. On 5th October 1917 he left England for Egypt, arriving there two weeks later and was posted to 32nd Field Ambulance, 10th (Irish Division) which was serving in Mesopotamia and based at Sheikh Sa'ad on the Tigris river. In 1916, Sheikh Sa'ad had been the site of one of the first battles fought between British and Turkish troops during the failed attempt to relieve the besieged city of Kut-al-Amara. The British had subsequently set up a supply base there and used it to support their advance north up the Tigris towards Bagdad in early 1917. By the time Frederick joined his new unit there was little fighting taking place, and 32nd Field Ambulance's main task was to ensure that hygiene standards were being maintained.

He returned to the RAMC Depot in Egypt in June 1918, along with several other RAMC men. The following month they were compulsorily transferred to 6th Battalion, Essex Regiment, in accordance with Army regulations that enabled support troops to be transferred to front line duties when the need arose, such as replacing the casualties lost during the German Spring Offensive. However, with Turkish and German surrenders later that year, he remained in Egypt and on 28th June 1919, Frederick arrived at Alexandria, leaving for home the following month. On demobilisation, he returned to his job as a gardener at Rossway.

In 1921 Frederick married Hilda Harnott and he continued working at Rossway until 1924, when he moved away. By 1939, he was working as the head gardener at Shenley Park in Newport Pagnell, Buckinghamshire, and regularly acted as one of the judges at the local flower festival. Frederick Batchelor died in 1983, aged 86.

Gilbert Henry Belshaw (1898 – 1967)
Private 511625, RAMC

Gilbert Belshaw was the youngest of the Belshaw brothers, who were registered at their mother's home in New Road, Northchurch in the 1918 Absent Voters List. Born in Dublin in February 1898, he was just seventeen years old, and a year below the minimum age, when he enlisted with the Kings Royal Rifle Company in 1915. On completing his training, he was sent to France in October that year to join his unit.

Gilbert's service record has not survived, and much of the detail of his army service is based on the few facts available. He would have been posted to either the 3rd or 4th Battalion of the Kings Royal Rifle Company in France, but both battalions were sent to Salonika soon afterwards.

From a surviving medical record, it appears that Gilbert was shot in his left shoulder soon after arriving at Salonika and that after recovering he transferred to the RAMC and started work as an orderly at a local casualty clearing station. In the late spring of 1916 he was admitted to 28th General Hospital suffering from mitral vascular heart disease, and was later transferred to another hospital, probably in Egypt.

Gilbert next appears in 1918, working as a Private in the RAMC at the hospital based at the Imperial School of Instruction in Zeitoun, a suburb of Cairo. At that time Zeitoun was a training camp for officers and non-commissioned officers from Australia, New Zealand and India.

As was the norm, the medical classifications of men serving in the RAMC were reviewed regularly, and later in 1918 Gilbert and several of his colleagues were reclassified as 'fit for front line service' and posted to 1/11th Battalion, London Regiment. It appears however, that the war ended before the posting could take effect. On 27th January 1919, he was demobilised and came back to Northchurch.

He did not remain in the village for long, for within months he had left England bound for Hong Kong, where he joined the local police force. In 1923, he decided to emigrate to the United States of America, arriving at San Francisco on board the *Tenyo Maru* on 5th April. He made his way to New York, where he found work as a gardener, and in 1930 he married Gudrun Elfrid, a Norwegian immigrant. Gilbert subsequently became an American citizen and died in New York in 1967, aged 70.

Alfred Bignell (1895 – 1965)
Private 265422, 1st/1st Battalion, Hertfordshire Regiment

Alfred Bignell, one of George and Elizabeth Bignell's eight children, was born in Orchard End, Northchurch, in August 1895. On leaving school, he started work as a houseboy doing odd jobs around the house for retired army officer, Major Frederick Gosselin, at his home at Sandfield, in Berkhamsted High Street. At that time Alfred's family was living in Alma Road, Northchurch.

In the spring of 1914, aged nineteen, and possibly encouraged by Major Gosselin, Alfred enlisted as a Territorial with the 1st Battalion, Hertfordshire Regiment (TF). His first, and only, annual camp with the battalion was at Ashridge in late July 1914. Having been embodied along with many of his fellow Hertshires, he left for France on board the SS *City of Chester*. After fighting as an infantryman during all the early Western Front battles, in July 1916 Alfred became a member of 118th Trench Mortar Battery.

In 1914, the British army did not possess any light trench mortars, although the Germans already had three versions in limited use. In January 1915, a new mortar was invented by Wilfred Stokes and came into service with the British army during the late summer. The new Stokes mortar, known by the troops as a 'Flying Pig', was designed to be operated by specially-trained crews made up of infantrymen who could fire up to 25 bombs per minute, each bomb having a maximum range of 800 yards.

Being a member of a trench mortar battery was an extremely dangerous role and if not operated correctly, the mortar could cause serious injury to the crew. Mortar batteries soon became key enemy targets as, once their location was identified, they would be at the receiving end of any retaliatory strikes.

The Hertshires incurred significant casualties during the German Spring Offensive in March 1918. Retreating north towards Ypres, Alfred and what was left of his battalion regrouped near Voormezele, south of Ypres, arriving there on 15th April. Two days later, the Germans launched their last-ditch offensive to defeat the British troops in the area and reach the Channel coast before fresh American troops arrived. On 26th April, German troops attacked Wyschaete Ridge, where the Hertshires had dug in, forcing them to retreat once again under fierce artillery and machine gun fire and gas shells. Casualties were high, and the only way to continue the fight was for the survivors from battalions in the area to reform into a single composite battalion. A second attack four days later caused further casualties, but by this time the German momentum was slowing and they failed to achieve their planned breakthrough. At some stage during the fighting, Alfred Bignell was gassed.

News of his injury appeared in the *Hertford Mercury and Reformer* on 6th July 1918, along with the names of numerous other Hertshires who had been killed or injured during the German offensive. It is unclear whether he was invalided back to England or treated in a hospital France, but he never returned to frontline service. Awarded a Silver War Badge, he was discharged from the army on 18th February 1919.

On his return, Alfred moved back to his parents' home and stayed there until 1929, when he married Rose Edney. They moved to Aston Clinton and he later worked as a storeman at RAF Halton, near Wendover. He died in 1965, aged 68.

William Henry Bignell (1885 – 1937)
Corporal 45461, Machine Gun Corps

William Bignell was born in Northchurch in the spring of 1885 and was the first son of George and Elizabeth Bignell. William grew up in the family home, first in Alma Road and later in Orchard End, and after finishing his schooling followed his father by working at Coopers chemical factory in Berkhamsted.

In January 1904, William enlisted for six years with 4th Battalion, Bedfordshire Regiment, the local militia battalion. His service record from that time shows him standing 5ft 5½ins tall, weighing 112lbs, with a fresh complexion, brown eyes and brown hair. As a militiaman, William attended the annual training sessions, only missing the one in 1907 due to him being unwell.

By 1911, and his time with the militia completed, he had moved to Abbots Langley and was working as attendant at the Metropolitan District Imbecile Asylum in nearby Leavesden. This was one of the first institutions built for the Metropolitan Asylums Board which was responsible for the care of certain categories of the sick and the poor in London. The Leavesden asylum cared for the "quiet and harmless imbeciles" from the north of the capital. In 1912, William married Elsie Louise Cooke, and they became parents soon afterwards.

It was not until December 1915, shortly before the introduction of conscription, that William attested under the Derby Scheme at Watford. It would be six months before he was mobilised and posted to 9th Battalion, Bedfordshire Regiment, which was then based at Colchester. Within a month, probably as a result of his earlier service in the militia, he was appointed acting Corporal and soon afterwards was transferred to the Machine Gun Corps at Clipstone Camp, near Mansfield.

In March 1917, shortly before leaving for France, William was appointed Corporal and posted to the Machine Gun Corp's No2 'D' Coy. He was taken ill in October 1917 and admitted to 46 Stationary Hospital at Étaples where 'DAH' (Disorderly Action of the Heart) was recorded on his medical record. He returned to England and spent the remainder of the war there serving in several MGC reserve battalions.

He was demobilised in February 1919 with a medical classification of B3 and returned to Abbots Langley and resumed his role as an attendant at the Leavesden Asylum. The following year William became a father for the second time. He continued working as an attendant at the Asylum until January 1937, when he died of heart failure, bronchitis and asthma, aged 51.

Thomas Bunn (1885 – 1948)
Private 13881, 8th Battalion, Bedfordshire Regiment

When Thomas Bunn was born in Northchurch in the summer of 1885 his father, William, was in the rag and bone business. Thomas, or Tom, as he is recorded in the 1891 Census, was one of five sons born to William and his wife, Mary, between 1878 and 1887. Initially, the family lived in Orchard End, but by 1901 they had moved into a cottage opposite the village school in Northchurch High Street.

Tom's father died in 1909, and not long afterwards he moved out of the family home, having found work as a groom and gardener in Kings Langley. In the late summer of 1911, he married Lilian Mary Draper at St Mary's, Northchurch. Lilian worked as a machinist at the Mantel factory in Lower Kings Road, Berkhamsted and the newlyweds moved to a house in Gallows Hill, Kings Langley.

Within days of Lord Kitchener's 'call to arms' Tom decided to sign-up with the Bedfordshire Regiment and was posted to their 9th Battalion for training. Initially based in Felixstowe, the battalion later moved to Mill Hill, north London, and then to Colchester. His training over, he was posted to the Bedford's 8th Battalion, which at the time was camped near Woking awaiting orders to move to France. On 28th August 1915, Tom and his battalion left for Dover, bound for Boulogne. By this time, his wife was pregnant with their first child.

On their arrival in France, 8th Battalion was one of the few newly-trained units to be sent immediately into battle, taking part in the Battle of Loos at the end of September. Tom's service record has not survived, but sometime during the autumn or winter of 1915 he fell sick and was invalided home. In October 1916 he was formally discharged from the army and later awarded a Silver War Badge.

After his recovery, he returned home to Kings Langley and in 1922, Lilian gave birth to their second child. In 1939, they were still living in Gallows Hill and he was working as a builder's labourer. He died in 1948, aged 62.

George Chandler (1891 – 1956)
Private 13/71187, 108th Training Reserve Battalion

George Chandler, the third child of domestic gardener, George Chandler, and his wife, Fanny, was born in Farnham, Surrey in December 1890. After the family's move to Northchurch around the turn of the century, he completed his schooling in the village and by 1911 had followed his father and brothers into becoming a domestic gardener. Although there was no shortage of gardening jobs in the Northchurch and Berkhamsted area, by 1913 George had left home and was working as a gardener for the Leigh family at The Manor House in Sherbourne, Dorset. That December he married Ellen Hills at St Phillip's Church, Kensington. She was a lady's maid and was probably employed at The Manor House. A year after their marriage George and Ellen became parents.

By 1916, George and his family had moved to Loughton, Essex, where he had found new work as a gardener. In May 1916, he attested at nearby Epping, but was not called up until the following March, by which time he had moved with his family to Kilburn. After passing his medical he was posted to 109th Training Reserve Battalion based at Wimbledon for three months' army training.

In June 1917 he transferred to 108th Training Reserve Battalion, which was also based in Wimbledon, but a week after his arrival he was admitted to the Military Orthopaedic Hospital in Shepherds Bush, London, suffering from *Hallux Rigidus*, the most common form of arthritis in the foot and which affects the big toe and makes walking painful. At the hospital George underwent a successful operation to remove part of one of the bones in his foot. Released from hospital after 161 days spent there, he was deemed unfit for further military service and discharged in December 1917. A note on his service record states that his case was subject to review after a year to see whether he could return to military service and this may be the reason why he was not awarded a Silver War Badge. By the time his review was due in December 1918 the war had ended.

It is currently uncertain whether George resumed his gardening career after his discharge from the army, but in 1939 he and Ellen were living in the village of Sutton Valence, Kent, close to his younger brother, Sam, and running small holding. Like his brother, he was a Special Constable in the Malling District of the Kent County Constabulary.

George Chandler remained in Sutton Valence until his death in 1956, aged 67.

Sam Chandler (1898 – 1987)
Lance Bombardier 111242, 177th Heavy Battery, RGA

Sam Chandler was born shortly before the Chandler family moved to Northchurch from Bagshot, Surrey. Out of school hours, Sam worked alongside his elder brother, Jim, in his mother's grocery shop in Northchurch High Street. Having left school, he followed his father, George, into becoming a gardener. However, he soon started to experience problems with his left eye and a subsequent examination at Kings College Hospital, London revealed that he was suffering from iritis, inflammation of the iris. It appears that little could be done by the hospital, and he returned home.

In June 1916, aged 18, Sam was conscripted and reported to the Watford Recruiting Office. A medical examination took place a few weeks later in Bedford. Standing over 6ft 3ins tall and weighing 135lbs, Sam was passed by the medical examiner, despite being extremely short-sighted in his left eye which only registered 6/24. His right eye, however, registered a perfect 6/6. Shortly afterwards, he was posted as a gunner with 177th Heavy Battery, RGA.

Raised at Portland, Dorset, the previous June, 177th Heavy Battery was equipped with four tractor-drawn 60-pdr guns. In October 1917, Sam, now appointed Acting Lance Bombardier, and his battery joined 13th (Western) Division in Mesopotamia. The Division had been there since 1916 and had taken part in the recapture of the Kut-el-Amara and later the capture of Bagdad. 177th Battery's role was to assist in the consolidation of the earlier gains by setting up defensive positions to the north of Bagdad to prevent any chance of a Turkish counter-offensive being launched. The following month, he was promoted to the rank of Lance Bombardier.

The hot, dry conditions in Mesopotamia, combined with the bright sunlight, did nothing to help Sam's weak eye, and in September 1918 he was finally invalided home and spent two months in Winchester Hospital, where a severe recurrence of iritis in his left eye was diagnosed. As this was a result of a pre-war condition, the army refused to make any allowance for its recurrence in his subsequent pension, despite the fact that it had been severely aggravated by his war service. Reclassified with a medical category of B2, he left Winchester Hospital on 15th November 1918.

Demobilisation came on 24th February 1919 and Sam returned to Northchurch where he resumed his job as a gardener. Two days later, Sam's brother, Jim, who was serving with the Royal Military Police in Cologne, died of influenza[37]. Shortly afterwards Sam left Northchurch and on 26th June 1923 he married Ethel Sprackland in Wonston, near Winchester. They had probably met during his time in hospital. By 1939 they were living in Sutton Valence, Kent, where Sam ran a small holding of pigs, chickens and vegetables. Living close by, and running a similar small holding, was his elder brother, George, who was also serving as a Special Constable for the Kent County Constabulary. Sam Chandler died in 1987, aged 69.

James Herbert Dancer (1892 – 1960)
Lance Corporal 10974, 1st Battalion, Kings Royal Rifle Corps

James Dancer was the third son of Thomas and Martha Dancer, who lived in Bourne End Lane. Born in December 1892, James later started work as a brush hand at GB Kent & Sons in Apsley. In 1913, aged 21, he decided to join the army, enlisting with 1st Battalion, Kings Royal Rifle Corps. Early the following year, he married Ethel Margaret Trowles.

In August 1914, James was based at the Salamanca barracks in Aldershot, and his battalion was one of the first to be sent to France, landing at Rouen and making their way north-east by train to Belgium to face the advancing German army. Forced south after the defeat at Mons, the Kings Royal Rifles fought during the subsequent battles of the Marne and the Aisne. During the First Battle of Ypres in October 1914, James was fortunate to survive, as his battalion was overwhelmed by the Germans, with over half of them becoming casualties.

---

[37] Jim Chandler's story is told in *For Them's Sake*

He returned home on leave towards the beginning of 1915 and later that year, Ethel gave birth to their first child. Back in France, James took part in all the major battles of 1915 and 1916. Following the end of the Somme Offensive, he was transferred to the Rifle Corp's 16th Battalion, but shortly afterwards he received treatment for a hernia at No34 Casualty Clearing Station at Daours, east of Amiens.

At the beginning of 1918 and now a Lance Corporal, he came back to England on leave, returning to France just prior to the launch of the German Spring Offensive. After the Battle of Amiens, the following August, James and his battalion slowly advanced north-eastwards and by the middle of September, having broken through the heavily fortified German Hindenburg Line, they were west of Cambrai.

Between them and the town stood the incomplete Canal du Nord. In 1913 work had started on digging this waterway, which was meant to provide a link between the Oise River and the Dunkirk–Scheldt Canal. On the outbreak of war, however, all work was suspended and it now formed a man-made barrier in front of advancing British troops. On 28th September, James's battalion launched a successful surprise attack against the defending Germans, capturing several enemy troops and artillery pieces in the process. Having consolidated their position, the battalion launched a follow-up attack, and during the subsequent advance James was severely wounded.

He was once again taken to No34 Casualty Clearing Station, which had moved eastwards with the advancing British forces and was now based at Grevillers. His medical record reveals that he had been wounded in his left arm, both buttocks and had a compound fracture of one leg, probably caused by machine gun fire or an exploding mortar shell. His war was over, and by the end of the year he had returned to England and was awarded a Silver War Badge. He was formally discharged from the army on 8th May 1919.

On his return home James discovered that he was now the father of two children, Ethel having given birth to a daughter a week before he had been wounded. She would give birth to a second boy later in 1919.

James and his family remained in their home in Bourne End Lane for several years, but by 1939 he was working as a postman, and had moved to Swing Gate Lane in Berkhamsted, where he lived for the rest of his life. He died in 1960, aged 67.

Edwin Charles Dell (1898 – 1979)
Private 29432, 14th Battalion, Highland Light Infantry

Edwin Dell, the fourth and last child of Joseph Dell and his second wife, Ellen, was born in Gossoms End in May 1898. Sadly, by 1910 both of his parents had died and, with his elder brothers no longer living at home, he was looked after by his elder sister, Florence. In 1911 she married William

Gurney who worked for the Rothchild family on the Tring Park Estate. The Census taken that year shows Edwin living with his sister and new husband at a cottage at Wigginton Bottom.

One of Edwin's elder brothers, Walter, was already serving as a regular soldier when the war broke out in August 1914 and, tragically, became the first Northchurchman to be killed in the war just two months later. This event did not discourage Edwin from attempting to enlist in the army, nor did the fact that he was underage at the time, but he failed to be accepted by an English Regiment as he was under the minimum regulation height of 5ft 3inches. However, he was not prepared to give up, and later enlisted in Scotland with 14th Battalion, (City of Glasgow Regiment) Highland Light Infantry.

Despite being overwhelmed by volunteers following Lord Kitchener's call to arms in 1914, the British Army kept to its pre-war standards, and rejected all men below the regulation height. Many miners from the north of England who had volunteered fell into this category and consequently Alfred Biglan, the Member of Parliament for Birkenhead, suggested that able-bodied men below the regulation height should be allowed to join special battalions. With no objection being offered by the War Office, Biglan proceeded to raise his own battalion calling for 'small and pugnacious' men between the height of five foot and five foot two,

Private Edwin Dell
Courtesy of Clive Blofield

with an expanded chest measurement of 33 inches, to volunteer for a new 'Bantam' battalion. Within days, there were enough volunteers to form two battalions from the Birkenhead area. The idea caught on, and soon many County Regiments had created their own 'Bantam' battalions. Among these was 14th Battalion, Highland Light Infantry, which was formed at Hamilton in July 1915 with Edwin Dell as one of its first recruits.

It was not until June 1916, that he landed in France with his battalion. Moving to the Loos area, they saw little action for some months, possibly due to the reluctance of the army to use 'Bantams' as frontline troops. By early 1917, however, increasing numbers of taller men began to join Edwin's battalion, which resulted in the loss of its 'Bantam' status. In April 1917, his other brother, Albert, was killed during the Battle of Arras[38]. Later

---

[38] Edwin and Albert Dell's stories are told in *For Them's Sake*

that year, Edwin's battalion took part in the advance eastwards, following the German retreat to the newly-built Hindenburg Line.

Although Edwin's service record has not survived, from other documentation, it appears that he was wounded in the leg, either by a bullet or shrapnel, during the summer of 1917. Invalided back to England, he was treated at St Luke's Auxiliary War Hospital in Bradford and the nearby Clayton Auxiliary War Hospital. It would appear, however, that he was suffering from more than a leg wound, as he was later transferred to the recently-opened Abram Peel Hospital in Bradford, which was one of only eight hospitals in the country at that time that specialised in treating solders suffering from shellshock.

The word 'shellshock' had only recently been coined by a medical officer called Charles Myers. The condition manifested itself in many forms ranging from hysteria and anxiety, depression and dizziness to paralysis. One of the therapeutic activities used at the hospital to ease the symptoms of the soldiers diagnosed with shellshock was handicraft, particularly the making of string bags, raffia baskets and embroidery. All the items made were then sold to raise funds for the hospital. It is not clear how long Edwin spent under treatment at this hospital before being discharged. He was subsequently awarded a Silver War Badge and formerly discharged from the army in May 1919, aged 23.

Returning to Northchurch, and now walking with a permanent limp because of his wound, he found work as a postman in Berkhamsted and started to help with the running of the Northchurch Scout Group. Unfortunately, like many shellshock sufferers, his symptoms returned and in 1923, Edwin was forced to seek treatment at Netley Hospital, Southampton, the main centre for shellshock cases in the country.

Over time Edwin's recovery continued and he became heavily involved in Northchurch village life, joining the Parochial Church Council at St Mary's and later he became a Churchwarden there. In 1933, he was appointed Group Scoutmaster of the 1st Northchurch Scout Group and later entered local politics, serving on both the Northchurch Parish Council and Berkhamsted Urban District Council, eventually becoming chairman of both bodies. He also served as a governor of Berkhamsted School and Berkhamsted School for Girls, and for over 30 years was a governor of Northchurch village school. Edwin Dell died in 1979, aged 81.

George Dell (1883 – 1946)
Acting Corporal 25689, 1st (Reserve) Garrison Battalion, Suffolk Regiment

George Dell was born in Northchurch in June 1883 the son of Joseph Dell and his first wife, Mary Ann. Two months later he was one of eleven babies christened on the same day by Revd Augustus Birch at St Mary's,

Northchurch. Mary Ann Dell died aged 37 and when George was just over eighteen months old, leaving his father to bring up the family with the help of some of the older children. Joseph Dell remarried in 1887 and with his new wife, Ellen, started a new family which included Albert and Edwin Dell. By 1891 George was living separately with his 20-year-old brother, William, in a cottage in Northchurch High Street.

George presumably remained in Northchurch until he left school, but by 1901 he was living in Atherstone Mews, Kensington with his recently-married sister and her coachman husband and was working as an assistant in a pill factory. By 1904 he had moved to East Ham, Essex, where he became a member of the part-time Territorial Army artillery. In a letter back to an aunt in Northchurch that year he wrote that he had recently attended another annual camp of his unit at the Royal Field Artillery gunnery ranges at Shoeburyness. Unfortunately, no records have been found to identify which unit George joined, or how long he served.

He next appears in 1915 living in Cheam, Surrey, where he was working as a gardener. When he attested under the Derby Scheme at nearby Epsom he was described as being 5ft 5ins tall and weighing 130lbs. He appears however, to have been given a 'B' medical classification as, when he was called up in January 1916, he was posted to 3rd Battalion, East Surrey Regiment, a garrison and training battalion based at Dover, and a few weeks later he was transferred to the newly created 1st (Reserve) Garrison Battalion, Suffolk Regiment.

Despite being a battalion of the Suffolk Regiment George's new unit was formed in Wendover, Buckinghamshire, in March 1916 and the following May moved to the Thames estuary with bases initially being set up at Tilbury and Gravesend. On 17th June he married Beatrice Horne at Fobbing Parish Church, Essex. At the time she was living in Sutton, Surrey, close to his home in Epsom.

It appears that George continued to serve with his unit in England until early 1918 when he was diagnosed with 'Valvular Disease of the Heart' (VDH), which may account for his earlier 'B' medical classification. In May 1918 he was discharged from the army and awarded a Silver War Badge.

Nothing is known about George's subsequent movements until 1939 when he was recorded as living in Bedford with Beatrice and working on a local farm. He died in 1946, aged 63.

John William Engeldow (1888 – 1920)
Corporal T4/107990, ASC

John Engeldow was born in the late summer of 1888 in Marylebone, north London, where his father, Frederick, worked as a whitesmith, sometimes known as a tin worker. John grew up in London, but by 1901 his father had moved the family to Gossoms End, presumably having found new work in the Berkhamsted area which was closer to his wife, Ruth's, family in Chesham. Sadly, Frederick Engeldow died a few years later leaving his eldest son, Frederick, a lithographer's apprentice, and John to support the family. By 1911, Fredrick had married and moved away, and so, to make ends meet, John's mother took in a boarder, Edwin Dell's brother, Albert, who was later to lose his life in the war.

At the end of May 1915, John travelled to Watford to enlist with the ASC. Following a medical examination, he was classified as B2, which precluded him from frontline service in the infantry, but did not prevent him from joining the ASC and he was posted to Aldershot to start his training.

That September, John returned home on leave and married Ethel Maud Wilder from the village of Markyate. In the spring of 1916, Ethel gave birth to a boy who was christened William George Verdun Engeldow, the name 'Verdun' coming from the bloody battle fought by the French army against the Germans the previous year. Tragedy was to hit the Engeldow family shortly afterwards, with the death of John's mother, and also Ethel's brother, Henry Wilder, who was serving with the Bedfordshire Regiment in France.

John was sent to France in the summer of 1916 and worked with No1 Railhead Supply Detachment. Such units were responsible for the unloading of supplies brought by train from the Channel ports onto either horse-drawn wagons or motor vehicles, which would then take the supplies on to their destination. In February 1918, John became an acting Corporal and two months later a Corporal. Around this time, he was also Mentioned in Despatches, but unfortunately no further details have been found of his actions which merited this recognition.

John was demobilised in May 1919, but by then he was an ill man. Ethel was now living back at Markyate with her son, and by March 1920 John was so ill that he could not venture out of his house. A military medical examination at that time revealed that he was very thin and emaciated and he had difficulty breathing. John was subsequently diagnosed with advanced pulmonary tuberculosis, entirely due to his time spent in the army. Two weeks after his medical examination, John died, aged 31. His body now lies in the Crawley Green Road Cemetery in Luton, under a Commonwealth War Graves headstone.

Alfred Thomas Fenn (1888 – 1971)
Private 25397, 6th Battalion, Northampton Regiment

Alfred Fenn was born in Aldbury in January 1888, the son of farm labourer, Edwin Fenn, and his wife Elizabeth, and was the younger brother of Frederick Fenn. After leaving school, Alfred started work for Samuel Dickens, who ran a bakery in the village, but in 1907 he decided to become a gardener, working for Arthur Dye, the head gardener at Lord Rothchild's

Tring Park estate. Sometime later he met Wigginton-born Louisa Delderfield, who was working as a domestic servant at one of the large houses in Berkhamsted. They married at St Mary's Northchurch in June 1912 and moved to a cottage in Charles Street, Tring, close to Tring Park. A year later, Louisa gave birth to their first child.

In November 1915, four months after the birth of a second child, Alfred attested at Watford under the Derby Scheme and was placed in the army reserve. Mobilised six months later, he reported to Bedford where he was posted to the Northamptonshire Regiment, joining their 3rd (Reserve) battalion based at Gillingham, Kent. In September 1916, his training completed, Alfred was posted to 6th Battalion, Northampton Regiment, and a few days later arrived in France as part of a draft of 100 men joining the battalion at Mailly-Mallet in the Somme Sector. The battalion had already fought during the early stages of the Somme Offensive and Alfred first saw action with them the following month during the Battle of the Ancre, the final British attack in the area.

In March 1917, he was severely wounded by shrapnel, receiving what his service record described as a 'penetrating lung wound' during an artillery bombardment on the battalion's trenches near Thiepval Wood. Following treatment at a local casualty clearing station Alfred was transported back to a hospital in England to continue his treatment. By then, his wife and their two children had moved to a cottage in Gossoms End, where, after having recovered from his wound in a convalescent hospital, he was able to join them for a short period of home leave.

In October 1917, three months after his return to France, Alfred's battalion took part in the Battle of Poelcappelle, which formed part of the Third Battle of Ypres. Under heavy artillery fire for much of the time, he was again wounded when a mustard gas shell exploded nearby. Not only was he affected by the mustard gas, but the explosion also caused a diaphragmatic hernia, which was probably exacerbated by being wounded some months before. Alfred was again rushed to a casualty clearing station and then back to England, where he spent the next seven months under treatment at 1st Western General Hospital at Fazakerley, Liverpool.

On 29th May 1918, Alfred was discharged from hospital. Having been deemed unfit for further military service and given £1, a new suit of clothes and an overcoat, Alfred returned to his family in Gossoms End. The following month, he was formerly discharged from the army and awarded a Silver War Badge.

Fortunately, his injuries did not prevent him from returning to his gardening profession. It is currently not known whether he was able to resume his job at Tring Park, but by 1939, Alfred and his family were living in a cottage on the Standen Manor estate at Hungerford, Berkshire, where he worked as a gardener. Alfred Fenn died in 1971, aged 83.

Arthur Garner (1888 – 1919)
Driver T3/029137, ASC

Arthur Garner was born in Dudswell during the early summer of 1888, the second child of David Garner, a farm labourer from Hawridge, and his wife, Emily. He grew up in the hamlet with his three siblings and then became a farm labourer, possibly working alongside his father. He also became a regular worshiper at the Baptist Chapel in Northchurch High Street.

Although his elder brother, Frank, enlisted at the start of the war and would later to be killed during the German Spring Offensive in 1918[39], it appears that Arthur deliberated for some months before finally enlisting with 7th Battalion, Royal Berkshire Regiment. After completing his training, he joined them in Salonika where they had been serving since November 1915. By the middle of 1916, however, Arthur had transferred to the ASC, becoming a driver.

Salonika, particularly the Struma Valley, was one of the worst areas in Europe for disease, particularly malaria, and over the duration of the campaign, more than 162,000 British troops were infected by mosquito bites. In June 1916, Arthur was admitted to 28th General Hospital suffering from enteritis, but after treatment he was able to return to his unit.

Although his service record has not survived, no evidence has been found to suggest that he was discharged early due to illness. After his demobilisation from the army in early 1919, Arthur returned home to his father's home in Bell Lane, Northchurch and found work as a labourer with the local council. Within weeks however, he started to feel unwell, suffering a high temperature and vomiting. The doctor was called and he was diagnosed with malaria.

Arthur Garner died of the disease in June 1919, aged just 31. The following year, his name was one of those included on the war memorial plaque placed on the inside wall of the porch of the Baptist Chapel in Northchurch.

Ephraim Garner (1881 – 1959)
Private T/388754, ASC

Ephraim Garner was one of only four of Thomas and Frances Garner's children to survive beyond infancy. Born in Orchard End, Northchurch, in May 1881, he grew up in the village and later became a bricklayer's labourer, possibly working alongside his father. By 1901 he had left the family home and was lodging in Northchurch High Street and six years later he married Sarah Ann Scutchings at St Mary's, Northchurch. They set up

---

[39] Frank Garner's story is told in *For Them's Sake*

home in a cottage in Gossoms End, but the marriage did not last for very long, as the couple separated and eventually divorced.

By 1915 34-year-old Ephraim had left Gossoms End and was working in London for the building firm, Higgs and Hill, which was responsible for the construction of several prestigious buildings in the capital. In May 1916, he was conscripted and reported to the Watford Recruiting Office, giving the name of his father as his next of kin. Following a medical examination, which resulted in an A1 classification, he was posted to 2nd Battalion, Suffolk Regiment.

On 25th October 1916, Ephraim left Folkestone with his battalion bound for France. Within two weeks of arriving, however, he was transferred to 2nd Battalion Essex Regiment, which had suffered catastrophic losses on the first day of the Somme Offensive. He joined his new battalion on 10th November as part of a draft of 56 men, and was to remain in the Somme sector over the cold winter months before moving north the following spring to take part in the Battle of Arras.

The British launched a heavy artillery attack on the German lines west of Arras early on the morning of 3rd May 1917, but despite this, the infantrymen advancing across no-man's land, including 2nd Essex, were met with fierce opposition and nearly wiped out. Ephraim was one of the casualties, receiving a wound to his right thigh, and was evacuated to 22nd General Hospital at Camiers, before returning to England aboard the hospital ship *St Andrew*.

Treated at the North Evington Military Hospital in Leicester, followed by a time of convalescence at the VAD Hospital in Uppingham, Ephraim was discharged by the medics at the end of June 1917, having spent fifty days under treatment. He now walked with a slight limp and his wound, or the shock of it, had created an issue with his lungs. As a result, his medical classification was downgraded from A1 to B2.

Once recovered, Ephraim was sent to the Essex Regiment's Depot to await a new posting. Considered no longer fit for frontline service, at the end of 1917 he was transferred to 776th (MT) Coy ASC and worked at loading and unloading their vehicles near Redhill, Surrey.

Ephraim's next admission to hospital was avoidable, and was a direct result of his own actions during a visit to Watford in April 1918. About half of all venereal disease cases within the British army during the war were contracted in the UK. Not only did this reduce the number of soldiers available to fight, but put an immense strain on the army's medical facilities as the treatment was lengthy and time consuming. He spent over three months being treated at Warlingham Military Hospital near Caterham, Surrey before returning to duty.

Demobilised in April 1919, he moved to Willesden, North London and returned to building work. He remained in Willesden for the rest of his life. Ephraim Garner died in 1959, aged 77.

Charles Geary (1896 – 1951)
Private 36983, ASC

Charles Geary, known as Charlie, was born in New Road, Northchurch, in December 1896, the seventh child of farm worker, William Geary, and his wife Annie. Having completed his schooling, he became a farm worker.

By the time Charlie was fifteen, two of his elder brothers, Walter and Frederick, were overseas serving with the Border Regiment. Walter Geary returned home in 1912 to become a Reservist, whilst Frederick continued to serve on garrison duty in Burma. Following the outbreak of war, Walter was recalled to his unit, leaving Charlie at home.

On 3rd May 1915 Charlie enlisted as a driver with the ASC at Watford and after passing his medical he was sent to Woolwich for training. Charlie's service record shows him as standing 5ft 3¾ins tall, weighing 112lbs, with brown eyes and brown hair. He was later posted to an ASC base at Aldershot.

Shortly after he enlisted, both Walter and Fredrick Geary were killed during the Gallipoli Campaign. Initially, there was some confusion over what had happened to Walter as *The Times* of 6th August 1915 listed him as one of those wounded at Gallipoli, which led to several enquiries about his condition being passed to the War Office. On 16th August, on behalf of his mother, Charlie wrote from Aldershot asking for further information, but it subsequently transpired that the report in *The Times* was incorrect; Walter had died on board a hospital ship, en route to Malta, the previous May and had been buried at sea.

Charlie remained in Aldershot until 19th November 1915, when he was discharged from the ASC. A further medical examination revealed that he suffered from a mild form of epilepsy and consequently he was not deemed fit for military service. He returned to Northchurch, and was later awarded a Silver War Medal.

By 1919, Charlie had moved to Hendon, north London. He later married and moved to Birmingham where, in 1939, he was living with his wife and child and working as a Consulting Motor Engineer. Charlie Geary died in Birmingham in 1951, aged 55.

Francis William Gomm (1892 – 1948)
Private S/24637, 1/6th Battalion, The Black Watch (Royal Highland Regiment)

Francis Gomm was born in Berkhamsted in September 1892, the son of James Gomm, a painter from Portsmouth, and his Berkhamsted-born wife, Caroline. In 1901, the family was living in Victoria Road, Berkhamsted, but by 1911 they had moved to Ellesmere Road in the eastern part of

Northchurch Parish. Francis was now working locally at the Locke & Smith brewery, but later found work as a machinist at William Cooper & Nephew.

He was conscripted in June 1916 and had the usual medical examination, his service record showing him as standing 5ft 6ins tall, weighing 122lbs and with a good physical development. The examination also identified some skin discolouration, probably because of his work at Coopers, and a slight problem with the hearing in one ear, but neither were enough to stop him from being awarded an A1 medical classification.

In the spring of 1917, several months before he was mobilised, Francis married Louisa Dell at St Michael and All Angels, Sunnyside. The following July, he was told to report to the Watford Recruitment Office and posted to 103rd Training Reserve Battalion based in Edinburgh. In 1916, the training structure of the British army changed, with the creation of new training reserve battalions, which replaced the previous regimental training structure. This meant that once trained, a conscript did not know to which regiment he would be posted.

His training completed, Francis was posted to 2/3 Scottish Horse Yeomanry which had been formed in Scotland shortly after the outbreak of war as a second line unit, and was then based at Fife. By the time he joined them in September 1917, the unit had lost all its horses and become a cyclist unit.

The need for urgent reinforcements in France following the German Spring Offensive in March 1918 resulted in Francis being transferred to 1/6th Battalion, The Black Watch (Royal Highland Regiment). He joined them in France two months later.

In July 1918, the Black Watch marched towards the Forest of Rheims prior to launching a joint attack with the French on the German defences in the area. During the fierce fighting that ensued, an artillery shell exploded next to Francis's position. Although not visibly injured, the blast had severely damaged the hearing in his left ear, leaving him deaf. It appears that he did not immediately report sick, possibly hoping that the deafness would clear, but on 14th August he was admitted to a local Field Hospital and transferred to No10 Field Hospital at St Pol where mastoiditis[40] was diagnosed. Francis had surgery on his ear shortly

Norfolk War Hospital
Author's collection

---

[40] A bacterial infection that affects the mastoid, a delicate bone behind the ear

afterwards and was then was invalided back to England on board the hospital ship *St David*. He spent the next few weeks receiving further treatment at the Norfolk War Hospital at Thorpe, near Norwich, followed by a period of convalescence at nearby Coonoor. A medical report from the time indicates that Francis was now totally deaf in one ear and suffered regular vertigo attacks and headaches.

Back in Northchurch his wife gave birth to a boy who was christened Dennis[41]. Following further treatment, Francis was discharged from the army in March 1919 and returned home and his army pension was increased to reflect his deafness. Fortunately, he was able to return to his job at William Cooper & Nephew in Berkhamsted. In 1939, he was still working there and was now living with his family in Gossoms End. Francis Gomm died in 1948, aged 55.

James Green (1879 – 1963)
Lance Corporal 57965, 39th Field Ambulance, RAMC

James Green was born in Dudswell in May 1879, the fourth child of Joseph Green, a shepherd, and his wife, Sarah. After leaving school he also started work on a farm, probably alongside his father. In 1903, James married Mary Jane Cadmore, the daughter of a brewery worker from Rickmansworth and over the next seven years Mary would give birth to four children at their four-roomed cottage in Bell Lane, Northchurch.

Although his service record has not survived, it is known that he enlisted with the RAMC in the opening weeks of the war, and was later posted to 39th Field Ambulance, part of 39th Brigade, and probably served with them as an orderly or a stretcher bearer. June 1915 saw James and 39th Field Ambulance sailing for Egypt and then to Gallipoli, where they landed on 5th July.

For a member of a Field Ambulance, the Gallipoli peninsula in 1915 was one of the worst places to serve. Apart from the daily risk of being hit by enemy rifle or artillery fire, the rocky terrain meant that most latrine trenches were shallow and open to the elements, and the flies and stench coming from them were often unbearable and frequently resulted in outbreaks of dysentery. Meanwhile, wounded soldiers on the battlefield often had to wait for hours for stretcher bearers to reach them due to the lack of adequate cover. By the time the men had been found, the ever-present flies had often got there first causing even minor wounds to become infected. Frequently, the lack of cover also meant that the bodies of dead soldiers had to be left to rot and putrefy in the heat. Even when brought back to the nearest field

---

[41] Petty Officer Dennis Gomm would be killed during a German bombing attack on Great Yarmouth on 28th April 1942 whilst serving at the Royal Navy storage depot HMS *Watchful*

hospital, men usually had to wait for hours in bloodstained uniforms to be examined and the overstretched orderlies often could not keep up with the need to change bandages on a regular basis. Washing facilities on the front line were minimal, except for when the soldiers returned to the beaches. For those who managed to avoid being wounded, the constant poor diet of tinned bully beef and undigestible army biscuits, together with the lack of fresh fruit and vegetables, slowly led to a deterioration in their health.

As the hot summer turned into autumn and then winter, conditions changed, but not for the better. The frequent rain saw an increase in cases of trench foot and later, as it got colder, frostbite. Eventually at the end of 1915, the British government acknowledged the futility of continuing the Gallipoli campaign and, along with their French allies, decided to evacuate its troops. James and 39th Field Ambulance were evacuated to Egypt on the nights of 19th and 20th December.

In February 1916 39th Field Ambulance was sent to Mesopotamia to join the relief force being assembling at Sheikh Sa'ad to break the besieged garrison at Kut-al-Amara. Arriving at Basra on 1st March on board the *Japanese Prince*, SS *Briton* and the SS *Oriana*, the Field Ambulance had to wait a further eight days before moving north on board the paddle steamer SS *Mozuffri*, but without their animals and vehicles. Despite a collision with another paddle steamer en route, the journey inland continued. After two weeks James and his field ambulance arrived at Sheikh Sa'ad and set up a base to deal with the casualties being brought down river from the fighting further north.

A planned attack on Turkish positions at the start of April required 39th Field Ambulance to move further north and closer to the fighting. It now operated in two main sections; the 'stretcher bearer division' was responsible for bringing the casualties into the field ambulance, together with the evacuation by boat of the seriously sick and wounded, whilst the 'tent division' was responsible for the erection of tents, provision of paillasses, blankets and all other non-medical items.

Within days of setting up the new camp, 39th Field Ambulance was again ordered further north and travelled up the river Tigris to Falahiyeh. The fighting on 9th April saw it's stretcher bearers pushed to their limits with the heavy number of casualties being brought back from the front and using up all the available stretchers. The stretcher bearers consequently had to resort to carrying the wounded using blankets. That day, the SS *Medjidieh* left with 455 casualties on board and returned twelve hours later to collect a further 385 men. During the first three days of the fighting, 39th Field Ambulance received, treated and evacuated a total of 1,559 casualties. A further 43 men died whilst under treatment.

On 29th April 1916, the besieged British garrison at Kut finally surrendered. As for the relief force, they suffered just under 10,000 casualties between 5th and 23rd April, more than a quarter of its strength.

James and 39th Field Ambulance were to remain at Falahiyeh for a further four weeks before returning to Sheikh Sa'ad.

In late August, 39th Field Ambulance were ordered to advance north with 13th Division in a move that would eventually lead to the capture of Bagdad. After securing the city, 13th Division continued the slow advance, pushing the Turks northwards. 39th Field Ambulance came behind, setting up temporary camps to process the sick and wounded and ship the severe cases south via riverboat. Around September 1917, James returned to Northchurch on leave, probably the first time that he had been there since enlisting back in 1914. In June the following year, James' wife, Mary Jane, gave birth to twin girls.

James had probably returned to his unit by the time that 13th Division were engaged in the fighting around the Hamrin mountains, some 150 miles north of Bagdad. The final major fighting in the area took place to the east at Tuz Khurmatli in April 1918, but by now the daytime temperatures were around 43 degrees Celsius, making it too hot to continue the campaign. Cases of cholera and typhus now began to increase and later influenza became a major problem.

On 30th October 1918, Turkey signed the Armistice of Mudros, but their defeat made little difference to the work of 39th Field Ambulance. James and some 260 other ranks in the unit continued to deal with the incessant stream of sick soldiers as they came in. The following month, 39th Field Ambulance moved its main camp eastwards to Qarah Tabbah, leaving three smaller camps in the nearby towns for the small garrisons based there.

James was demobilised in 1919 and returned to his family in Bell Lane. In 1922, they moved from their 4-roomed cottage into one of the newly-built council houses on Tring Road, Northchurch, where James lived for the rest of his life. In 1939, James was working as a furniture porter. He died in 1963, aged 84.

Joseph Hales (1897 – 1959)
Private 203212, 2/5th Battalion, Notts & Derby Regiment

Joseph Hales was born in December 1897 in the family home in New Road, Northchurch and was the fourth of Joseph and Elizabeth Hales sons to go off to war. In May 1916 he received his conscription papers and was mobilised the following month. On completion of his training, he was posted to 'B' Coy, 2/5th Battalion, Notts & Derby Regiment.

In 1916, 2/5th Battalion were based in Ireland, having taken part in the suppression of the uprising earlier in the year by Irish Republicans and, as they did not leave Ireland until the following January, it is possible that Joseph spent some time with his new battalion there. 2/5th Battalion arrived in France on 26th February 1917 and first saw action during an attack on a village near the German Hindenburg Line. Later that year its troops fought in the Third Battle of Ypres.

Back in the Somme sector by the beginning of March 1918 and three weeks before the Germans launched their Spring Offensive, the strength of Joseph's battalion totalled 998 officers and men. On the morning of the offensive, Joseph was with 'B' Coy in the trenches north of the village of Noreuil. Opening fire on the British positions with a mixture of high explosive and gas shells, German stormtroopers were soon reported to be advancing at a fast rate through the fog and smoke. As they advanced, so did the creeping barrage in front of them, and soon it was targeting Joseph's battalion. By 13:00 on 22nd March, Noreuil village was in enemy hands and the stormtroopers were sweeping past 2/5th Battalion's positions, and surrounded them shortly afterwards. The roll call taken on 31st March revealed the losses the battalion had suffered during the attack; of the 998 officers and men present on 1st March, only 210 men remained. The others were either dead, wounded or missing.

Among the wounded was Joseph Hales. The extent of his injuries is not known, but they were serious enough for him to be invalided back to England. On 14th October he was formally discharged from the army and awarded a Silver War Badge.

In due course Joseph returned home to Northchurch, where he lived with his parents for several years in a cottage on the High Street. In the early 1930s Joseph met and fell in love with Jane Reay Minto, the daughter of a licenced victualler from Tyneside, and they were married in the autumn of 1933. Joseph and Jane became parents the following year upon the birth of a daughter, with a second daughter being born in 1936.

In 1939 he and his family were living at a house named Arizona on Berkhamsted Common and he was working as a house painter. The family later moved north to Tyneside, where he died in the spring of 1959 aged 62.

Frederick James Harris (1883 – 1968)
Private 113351, RAMC

Frederick Harris only spent a short time in the Northchurch area. Born in Exeter in September 1883, the son of Albert Harris, a bookdealer, Frederick later became a chemist. In 1910 he was living in the village of Trentham, Staffordshire, when he married 27-year-old Matilda Mothersole, the daughter of a bricklayer from Northchurch. How they met each other, miles away from where they grew up, is unknown. Around that time, Frederick was working as an analytical chemist for a brewery in the Trentham area, and following their marriage he and Matilda moved into a 6-roomed house in Hem Heath, just outside Trentham village. They did not stay there for long, as Matilda gave birth to their first child in Devon in 1915, with a second child being born the following year.

Frederick was probably conscripted in the summer of 1916. Although his service record has not survived, it is known that he put his skills as a chemist to good use by when he joined the RAMC. Meanwhile, Matilda returned to Northchurch, along with her two children, to be closer to her parents and set up home in a small cottage in Eddy Street, Gossoms End. Here, in September 1918, Matilda gave birth to a third child.

In 1918, Frederick was serving with 38th Mobile Laboratory, RAMC. By that stage of the war, each army division had four mobile laboratories. The first mobile laboratory had been introduced in October 1914 by adapting a bespoke motor caravan built by the Austin motor company for the wealthy Dunlop pneumatic tyre magnate, William Harvey du Cros. The caravan part of the vehicle was sufficiently large enough for a medical laboratory to be installed inside. Later, vehicles used as mobile medical laboratories were built on the chassis of standard 3-ton lorries. Being mobile, the laboratories could operate close to the frontline troops, testing the local water supply to ensure that it was drinkable so that any outbreaks of disease could be identified quickly and precautions put in place. The work of chemists like Frederick working in the field was dangerous, with samples of all types from the troops and their surroundings being delivered to the laboratories for speedy analysis, and it was not uncommon for the chemists to become infected via the samples they were analysing.

Frederick was demobilised in 1919, and shortly afterwards he and his family returned to Exeter, where he worked as a chemist for a local industrial company. In 1924, Matilda gave birth to a fourth child. By then, the couple were considering their future, and in July 1925, they arrived with their family in Queensland, Australia. They settled in Wynnum, a small town on the coast east of Queensland's capital, Brisbane, where he continued to work as a chemist. Frederick Harris died in Queensland in 1968, aged 84.

Reginald (Reg) Hucklesbee (1893 – 1967)
Air Mechanic 90647, RFC

Reginald Hucklesbee's conscription into the armed forces highlights the difficulties faced by those appealing their case at the local military tribunals. Born in Boxmoor in August 1893 to timber yard worker, Micah Hucklesbee, and his wife, Mary Ann, Reginald, known as Reg, was one of ten children, with eight surviving beyond infancy. On leaving school he followed the recently-established family tradition of obtaining work at the Apsley paper mills, where in 1911 he was working as a machine ruler[42].

---

[42] A machine ruler sets up and overseas the operation of a machine that draws lines on paper for use in account books and ledgers.

Whilst working at the paper mills, Reg met and fell in love with Annie Dell, whose family originally came from Wigginton, and were now living in Northchurch. They were married in the summer of 1915 and moved into a cottage in Alma Road, Northchurch. Their only child Ronald, was born in October the following year.

Reg's conscription papers arrived in December 1916 and he appealed to the Berkhamsted Military Tribunal on grounds of ill health. Appearing before the Tribunal in April 1917, having previously been awarded an A1 category at his medical examination, Reg stated that he had been under the doctor since December 1915 and had been unable to work since the previous Easter, and that his attendance at the tribunal had been one of the few times he had left his home. Despite his plea, the Military Advisor on the tribunal, Colonel Blest, stated that *"In face of his classification, we can only assume he is a fit man, in fact one of the fittest"*. Reg's case was adjourned for an examination to take place at a Special Medical Board. It would appear that Reg's appeal was subsequently dismissed and he was posted to the Royal Flying Corps becoming a 3rd Class Air mechanic based in England.

It soon became obvious that Reg was not fit enough to serve in the military, albeit even in a support role, and in March 1918 he was discharged from the RFC on grounds of sickness. Reg returned to Northchurch with a small military pension and in due course to his job at the Apsley paper mill.

In 1920 Reg and his family moved from Alma Road into one of the newly-built council houses in Tring Road where the family lived for many years. By 1939 Reg had become a foreman at Apsley, and shortly afterwards his son, Ronald, who was now also working at the paper mill, was called up, joining the Bedfordshire & Hertfordshire Regiment. Tragically, Ronald was to be killed in North Africa in 1941 and was posthumously awarded the Military Medal[43].

Reg and Annie later moved to Hemel Hempstead. He died there in 1967, aged 73.

Frank Humphrey (1889 – 1944)
Private GS/53042, 2nd Battalion, Royal Fusiliers

It was probably his work as a gardener that brought Frank Humphrey to Hertfordshire. Born in February 1889 in the market town of Wadhurst, Sussex, he was one of Charles and Catherine Humphrey's seven children. Charles worked on a local farm, but by 1901 he had moved his family to a stud farm near Tonbridge, Kent, where he was now working as a shepherd, whilst Frank's brothers worked locally as gardeners. Ten years later, Frank had also become a gardener and was boarding in a house in Tonbridge. Soon afterwards, he moved to Berkhamsted, having found work at one of

---

[43] Ronald Hucklesbee's story is told in *For Them's Sake*

the large houses in the area. In 1913, he married Alice Wilkin at St Andrew's, Otshott, Surrey and moved into a cottage in Northchurch High Street. In the spring of 1915, Alice gave birth to a boy, who sadly died soon afterwards.

With the threat of conscription growing closer, Frank decided to attest under the Derby Scheme in November 1915, and having been mobilised, he was posted to 20th (Service) Battalion (3rd Public Schools), Royal Fusiliers. Formed at Epsom at the start of the war for men from university and private schools in the Surrey area, 20th Battalion had suffered heavy casualties in France. Frank's service record has not survived, so it is unclear when he joined them, but it is likely that he was in a draft of new recruits to help replenish the casualties from the opening days of the Somme Offensive.

He was to remain with 20th Battalion until the end of January 1918, during which time he would have seen action several times, including the German retreat to the Hindenburg line and the Third Battle of Ypres. By the end of 1917, plans were being made to decommission his battalion as many of the remaining public-school members had been awarded commissions. As a result, Frank was transferred to 2nd Battalion, Royal Fusiliers.

According to his medal record, his time with 2nd Battalion ended on 10th June 1918. He was subsequently awarded a Silver War Badge after being discharged from the army due to being wounded. Without his service record it is impossible to identify exactly when and where he had been injured, but 2nd Battalion's last major action was during Battle of the Lys in April 1918, when it suffered significant casualties. Formal notification that Frank had become a casualty appeared in the 9th July 1918 edition of the *Weekly Casualty List*. He was probably evacuated back to England for treatment and recuperation; the Absent Voters List for the spring of 1919 still records him being away from home, and he was probably continuing his recovery in a convalescent hospital at the time.

On his return to Northchurch, he decided to become a boot and shoe repairer and obtained a £40 grant from the Army to start his new business in the village. Frank Humphrey died in 1944, aged 55.

Harold Garnett Janion MC (1885 – 1946)
Captain, RAMC

In November 1885, Mary Janion, the wife of successful barrister, Richard Garnett Janion, gave birth to twin boys, Harold and Cecil, at their home in Warwick Gardens in the fashionable area of West Kensington, London. Not long after the birth of their last child two years later, Richard Janion commissioned the building of Alderley on Chesham Road, Berkhamsted, the family moving there on its completion. For some reason, Harold and his twin brother were sent to different schools, Harold boarding at Felstead School, Essex, whilst Cecil went to Berkhamsted School. Richard Janion died in 1899, aged only 46.

After leaving Felstead School, Harold studied medicine at University College London, graduating in 1908. One of his maternal great-grandmothers had been born in Brazil, and following his graduation Harold decided to visit the country, leaving Liverpool on a round voyage on board the RMS *Augustine*.

While he was away, tragedy again hit the Janion family with the death of his twin brother. Cecil was a law student and a member of the Yeomanry and it was at his unit's annual camp on Salisbury Plain that he was suddenly taken ill and died a few days later.

After his return to England, Harold qualified as a doctor and later became a senior registrar surgeon at the Royal Sea Bathing Hospital at Margate, Kent, an infirmary founded in 1791 to provide treatment for the poor of London suffering from skin diseases.

Upon the outbreak of war, Harold joined the RAMC and on 16th September 1914, having obtained a temporary commission, he was attached to 2nd Battalion Prince of Wales Own (West Yorkshire Regiment) as the battalion's medical officer. Harold's battalion had recently returned from Malta to become part of 23rd Division and was based at Hursley Camp near Winchester. On 5th November, 2nd Battalion left Southampton bound for Le Havre onboard the SS *Mount Temple* and within days the men were in the trenches at Neuve Chapelle. The following March, 2nd Battalion took part in the Battle for Neuve Chapelle, and despite achieving their objective of breaking through the German defences, their success could not be exploited. For his role in providing medical support to the casualties during the battle, Harold was subsequently awarded the Military Cross and in September 1915, he was promoted to Captain. He remained with 2nd Battalion for another year, having seen them incur heavy casualties on first day of the Somme Offensive.

Returning home on leave in September 1916, Harold was reassigned as medical officer attached to the Royal Horse Artillery. Back in France in August the following year, Harold gained a bar to his Military Cross whilst helping to remove the pilot from a wrecked aeroplane close to the front line. Realising that the pilot was being rescued, German artillery opened fire on the rescuers, injuring Harold and several of the stretcher bearers. Fortunately, suffering only minor wounds and despite being under constant shellfire, Harold managed to return to the British lines to collect new stretcher bearers and brought the wounded soldiers and pilot back to safety.

At the end of the war, Harold decided to remain with the RAMC and the 1921 Absent Voters List records him registered at his mother's address at Lane End, Shootersway, Northchurch and attached to the Ministry of Pensions. Not long after, he was transferred to the British Army in India where he remained for several years. In 1926, Harold was registered at Briarcroft in Cross Oak Road, Berkhamsted. By now, he had left the RAMC and started work with the medical department of the East India Railway Company in Allahabad, India. By 1930, he had returned to Berkhamsted and the following year he married a widow, Brynhild Lucy Chalmers, the daughter of Sir Francis 'Frank' Robert Benson a well-known actor of the day. Harold and Brynhild returned to India shortly afterwards and Harold became a District Medical Officer for the East Indian Railway Company.

By 1938, Harold and Brynhild were back in England again and settled at Cheeleys in the village of Horsted Keynes, Sussex. They later moved to Hartley Witney, Hampshire. Harold Garnett Janion died in 1946, aged 60.

Arthur Kempster (1896 – 1956)
Private 83384, Machine Gun Corps

Arthur Kempster was born in January 1896 at The Ferns, Hog Lane, on the southern edge of Northchurch Parish, and was one of ten children born to William Kempster, a horseman from nearby Ashley Green, and his Northchurch-born wife, Emily. He went to school at Ashley Green and later started work as a farm labourer.

On 17th May 1915, aged 19, Arthur travelled to Aylesbury, where he attested with the local territorial force unit, the Bucks Battalion, Oxfordshire & Buckinghamshire Light Infantry. Passing the medical, Arthur was posted to the Regiment's 2/4th Battalion and his training took place at Broomfield, near Chelmsford, Essex. On 4th April 1916, he was appointed Lance Corporal. Preparations for the battalion's departure for France commenced the same month and it left Southampton for Le Havre on 24th May as part of 61st (South Midlands) Division on board the SS *Arundel* and SS *City of Dunkirk*. Subsequently moving to billets near Merville in northern France, Arthur and his battalion entered the front line near Laventie, west of Loos on 1st June.

German gas attacks were expected in the area at any time, and on 18th July, Arthur was caught in one whilst in a working party. Taken to Lady Hadfield's Hospital at Wimereux, named after a wealthy and philanthropic American wife of a British businessman, he remained there for six days before being invalided back to England. He was later treated at the Duston War Hospital on the outskirts of Northampton, which specialised treating in gas casualties.

In November 1916, having recovered from his injuries, Arthur was transferred to the MGC and started his training at Belton Park. The following March, Arthur once again left for France, arriving at Camiers where he joined 175 Coy MGC and moved to the Somme sector two weeks later. Within days, Arthur had gone down with a very nasty bout of dysentery and reported to No38 Casualty Clearing Station at Heilly and was then moved to No25 Stationery Hospital at Rouen. Arthur's case was severe enough for him to invalided back to England for treatment for a second time, arriving on board the hospital ship *St David*. Initially treated at University Hospital in Southampton, Arthur was sent to convalesce at the Dysentery Convalescent Hospital at New Milton, Hampshire.

Once recovered, Arthur returned to Belton Park on 8th September 1917 and was assigned to No7 Battery, MGC for a period of retraining. Two months later, Arthur boarded the SS *Corina* with a draft of inexperienced troops bound for India. For the duration of the journey Arthur became an Acting Corporal, reverting to the rank of Lance Corporal on their arrival at Bombay. In India, Arthur was assigned to 222 Coy, MGC which was based in Abbottabad, located on the North West Frontier with Afghanistan.

Arthur was promoted to Corporal in September 1918 and later the same month was transferred to 286 Coy MGC. Although his dysentery had been successfully treated in England, the conditions in India frequently caused it to flare up. Following a particularly bad experience, it was decided to invalid Arthur home as it was felt unlikely that he could deal with another hot summer in India. He left India in April 1919 and on arrival in England he was taken to Bermondsey Military Hospital in Lewisham for three weeks of treatment. A further two months of convalescence followed at the Military Hospital, Addington Park, Croydon. Two days before he left Croydon, he was demobilised.

Arthur returned to the family home in Hog Lane in Northchurch and in early in1921 he married Lily Simmonds, the daughter of a local gamekeeper. In 1939 he was living with Lily and their two children in Watford and working as a ploughman. Arthur Kempster died in 1956, aged 60.

James Meager (1891 – 1961)
Driver T3/029079, ASC

James Meager was born in June 1891, and was the son of Frederick Meager, a local bricklayer, and his wife, Lucy. He initially followed his father's trade, but later started working at Norcott Hill Farm. In the summer of 1912, James married Alice Collier from Tring and the couple moved to a cottage in the picturesque village of Aldbury, where she gave birth to a child the following year.

He was still working at Norcott Hill Farm when war broke out. With the harvest still to be brought in, and preparations made for the forthcoming winter to be completed, it was not until the following December that James, then aged 23, decided to volunteer and travelled to Watford to enlist as a driver with the ASC. In his service record, he is described as being 5ft 5½ins tall, weighing 140lbs and with good physical development and vision. Following his medical, James was sent to the ASC depot at Woolwich for training.

James left for France in September 1915 as a driver for 80th Field Ambulance, RAMC, part of 26th Division. Like the other units of the British army, the RAMC employed ASC servicemen as drivers for both their horse-drawn and petrol-driven vehicles and wagons. James remained in France for some three months before his unit was transferred to Salonika. Before he left however, boredom must have set in a few days before Christmas as he, and possibly others, broke out of camp and were absent for a whole day, which resulted in him being fined 17 days' pay on his return.

In January 1916, James and his unit left Marseilles onboard the SS *Menominee*, and arrived at Salonika nine days later. Within three months he was admitted to his own field ambulance when he started to suffer from synovitis of the knee, inflammation of the lining of the knee joint. After treatment he was discharged, but the symptoms soon reappeared, necessitating another spell in hospital. This time he was transferred to a hospital on the island of Malta and he left Salonika onboard HS *Formosa* on 24th June. He was discharged after seven weeks of treatment and returned to Salonika, where was posted to No3 Base Horse Transport Depot, and later transferred to 12th Labour Battalion.

There were several labour battalions serving in Salonika, each with an establishment of some 500 men of various ranks, who had served in front line units, but had been given a lower medical category due to sickness or injury. James remained with 12th Labour Battalion for the next eleven months throughout the cold winter and the hot, steamy summer. In August 1917, he was admitted to 66 General Hospital and was found to be suffering from malaria. Following treatment, he was sent to No2 Convalescent Depot to recover, but within days of being discharged, the malaria returned and he was admitted to 29th Stationary Hospital for further treatment, followed by a spell at No6 Convalescent Depot. The malaria returned for a second time just before Christmas 1917, which resulted in James returning to England under the 'Y' Scheme. This scheme was established in 1917 by the War Office following the recommendation of Sir Ronald Ross, an expert in tropical diseases, who had recently discovered the link between mosquitos and malaria. His solution was a simple one, remove the infected serviceman from the area where he had contracted malaria and move him to a more suitable environment where recovery was more likely, whilst retaining him in a reserve capacity in the army. James left Salonika in February 1918 onboard the SS *Londonderry* and his service record was marked '*Not to be sent to theatre of war apart from France or Italy*' in accordance with the 'Y' Scheme guidance.

On arrival at Southampton, James was posted to 661 Company, ASC, which was based at Park Royal, west London. A subsequent posting to 833 Company, ASC, at Shorncliffe near Deal, followed a few months later. His final posting was to the newly-established No1 Malarial Concentration Centre at Great Baddow, near Chelmsford. This was a specialist unit created as a result of another of Sir Ronald Ross's ideas, which aimed to prevent infected servicemen passing malaria to the civilian population. To do this effectively, the servicemen were 'concentrated' in dedicated centres, where specialist control and treatment measures were put in place. James was to spend a month at Great Baddow before returning to 661 Company to await his demobilisation.

He was demobilised in March 1919 and returned home to Aldbury. It is not currently known whether he resumed his work at Norcott Hill Farm, nor what the impact of malaria had on his subsequent life. In 1939, James was once again working as a bricklayer and still living in Aldbury. He died in Harrow in 1961, aged 70.

George Monger (1886 – 1919)
Sergeant 18181, Royal Army Veterinary Corps

On 5th May 1887, Frederick and Elizabeth Monger witnessed the christening at St Mary's, Northchurch of three of their boys, George, Henry and Frederick. The family lived in the easternmost part of Northchurch Parish, where Frederick worked as a general labourer.

George Monger was born in 1886 and later became a blacksmith's striker. In 1902, adding two years on to his age to appear to be eighteen years old, he managed to enlist with the 1st Battalion, Bedfordshire Regiment for a twelve-year term. His service record dating from that time shows him as being 5ft 3ins tall, weighing 114lbs, with brown hair and grey eyes.

The following year, George transferred to the Bedford's 2nd Battalion, which had recently returned from fighting the Boers in South Africa. The battalion's first role on its return was to form the Colchester garrison and it later moved to Borden Camp, Hampshire, where George was later awarded the good conduct medal. Returning to Berkhamsted in 1905 at the end of his first three years in the army, he transferred to the Reserves and started work as a plumber's fitter. On 11th May 1911, he married Florence Eggleton at St Michael and All Angels, Sunnyside. The newlyweds moved to a cottage in Gossoms End and Florence gave birth to a daughter two years later.

In August 1914, just days before the end of his time in the Reserves, George was mobilised and reported to the Bedford's headquarters. Here, he was posted to the Bedford's 3rd Reserve Battalion and then to their 1st Battalion. He arrived in France on 26th August, the same day that the main battalion were making a stand against the advancing German army at the Battle of Le Cateau. He joined them shortly afterwards and first saw action during the battles of the Marne and the Aisne.

Conditions in the trenches during the winter of 1914/15 were particularly harsh. Living in the open left soldiers vulnerable to the freezing winter weather and George was no exception. In March 1915, he reported to No3 Casualty Clearing Station at Hazebrouck and was subsequently admitted to

No4 General Hospital at Versailles suffering from frostbite. Two weeks later, he was transferred back to England to continue his recovery.

On his return to duty the following June, George was posted back to the Bedford's 3rd Battalion for his final two months in the army. By then he had come to the end of his contracted twelve years in the army, which had automatically been extended by a year upon the outbreak of war. He was formally discharged on 24th August 1915 and returned home to resume his civilian occupation of plumber's fitter.

As a discharged soldier who had already served his country, George was initially exempt from the Military Service Act when it came into force in 1916. Later in the year, however, many of the previous exemptions were removed and George, now 31 years old, joined the Army Veterinary Corps (AVC) as a Private. He duly reported for duty at 18th Veterinary Hospital in August 1916 and left Devonport on board the HT *Hororata* bound for Salonika.

Here the rocky, mountainous terrain meant that horses and mules were used extensively to carry stores and equipment to the troops. The animals needed to be well looked after, so the work of 18th Veterinary Hospital was essential. George spent the next thirty months serving with the unit, during which time he rose to the rank of Sergeant. Unsurprisingly, being in Salonika for a lengthy period, he contracted malaria and spent six weeks under treatment at 63rd General Hospital and he was still at Salonika when the war ended in November 1918.

Early the following year, whilst he was waiting to return home, George received the sad news that his 33-year-old wife, had died of influenza and cardiac failure at their home in Gossoms End. Around the same time, he began to feel ill again and a medical examination at 20th General Hospital in Salonika revealed that his malaria had returned. He left for home the following month.

Back in Gossoms End following his demobilisation, his malaria continued to worsen and he died at his sister's home in George Street, Berkhamsted on 20th November 1919, aged just 33. His daughter was subsequently adopted by her uncle and aunt.

As he died after being discharged from the army, George does not currently have a Commonwealth War Grave Commission headstone, nor does his name appear on any war memorial.

James William Newell (1882 – 1944)
Rifleman 47605, 2nd Battalion, Royal Irish Rifles

James Newell was born in Bridge Street, Berkhamsted in June 1882, the son of David Newell, a bricklayer, and his wife, Mary Ann. By 1901, the family had moved to a four-roomed house in Manor Street with James now working as a painter's apprentice. He left home soon after his mother died in 1909 and two years later he was boarding at a house in Cross Oak Road, Berkhamsted. In 1912 James married 30-year-old Charlotte Maria Curl, a parlour maid, who worked for the Barnett family at Northchurch Hall and the newly-weds set up home nearby in a cottage in Northchurch High Street.

In December 1915, James attested under the Derby Scheme and having been mobilised he was posted to 4th Labour Corps, Hampshire Regiment, joining his unit in France the following year. In April 1917, as a result of the formation of the Labour Corps, 4th Labour Corps became 181st Coy, Labour Corps.

As his service record has not survived, it is not clear when James was compulsorily transferred to 2nd Battalion, Royal Irish Rifles, but by the end of 1917, in anticipation of a German offensive on the Western Front, numerous small drafts of men had joined 2nd Battalion, Royal Irish Rifles. A larger draft of men joined the battalion two days after the start of the German Spring Offensive in March 1918. At that time the battalion was setting up a new defensive line at the village of Cugny, some 13 miles south-west of Saint Quentin and over the next few days it suffered very badly and by the end of March, having incurred 703 casualties, it effectively ceased to exist as a fighting unit.

James was among those wounded, having been shot in his left arm. First treated at No2 General Hospital at Le Havre, he was then repatriated to England. He was discharged from the army in January 1919 and later received a Silver War Badge.

Once he had recovered he returned to Northchurch and with the help of a £30 grant from the Army, James was fortunate to be able to resume his job as a painter and decorator. In 1939, he and Charlotte were living in one of the council houses in Tring Road, Northchurch. James Newell died in 1944, aged 62.

Ernest John Osborne (1898 – 1924)
Private 56772, 24th Battalion, Kings Royal Rifle Corps

Ernest Osborne was born in Berkhamsted in the spring of 1898 and was the only son of Archibald Ernest Osborne and his wife, Lily. The family lived in Gossoms End and Ernest's father worked as a sawyer at East & Son's timberyard.

In January 1901, leaving his wife and young Ernest at home, Archibald Osborne was among a group of Berkhamsted men who volunteered to join 2nd Bedfordshire Regiment to fight the Boers in South Africa. Sadly, soon after arriving there, he died of enteric fever and was buried in a cemetery in Bloemfontein. By then, Lily and Ernest had left Gossoms End and moved into a small cottage in Highfield Road, Berkhamsted. In 1908, she married Edward Gray, and she and Ernest moved to Bank Mill Lane in the eastern part of Northchurch Parish.

Ernest's service record has not survived, but he would have been conscripted in 1916. His military medal records show that he initially served with 1st Battalion, Cambridgeshire Regiment, so he would certainly have seen action in Flanders during the Third Battle of Ypres in 1917. How long he served in the Cambridgeshire Regiment is unclear as, at some point, he was transferred to 1/5th Kings Own Yorkshire Light Infantry (KOYLI), possibly due to the army reorganisation after the German Spring Offensive, as the KOYLI had suffered significant casualties. In August 1918, Ernest was admitted to 25th General Hospital at Hardelot on the French Coast suffering from a mild form of dermatosis. It appears that after treatment, Ernest was posted to 24th Battalion, Kings Royal Rifle Corps, a training battalion, whilst awaiting reassignment to a fighting unit. However, during this time he was re-admitted to hospital suffering from eczema.

Following his demobilisation in 1919, Ernest returned to Gossoms End, where his mother and step-father were now living, and started work as a gas fitter. Two years later, in June 1921, he decided to rejoin the army and enlisted at Watford with the Royal Engineers. Unfortunately, he was only to serve with them for two years before becoming ill with tuberculosis. Discharged from the army, Ernest Osborne died of tuberculosis in March 1924 aged just 25, and he was buried in the Rectory Lane Cemetery in Berkhamsted. Whether his early death was attributable in part to his war service is unclear.

Archibald Parsley (1875 – 1959)
Private 4/7099, 2nd Battalion, Bedfordshire Regiment

Archibald Parsley, known locally as Arch, was born in 1875, the first child of Charles Parsley and his wife, Amelia. After his father's death, Arch started work as a labourer at East & Son in Gossoms End, supporting his widowed mother and younger brothers, Frederick and Frank, and sister, Emily. The family lived in a cottage in Orchard End, Northchurch.

In August 1893, eighteen-year-old Arch decided to join the local militia, 4th Battalion, Bedfordshire Regiment, for a six-year term. His service record shows him as being 5ft 6½ins tall, weighing 125lbs with a fresh complexion, hazel eyes and brown hair. Having served four years in the militia, Arch decided to join the Militia Reserve. This was not, as its name might imply, a reserve force for the militia, but a reserve for the regular army, and consisted of men aged between nineteen and thirty-four who had served at least two years in the militia. Any militiaman joining the Militia Reserve received an extra one pound per year and agreed to remain with them until the end of their six-year term and partake in the annual drill practice of 56 days. In the event of a war breaking out, they would automatically enter the regular army.

At the end of his six-year term, Arch decided to become a full-time soldier and joined the Grenadier Guards and in 1901 he was based at the Guards Barracks in Kensington. It is unclear how long he served with them, however, as by 1911 he was back in Northchurch, and working again at East's timber yard.

In August 1914, Arch was at the upper end of the recruitment age, but that did not stop him enlisting with 2nd Battalion, Bedfordshire Regiment six days after the outbreak of war. After a short period of retraining, he was sent to France, joining his battalion at Bailleul. In February 1916, he appeared before a court martial charged with being absent without leave. Found guilty, he was sentenced to 12 months' imprisonment. The sentence appears to have been suspended however, as four months later he fought with his battalion during the opening days of the Somme Offensive. He was severely wounded a month later which resulted in the amputation of one of his legs. His name appeared in the list of wounded published in *The Times* on 18th August. The following year, aged 40, he was discharged from the army and awarded a Silver War Badge.

Arch never married and continued to live with his mother in Orchard End until she died in 1931. Eight years later, Arch was still living alone in the same house, which he called 'The Dugout'. In the 1939 Register he was described as 'incapacitated', presumably due to his lost leg, but he lived another twenty years and died in 1959, aged 82.

William Henry Parsley (1883 – 1929)
Private G/26400, 13th Battalion, Middlesex Regiment

William Parsley was another of the multitude of gardeners employed on the Rossway estate. Born in the late summer of 1883, he was the third child of William Parsley and his wife, Many Ann. His father worked on the estate as one of the gardeners for the McCorqudale family, and the Parsley family lived at Berkhamsted Lodge, one of the three lodges built in the early years of the nineteenth century. He grew up on the estate and, unsurprisingly, after leaving school he started working there as a gardener alongside his father. In 1903, Rossway's owners, the Hadden family, returned to the estate and retained the existing staff. William Parsley (snr) died in 1909 and William took over the tenancy of Berkhamsted Lodge.

Unlike many of his fellow gardeners on the Rossway estate, William decided not to volunteer during the first few weeks of the war and was conscripted in February 1916. Posted to 5th Battalion, Middlesex Regiment, he was later transferred to their 13th Battalion. Unfortunately, his service record has not survived, but it is likely that he was one of the men who joined 13th Battalion on the Western Front in the early autumn of 1916.

The battalion spent the winter of 1916/17 in the relatively quiet Loos sector before taking part in the Battle of Arras the following April. In June and July 1917, the battalion took part in the opening weeks of the Third Battle of Ypres, and it was during this time that William fell sick, his name appearing in the *War Office Weekly Casualty List* on 3rd September 1917. Whether this was the result of a gas attack or sickness is unclear, but he was repatriated to England for treatment and never returned to France. In June 1918 he was formally discharged from the army on the grounds of sickness, and awarded a Silver War Badge.

After his recovery William returned to Rossway and his work as a gardener on the estate. In 1926, aged 42, he married Rosa Reading at the Berkhamsted Registry Office. She was the daughter of a former farmer from Marlins Farm, which formed part of the Rossway estate. Sadly, William died of phthisis, the most common form of tuberculosis, three years later, aged just 45.

Albert Scott (1893 – 1955)
Private 6039, 5th Battalion, Bedfordshire Regiment

The 'A Scott' named on the War Shrine in St Mary's Church is thought to be that of Albert Scott, who served with 5th Battalion, Bedfordshire Regiment in 1915 and 1916.

Born in May 1893 to James and Emma Scott, Albert grew up in the family home in Northchurch High Street alongside elder brothers Frederick, Harry and Charles and sister, Florence. By 1911, he had left school and was working as a draper's shop boy.

It was not until May 1915 that Albert decided to enlist with the Bedfordshire Regiment and once he completed his training he was posted to the Bedford's 5th Battalion.

The battalion had suffered severe casualties during the Gallipoli Campaign and was now in the process of being rebuilt in Egypt. The main draft of 420 men who joined the battalion at Mena Camp, near Cairo in February 1916 was a mixture of soldiers from the Bedford's 1st and 2nd battalions, who had been wounded earlier in the war, together with several new recruits, which probably included Albert Scott. Shortly after their arrival the battalion moved to the Canal Zone.

It was not long before Albert fell sick and had to return to England for treatment. Unfortunately, no further information has been found except that he was subsequently deemed unfit to continue in the army and on 25th August 1916 he was discharged and later awarded a Silver War Badge.

No details of Albert's occupation in the years following his discharge have yet come to light, but in 1939, and still single, he was living in Northchurch High Street with other members of the Scott family and working as an auxiliary postman. He died in 1955, aged 61.

Charles Scott (1889 – 1918)
Private 23537, 3rd Battalion, Bedfordshire Regiment

Charles Scott was born in the family home in Northchurch High Street in the summer of 1889 and was James and Emma Scott's third son. The following November Charles was christened alongside his older brother, Harry, at St Mary's, Northchurch. By 1911, Charles had become a farm labourer but later turned his hand to gardening.

On 22nd November 1915, just before the introduction of conscription, Charles travelled to Bedford where he joined the Bedfordshire Regiment. His medical took place at the regiment's Training Depot at Ampthill Park, which was owned by the Duke of Bedford, and it showed that he had a sallow complexion, dark brown hair and blue eyes. His height was recorded as 5ft 2¾, marginally shorter than the minimum required to be a soldier, but this was apparently ignored.

His training took place at Ampthill Park, but it appears that Charles did not fit in with army life and discipline, and on 12th April 1916 he disappeared. Six days later he was declared a deserter and the police were informed. He was apprehended on 5th May and returned the Ampthill Park. The following day he absconded again but was recaptured two days later. The reason why Charles absconded has not come to light, but he was treated leniently only losing a total of 29-day's pay, the length of time he was absent without leave. By the end of May Charles had been discharged from the army, considered unfit for military service. A note on his service record simply states 'mentally undeveloped'.

In 1917, Charles was awarded a Silver War Badge, the medal record showing that he was discharged due to 'sickness'. After his dismissal from the army Charles returned to Northchurch and became a farm worker again. Unluckily, he was to die in November 1918 during the influenza epidemic, his older brother, Harry being present at his death.

Ernest Arthur Seabrook (1898 – 1987)
Private 55266, 2nd Battalion, Welch Regiment

Ernest Seabrook was the youngest of the three Seabrook brothers who served in the war. He was born in Ruislip in January 1898, and later moved with his parents to Gossoms End. In due course he started work at a printing company in Berkhamsted, possibly G Loosley & Sons.

Ernest was conscripted in May 1916 and posted to the Bedfordshire Regiment. Mobilised five months later, he reported to Bedford where, following his medical examination, he was classified as A2 and posted to the Bedford's 3rd Battalion for training. In February 1917, his training complete, he was transferred to the Bedford's 2nd Battalion and departed for

France. Whilst still waiting at a military depot at Calais to join his unit, he was transferred to 16th Battalion, Welch Regiment, which badly needed new recruits, having suffered a significant number of casualties during the Somme Offensive. He joined his new battalion at Boesinghe, near Ypres, on 15th March.

The Third Battle of Ypres opened four months later and Ernest's battalion was one of the first to attack the German lines. After three days of heavy fighting, Ernest was hit in the right leg by a piece of shrapnel and taken to 61 Casualty Clearing Station at Lozinghem. His wound was severe enough for him to be invalided back to England on board the hospital ship *St Patrick,* where he was admitted to 54th London General Hospital and later transferred to 5th Northern General Hospital in Leicester, where he was to remain until January 1918.

5th Northern General Hospital, Leicester
Author's collection

With his wounds healed and convalescence complete, Ernest was transferred to 3rd Battalion, Royal Welch Regiment, a reserve battalion, where he spent the next three months in training. Upon his return to France, he was posted to 13th Battalion, but within days he was transferred again, this time to the Royal Welch's 2nd Battalion, which had suffered badly during German Spring Offensive in Flanders.

By October 1918, the strategic city of Cambrai had been taken by the British and the retreating German troops had fallen back to a series of newly-constructed defensive positions on the River Selle, which they called the *Hermann Stellung.* On 18th October, Ernest's battalion attacked the enemy troops there and during the vicious fighting that ensued, his steel helmet deflected a German machine-gun bullet which knocked him to the ground, the impact leaving him with severe concussion. He was taken to No5 Casualty Clearing Station at Bihecourt and then transferred to 56th General Hospital at Étaples. Five days later, he was invalided back to England for a second time on board the hospital ship *Ville de Liege.* He was then admitted to the West Dene Hospital at St Leonards-on-sea, Sussex, and put under observation before being transferred to the Kempston Auxiliary Hospital in nearby Eastbourne. He was discharged from hospital on 27th January 1919 and demobilised the following month. It does not appear that he was awarded a Silver War Badge.

On his return to Northchurch, Ernest initially lived with his parents, who had now moved to a cottage in Norris's Terrace in Gossoms End. He later moved to Putney, where he started work as a printer's compositor. Here he met Victoria Stops, a domestic servant who lived three houses away from his home, and in 1923 the couple were married at Putney Parish Church. They spent most of their married life in the same area, moving to nearby Wandsworth just before the start of the Second World War. Ernest Seabrook died in 1987, aged 89.

Charles Herbert Simmonds (1900 – 1967)
Guardsman 29153, 5th Reserve Battalion, Grenadier Guards

Charles Simmonds was born in the hamlet of Heath End, near Wigginton in January 1900, and was the second, and last, child of domestic gardener, Herbert Simmonds, and his wife, Maria. Soon after his birth the Simmonds family moved to Rossway Lodge on the Rossway estate where his father had been appointed the estate gamekeeper. Also working on the estate as carpenters were Charles's uncle and cousin.

On his 17th birthday in January 1917 Charles, although underage, managed to enlist as a Guardsman with the Grenadier Guards at their barracks at Chelsea, becoming part of their 5th (Reserve) Battalion. His time as a guardsman was relatively short, however, as the following November he was discharged as medically unfit and later awarded a Silver War Badge and a small military pension.

Charles returned to his parents' home, and it is assumed that he became an estate worker. In 1923, he married Dorothy Caffall, the daughter of the railway signalman at Boxmoor and the couple moved into Shootersway Cottage on the estate. Two years later Dorothy gave birth to a daughter.

By 1930, the Simmonds family had left the Rossway estate and moved to Bovingdon, where a second daughter was subsequently born. The 1939 Register records Charles still living in Bovingdon and working in one of the testing laboratories at the De Havilland factory at Leavesden, near Watford, and serving as one of the factory's ARP wardens.

Charles died in Garston, Watford in 1967, aged 67.

Robert William Smith (1896 – 1983)
Private 521719, 581st (Home Service) Employment Company, Labour Corps

Robert Smith was born in November 1896 in Saffron Walden, Essex, and, along with James Whent, the family's chauffeur, moved with the Tuke family from Suffolk to Norcott Court near Dudswell soon after the start of the war. It is not clear in what capacity Robert was employed by the Tukes as, although his father, William, was a gardener, after leaving school he started work as a grocer's apprentice.

Robert's service record has not survived, but it is known that he enlisted with the Essex Regiment on 29th June 1915. Unfortunately, no further details of his military service exist, except that sometime before 1918 he was back in England and serving with 581st (Home Service) Employment Company, Labour Corps which was based in the Bedford area. In 1918, Robert would have been 22 years old, so it is likely that he was either wounded or fell sick during his time serving in the Essex Regiment. By the August of 1918, he was deemed unable to continue working in the Labour Corps, and he was discharged from the army and awarded a Silver War Badge on the grounds of sickness. After his discharge he returned to Norcott Court.

Robert moved to the village of Bengeo, just outside of Hertford, sometime towards the end of 1919 or early 1920. By then he had met Sylvia Powell, the daughter of a coachman from London, whose mother originally came from Saffron Walden, and it is therefore possible that Sylvia also worked for the Tuke family. Whatever the connection, Robert and Sylvia were married at St Mary's, Northchurch on 3rd November 1923. Their wedding certificate records Robert as now working as a builder's clerk. The couple continued to live in the Hertford area for many years and in 1939 he was working as a builder's estimator and surveyor during the day, whilst serving as an ARP warden at night. Sylvia was also playing her part in the war effort having joined the Women's Voluntary Service. Robert Smith died in 1983, aged 86.

Frederick John Tipping MM (1896 – 1970)
Private 65038, RAMC

Frederick Tipping was born in March 1896 in the village of Ickford on the border between Buckinghamshire and Oxfordshire, where his father, also called Frederick, worked as a cowman. He spent his early years in Ickford, but by 1907 his family had moved to Winkwell in the eastern part of Northchurch Parish, where, presumably, his father had found new work at a local farm. By 1911, Frederick had left school and was working as a carter at one of the nearby mills.

Little is known about his time or role in the RAMC. Having volunteered early in the war, Frederick arrived in France on 7th September 1915 and spent the rest of his time with the RAMC serving on the Western Front. The 1918 Northchurch Absent Voters List shows him serving with 2/3 West Riding Field Ambulance but as this unit only arrived in France in 1917, he must have served in at least one other medical unit before that. Later in the war, Frederick was awarded the Military Medal whilst serving with 3rd Field Ambulance, 3rd Brigade. Unfortunately, no further details of how he earned this medal have come to light.

After demobilisation, he returned home and in 1919 married Gladys Winifred Walker in Berkhamsted. The couple became parents the following year. In 1939, they were living in Apsley, where Frederick worked on a local farm. He died in 1970, aged 74.

Nelson Norman Wimbush (1880 – 1965)
Lieutenant, 2ⁿᵈ Battalion, Lancaster Regiment

About two thirds of the casualties on the Western Front were caused by exploding artillery shells. Many were designed to explode in mid-air over the enemy trenches using a timer fuse and this resulted in hot, sharp shards of metal and shrapnel bullets raining down on the soldiers below. The effect on a soldier's body hit by any of these metal fragments could range from a simple scratch through to devastating life-changing injuries and death.

Nelson Norman Wimbush, (known as Norman), was born in Birmingham in August 1880, and moved to Northchurch in the mid-1920s. The Wimbush family originated from the area around the village of Tingewick, to the

Lieutenant Norman Wimbush
Courtesy of Mark Todd

west of Buckingham, but Norman's father, Nelson Wimbush, left the village and moved to Birmingham in the 1870s where he met and married Annie Hill. Here he worked as a baker and confectioner.

Norman grew up in the centre of Birmingham, and in 1894, aged 13, he was christened at Christchurch, Colmore Row, along with his younger sister and brother. After leaving school, he studied at Oxford University, graduating with a BA. Deciding to become a teacher, he started work at Salisbury School, and later taught at the Royal Masonic School in Bushey, Hertfordshire. In 1911, aged 31, Norman moved to South Hill Park Gardens in Hampstead and started work at the nearby University College Junior School. Deciding to join the Territorial Force shortly afterwards, Norman enlisted with 28ᵗʰ Battalion (County of London Regiment), otherwise known as the 'Artists Rifles'.

Following the declaration of war in 1914, the Artists Rifles were mobilised at their headquarters at Duke Road, close to Euston Square. Initially based at the Tower of London, Norman and his battalion, whose members also included Lancelot Desmond Fellows and Nigel Keith Farrar

Porter, spent the next few weeks subjected to multiple route marches to get the men fit before they moved to Abbots Langley, Hertfordshire, prior to being sent to France at the end of October. On 14th February 1915, Norman obtained a temporary commission with 2nd Battalion, Lancaster Regiment, but before he joined his new regiment near Ypres, he returned to Birmingham for a week's home leave.

Officially known as 2nd Battalion, The King's Own (Royal Lancaster Regiment), Norman's new battalion had arrived in France at the end of 1914 and had already suffered significant casualties from enemy shelling whilst in the frontline trenches at Ypres. The atrocious wet and muddy conditions there also meant that considerable numbers of men regularly reported sick, suffering from 'trench feet', and by the end of February 1915, new drafts of men were arriving as replacements.

On 22nd April 1915, the German Army launched what would later become known as the Second Battle of Ypres, unleashing a new weapon, chlorine gas, on the trenches held by French and Algerian forces. Within minutes the noxious yellow gas cloud had caused the death of some 5,000 soldiers leaving a further 10,000 injured. With any effective opposition removed following their attack, the German troops were able to make substantial advances north of the British-held trenches in the area, leaving the British troops in a precarious position. On 3rd May, orders came for Norman's battalion to retreat to Frezenburg Ridge, where new trenches were hastily dug whilst under constant fire from the German artillery. The term 'ridge', when applied to Frezenburg Ridge, was something of a misnomer. The terrain there was only slightly higher than the surrounding countryside, and was nothing compared to the better-known Vimy Ridge which dominated the area to the north of Arras. The defences that the battalion hastily constructed there were soon to prove woefully inadequate.

On 6th May, the Germans turned their full attention to this battalion, launching a heavy artillery attack. Over the next twenty-four hours the exposed British troops attempted to hold the line, but heavy shelling and machine gun fire eventually forced them to retreat westwards. A roll-call of the battalion three days later revealed that of the original 963 troops at the start of the attack, 40 had been killed, 115 had been wounded, 2 had been taken prisoner, 32 were known to be wounded, but classified as missing, and 725 were classified as missing. Among the casualties was Norman Wimbush.

He had been an early casualty of the German attack. The hastily dug, shallow trenches on Frezenburg Ridge, offered little or no protection against the thousands of hot, sharp pieces of metal cascading down onto the troops below. The 'Brodie' metal helmet had still to be introduced into the British army, and the standard caps worn by the British troops offered absolutely no protection. One piece of the falling shrapnel hit the front of Norman's face, effectively slicing off most of his nose and upper lip and destroying the upper part of his palate. Another piece of shrapnel hit his left leg, causing a five-inch wound whilst fracturing and destroying part of the bone. A further piece of shrapnel hit his right leg, but only caused a superficial wound. Fortunately, none of Norman's major organs were damaged.

In excruciating pain, Norman was evacuated from the front line, passing down the standard evacuation process until he was admitted to one of the military hospitals in Boulogne for emergency surgery. On 14th May, eight days after being wounded and still in the Boulogne hospital, Norman was visited by his mother. Subsequently writing to her nephew, Roland Wimbush, in Birmingham, Annie Wimbush wrote that "… *Norman lies just the same. Does not say he will recover, but does not give me much hope. He had a piece of bone taken from his cheek today*".

As soon as he was fit to travel, Norman was sent back to England and admitted to St Thomas's Hospital in London where the military had taken over 200 beds soon after the outbreak of war renaming it 5th London (City of London) General Hospital. Here, Norman's wounds continued to be treated. The following month, his case was reviewed by the Medical Board at the hospital which noted that the although the major wound to his face was irreparable, it was healing, whilst the one to his left leg was suppurating. His general state of health however, was noted as good. Following deliberation, Norman was classified as 'not being fit for six months' (sic).

In October 1915, whilst still being treated in St Thomas's Hospital, Norman was promoted to acting Lieutenant. Norman's next Medical Board, held the following December, heard that his left leg had nearly healed, but an attempt to deal with his facial wound had failed. A further Medical Board, held in March 1916, noted that the wound to his left leg had not healed as well as expected, and that as a result he was still unable to walk. Attempts were also being made to provide him with a denture to cover the damaged part of his upper mouth, but that this was proving difficult due to the lack of surrounding supporting tissue.

The medical expertise to deal with severe facial wounds like Norman's was effectively non-existent in Great Britain at the time, but fortunately this was not the case the other side of the English Channel in France and Sir George Makins, the surgeon who had been tending Norman's wounds at St Thomas's Hospital, had been in communication for some time with a French surgeon with considerable expertise in facial replacement surgery, Dr Hippolyte Morestin.

Morestin, the son of an eminent doctor, was born in the French overseas department of Martinique in the Antilles in 1869. He grew up on the island until, at the age of 14, his father sent him and his elder brother to continue their studies in Paris, and later enrolled them both at the Faculty of Medicine. Obtaining his doctorate in 1894, Morestin began to specialise in surgery, specifically relating to cancers associated with the mouth, and experimented with early cosmetic surgery to various parts of the body. By

1914, Morestin had become an acknowledged expert in his field, and shortly after the outbreak of the war he began operations at the Val-de-Grace Military Hospital in Paris, gradually perfecting techniques in restorative surgery to the faces of severely wounded French soldiers. Key to Morestin's work was the use of transplanted cartilage from the wounded patient, together with skin grafts from areas close to the wound which were not disconnected from their original blood supply until the grafts had taken.

In December 1915, at the suggestion of Sir George Makins, Norman wrote to the War Office, formally requesting that he be allowed to travel to Paris to be examined by Dr Morestin. The British authorities deliberated over Norman's request for some time and it was not until seven months later that he was told that he could travel to Paris for treatment, but at his own expense.

By the beginning of November 1916, Norman had undergone three operations supervised by Dr Morestin at the American Ambulance Hospital at Neuilly-sur-Seine, Paris, which enabled him to breathe and eat more easily. Further operations were planned for early the following year. Whilst waiting for the new surgery to take place, Norman returned to his home in Birmingham to find that his temporary commission was about to be revoked on the grounds of his ill health. Writing to the War Office in December 1916, Norman stated that this move was 'a little unjust' considering that he was now paying for his own treatment in France. With no response from the War Office, Norman wrote again from the hospital in Paris the following March, requesting that he be awarded the honorary rank of Lieutenant. The War Office finally approved his request later that month.

Norman underwent a further series of operations in Paris during 1917. A Medical Board, held on 31st December, heard that one operation to graft additional bone onto Norman's fractured left leg had only been partially successful, but that Dr Morestin and his team of surgeons had managed to rebuild his upper lip and hard palate on the roof of his mouth.

Returning home in 1918, Norman came under the care of Dr Howard Gillies, who had brought and developed Morestin's pioneering work to England. Born in New Zealand in 1882, Gillies excelled in almost everything he did, becoming a talented musician, sportsman and student. Whilst a student at Gonville and Caius College, Cambridge, in 1904 Gillies had represented the University in the University Boat Race, and his boat had won by of four-and-a-half lengths. After qualifying as a surgeon, Gillies started work at St Bartholomew's Hospital, London, concentrating on ear, nose and throat surgery and in 1915, he became a Major in the RAMC, initially taking up general surgery duties. After being posted to a military hospital in Boulogne, he soon became aware of the number of soldiers returning from the front line with severe facial injuries. Gillies later met Morestin in Paris and enthused and motivated by his work, lobbied the British authorities to allow him to set up a specialised unit in England along the same lines as those at the Val-de-Grace Military Hospital. It was the lack of such a specialised unit in England at the time that had forced Norman to seek treatment in Paris.

In January 1916, Gilles set up a unit at the Cambridge Military Hospital in Aldershot, but the numbers of severely wounded soldier referred there soon proved overwhelming. Consequently, in August 1917 a new unit, the Queen's Auxiliary Hospital, opened at Frognal House in Sidcup, dedicated to facial and jaw surgery. Starting with 300 beds located in wooden huts, it rapidly expanded to 650 beds. It was here, starting in November 1918, that Norman's final major surgery took place.

Using vulcanite implants, Gilles first operation was to restore the shape of Norman's face and to strengthen the upper lip which Morestin had built. Once healed, this allowed the fitting of a permanent denture. The final major operations concerned the rebuilding of Norman's nose. For this, Gilles took skin from Norman's forehead, and whilst still attached to the blood supply,

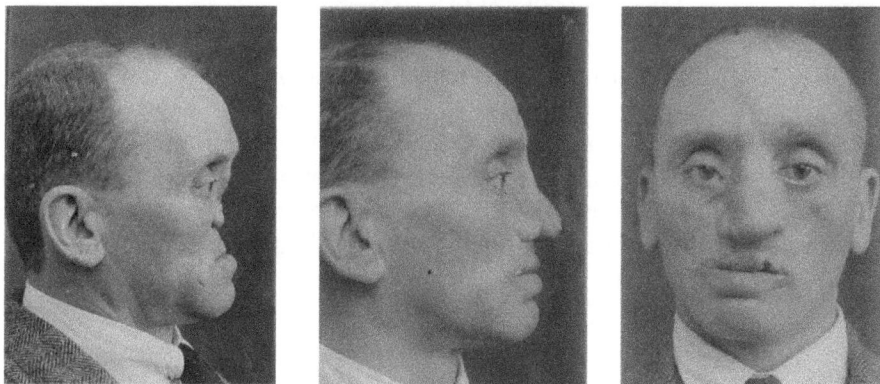

Images from the final stages of the rebuilding of Norman Wimbush's face by Dr Howard Gillies Courtesy of Mark Todd

with the aid of cartilage implants, moulded it into a nose shape, grafting it to the front of his face. With the blood supply to the transplanted skin still in place, the graft soon took. Further surgery was later necessary to repair the new wound to the forehead and reshape the nose. By January 1920, nearly five years after being wounded on Frezenburg Ridge, Norman's face had been restored to as close to its original as it could be. Later that year Norman was discharged from the army.

Shortly after Norman's treatment had ended, Howard Gillies wrote his defining work *Plastic Surgery of the Face*, which featured highly graphic photographs and diagrams of the work of his unit, including several of Norman. He is known today as the father of plastic surgery, becoming a CBE after the war and was knighted in 1930. During the Second World War, his operations at Sidcup were moved to locations in southern England to be away from the flight path of German bombers. He died in 1960. Dr

Hippolyte Morestin, who had influenced much of Gilles early work, sadly died in Paris in 1919 during the influenza epidemic, aged just 40.

In 1921, Norman obtained a Third-Class Honours degree in Economics at the London School of Economics. In the summer of the same year, he married Ida Margaret Hughes in Bromsgrove. Ida was a divorced woman whose first husband, Baron Hugo Ernst Hermann Peter von Grundherr zu Altenthann und Weyherhaus, was a German racehorse trainer, who had subsequently gone bankrupt. Their wedding in 1908, was notable by the inclusion on the guest list of the future German air ace Baron Manfred von Richthofen. Norman and Ida moved to Kenton, north London, where he resumed his teaching career as an instructor in economics and citizenship at various evening institutes for the London County Council. It is possible that Norman felt embarrassed being seen with his facial injuries during daylight hours, choosing to work during the darker evenings instead. Ida Wimbush gave birth to their first daughter, Joanna, in the late spring of 1922 with a second daughter, Mary, being born two years later[44].

In 1929, Norman and his family moved to The Chalet, a large house off Shootersway Lane, Northchurch. There is no record of Norman resuming his teaching career after this move. In 1961, the family moved to Edgehill, Kingsdale Road, Berkhamsted. Around this time Norman decided to upgrade the BA that he had gained in Oxford some fifty years earlier to an MA. This apparently only involved a ceremony, with no studying or examination being required. Norman Wimbush died in 1965, aged 85.

---

[44] Norman's daughters, Joanna and Mary, both attended Berkhamsted School for Girls and Joanna also briefly worked there during the late 1940s. Mary Wimbush became an actor, appearing in many films and on television during her long career. It was in the radio studio however, that she made her name, appearing in numerous plays and for thirteen years she played the part of Julia Pargetter, of Lower Loxley Hall, in the long-running BBC radio series *The Archers*. She died suddenly at the BBC studios in Birmingham in 2005 after recording an episode of the programme.

17 – The Prisoners of War

Germany's plan for the invasion of France in 1914, commonly known as the Schlieffen Plan, was based on the premise of a short, sharp war. Troops would invade France from the north though neutral Belgium and Luxembourg, before swinging south, and then due east, cutting Paris off from the Channel ports. With any help from Great Britain now impossible, the French army would quickly surrender and the war would be over. The Germans estimated that their plan would take six weeks at the most to complete and consequently they saw little need to consider the added complication of dealing with long-term prisoners of war.

In 1874, three years after the defeat of France in the Franco-Prussian War, the major European Powers met in the Belgian capital, Brussels, to define and agree a set of rules for the waging of war. The resulting draft document, although never formally ratified by the participating countries, set out guidelines to be followed should another European war break out. The Hague Conventions of 1899 and 1907 built on the Brussels guidelines, and set down a series of rules for warfare, together with the treatment of prisoners or war. Once again, the European Powers failed to ratify what had been agreed, but following the outbreak of war in August 1914, all sides sought to adhere to the principles as best they could. The 1907 Hague Convention stated that each side should set up a Prisoner of War Enquiry Bureau, which would record the details of every Prisoner of War (PoW) captured, together with where they were being held. This information would then be passed to the equivalent Bureau on the opposing side.

The failure of the Schlieffen Plan in the late summer of 1914, and the subsequent stalemate that enveloped the Western Front, highlighted the lack of planning on both sides for the handling of captured servicemen. Consequently, many of the British and French PoWs captured by the Germans in 1914 faced their first few weeks of captivity in hastily-built camps and living under canvass. The Germans captured by the British and the French fared little better. By the start of 1915 however, the Germans had introduced a basic system of PoW camps consisting of two main types, the *Mannschaftslager*, or basic soldiers' camp, and the *Offizerslager*, or Officers' camp.

The *Mannschaftslager* varied in size and facilities. Some, like those in the *Sennelager* complex at Paderborn, Westphalia, were set up at existing army camps with the PoWs housed in former barrack blocks or purpose-built wooden huts, whilst others, like the one in Königsbrück, Saxony, were purpose-built camps constructed in pine woods and consisting of huts built from wood from the felled trees. A typical *Mannschaftslager* hut held 250 prisoners who slept in bunk-beds on straw and sawdust-filled paillasses either side of a central corridor. Apart from a few chairs and a table, the only other item in the hut was a stove. Situated outside the huts were latrines and a cook house. Some camps later had a library, and a building where concerts, theatre productions and religious services could take place. Surrounding each camp would normally be a three-metre-high barbed-wire fence built to contain the PoWs and which would be regularly patrolled by the camp guards. PoWs held in *Mannschaftslager* were expected do some form of work not associated with the war effort. This would range from basic maintenance activities to helping the farmers in the local fields. Recreational facilities were normally limited, and it was left to the PoWs to develop their own. Some camps had a small hospital, whilst others sent sick PoWs for treatment at the hospital in the nearest town. Poor hygiene, often caused by insufficient latrines, occasionally led to outbreaks of typhus and cholera, and resulted in camps being put under quarantine.

Offizerslager, by comparison, were generally created in requisitioned buildings and ranged from castles, like the one in Königstein, or university complexes, as in Freiburg, to hotels such as the one in Augustabad. Living conditions for officers were consequently less severe than those in the *Mannschaftslager,* and unlike the PoWs held in the basic soldiers' camps, captured officers were not expected to work. The main problem experienced by officers, therefore, tended to be that of tedium, and consequently life in the *Offizerslager* mainly revolved around sport, concerts, theatrical productions and lectures.

The standard of food provided to the PoWs also differed between the two types of camp. In many of the *Mannschaftslager,* food was basic and of poor quality. That provided in *Offizerslager* was, in the main, of a far higher standard, at least until the British blockade of German ports later in the war led to general food rationing among the civilian population. The men in both camps were, however, allowed to receive supplementary food and clothing parcels sent from home under the auspices of the International Committee of the Red Cross (ICRC). Each PoW could send mail home, the men in the *Mannschaftslager* being allowed to write two letters consisting of up to four pages each month, together with four postcards, which the PoW had to purchase out of his weekly allowance. Officers were allowed two letters of up to six pages, together with four postcards per month. All items of correspondence leaving the PoW camps were subject to regular censorship.

Members of the ICRC, together with delegations from neutral countries, inspected the PoW camps from time to time. Being pre-arranged, their imminent arrival was often marked by a substantial improvement in the PoW's conditions, both in terms of accommodation and in the food provided. The ICRC maintained a detailed record of the whereabouts of each PoW, together with their subsequent movements, as it was not unknown for PoWs to be transferred between camps for a variety of reasons.

Arthur Chapman (1890 – 1959)
Lance Corporal 18699, 4th Battalion, Bedfordshire Regiment

Relatively little is known about Arthur Chapman's military service before March 1918. Born in March 1890 in a cottage in Bourne End Lane, in the eastern part of Northchurch Parish, Arthur was one of eight children of William Chapman, a farm labourer and his wife, Lucy, both of whom came from the nearby village of Bovingdon. After leaving school Arthur started working in the watercress beds fed with water from the river Bulbourne in nearby Winkwell. In the spring of 1910, Arthur married Alice May Latchford, who worked at the paper mill at Apsley. They moved into a cottage near his parents' home and there Alice later gave birth to a boy.

It is not clear when Arthur joined the Bedford's 4th (Special Reserve) Battalion, he either attested under the Derby Scheme at the end of 1915, or was conscripted in the summer of 1916. He would have served with his battalion throughout 1917, seeing action during the Battle of Arras and the Third Battle of Ypres and rising to the rank of Lance Corporal. On 21st March 1918, 4th Bedfords were in their newly-created defensive positions near Ribecourt-la Tour when the Germans launched their Spring Offensive. Driven back by the force of the attack, a roll-call taken a few days later revealed that 124 men from the battalion were missing, one of them being Arthur Chapman.

It later transpired that he had been captured on 23rd March. Some three months later he appears in the records of the *Mannschaftslager* at Güstrow, Mecklenburg in northern Germany. The camp was situated in pine woods some three miles from the town and was designed to hold 25,000 PoWs in wooden barracks. Here he remained until the end of the war.

Arthur returned home in 1919 and resumed his occupation as a watercress grower. In 1939 Arthur and Alice were still living in Bourne End Lane and Arthur had now become a market gardener. He died in 1959, aged 69.

John Cripps (1891 – 1974)
Corporal 9585, 2nd Battalion, Bedfordshire Regiment

John Cripps, the elder brother of Charles Cripps, was serving with 2nd Battalion, Bedfordshire Regiment, at the start of the war. Born in March 1891 in Gadebridge, Hemel Hempstead, he was the first son of John and Elizabeth Cripps and grew up initially in Gadebridge and later in the nearby villages of Piccotts End and Potten End. In 1910, aged 19, John enlisted with the Bedfordshire Regiment and started his training at Aldershot Barracks before being posted to the Bedford's 2nd Battalion, going with them to South Africa in 1912 on garrison duty.

John returned to England with 2nd Bedfords on the outbreak of war and served with them in France and Belgium until March 1918, rising to the rank of Corporal. He was captured by enemy troops near the village of Savy early in the morning of 21st March 1918, the first day of the German Spring Offensive, and was probably part of the 2nd Bedford's 'A' Coy which bore the brunt of the German attack on that day. He next appears in early June being held as a PoW at the *Mannschaftslager* at Sagen, Silesia, a small camp some five miles from the main town and built on a flat sandy plain surrounded by forests[45], though he would only remain at Sagan for a few days, for by the end of the month he had been moved to the larger camp at Kassell, some 100 miles north of Frankfurt. The *Mannschaftslager* at Kassel had a capacity of 20,000 and was built on a hillside overlooking the Fulda Valley and consisted of wooden barracks built on stone foundations. John remained at the Kassel *Mannschaftslager* until the end of the war, by which time the camp was used mainly to hold captured American troops.

The war over, John returned to his parents who were then living in the hamlet of Frithsden, part of the Northchurch Parish polling district. Later that year, he married twenty-year-old Lily Tompkins, whose family lived close by, and the couple moved to a cottage in nearby Nettleden, where they raised four children together. Around 1930, having gained employment working as an electrician in north London, John and his family moved to Uxbridge. He died in 1974 aged 82.

Jocelyn Lee Howard Hardy, MC, DSO and bar (1894 – 1958)
Captain, Connaught Rangers

The phrase 'escape plan', when associated with PoWs, normally conjures up thoughts of the Second World War like the ill-fated escape from Stalag Luft III, or the prisoners held in the supposedly escape-proof Colditz Castle. These stories are well known, but such daring deeds also took place some thirty years earlier.

Jocelyn Hardy was born in Kensington, London, in June 1894. His father, Howard Hardy, was a wealthy wool merchant from Donegall, County Down, who had moved to London around 1880 as a woollen manufacturer's agent. Howard met his future wife, Katherine Plaskitt, in London in the late 1880s and they were married at All Soul's, Langham Place, in 1891. By this time, his business was thriving and he and Katherine set up house in Edwardes Square, a fashionable part of Kensington, where Jocelyn was later born. By 1909, Howard Hardy had moved his family to Berkhamsted,

---

[45] The camp at Sagen would become world famous during the Second World War under its new title *Stalag Luft III*, the site of 'The Great Escape'

initially living at Hillside Cottage in Doctors Common Road, before moving to the other side of the valley and settling at Hillsbrook a large house on Gravel Path, on the eastern parish boundary with Northchurch. In the 1911 Census, Jocelyn Hardy was described as a schoolboy living at home, and it is likely that he attended Berkhamsted School as a day boy.

On leaving school, he joined the army, and in January 1914 he obtained a commission with the Connaught Rangers, possibly because of his father's Irish connections. The Connaught Rangers were training at Frensham near Aldershot when war was declared and nine days later they left Aldershot bound for France with Hardy a member of their 'D' Coy.

As the German armies swept across Belgium, the Connaught Rangers moved to the village of Bougnies, near Mons, where they dug in. With all efforts to stem the German advance failing, the BEF were forced south and the 'Retreat from Mons' began. On 27th August, Hardy took part in a rear-guard action at Le Grand Fayt, some 27 miles south of Mons, but he and some 50 fellow officers and men became stranded behind enemy lines. Making their way to the village of Maroilles, now famous for its cheese, the men attempted to evade the advancing Germans and return to their unit, but were surrounded in two buildings being used as temporary hospitals and captured. The subsequent investigation into the incident by the British army cleared Hardy of any blame in his capture.

Following his capture, he was taken to nearby town of Saint Quentin, before being transported by train to Germany. Separated from the 'other ranks', Hardy found himself in the *Offizerslager* at Magdeburg, where he was kept in a locked room for five days and only allowed two hours of exercise each day. On 5th September, he was moved to the *Offizerslager* at Torgau, a town on the banks of the river Elbe, in north-western Saxony. The camp had quickly been converted from an old army barracks close to the river and Hardy was to spend the next five weeks here, before being moved to the *Offizerslager* at Burg and then, at the beginning of December, to Halle.

The university town of Halle is situated on the river Salle and in 1914 had a population of some 180,000 people. The *Offizerslager,* where Hardy was incarcerated, was a disused factory in the manufacturing district and was built around three sides of a square. Officers from the British, French, Belgian and Russian armies were held at Halle, which made communication between them particularly difficult. However, Hardy was fortunate as he was fluent in both French and German, the latter becoming extremely useful during his subsequent escapades.

Being captured so early in the war, Hardy felt cheated and he was determined to escape and return to the fighting if possible; sitting out the war in a PoW camp in eastern Germany was simply not an option he was prepared to consider. Consequently, during the next few weeks, he used every opportunity to spot any weaknesses in the camp's security which he could later exploit. Using the help of some fellow PoWs, Hardy's first escape attempt involved breaking through a dormitory wall into a disused area in an adjacent ammunition factory. As this involved the careful removal of brickwork, it was only possible to work at night-time when the ammunition workers had ended their shift. The hole on the dormitory wall side was then disguised with wooden planks, covered by thin pieces of wood carefully coloured to look like bricks. After several weeks' work, Hardy broke through to the ammunition factory and found himself in a disused shed overlooking a courtyard. For the escape itself, he had managed to acquire some civilian clothes and would attempt the escape with a Russian PoW. The Russian withdrew at the last minute, so Hardy attempted to escape alone. It was only after entering the ammunition factory that he discovered that he could go no further due to the constant presence of sentries in the factory courtyard whose only entrance was through a heavily guarded gate. Reluctantly giving up, he returned to the dormitory and disguised the hole for a final time. Within hours, Hardy heard that he and some eighty other officers were about to be transferred to the *Offizerslager* at Augustabad. The hole in the dormitory wall leading to the ammunition factory was not discovered by the German guards until well after he had left the camp.

The *Offizerslager* at Augustabad, near the little town of Neu Brandenburg, north Germany, was a converted hotel situated on a slope above a nearby lake called the Tollensee. Here, Hardy found the sentries polite and the rooms clean and comfortable and the food good, but not plentiful. Having failed in his first attempt to escape, he felt downhearted and the location of the *Offizerslager* made escape practically impossible. However, being close to the lake, the PoWs were allowed to bathe every day and Hardy started wondering whether this could be exploited to his advantage. Armed sentries were posted along the route to the lake and also on board a boat just off the shore to ensure that no PoWs escaped. Having acquired another set of civilian clothes, together with food and money wrapped in a towel, Hardy's new escape plan was to evade the sentries on the lakeside by hiding in nearby bushes. He had discovered that the security on the 'lake parades' was often lax, in that the number of returning PoWs were not always counted. Planning to escape alongside him was a Russian PoW who had been with him in Halle. One day in July 1915, as the remaining PoWs returned to their camp, Hardy and the Russian disappeared into the bushes, changed into their civilian clothes and started off through the nearby woods. Nearly captured by a German guard who was on duty outside a nearby inn, Hardy and the Russian make their escape from the immediate area using the local woodland for cover and after sunset they headed north. Avoiding men working in the fields and managing to cross several streams, they reached the outskirts of Griefswald, a small town close to the Baltic coast, some forty-four miles north of Augustabad. By now their food was running out and Hardy, being fluent in German, managed to purchase some sausage and cheese in a local shop, together with some cigarettes. He had previously ascertained that it was possible to take a boat from the nearby harbour to the old Hanseatic town of Stralsund, and from there to neutral Sweden. The plan fell apart however, when Hardy tried to hire a boat, and with suspicions aroused, he and the Russian were captured. The following day, they were escorted back to the camp, where the Kommandant congratulated them on having nearly escaped. A short period in solitary confinement followed, before Hardy was told that he would be being returning to the *Offizerslager* at Halle.

Back at Halle, Hardy's new-found experience meant that he was normally invited to join in many of the plans to break out of the camp. None got very far, however, as the plans were either discovered or proved impracticable.

By March 1916, having been a PoW for over eighteen months, Hardy was getting desperate and he decided to attempt an escape that he had been considering for some time, but deemed very risky. This involved breaking into the quartermaster's stores by picking the lock, a skill in which he had already gained some experience, and then climbing onto the store's roof via a skylight, which would provide access to a nearby street. His destination this time was the city of Bremen on the Baltic coast, from where he would travel westwards towards Holland and freedom. On the night of his escape, it was raining heavily and Hardy was able to climb onto the roof as planned and then jump down into the street without being seen, the heavy rain having forced the sentries to stay indoors and so providing extra cover. Dripping wet, as he did not have a raincoat as part of yet another set of civilian clothing, he moved off cautiously, and headed for Halle railway station. At the ticket office, he deliberately purchased a fourth-class ticket to Berlin, although he intended to catch a train heading north-westwards towards Bremen. His plan nearly failed on the Bremen train however, when a ticket inspector discovered that he had the wrong ticket and forced him to get off at the next station and purchase a return ticket to Halle. Deciding to the remain on the train when it reached Halle, where no doubt troops would be searching for him, he eventually reached Leipzig. Yet more bluffing at the ticket office enabled Hardy to purchase a ticket to Bremen, where he arrived in the early evening. Leaving the station without any real sense of direction, he wandered the streets before finding a tram that travelled west out of the town. Tiredness eventually forced him to seek cover and sleep. Discovered the following morning and recaptured, he was returned to the *Offizerslager* at Halle and a month's stay in the local military prison.

On his release from the prison, Hardy was moved to the *Offizerslager* at Magdeburg, which had been converted from an old fortress, complete with a dry moat overlooked by sentry points. It was not long before Hardy and a Belgian PoW called Baschwitz, whom he knew from his time in Halle, worked out an escape plan. Watching from a window outside their dormitory, they worked out the daily routine of the German guards and orderlies and spotted that a latrine in the courtyard, which backed onto a railway embankment, was always locked at night-time. If they could hide there during the night, they might be able to break through the rear wall and reach the railway. Acquiring the obligatory civilian clothes, together with some money and a compass, Hardy and Baschwitz decided their destination would be the port of Sassnitz on the Baltic coast, from where they could get a boat to Sweden. Their absence from the roll-calls whilst they were breaking out of the latrine would be covered by the construction of two life-size dummies, and to reduce the risk of being seen the escape would again need to take place during heavy rain to keep the sentries inside.

On the day of the escape, Hardy and Baschwitz were helped by other PoWs who distracted the German guards whilst they climbed over the wall into the locked latrine. They then set to work removing wooden planks with a small saw they had managed to acquire. After several hours, and in constant rain, they were able to break through to the railway embankment. Carefully replacing the wood, and avoiding a sentry, they set off for Magdeburg station. Their route would take them to the German capital, Berlin, where they would catch another train to the Baltic coast. Arriving at Sassnitz without being detected, they took a ferry to Rügen, from where the Swedish coast was visible in the distance. It was now just a matter of finding a way to cross the last mile or so of water. Unfortunately, they had underestimated the size of the harbour, and only one small boat was moored there. Deciding to look for some food, they went into a nearby tavern, but were spotted and apprehended by a local policeman who had them put under guard in the tavern's back room. They decided to take a nap and woke up to discover all their guards were asleep and, finding that the door had been left unlocked, they made their escape. Three hours later, they were recaptured and taken to the jail at Stralsund where Hardy had been imprisoned following his capture the previous year. On their return to Magdeburg, they spent several weeks in prison and immediately after their release at the end of August 1916 they were both moved to the *Offizerslager* at nearby Burg.

This move proved to be temporary, and within days of arriving there, Hardy was moved to Fort Zorndorf, one of the many forts surrounding the town of Cüstrin, due east of Berlin. Surrounding the main fortress was a 40-foot deep, dry moat, with brick walls and only one entrance. From the entrance a series of underground tunnels led into the fortress itself which was considered by the Germans to be escape-proof, hence the reason why most of the PoWs held there had previously attempted to escape from other camps. One of the prisoners held at Fort Zorndorf was Roland Garros, a French aviator, whose name would later be given to the French Open Tennis

Tournament[46]. The Germans had created Fort Zorndorf as a 'correctional facility', thinking that as it was escape-proof, the prisoners would give up any thought of freedom and see out the war there. Just like Colditz some twenty-five years later, it had the opposite effect, with all the PoW's escape experiences contained within Fort Zorndorf's walls effectively turning it into a centre of expertise. Whilst he was incarcerated at Fort Zorndorf, back in London Hardy was promoted to the rank of Captain.

A week before his arrival at Fort Zorndorf, the German guards had discovered a tunnel which started in one of the dormitories and after going under the dry moat was due to end in the nearby woods. Another attempt by a Russian PoW, disguising himself as a German officer, had also failed when he was stopped at the fort's gates. None of these previous failures deterred Hardy on his arrival and, as usual, he spent most of his time looking for potential weaknesses in the fort's security. He soon discovered that in one of the passages there was a nailed-up door, behind which was a barricade, which appeared to lead to another passageway prohibited to PoWs and provided access to the kitchens and the guards' washroom and eventually would lead to the outer gates of the fort. Devising a new escape plan and with the help of other PoWs, he started to remove the nails that held the door in place, replacing the nails with screws. He found that there was just enough room for a small man, like himself, to hide behind the door and start work on carefully removing the barricade behind. Meanwhile, others in the camp were busy producing forged passes and other documents, whilst the camp tailor, another PoW, was able to build up a stock of German field-grey material to make new uniforms in secret.

It took Hardy four days to break through the barricade and replace the missing pieces with a temporary cover to disguise the hole. It was now time for a dress rehearsal, followed by the escape. The plan was that Hardy would attempt the escape along with two other PoWs, pretending to be military orderlies wearing fake field grey uniforms over civilian clothes. They would then break through the hole in the barricade and join other German orderlies collecting their food from the kitchens and then walk out through the fort's gate. Bluffing their way past several real orderlies, the three PoWs were held up by a sentry and then an officer who, after initially being helpful, suddenly realised that they were prisoners attempting to escape and ordered their immediate arrest. It was the first time that Hardy had been caught 'red handed' whilst attempting to escape from a PoW camp. Two further escape attempts followed within weeks, the first resulting in Hardy getting a short distance from the fort, only to be caught within hours of escaping by a policeman. He spent the next few weeks back in prison, charged not only

---

[46] Roland Garros escaped from the *Offizerslager* at Magdeburg in February 1918 and returned to the French air force, but was killed during a 'dog-fight' over the Ardennes eight months later.

with attempting to escape, but also with the theft of items he had used for the break out.

After his release from prison in February 1918, Hardy was moved to the *Offizerslager* at Aachen, where he was offered the choice of remaining there or be transferred and interned in neutral Holland, to await the end of the war. Hardy, still eager to play his part in the war effort, chose to remain in Germany and take his chances as to whether or not he could escape. The following month, he was moved to the *Offizerslager* at Schweidnitz.

Located some 150 miles due west of Dresden, the *Offizerslager* at Scweidnitz was a former army barracks and workhouse. Consisting of a large courtyard and surrounding buildings, all encircled by a ten-foot brick wall topped with glass shards, Hardy's new 'home' had only been open for some five months. Here, he was greeted on his arrival by Captain William Loder-Symonds of the Wiltshire Regiment whom Hardy had met at his first PoW camp soon after his capture. Loder-Symonds had also attempted to escape from his previous PoW camps and had already spotted a weak spot in the Scweidnitz camp's security – part of the surrounding wall was not always in view when one of the sentries went for a patrol around the nearby huts. The same part of the wall also had two large plum trees growing conveniently close to it.

It was not long before Hardy and Loder-Symonds acquired photographs from a local photographer who occasionally visited the camp to take photographs of the Germans guards and the PoWs interred there, provided they were in military uniform. These, together with forged permits and other documents containing the imprint of rubber stamps made by Hardy himself, some civilian clothing and German money, were kept carefully hidden away awaiting a suitable time to escape.

Choosing 1st March 1918 as the date for the escape, Hardy and Loder-Symonds asked a fellow PoW to distract the remaining sentry whilst they climbed the wall. On the day, everything was ready, one of the sentries was engaged in conversation by the PoW whilst Hardy and Loder-Symonds discarded their military coats and made a run for the wall. Fortunately, the plum trees took their weight and within seconds they were both over. They had still to get over the unguarded outer fence, however, which surrounded the *Offizerslager*. On the other side of the outer fence was a canal and towpath that was popular with strolling couples. Waiting until there was no one around, Hardy and Loder-Symonds climbed over the second fence and headed for Scweidnitz railway station. Their plan was to travel westwards across Germany using their forged papers as cover, and then head for the Dutch border.

They reached Dresden just before dawn and then took another train to Leipzig. During the journey, Hardy was once again able to bluff his way past several ticket inspectors. At Leipzig, they purchased tickets to Cologne and then on to Aachen, where they took a tram heading west. From the tram terminus, Hardy and Loder-Symonds set off in the dark without a map, in what they hoped was the direction of the Dutch border. Not encountering any guards, they crossed the border into Holland not realising they were there until they were challenged by two soldiers who Hardy initially thought were German. Discovering who they were, the Dutch soldiers took Hardy and Loder-Symonds to a local inn. The following morning, no doubt having celebrated at the inn the previous evening, Hardy and Loder-Symonds were put on a train to the British Consulate at Maastricht. Given new clothes, they then travelled to Rotterdam where they were given temporary documents and put on board a ship heading for England. In the middle of March 1918, they stepped foot onto British soil for the first time in four years. By now their exploits were well-known and on 18th March they were received by King George V at Buckingham Palace. Hardy spent the next month back at his parent's home in Berkhamsted.

On 19th April 1918, he reported for duty with 6th Battalion Connaught Rangers, who were then training some of the recently-arrived American troops in France. Still wanting to see action, and not wishing to spend the remaining months of the war training troops, he immediately asked for an attachment to a fighting unit. His transfer came through within days, and Hardy found himself attached to 'C' Coy, 2nd Battalion, Royal Inniskilling Fusiliers which was being held in reserve near Ypres, having been badly mauled during the recent German Spring Offensive. The following month Hardy had his first

Captain Jocelyn Lee Hardy in 1918
Author's collection

experience of trench warfare when the Germans launched artillery attacks on his new battalion's positions.

On the night of 1st August, he led a patrol from 'C' Coy to discover the location of the enemy positions close to the British lines. His patrol suddenly came across a group of German soldiers, one of whom Hardy shot, whilst the others retreated. A German machine gun then opened fire and grenades were thrown. Hardy was slightly wounded by an exploding grenade, but a Sergeant in Hardy's patrol suffered worse injuries. Ordering his patrol back, Hardy stayed with the Sergeant before dragging him some 200 yards to safety. For his action that night, Hardy was Mentioned in Despatches and on 25th September 1918, he was awarded the Military Cross.

On 2nd October, one of 'C' Coy's positions near the village of Dadizeele, Belgium, was attacked by German troops, forcing the company to retreat.

Before the Germans could consolidate their gains however, Hardy led a successful counter attack, but was seriously wounded in the process. Taken to a nearby field hospital, it was discovered that he had been shot in the stomach and one of his legs had been badly damaged and later had to be amputated below the knee. Once fit to travel, Hardy was evacuated back to England where he was treated at Queen Alexandra's Military Hospital in London.

Determined that the loss of a limb would not turn him into an invalid for the rest of his life, Hardy mastered the use of a prosthetic leg as soon as he could. With practice, he could now walk at a very quick pace which subsequently gained him the nickname 'Hoppy'. In September 1919, nearly a year after being wounded, Hardy was finally discharged from hospital.

Two months later, Hardy married Kathleen Hutton-Potts, the daughter of a London stockbroker. By now, he was renting rooms in Langham Street, London and his wedding took place at the nearby church of All Souls, Langham Place where his parents had got married. In February 1920, he was awarded a DSO together with a bar to add to the Military Cross he gained in 1918.

Around this time, Hardy was attached to Military Intelligence and in January 1920, it was reported that he had been placed on the half-pay list, but remained employed by the War Office. Hardy was subsequently seconded as an Intelligence Officer to the Auxiliary Division of the Royal Irish Constabulary (ADRIC), the same organisation that former Northchurch policeman, William Hunt, had joined. Hardy's role in the organisation has never been totally revealed, but it is known that he frequently acted as an interrogator of Irish Nationalist suspects and prisoners during the Irish War of Independence, whilst based at Dublin Castle. In this role, despite his prosthetic leg, Hardy was still able to lead raids on IRA hideouts, with the suspected IRA members, along with any documents or weapons found during the raids, being taken back to Dublin Castle. Here he or one of his colleagues, would interrogate the suspects.

As the violence continued to escalate, both the IRA and ADRIC regularly sent out squads to murder their opponents, often killing family members if the 'target' was not found to be at home. By now, the IRA had identified Hardy as a potential target, and under the direction of Michael Collins, the leader of the main IRA murder squad, he was put under observation. He was subsequently spotted entering a hotel in Harcourt Street in Dublin where he was living with his wife. On 21st November 1921, Collins authorised the murder of fifty British Military Intelligence officers and their informants. One of those on Collins' death list was Jocelyn Hardy. That morning, IRA murder squads went out across Dublin, shooting dead twelve British Intelligence Officers and two policemen. Hardy, however, was not at his hotel when the IRA assassins arrived.

News of the deaths quickly reached Dublin Castle where three leading IRA men were being held for questioning by Hardy and others. That afternoon, British auxiliary troops in trucks, accompanied by two armoured cars, drove to Croke Park in Dublin where a match of Gaelic football was being played. Within seconds of their arrival, shooting started and soon fourteen Irish civilians lay dead. That evening, the three IRA men being held in Dublin Castle were killed whilst 'trying to escape'. Whether Hardy was involved with the IRA men's killing, or of the killing of other IRA men during this period, has never been satisfactorily answered. The events of 'Bloody Sunday', as it later became known, was one of the defining moments in the Irish fight for independence.

The IRA continued to track Hardy's movements and when he went on leave to London he was followed by an IRA assassin. At Euston Station in London the IRA assassin lost him, and it highly likely that he had been spotted by Hardy, either on the ferry from Dublin, or on the train to London. All subsequent IRA attempts to assassinate Hardy failed and were later put down to the level of the security put around him when visiting Dublin.

On 6th December 1921, the Anglo-Irish Treaty was signed and it was ratified by the *Dáil Éireann* the following month. Hardy returned to England with his wife, settling back at Hillsbrook in Berkhamsted. He remained on half-pay, still working for Military Intelligence until 1st April 1925, when he retired on the grounds of ill health caused by wounds.

Moving to Kings Lynn, Norfolk, Hardy started breeding chickens on a farm and writing several books including *I Escape!* which told the story of his time as a prisoner of war and *Never in Vain*, a novel based loosely on his time in Ireland. Two other books were made into films in the 1930s. He was also a regular attendee at the annual Connaught Rangers' Regimental Dinner throughout the 1930s. By 1939, he and his wife had moved to Washpit Farm at Rougham, Norfolk where he continued to breed chickens.

During the Second World War, Hardy was once again in uniform, leading a troop of men manning the Bofors guns of No121 Light Anti-aircraft Battery at RAF Coltishall in Norfolk and his battery is credited with shooting down at least one enemy airplane. In addition to Washpit Farm, Hardy owned another property at Wells-next-Sea in Norfolk.

Having had a lifetime of adventure and seen a variety of action, Captain Jocelyn Lee Hardy died peacefully at his home in 1958, aged 63.

Arthur Hosier (1893 – 1934)
Lance Corporal 9799, 2nd Battalion, Bedfordshire Regiment

Arthur Hosier was the youngest of Charles and Esther Hosier's three boys, and was born in Berkhamsted in 1893. He grew up in Northchurch alongside his two older brothers, Frederick and Joseph, and his two sisters. On at least two occasions during his youth, Frederick found himself on the wrong side of the law, once for shoplifting, and another for being with a group of six friends, including Frederick Geary and George Bignell, whilst setting off fireworks close to Northchurch Hall on a Sunday evening[47]. On both occasions he appeared before the local magistrate, the first offence resulting in a birching.

In June 1911, eighteen-year-old Arthur joined the Bedfordshire Regiment. His initial training took place at the Militia Barracks at Hertford with the Bedford's 4th (Special Reserve) Battalion before being posted to their 2nd Battalion, the same battalion in which his older brother, Joseph, would later serve.

Recalled on the outbreak of war, 2nd Battalion returned to England and less than a month after its arrival embarked for France. Arthur and his mates landed in Zeebrugge on 7th October as part of 7th Division and within days they had fought a brief skirmish with enemy troops near Ypres. Like his older brother, Joseph, Arthur would be present during what would later be known as the 'Christmas Truce' in December 1914.

By the early autumn of 1915, he had become a Lance Corporal. Returning to the frontline trenches from their billets that September, Arthur and his comrades started preparing for a major attack on the German lines near the town of Lens in north-east France. The Battle of Loos, as it later became known, would be the first time that British forces used gas shells again the German troops.

Just after midnight on 25th September, the Bedfords moved to the assembly position at Noyelles-sous Lens and then, in platoons, down the trench network to the launch point for the attack near Cité-St-Elie. Initially, the attack went to plan with the troops incurring very few casualties. Entering open ground however, the Bedfords encountered heavy rifle fire from nearby German positions and the casualties began to mount. Two platoons got beyond the next German trench, which the British called *Gun Trench*, but unsupported by other troops, they were forced to retire. The battalion then consolidated their hold on *Gun Trench*, digging an additional defensive support trench about 100 yards to the rear from which they were able to repel a subsequent German counter attack. The battalion held their position until the following day, when they were relieved by fresh troops. A subsequent roll call revealed that Lance Corporal Arthur Hosier was missing.

He had received a serious leg wound during the attack, and had been captured by the Germans and spent several months at the *Kriegslazarett II* (War Hospital) in the *Palais des Académies* in Brussels. At the start of March 1916, Arthur was moved to another military hospital, this time in Aachen, where he remained for three weeks, before being moved to a

---

[47] Both Frederick Geary and George Bignell would be killed during the war

hospital in Cologne and finally, having recovered, to the *Mannschaftslager* at Stendal.

Stendal, a city in the German state of Saxony, is located some 78 miles west of Berlin. The PoW camp there was situated one mile north-east of the city and, like many others in the area, was built on sandy soil. It had a capacity for 15,000 PoWs and was made up of several work camps. Arthur would later recall that the PoWs in Stendal were badly treated by the civilians living near the camp, especially the women, who would regularly throw things at them as they passed. His stay in Stendal, however, would not last long fortunately, as he was about to be moved to neutral Switzerland.

Following the agreement negotiated in 1914 by the ICRC between Great Britain, Germany, France, Russia and Belgium, captured servicemen whose wounds or sickness would prevent them returning to military service, could be repatriated via a neutral country such as Holland or Switzerland. Another agreement, covering sick and wounded servicemen who might still be capable of military work away from the front line, came into force in 1916. The aim was to intern those who had been selected in better conditions in neutral Switzerland and so aid their recovery. Following this agreement, Swiss doctors visited the PoW camps to select potential internees. Once selected, the PoW would come before a board made up of two Swiss Army doctors, two doctors from the country where he was being held captive, and a representative from the prisoner's home country. Arthur Hosier was one of the few British PoWs selected from the *Mannschaftslager* at Stendal, selection being based on individual need as opposed to a set quota of men.

The first contingent of some 300 British PoWs, including Arthur, arrived by train at the small Swiss village of Chateau d'Oex, some 31 miles east of the city of Montreux, on 30th May 1916. Thousands of Swiss turned out to welcome them on their arrival, and a hotel in the village was decked out in Union Flags to make the newly arrived internees feel at home. After being given a meal, they were allocated lodgings in and around the village, with Arthur being sent to the *Hotel Pension du Torrent*.

Chateau d'Oex, Switzerland where Private Arthur Hosier was interned Author's collection

What seemed a perfect solution of a (hopefully) temporary stay in the beautiful Swiss countryside soon turned out to be anything but. A visiting group of women from the British Red Cross Society visited Chateau d'Oex in

October 1916, five months after Arthur's arrival. They found that the interned men had nothing to do, nor had they been provided with any form of recreation or tuition, and many of them were becoming demoralised. Some had turned to alcohol, and crime was beginning to be a problem. As a result, despite several differences between the various organisations involved, it was agreed that a Hut be built in Chateau d'Oex based on those provided on military bases elsewhere by the Red Cross and YMCA, which would give the internees somewhere to go and socialise amongst themselves. The Hut, which was run by Voluntary Aid Detachment (VAD) staff, opened in January 1917 and was an immediate success, with the men organising various games and debates among themselves, as well as participating in educational classes. Within two months of the Hut opening, crime had fallen by 90% and drunkenness had effectively disappeared.

Arthur remained at Chateau d'Oex until September 1917, when he was one of 425 officers and men repatriated to England under the auspices of the ICRC. Travelling to the French coast by train, they arrived at Southampton on 14th September and were taken to London for medical checks. Arthur returned home to Northchurch the following day. He was formerly discharged from the army on 15th November 1917 and awarded a Silver War Badge.

The Hut at Chateau d'Oex remained open until December 1918 when the last batch of internees left for England. The building was later used by a Swiss children's charity. Today, all that remains of the British PoW's stay at Chateau d'Oex is a plaque in the village church which reads *'In memory of the British soldiers who were interned in Switzerland from 1916 to 1918'*.

Two years after his return, and now working as a carman, Arthur married Emily Lucas and settled in Linslade, just outside Leighton Buzzard. He died in 1934, aged 40.

Charles Eustace Harman (1894 – 1970)
Lieutenant, 13th (Service) Battalion, Middlesex Regiment

Charles Harman's connection to Northchurch comes via his mother and grandfather. His mother, Ethel Frances Birch, was the daughter of Revd. Augustus F Birch, the Rector of St Mary's, Northchurch in the 1890s. It was here, in April 1892, that she married John Eustace Harman, an up-and-coming barrister at Lincoln Inn Fields in London. A second connection between the family and Northchurch came about in 1900, when the then Priest in Charge, (and later Rector), of St Mary's, Revd. Reginald Henry Pope, married Ethel's younger sister, Alice Mary Birch, thus becoming Charles Harman's uncle.

John and Ethel's first son, John Augustus Harman, commonly known as Jack, was born in 1893 with Charles Eustace Harman being born in November the following year. Unlike Jack, who was christened by his maternal grandfather at St Mary's, Northchurch, Charles's baptism took place at All Saints, Pickwell, Leicestershire, where his paternal grandfather, Revd. Edward Harman, was Rector. The Harman family home was in the fashionable area of Onslow Square in South Kensington.

Charles's parents broke with family tradition when considering his schooling; both his father and uncle and also his brother, Jack, had been educated at Uppingham School, whereas Charles was sent to Eton College. From there, in October 1913, he won a Classical Scholarship to Kings College, Cambridge.

In 1914, Jack Harman emigrated to Ceylon with the aim of becoming a tea farmer. Following the outbreak of war however, he returned to England and obtained a commission in the Army Service Corps and later transferred to the Royal Flying Corps, becoming a pilot.

Meanwhile at Cambridge, on 27th August 1914, Charles Harman successfully applied for a commission with the recently-formed 13th (Service) Battalion, Middlesex Regiment (Duke of Cambridge's Own). The new battalion's training took place on the South Downs near Hove and that November, Harman held a party to celebrate his twentieth birthday with his Cambridge friends in nearby Shoreham.

In August 1915, Harman's battalion received notification that they were about to be sent to France and would probably embark later that month. Just before they departed, King George V, Queen Mary and Princess Mary inspected the battalion in their practice trenches at Chobham Common. Harman and his battalion entrained at Brookwood station in the early evening of 1st September bound for Folkestone and arrived there in pouring rain before embarking on SS *Duchess of Argyll* and landing at Boulogne around midnight. They immediately marched to a rest camp just outside the town.

On 21st September, the battalion were ordered to move east to Vermelle, near Loos, a large coal mining area, ready to take part in an attack against the German positions in the area. Marching along the Vermelle Road during the afternoon of 25th September, Harman and his battalion met numerous wounded soldiers belonging to a Scottish battalion, together with several German PoWs returning from the front. That evening, in the gathering darkness, the battalion assembled at the end of a long communication trench some three-quarters of a mile from the front line. It was here that they first came under enemy artillery and rifle fire. At 23:00 the battalion entered the trenches, which were knee-deep in water in places. About 03:00 the following morning, Harman, leading 'D' Coy, together with the men from 'A' Coy, made his way towards a nearby slag heap known as 'No 8 Fosse'. Under constant enemy fire, Harman's' company soon began to run out of food and water. With no immediate prospect of new supplies arriving, a neighbouring battalion was able to share what little rations it had with the men. Around this time, Harman received a minor shrapnel wound to his right leg.

Two days later, an urgent request for help was received from 9th Battalion, Royal Sussex Regiment, whose Lewis machine-gun had been damaged and its team injured during an exchange of rifle and artillery fire. Harman, who had experience of handling Lewis guns, volunteered to help and handed over leadership of 'D' Coy to a fellow lieutenant. Whilst he was with the Royal Sussex men, orders came to withdraw and Harman was ordered to remain behind to cover their retreat with hand grenades. He was joined from a nearby trench by a Captain Waddell of 12th Battalion, Royal Fusiliers. Together, they blocked the trench and waited for the Royal Sussex men to leave their positions and make their way down a congested communication trench which was the only route away from the front line.

To assess how the retreat was progressing, Captain Waddell left Harman alone, but did not return, and it was subsequently discovered that he had been killed. With the Germans advancing from the left, Harman decided to pull back, but in the confusion and darkness found himself in a support trench which had been dug by British troops the previous night. Cut off from the British line, he found an operational Lewis gun and fired it at the approaching Germans. Running out of ammunition, he attempted to destroy the Lewis gun, but was rushed by three German soldiers from 7th Bavarian Infantry Regiment who shot at him at close range. Two bullets went through his uniform jacket, missing his body by millimetres, but the third hit Harman's right leg, which had already been grazed by shrapnel. It was only the quick intervention of a German officer that prevented him from being shot again and killed. The following day, Charles Harman was listed as 'Missing in Action'.

He was taken to a military hospital where his wounds were tended. As soon as he was able to be moved, he was sent under guard to the nearby town of Douai, where he joined other British officers who had recently been captured, among them, Second Lieutenant John Hudson Alcock, of 8th Battalion, Lincolnshire Regiment. Alcock was later to keep a meticulous diary of his time as a PoW. He recorded that before boarding a train for Germany on 29th September, some ladies from Douai gave each officer a parcel containing clothes, cigarettes and a tin of sardines, together with a French novel to read. At the railway station, Harman and his fellow officers were put in 2nd Class railway carriages, their destination being the *Offizier Kriegsgefangenenlager* at Gütersloh, north-east of Dortmund in Westphalia.

It was a long, slow journey, and the PoWs shared what meagre rations they had. Arriving at Dortmund the following day, they were given a small bowl of soup by Red Cross nurses, but on entering the camp early the next morning, the extremely hungry PoWs were horrified to find that breakfast only consisted of a cup of coffee and a slice of black bread. Additional slices of bread were available to buy, but only in German currency, which none of them had. The main meal at lunchtime was more substantial and consisted of a piece of fish and lots of boiled potatoes.

Soon after their arrival, Harman and the other PoWs were given a medical examination and a hot bath. They were then put in a building separated from the main camp as a form of quarantine, and given a postcard to complete which would be sent to their homes saying that they were alive and providing details of their location. On 13th November, Harman received a letter from one of his friends at Cambridge. Writing back, Harman's mental state at that time can be determined as he wrote that, as far as he was concerned, "*as he was out of sight, he must soon be out of mind*".

Harman's daily routine whilst in quarantine at Gütersloh started at 08:00 with breakfast, consisting of coffee, bread and occasionally ham. Dinner was at 12:00 and comprised some tepid 'meat', a slice of bread and boiled potatoes, or sometimes a kind of vegetable stew. Many of the PoWs saved their bread to have later that day with some jam or honey which, having been given some German money, they could purchase from the camp's canteen. Supper was at 19:00 and consisted of black tea or coffee, a piece of bread and either soup, cheese or sausage. Time in between these meals was spent as best they could. There were some books available, and it was possible to walk around an enclosure for exercise. With a little ingenuity, it was also possible to play cricket using a piece of wood as a bat and a rag tied up in a sock as a ball. Canadian PoWs later taught the British PoWs how to play baseball. Indoor activities were limited to various card games. 'Lights Out' was at 22:00. The guards were mainly older soldiers and most of them, not surprisingly, only spoke German.

Harman, and the other newly arrived PoWs, were moved to the main camp on 21st October and initially put in a building full of Russian PoWs. John Alcock describes in his diary that the Russians seemed to only wash once a week and never took baths, nor did they like fresh air, closing all the windows at night

Gütersloh Kriegsgefangenenlager in Westphalia
Author's collection

time. Within a few days however, the accommodation was reorganised and Harman and his fellow British officers were put together in one building with about seven men to a room. The camp itself consisted of ten main buildings in some five acres of land surrounded by pine trees and was enclosed by two rows of barbed wire with armed sentries patrolling the perimeter. The daily routine in the main camp was different to that experienced during their time in quarantine. Breakfast was between 08:00 and 08:30 with daily roll calls at 09:00 and 16:00. With more PoWs to feed, the meal times for the main camp were split into three sittings. The food was markedly better, with the PoWs being able to purchase steak and kidney in addition to their basic ration. By now, most PoWs were also receiving regular food parcels from home. There were also more sporting opportunities, with the British PoWs creating pitches on which they could play football, rugby and hockey. There was also a tennis court, the use of which had to be paid for. A library of some 1,000 books was available, together with censored translations of recent German newspapers. The camp also included a barber's shop, run by French PoWs.

In December 1915, some of the British PoWs that had arrived with Harman were moved to another camp and were replaced by new PoWs. To accommodate the additional men, a new dining hall was constructed, but less time was allowed to eat each meal before the next sitting was due. Later that month, several Russian PoWs made a successful escape by tunnelling under the barbed wire, but within a few days they had all been recaptured. On 19th December, Harman witnessed the Russian PoWs celebrating the Tsar's birthday with a Russian Orthodox open-air service being held during the morning which concluded with the singing of the Russian National Anthem. During the afternoon, some Russians managed to acquire some wine and went about the camp encouraging all the PoWs to toast the health of the Tsar. That evening, a concert was held by a choir and orchestra made up from the Russian PoWs and concluded with the singing of the Russian, French and British National Anthems.

Christmas 1915 was met with mixed feelings. Harman and his fellow PoWs naturally thought of home, but were grateful that their conditions at Gütersloh could have been far worse. Christmas Day started with a church service at 11:00 with the afternoon being spent playing the usual games. The evening however, consisted of a festive meal of venison, goose, plum pudding and other desserts, followed by coffee. The meal was washed down with copious amount of local Rhine wine. After numerous toasts, the evening once again concluded with the singing of the National Anthems, much to the annoyance of the German Commandant. The PoWs on parade during the roll call the following morning were an interesting sight.

On 27th December, a list of names of fifteen PoWs to be transferred to another camp was read out. Among them were those of Charles Harman and John Alcock. They left Gütersloh by train on 28th December and arrived at their new camp at Fürstenberg the following day.

The *Offizier Kriegsgefangenenlager* at Fürstenberg, located in the Grand Duchy of Mecklenburg-Strelitz, some 55 miles north of Berlin, was smaller than Gütersloh and contained about 200 officers, of which only 24 were British. Recreational facilities were also limited – there was no football pitch, but there was a garden. Escorted walks in the nearby sandy countryside was also allowed. John Alcock describes in his diary that a Scottish officer would frequently go on the escorted walks and caused some amusement as the local children had never seen a Scotsman wearing a kilt before.

Soon, Harman was once again receiving food parcels and books from his family and his Cambridge friends. The newly-arrived British PoWs quickly created a new football pitch which proved extremely popular and a tennis court soon followed.

In the spring of 1916, three British PoWs attempted an escape. Wearing the clothes of German orderlies, they managed to walk through the camp's main gates without being spotted by the guards, but unfortunately a local German with a cart was standing outside waiting to collect some items from the camp. Thinking that the fake orderlies were bringing the items out, he called out to them, and when they did not answer he alerted the guards. The following June, two Belgian officers attempted to escape, but were recaptured after a few days.

Meanwhile, relations between the Russian and non-Russian PoWs started to deteriorate. The British PoWs discovered that many of the Russians came from German-speaking lands near the Polish border, and that many of them were sympathetic to the German cause, with some even agreeing to join the German Army. The British and Belgian PoWs therefore kept themselves apart, but it was not unknown for the occasional fight to break out.

In May 1916, Harman wrote home saying that he had decided to learn German. Other British PoWs also started learning a foreign language, with John Alcock being taught French by a Belgian PoW.

At the beginning of July 1916, it was announced that all non-Russian PoWs would be moved to new camps and on 5th July, Harman and the other British PoWs left Fürstenberg by train and arrived in Berlin in the late morning. They were then marched through the streets to the Potsdamer Bahnhof where crowds gathered to watch them pass. En route, they passed the Reichstag and Brandenburger Tor. John Alcock noted in his diary that there were not many motor cars on the streets and that he saw a lot of civilians in mourning clothes. All the tram drivers and conductors appeared to be women, which he presumed meant that the menfolk had been sent to fight.

Harman, Alcock and the other British and Belgian PoWs arrived at their new camp at Burg, near Potsdam around 14:30 and found it nowhere as good as their previous camps. Of the 800 PoWs in the camp, most were Russian only 45 being British. Many of the buildings were merely wooden huts divided into small four-man units. On their arrival, all German money was taken away and exchanged for new 'Lager-geld', camp money which consisted of vouchers or tokens depending on the value. Another major difference was that there were more guards on duty and they tended to be more aggressive and had fixed bayonets on their rifles. Recreation facilities were better however, as there was a tennis court and football pitch, albeit that both were in poor condition.

Soon after Harman's arrival, a Russian escape tunnel was discovered, with two officers being caught red-handed in the act of digging it. Hauling the Russians out, the guards proceeded to hit them with their rifle butts in full sight of the camp Commandant. Protests from the other PoWs resulted in the Commandant losing his temper and ordering everyone to their huts. When they refused, the guards were ordered to take them to their huts at bayonette-point. Following this near riot, the British officers wrote to the German War Ministry requesting that the camp's Commandant be replaced.

Within days, Harman and his fellow British PoWs were transferred back to Fürstenberg, leaving their Belgian counterparts still in Burg. Harman's experience of the less than civil conduct of the German officers and guards at Burg seemed to unsettle him, as he became very homesick, saying that writing was becoming a pain and grief, and that he feared that the war would last for a long time.

In September 1916, possibly to ease the tension, the Commandant at Fürstenberg agreed to the British PoWs being allowed trips via motorboat on the nearby lakes, each connected by a canal system. Some of these trips lasted a full day, and on several occasions, they included time to look around nearby castles and churches. The following month, a film projector was set up in one of the large rooms where some German films were shown. At that time, food was still plentiful and, in a letter, written in October, Harman stated that he was getting fat due to lack of exercise.

Despite managing to purchase turkeys and other traditional items from the local village, Harman found Christmas 1916 a particularly difficult time. The previous month, representatives from the ICRC had visited the camp and one British officer had been selected to be moved to an internment camp in neutral Switzerland. Having built up a close relationship with each other, the loss of one from a close-knit group of PoWs left a significant gap which for some of them was particularly difficult to handle.

To help lighten the atmosphere, over the previous few weeks John Alcock had formed a Dramatic Society with Charles Harman joining the cast of a camp production. Several performances were held between Christmas and the new year, all of which were enjoyed, not only by the PoWs, but also by the Germans. 1916 ended at Fürstenberg with a fancy-dress ball preceded by a dinner. The PoWs managed to make half the costumes themselves, with the remainder apparently being hired from the local village. January 1917 saw the local lakes freeze over in the extreme cold and Harman and the other PoWs were able to go skating. The following March, the Dramatic Society put on a performance of Oscar Wilde's play, *The Importance of Being Ernest*.

In the confined environment of the PoW camp, news of any sort was always welcome. March and April 1917 were particularly newsworthy, with Germany's announcement that their submarines would sink any ship bringing goods to England, the revolution in Russia and the subsequent abdication of the Tsar, the German retreat to their newly-created Hindenburg Line on the Western Front and then, on 1ˢᵗ April, the entry of the United States into the war.

The Dutch Ambassador to Germany visited Fürstenberg in May 1917. He brought news of a proposal that all British and German PoWs who had been in captivity for over two years should be interned in neutral Holland, as opposed to remaining in German PoW camps. Despite this, a few days later a British PoW decided to escape and managed to avoid the sentries. Hiding in the nearby woods he planned to travel under cover of darkness towards a frontier. His absence was quickly noticed, however, and he was soon found and later sentenced to five months solitary confinement. Having served a few days of his sentence however, he was released and rejoined his mates in the camp.

As the year progressed, further details of the proposed internment in Holland began to emerge. Two thousand places were to be reserved for interned civilians, 7,500 places for sick and wounded servicemen of all ranks and 6,500 places for officers and NCOs who had been in captivity for over eighteen months. Lists of the PoWs were prepared and delivered to the ICRC which, it was agreed, would oversee the process. Hopes were high among the PoWs who were captured around the same time as Harman, although it did not deter two other British POWs from escaping from the camp in September, only to be caught in Hannover.

In October 1917, following the surrender of the Russian army, all the Russian PoWs left Fürstenberg and were replaced by French officers, many of whom had been captured at Verdun. As the last few weeks of the year dragged on, news from outside did nothing to encourage the PoWs at Fürstenberg. The Austrian army, with the support of German troops released from fighting the Russians, had broken the allied lines in Italy, whilst in Russia, the Bolsheviks had seized power. Letters from some of Harman's Cambridge friends stopped and he feared that they had been killed in the war. In December 1917, Harman's parents wrote, telling him that his brother, Jack, now a pilot serving with the RFC, had been killed in a flying accident in Lincolnshire[48].

By now, the absence of certain food items was becoming noticeable. Cooking arrangements were changed, with all food for the whole camp being cooked at the same time by German cooks, as opposed to French orderlies. Initially the Germans received their food first, with the PoWs being given what was left. This led to protests and eventually it was agreed

---

[48] Jack Harman's story is told in *For Them's Sake*

that the food would be weighed out in a raw state, with the PoWs food then being cooked by the French orderlies. Some of the recently-arrived French PoWs turned out to be very good actors, and soon joined the camp's Amateur Dramatic Society. The 1917 Christmas production featured John Alcock playing opposite Charles Harman as husband and wife!

In January 1918, Harman wrote to a Cambridge friend that he feared that he would be 'too aged and too ignorant' to become an undergraduate again once the war was over. In another letter a few weeks later, he wrote that he was expecting to be leaving Fürstenberg shortly and repatriated to neutral Holland.

The French prisoners of war were the first to leave. Harman left in April 1918 and was one of about 2,000 PoWs who were billeted in houses and hotels on the outskirts of The Hague and Scheveningen. In a letter, Harman wrote that he was ill in bed and had sent a message to London for new clothes to be sent to him. Two months later, he wrote that he still had not received any new clothes, but hoped to have a room of his own in a house just outside Scheveningen. July 1918 saw him in new lodgings, but conditions were not as good as he had hoped, as rations were poor and exchanging money was costly, with high commission charges being made. The following month, Harman wrote that he was not looking forward to spending the winter in Holland, no doubt due to the cold winds coming off the North Sea. In October, Harman wrote again saying that offers of lectures and other activities to keep the PoWs occupied had not materialised, and that he had spent his time birdwatching on the coast, and had been told to take a physical training course to keep fit.

Harman's three years of incarceration came to an end following the signing of the Armistice. He left Holland and travelled back to England on 22nd November, returning to his parent's home in Onslow Square. He later underwent a minor operation on his throat.

Having recovered from his ordeal, in 1919 Harman returned to his studies at Cambridge, winning both the *Charles Oldham Shakespeare Scholarship* and the *Winchester Reading Prize*. He also returned to amateur dramatics, playing *Falstaff* in *Henry IV Part 1* for the Marlowe Society.

Charles Harman graduated in 1920 and decided to follow his father in the Law and was Called to the Bar in 1921. Three years later, he married Helen Sarah Lewis, the daughter of Colonel Le Roy Lewis CB, CMG, DSO. He became a King's Council in 1935 and ten years later, Vice Chairman of the Bar Council. In 1947, he was appointed a Justice of the Chancery Division of the High Court in England and Wales and was given a knighthood. Twelve years later, he was promoted to be a Lord Justice of Appeal in the Appeal Court and shortly afterwards, became a Privy Councillor.

Lord Justice Charles Eustace Harman died in November 1970, aged 76, six months after his retirement from judicial office.

Shirley Morgan (1898 – 1971)
Lance Corporal 235594, 8th Battalion, Leicestershire Regiment

Shirley Morgan was born in the village of Totternhoe, near Dunstable in March 1898. His father, Amos, a jobbing domestic gardener from Luton, regularly moved his family around the south Bedfordshire and west Hertfordshire areas in search of work. As a result, Shirley's siblings were born in Bovingdon, Watford, Abbots Langley and Hemel Hempstead. By 1911, Amos Morgan had changed career and was working as a farm labourer and shepherd at Norcott Hill Farm with Shirley's 15-year-old elder brother, Lionel[49], helping his father. Two years later, the Morgan family moved into a cottage in New Road Northchurch. Shirley would have left school by then, but it is not known how he was employed.

Although his service record no longer exists, it is known from his service number that, despite being underage, in the late winter of 1915 he managed to enlist with 1st Battalion, Hertfordshire Regiment, the same battalion in which his brother Lionel was then serving, but it is unclear how long Shirley spent with the Hertshires. After being appointed a Lance Corporal, he was later transferred to 'D' Coy, 8th Battalion, Leicestershire Regiment. On 22nd March 1918, 8th Battalion was in the front line near Épernay, close to the Hindenburg Line, when the Germans launched their Spring Offensive. Suffering over 150 casualties the battalion was forced to retreat and moved north to recover and rebuild.

Two months later, the Germans launched the last of their offensives, attacking the British troops in the area where Shirley and his battalion were based. Although warned of the impending action following the capture and interrogation of two German pioneers, the ferocity of the German attack caught the British troops unprepared. It began with a heavy bombardment of the British front lines with the use of high explosive shells followed by a mustard gas attack. Stormtroopers wearing gas masks and brandishing hand-held machine guns and flamethrowers then advanced through the mist. Capturing the British front line, they began to advance up the communication trenches. The men who did not surrender were shot. The following day, Shirley Morgan was one of many listed as 'Missing in Action'.

It was not until the war had ended that his fate became known. During the German attack, he and several others from 'D' Coy were surrounded by German troops and had surrendered. It is likely that Shirley, like thousands of other British soldiers captured during the spring of 1918, never reached a PoW camp. Held to the rear of the battlefield they were kept under constant guard and used as labourers by the Germans. His release came five months later, following the signing of the Armistice.

---

[49] Lionel Morgan's story is told in *For Them's Sake*

On 2nd December 1918, Shirley, together with other men from the Leicestershire Regiment who had been captured during the offensives, boarded the SS *Cambria*, a former steamship of London & North Western railway, at Boulogne bound for Dover. After a basic interrogation and a short period of acclimatisation, he returned home to Northchurch.

In 1919, his parents moved to Manor Avenue, Hemel Hempstead. Three years later, Shirley married Edith Smith and around this time he found work at John Dickinson and Co in Apsley, where he was still working as an envelope cutter in 1939. Shirley Morgan died in 1971, aged 73.

William George Mustill (1894 – 1984)
Private 2306, 1st Battalion, Northumberland Fusiliers

William George Mustill, known as George, was born at Cow Roast in July 1894. William's father, George Mustill (snr), was a former career soldier who had served in the army for 25 years, including spells of duty in India and Afghanistan. After leaving the army in 1889, George (snr) and his wife, Florence Annie, moved to Cow Roast where he became the lockkeeper on the Grand Junction Canal. It was here that six of their eight children, including George's younger brothers, Henry and Edward, were born. George Mustill (snr) died in 1900, leaving Florence to raise her six surviving children alone.

As a son of a former soldier, George was eligible to attend the Duke of York's Royal Military School in Chelsea, and so in 1903, aged just nine, he was sent there, which no doubt eased some of the pressure off his mother. He was to remain at Chelsea for five years when, at the age of fourteen, he became a boy soldier with his father's old regiment, the Northumberland Fusiliers. Boy soldiers in the British Army served as either drummers or tailors and were not allowed to be sent abroad until they had reached the age of nineteen. The 1911 Census shows him at the Fusilier's barracks at Ecclesall Bierlow, Yorkshire.

At the outbreak of war, George, now a 20-year-old fully-fledged soldier with 1st Battalion, Northumberland Fusiliers, was serving at Cambridge Barracks in Portsmouth. Sailing from Southampton on board the SS *Norman* on 13th August 1914, George and his battalion arrived at Le Havre the following morning in extremely hot weather and marched to their rest camp. Although it was only a five-and-a-half-mile march, 82 men from the battalion fell out before reaching their destination owing to the intense heat.

By November, the allied and German front lines, which would effectively remain in place for much of the war, had been created. On 7th November, George and his battalion were entrenched near Ypres when they came under fire from German artillery. This was a prelude to a fearsome infantry attack which resulted in the capture of some of the British trench system. A counterattack by George's battalion was unsuccessful, and a new line had to be formed some 300 yards to the rear. At the next roll call, George was found to be missing. It later transpired that he had been captured by the Germans, having received a serious head wound during the attack that had resulted in the loss of one eye, and he had also been wounded in one arm.

Following his capture, George was probably taken to a German field hospital in the nearby town of Kortrijk, which handled the majority of the men wounded during the fighting at Ypres, and later moved to a military hospital at Mulheim, Germany. In view of his condition it is likely that he remained there for several weeks.

In February 1915, George was one of 150 soldiers transferred to neutral Holland before returning to England as part of an agreement arranged by the ICRC. In exchange, the British repatriated the same number of wounded German PoWs. He landed at Folkestone and was taken to Queen Alexandra's Military Hospital in Grosvenor Road, London, next to the then site of the National Gallery (now the Tate Gallery). The King and Queen visited the hospital shortly afterwards, speaking to all the wounded men. Interviewed from his hospital bed for the *Bucks Herald*, George said "… *we are very fortunate to be home again, though the majority are maimed for life. I shall want an artificial eye before leaving hospital. There are half-a-dozen young fellows' home who have lost both eyes, so I am fortunate*".

After his discharge from hospital, George returned to Cow Roast Lock and was discharged from the army in November 1915. A few months later he was awarded a Silver War Badge.

He subsequently moved to London, where he found work as a civil servant. In June 1921, he married Beatrice Page and they would later have two children. By 1939, the family was living in Southgate and he was working at the War Office. George Mustill died in London in 1984, aged 89.

Charles (Charlie) Henry Penn (1876 – 1949)
Private 201767, 4ᵗʰ Battalion, Suffolk Regiment

Charlie Penn was born in Shenley, Hertfordshire, in August 1876 where his father worked as a groom. After the Penn family moved to a cottage on the Haresfoot estate in Berkhamsted, Charlie started work as a shop assistant, probably for Samuel Dickens, who ran a baker's and grocer's shop in Aldbury and where his younger brother, William, later worked. Having grown up surrounded by horses, Charlie decided to become a groom and moved to London and in 1901 he was lodging with other grooms in Gloucester Terrace Mews, close to Paddington Station. By then, the Penn family had moved from the cottage at Haresfoot to 7 Bell Lane, Northchurch, which would later become Charlie's own home.

His service record has not survived, but he was probably conscripted in early 1916, by which time he would have been nearly 39 years old and still single. Having completed his training, he was posted to 4ᵗʰ Battalion, Suffolk

Regiment, a territorial unit that had been in France since November 1914. At the start of 1917, the battalion was training at Villers-sous-Ailly in the Somme sector and had recently taken on several drafts of conscripts, all of whom needed to be integrated. Charlie Penn was probably in one of these drafts, becoming a member of 'B' Coy.

On 23rd April 1917, British forces launched the offensive against the German lines at Arras. Charlie's battalion was given orders to capture the front and support trenches of the Hindenburg Line some 2,300 yards directly in front of their own positions. 'B' Coy's specific objective was to support the battalion's 'A' Coy in their attack on the support trench to their left. At 04:45 the British artillery barrage commenced and 'A' and 'B' Coys worked their way up the support trench, but met considerable resistance from the German troops. By 06:30 they were still some 200 yards from their objective when they came under heavy fire from rifles, machine guns and trench mortars. Unable to proceed, the two companies were forced to remain where they were for the next three hours. The Germans then launched a counterattack which forced them to choose between withdrawing or face being cut off. The battalion's 'C' and 'D' Coys fared little better, and were also forced to retreat. That evening the battalion was relieved, having captured some 650 German prisoners during the attack, but it had incurred substantial casualties, with 42 officers and men killed, 168 wounded and 104 men, including Charlie Penn, reported as missing.

Charlie had been shot in the chest during the attack and, having been captured, was taken to a military hospital in nearby Douai. It appears however, that his wound was not as serious as at first thought, since on 17th May he arrived on a crowded train with other captured soldiers at the *Mannschaftslager* at Dülmen, Westphalia. His family was advised of his location a week later.

The camp at Dülmen had only recently been built and was situated on sandy soil just outside of the town in a pine forest. To make the camp, an area of the forest had been cleared and the pine trees used to make the wooden barracks. Surrounding the camp was a barbed-wire fence which was illuminated by searchlights

Dülmen Mannschaftslager, Westphalia
Author's collection

during the night. Sanitary conditions were basic.

Coming from a hospital, Charlie may have foregone some of the usual PoW arrival procedures. Normally the PoWs would be placed in quarantine for 48 hours and then given a bath, followed by a short haircut. At Dülmen, no soap was provided and the PoWs had to wash themselves with sand. They were later vaccinated against smallpox, cholera and yellow fever.

The daily camp routine started with a roll call at 06:00. The PoWs would then queue up at the camp kitchen for breakfast, which was little more than coffee made from roasted acorns or chestnuts and a small piece of bread. Lunch, which the men again collected from the camp kitchen, normally consisted of some badly made cabbage soup, with the occasional potato floating in it. Having obtained their food, they returned to their huts to eat. At 18:00, more 'coffee' was served. Many of the PoWs tried to supplement their meagre diet as best they could by looking for potato peelings and other discarded food waste near the camp kitchen. Later, food parcels from home started to arrive which made life a little more tolerable.

After a month at Dülmen, Charlie was moved to the *Munster I Mannschaftslager*, one of four camps in the area and five miles from the city of Munster, the capital of Westphalia. Consisting of two large compounds formed by lines of barracks on each side, it also included a small isolation hospital. Here, Charlie shared a hut with PoWs of all nationalities, principally French and Belgian, this being a ploy by the Germans to hinder communication and thus reduce the risk of escape attempts. Each hut consisted of a series of two-tier bunks, the lower tier being formed by wooden frames containing straw mattresses, the upper tier consisted of hammocks. Each man was allowed four blankets. Ventilation in the huts was minimal. Unlike Dülmen, the camp was built on clay soil and consequently became very muddy after it had rained and often made the playing of outdoor games impossible.

On 19th July 1917, Charlie was transferred to the *Mannschaftslager* at Senne, where he was to remain for the next six months. His new camp was located near Paderborn, Westphalia, 50 miles southwest of Hanover. Known as *Sennelager*, it consisted of three camps (*Senne I, II and III*) with a fourth used for civilian internees. It transpired that a group of British North Sea trawlermen whom the Germans had captured in 1914, were interred in the civilian camp there. Being a former army barracks and summer training camp for the German army, the accommodation consisted of metal huts. In February 1918, Charlie was moved from *Sennelager* to the *Munster III Mannschaftslager* which was the largest of the Munster camps, and like *Sennelager* was a former army barracks.

By this stage of the war the British blockage of German ports was having a major impact on the food supply, with shortages becoming common. Over the coming weeks the failure of the German Spring Offensive, the arrival of fresh American troops in Europe, and the subsequent advance of the allies following the Battle of Amiens, led to a major fall in morale amongst the camp guards. More serious though was the breakdown of the German transport system, which meant that the food parcels from home, which were becoming increasingly essential, took longer to arrive, or did not arrive at all. Added to this was the outbreak of influenza across Europe which killed many of the PoWs and their guards. There was nothing Charlie and his fellow PoWs could do but survive as best they could until the war was over.

Following the signing of the Armistice in November 1918, he was transported by train to the French coast and arrived back in England on 17th December. Returning to his parental home in Northchurch, Charlie found work as a local road sweeper. He never married and remained at Bell Lane for the rest of his life. He died in 1949, aged 73.

Frederick Charles Rowe (1893 – 1959)
Lance Corporal 22195, 1st Battalion, Royal Irish Fusiliers

Frederick Rowe was born in Berkhamsted in the summer of 1893. His father, also called Frederick, came from the village of Pitstone, whilst his mother, Sarah, came from Berkhamsted. One of six children, he grew up in Berkhamsted where his father worked as a bricklayer. By 1911 Frederick (snr) had become the foreman at the sewage works at Broadway in the eastern part of Northchurch Parish and Frederick (jnr) was also working there as a labourer.

Deciding to join the army in the winter of 1913/14, Frederick was serving with the Bedford's 3rd Battalion when war broke out. Transferring to the Bedford's 1st Battalion, he arrived in France on 4th January 1915 and was probably in the draft of 60 men that joined the main battalion near Ypres later that month. He was later attached to 5th Battalion, Royal Irish Fusiliers and sent to Salonika the following October.

Two months after Frederick's arrival at Salonika, a three-day blizzard, preceded by heavy rain, set in. Whilst setting up their camp on the rocky, inhospitable terrain, the Irish Fusiliers were exposed to the full force of the weather and, with temperatures frequently at 20 degrees below zero, any damp clothing froze immediately. Although the troops were soon issued with warm underwear, it was often too cold to put them on and not surprisingly, Frederick was one of many men to go down with frostbite during this time. Admitted to 28th General Hospital in December 1915, he was later transferred by hospital ship to Malta to recover. On his return to service, he was posted to 1st Battalion, Royal Irish Fusiliers, which was then serving on the Western Front.

At the beginning of November 1917, the Fusiliers moved to the area near the village of Trescault, south-west of Cambrai, where they would take part in the next major offensive, which would include the massed use of tanks for the first time. In the days leading up to the attack, Frederick's battalion spent their time creating four new saps[50] called 'B', 'C', 'D', and 'E'. Work on these saps finished on 17th November and ten men were left to guard each one overnight. Among those guarding 'E' sap was Frederick, who was now a Lance Corporal. Early the following morning, the Germans launched a short barrage on the positions whilst troops attempted to cut through the barbed wire defences. The initial attacks were driven off by the Fusiliers, but the Germans managed to break through into 'E' sap and captured six of the ten defenders including Frederick.

After his capture he was taken to the *Munster II Mannschaftslager*, the first record of him being there dating from February 1918. Built on the racecourse at Munster, the barracks holding the PoWs were built of brick, and the former grandstand was used for administration. Frederick was to remain in the camp until his release at the end of the war.

After the war, he decided to remain in the army, but returned to Berkhamsted on leave in 1919 to marry Laura Giddings, a widow with two children. Her first husband had died suddenly in 1916 whilst his wife was pregnant with their second child. In 1921, Frederick was serving with 2nd Battalion, Beds & Herts Regiment and later became their Sergeant Major. By now, he was a father in his own right as Laura had given birth to a child the previous year.

Details of Frederick's subsequent life is not clear. In the 1939 Register, Laura was shown as still being married and living with her children and future son-in-law in Alexandra Road, Kings Langley. Frederick is not recorded as being there at the time however, and it is quite possible that he was again serving in some capacity in the army. After the Second World War, Frederick worked as a postman and he died in 1959, aged 66.

Arthur William Strange (1894 – 1956)
Sergeant 265195, 1st Hertfordshire Regiment

Arthur William Strange was born in Great Brickhill, Bedfordshire on 11th November 1894, the son of William, a painter's labourer from Newport Pagnell, and Sarah, who came from Cheddington. By 1901 the family had moved to Fenny Stratford, where Arthur grew up with his four sisters.

1911 saw the family living in Boxmoor and Arthur working as an office boy at Kent's Brushes in London Road, Apsley End, whilst two of his sisters were employed at the nearby papermill. Soon afterwards, on reaching the age of 18, Arthur became a part-time soldier, joining the local territorial unit, the Hertfordshire Regiment and went off to war with them in November 1914.

---

[50] A short trench dug into No Man's Land in the direction of the enemy trenches to enable soldiers to move closer without being seen

Arthur's service record no longer exists, but it is known that he was back in England in the spring of 1917, as this was when he married Lily Bunker from Bourne End Lane, a fellow worker at Kent's Brushes. At that time Kent's were making thousands of brushes for the War Office including a soldier's kit consisting of hair and tooth brushes, a shaving cloth, shoe blackening and shoe and button polishing brushes. Returning to France soon after his marriage, Arthur was to face the horror of the Third Battle of Ypres.

March 1918 saw Arthur, now a sergeant, and his battalion on the front line south of Cambrai near the village of St Emilie. In the early morning of 21st March, the Germans launched Operation Michael, the first of their Spring Offensives, with stormtroopers sweeping through the British lines and driving all before them. Arthur was one of thousands of British servicemen who were cut-off from the British lines as a result of the speed of the German advance and was captured the following day during the 'mopping-up' operation. The 1918 Northchurch Absent Voters List records him as a PoW and registered in Bourne End Lane.

After his capture Arthur was taken to the prisoner of war camp at Crossen near Frankfurt an der Oder in Brandenburg along with many other captured during the German attack. The camp was located near to the town and was a purpose-built facility in the shape of a wheel. At the centre was a circular mound surmounted by a large tower which provided excellent views across the camp. Three artillery pieces were located on the mound to control the camp in case of any attempted breakout. Surrounding the mound were a number of compounds for the prisoners and included a YMCA hut as well as various workshops. Previously used for Russian PoWs, by October 1918, when the camp was visited by Red Cross officials, the British were the main prisoners.

Arthur was to remain at Crossen until the end of the war and returned home in 1919. He and Lily moved to Apsley End. It is not known whether he returned to Kent's Brushes, but he later worked as steward at the British Legion Club in Hemel Hempstead. Arthur Strange died in 1956 aged 61.

Thomas Chandler (1876 – 1954)
Sergeant 13053, Military Provost Staff Corps

Germany was not unique in not having any defined plans at the start of the war to deal with the influx of PoWs. Great Britain was likewise unprepared, with the War Office being forced to send out a telegram to all Commands ordering that they make whatever temporary arrangements were necessary, including the requisition of buildings or the creation of new PoW camps. Newly arrived German PoWs, like their British counterparts, consequently found themselves accommodated at first in former industrial buildings or under canvas on racecourses or other suitable open spaces.

As the numbers of German PoWs slowly increased, purpose-built or adapted camps came into operation. By December 1916, apart from two PoW camps set up in France, there were thirty-eight camps in England, eight in Scotland, two on the Isle of Man, one in Ireland and one on Jersey. Cells in civilian gaols were also requisitioned when specific punishment was required. As with the German PoW camps, the British also created special camps for the 'Officer class', one of the largest being at Donnington Hall in Derbyshire.

The main influx of German PoWs took place in late 1917, following the Third Battle of Ypres, and increased significantly after the failure of the German Spring Offensive in 1918. By the summer of 1918, numerous PoW and internment camps had been established across Great Britain, the largest internment camp being on the Isle of Man, with large PoW camps at Frimley in Hampshire and Brocton in Staffordshire. The PoW camp at Eastcote House just outside the small village of Eastcote, Northamptonshire, was initially requisitioned by the Government as an internment camp and was later converted into a PoW camp for up to 4,500 men. Eastcote (or Pattishall as it was later known) created several separate 'work camps' camps in Norfolk, Essex, Bedfordshire, Buckinghamshire and several in Hertfordshire, including one in Hemel Hempstead and another at The Fryth, on Berkhamsted Common.

Generally, the PoWs in the work camps were happier than those housed in the larger camps, the main difference being that they at least had something to do. In January 1917, with German U-Boats in the Atlantic threatening food supplies, the Board of Agriculture proposed that German PoWs be employed to break up uncultivated land and use it for food production. Seventy-five German PoWs were set aside to do this work in Hertfordshire and went wherever they were needed on the condition that they were always provided with suitable accommodation and kept under guard.

In June 1918, another enquiry went out from the Board of Agriculture regarding PoW labour. As a result, the following month, thirty-eight German PoWs were allocated to farms surrounding Berkhamsted and Northchurch and by October, three special migratory PoW camps had been set up in Hertfordshire to help bring in the harvest. The existing camps were now working well, although local people often complained of some PoWs being allowed to walk wherever they wanted without any obvious supervision. With the numbers of PoWs working on the farms continuing to grow, it soon became apparent that there were not enough guards to supervise them, and eventually the responsibility was passed to the local farm owners.

One of the British servicemen assigned to guard German PoWs in England was Tom Chandler. Born in Battersea in September 1876, Tom's father, George Chandler, originally came from Paddington and worked as a journeyman gardener, travelling between various country estates. It was during his travels that he met his future wife, Fanny and Tom was the first of George and Fanny's eleven children.

Sometime between 1897 and 1901 George Chandler and his family moved to Northchurch. Meanwhile, one month short of his 22nd birthday, Tom, already in the Hampshire Militia, enlisted with the Grenadier Guards for the standard twelve-year term. He was the ideal height for a soldier, standing 5ft 11½ins tall, and weighed 139lbs and had brown hair and blue eyes. Declared fit at his medical, he joined 3rd Battalion, Grenadier Guards in August 1897. He remained in England until September 1899, when his battalion sailed to Gibraltar en-route to South Africa to take part in the Boer War.

Arriving at the Cape in November 1899, the battalion formed part of Lord Methuen's infantry force that advanced towards the Boers besieging the town of Kimberley, driving them back during Battle of the Modder River and the Battle of Belmont. Much of the following year was spent chasing the Boers and thwarting many of their offensives. The Treaty of Vereeniging, which ended the Boer War, was signed in May 1902. A few weeks later, Tom and his battalion sailed for home, each man having been awarded numerous medals and clasps in recognition of the role they had played during the war.

He returned to England in July 1902 and travelled to Northchurch where his parents were now living. On 7th October 1902, the same day that he was transferred to the Reserves, Tom married Rebecca Gamble in St Peter's, Berkhamsted. Soon afterwards, he followed his father's trade and became a gardener and left the army in 1909. By 1911, Tom and Rebecca were living in a cottage in Northchurch High Street with their four children and they later moved to a larger house in Orchard End.

With a family to support, and having already served twelve years in the army, Tom did not volunteer to rejoin in 1914. On 26th July 1915 however, aged 39, he decided to attest at Hertford, joining No1 Supernumerary Company attached to 3/1st Hertfordshire Regiment, which was one of several Territorial Force units raised to guard railways and other vulnerable areas in the country.

In March 1916, probably because of his previous army experience, Tom became an unpaid Lance Corporal, and the following month he was transferred to No43 Protection Company in the newly-created Royal Defence Corps (RDC). The RDC brought together the various Supernumerary Companies into a single unit and paid its men the same rates as the infantry. On 14th July 1916, Tom was appointed Corporal.

In April 1917, with the number of German PoWs increasing, Tom was transferred to 164 Protection Company, part of Northern Command which covered the area of England between Leicester and the border with Scotland, and had its headquarters in York. Four months later, he was attached to the

Military Provost Staff Corps (MPSC) with the rank of Provost Sergeant. The MPSC's role was to provide warders for military prisons, and later, PoW camps.

Tom was subsequently posted to Catterick Camp in north Yorkshire. The army had built a camp here at the start of the war and a PoW camp was established on the site in April 1917. Consisting of three compounds, each with its own kitchen, it provided accommodation for some 4,000 PoWs housed in concrete huts, all surrounded by the usual fences and watchtowers. All non-officer German PoWs, like their British equivalents, were expected to work and spent their time at Catterick on local road construction and building a new officers club on the army camp.

Following the increase in the numbers of German PoWs arriving in Great Britain in 1918, Catterick established a small separate working camp near the village of Stanhope, County Durham. Called Camp Eastgate, it was built on land at Rosehill Farm and consisted of two accommodation buildings with a separate building containing a kitchen and washing/bathing facilities. Tom transferred to the new camp in June 1918 and remained there until the end of the war. It is likely that the PoWs held there worked in the nearby fields to help bring in the 1918 Harvest.

Whilst awaiting his demobilisation in February 1919, Tom received the sad news that his younger brother, Jim Chandler, a Lance Corporal in the Military Police serving at Cologne in occupied Germany, had died of influenza[51]. Tom's demobilisation came through five months later and he returned to his family Northchurch. Shortly afterwards Tom and his family moved over the Buckinghamshire border to Chesham Bois, where he had found work as a gardener. By 1939, Tom and his family were living on the Isle of Sheppey, Kent and he was working as a landscape gardener at one of the large country houses. All his four daughters were working as domestic servants, possibly at the same house.

Tom Chandler remained in Sheppey for the rest of his life. He died there in the spring of 1954, aged 77.

The Armistice, signed in November 1918, stated that all Allied PoWs and internees must be handed over unconditionally and without reciprocity. In January 1919, *The Times* reported that 153,372 British PoWs had already returned home, with a further 4,081 awaiting transport in Holland. Meanwhile, in Great Britain, nearly 500,000 PoWs and Internees were still being held. These were dealt with under the Treaty of Versailles, which formally ended the war between the Allies and Germany. In the provisions of the Treaty it was stated that PoWs and civilians should be released "as soon as possible", with the German Government responsible for all the costs associated with their repatriation, including the provision of transport.

---

[51] Jim Chandler's story is told in *For Them's Sake*

Britain, not wanting the continued burden of the PoWs, started to repatriate their PoWs on 30th August 1919 and within a month, some 120,000 had already returned to Germany. Two months later, all but a few PoWs remained. The German officers were the last to leave that Christmas.

18 – The Women's Army Auxiliary Corps

The constant need for fresh troops to serve in the front line, particularly after the significant losses incurred during the opening days of the Somme Offensive in July 1916, resulted in a full review of all the non-combatant tasks performed by soldiers. With many men capable of firing a gun in the direction of the enemy being employed on less important tasks behind the lines, it was decided to create a new unit, manned by women, who could take over these tasks and thus release men for the front line. The Women's Army Auxiliary Corps (WAAC) came into being in December 1916, recruitment starting the following March. The women recruited were not allocated ranks, instead those working as controllers or administrators were known as officials, whilst ordinary workers were known as members. Members were divided into four categories – cookery, mechanical, clerical and miscellaneous. Like male servicemen, the members of WAAC wore a khaki uniform, each item being signed for upon allocation.

In April 1918, following the patronage of Queen Mary, the WAAC changed its name to the Queen Mary's Auxiliary Army Corps.

May Carter (1899 – 1988)
38804, Women's Army Auxiliary Corps
Lizzie Curl (1899 – 1992)
39215, Women's Army Auxiliary Corps

In April 1918, two young friends from Northchurch, 19-year-old Lizzie Curl and 18-year-old May Carter, decided to apply to join the WAAC. Lizzie was the daughter of George and Lizzie Curl and the younger sister of Alfred and George Curl, who had both been killed earlier in the war[52]. May was born in October 1899, the second youngest daughter of George and Ellen Carter. George was a farm labourer, whilst May's brothers, George, Harry and Fred had all worked as domestic gardeners before enlisting in the army at the outbreak of the war.

May Carter
Courtesy of Roger Emery

---

[52] Alfred and George Curls's stories are told in *For Them's Sake*

Both women had grown up together and had been in the same class at Northchurch village school. After leaving school aged fourteen, Lizzie started work as a clerk at John Dickinson & Co. in Apsley, while May joined her elder sisters working for HG Hughes and Co making high quality women's clothes at its factory in Lower Kings Road, Berkhamsted.

The WAAC application forms that Lizzie and May completed on 11th April 1918 are virtually identical, differing only when specifying personal details. Two of the references they quoted, schoolteacher Miss Constable Curtis, and Revd. RH Rope, the Rector St Mary's Northchurch, were the same, as was their educational history. The third reference for both women were their current employers. Both stated that their preference was to work in wireless telegraphy, and if not possible as general clerks.

Both women's applications were successful and they enrolled the same day at the Connaught Club Hotel in central London. Here they both received their uniforms and became

Lizzie Curl
Courtesy of Janet Stupples

members of the WAAC and were classified as clerks. After completing their basic training, Lizzie was posted to the ASC depot at Shortlands near Beckenham, Kent, while May was posted to the Royal Engineers Signal Depot in Biggleswade, Bedfordshire, an off-shoot of the RE Signals training base at nearby Bedford.

May remained at Biggleswade until March 1919 when she was posted to the Royal Engineer depot at Balsall Heath, Birmingham. She remained there until being discharged on 6th September 1919 and returned to Northchurch. In 1928 she married Herbert Emery, a salesman. At the outbreak of the Second World War, she and Herbert were living in Dudswell, along with her elderly father, George. May died in Watford in 1988 aged 88.

Lizzie remained at Shortlands working as a clerk until August 1919 when she was posted to Hazeley Down Camp at Winchester. She was discharged in January 1920, and in the summer of 1929, she married Alfred Coughtrey. Lizzie died in 1992 aged 94.

19 – Homecoming

By the end of 1918 the process of demobilising and returning the servicemen (and women) to civilian life had begun, with priority being given to those still serving under pre-war terms of enlistment and those whose discharge from the armed services had been delayed due to the war. In theory, this could have included Joseph Hosier, but the end of his term of service in 1915, and the subsequent confusion after he rejoined the army to become a Sapper, resulted in him being treated like any other soldier enlisting in 1916. Instead he had been transferred to another unit and sent to Ireland. He would have to wait for another year before returning home for good.

For many who had endured years of warfare, their return to civilian life came as a severe challenge. Many could not, or would not, speak of their experiences to their families, preferring to spend time with former comrades with whom they could still relate. During the war, St Mary's Church Room, which used to stand on New Road, in front of the village school, was used as a temporary club for local servicemen on leave, as well as those billeted in the area. Following the return of the ex-servicemen to the area the need for a permanent solution was quickly identified and in 1922 William Favill Tuke organised the financing and construction of a new wooden ex-servicemen's hut a few yards further up New Road. This later became the Northchurch Working Men's Club, open to all men from the village.

Being a largely rural area, many of the returning Northchurch servicemen were able to return to their former occupations, even if it was not necessarily with their pre-war employer. Consequently, the area avoided most of the problems associated with the increase in unemployment that the large towns and cities experienced. Other ex-servicemen from the area never returned, deciding to start new lives elsewhere, sometimes emigrating to countries such as Australia and Canada.

Over 70 of the demobilised servicemen were back in Northchurch in time to celebrate the nationwide 'Peace Day' on 19th July 1919 which followed the signing of the Treaty of Versailles. The start of the Northchurch festivities was signalled by the ringing the bells in St Mary's church at 8am. Later in the day, the former servicemen sat down for a meal of beef, pork, mutton and vegetables provided by the local famers, all washed down by copious amounts of beer and other beverages. For the children of the village there were games and musicians kept everyone entertained throughout the day. A cricket match between a team of single men and a team of married men from the village was won by the married men. Meanwhile in Berkhamsted, a larger event took place with a parade attended by many of the servicemen from the eastern part of Northchurch parish. Unfortunately, unlike the event in Berkhamsted, no photographic record of the Northchurch celebrations has so far come to light.

Despite the celebrations, it was also a time to remember those from the village who went off to war and did not return. The planning of a permanent memorial for them began in February 1919 and resulted in the unveiling of a new War Memorial in the churchyard of St Mary's, Northchurch in March 1920[53]. Almost exactly a year later, a memorial plaque and stained-glass window were dedicated to their memory in the church. For those who came from the former eastern part of Northchurch parish a separate war memorial, constructed in the churchyard of what is now St John's, Bourne End, was unveiled showing the names of fourteen local men who died. In addition, St John's churchyard contains the war graves of three servicemen who died in the UK.

---

[53] The story of the Northchurch War Memorial is told in *For Them's Sake*

Appendix 1: Northchurch Families at War

The following is a list of families who are known to have seen more than one family member go off to war between 1914 and 1918. The stories of those who did not return are indicated by either an * and are told in *For Them's Sake* or ** and are told in *Men of Berkhamsted, Lest we Forget*, produced by the Berkhamsted Local History & Museum Society

The Alcock Family
Frank Alcock, Lieutenant, 2nd Kings African Rifles*
John Forster Alcock, 2nd Lieutenant, Royal Air Force

The Badrick Family
Arthur Badrick, Gunner, 42nd Brigade, RFA
Horace Badrick, Gunner 326th Brigade, RFA

The Beasley Family
Sydney Beasley, Private, 2nd Battalion, East Kent Regiment
Richard Beasley, Lance Corporal, 4th Battalion, Bedfordshire Regiment*
Vincent Beasley, Corporal, Dorsetshire Regiment

The Belshaw Family
John Belshaw, Private, 615 Motor Transport Division, ASC
Robert Belshaw, Private, Unknown Motor Transport Unit ASC
Thomas Belshaw. Private, 1st Battalion, Dublin Fusiliers
Gilbert Belshaw, Private, RAMC

The Bignell Family
William Bignell, Corporal, Machine Gun Corps
Charles Bignell, Private, 4th Reserve Battalion, Royal West Kent Regiment
George Bignell, Private, 1st Battalion, Bedfordshire Regiment*
Alfred Bignell, Private, 1st/1st Battalion, Hertfordshire Regiment

The Blount Family
George Percy Cosmo Blount, Lieutenant Colonel, Royal Artillery
George Ronald Beddard Blount, Captain, Royal Navy
Oswald Blount, Captain, ASC
Harold Blount, Major, Royal Marine Artillery

The Brockman Family
William Drake Brockman, Private, Machine Gun Corps
Francis Drake Brockman, Captain, 1/4th The Buffs (East Kent Regiment)

The Bryant Family
William Bryant, Sapper, 115th Railway Company, RE
Bertie Bryant, Private, 52nd Division Military Transport Company, ASC

The Burney Family
Cecil Burney, Lieutenant, Signal Corps, RE
Edward Burney, Captain, ASC

The Carter Family
Harry Carter, Gunner, 54th Divisional Ammunition Column, RFA(T)
Fred Carter, Private, 7th Battalion, Norfolk Regiment
May Carter, Member, Women's Army Auxiliary Corps

The Chandler Family
Thomas Chandler, Sergeant, Military Provost Staff Corps
Ernest Chandler, Private, 9th Battalion, Cheshire Regiment
George Chandler, Private, 108th Training Reserve Battalion
James Chandler, Lance Corporal, Military Police Corps*
Sam Chandler, Lance Bombardier, 177th Heavy Battery, RGA

The Cripps Family
Charles Cripps, Private, 597th (HS) Employment Company, Labour Corps
John Cripps, Corporal, 2nd Battalion, Bedfordshire Regiment

The Curl Family
Alfred Curl, Gunner, Royal Garrison Artillery*
George Curl, Lance Corporal, 2nd Battalion, Bedfordshire Regiment*
Lizzie Curl, Member, Women's Army Auxiliary Corps

The Dancer Family
Thomas Dancer, Sapper, 114th Railway Company, RE
James Dancer, Lance Corporal, 1st Battalion, Kings Royal Rifle Corps
Alfred Dancer, Private, 8th Battalion, Queens, Royal West Surrey Regiment

The Davis Family
Arthur Davis, Driver, 207th Field Company, RE
Henry Davis, Private, Gloucestershire Regiment
George Davis, Private, 16th Battalion, Sherwood Foresters, (Notts & Derby) Regiment

The Delderfield Family (Wigginton)
James Delderfield, Private, Labour Corps
Ernest Delderfield, Gunner, Hampshire (Southampton) Fortress, RGA(T)

The Delderfield Family (Orchard End)
William James Delderfield, Gunner, 58th Brigade, RFA
Harry Delderfield, Gunner, 434th Siege Battery, RGA

The Dell Family
James Dell, Sapper, Canadian Royal Engineers
George Dell, Acting Corporal, 1st (Reserve) Garrison Battalion, Suffolk Regiment
Albert Dell, Private, 19th Battalion, Manchester Regiment*
Walter Dell, Drummer, 2nd Battalion, Grenadier Guards*
Edwin Dell, Private, 14th Battalion, Highland Light Infantry

The Dwight Family (Little Heath)
Sydney Dwight, Lance Corporal, Signals Service, RE
Percy Dwight, Lieutenant, 25th Battalion, Middlesex Regiment

The Dwight Family (Gossoms End)
Frank Dwight, Private, 587th (HS) Employment Company, Labour Corps
Fred Dwight, Sergeant, 102 Siege Battery, RGA
Alfred Dwight, Private, 11th Battalion, Essex Regiment*

The Eggleton Family
James Eggleton, Private, 396th Agricultural Company, Labour Corps
Arthur Eggleton, Private, 2nd Battalion, Northamptonshire Regiment**

The Garner Family
Frank Garner, Private, 7th Battalion, The Queens (Royal West Surrey) Regiment
Arthur Garner, Driver, ASC

The Geary Family
Harry Geary, Sapper, 260th Railway Company, RE
Charles Geary, Private, ASC
Walter Geary, Private, 1st Battalion, Border Regiment*
Frederick Geary, Private, 1st Battalion, Border Regiment*

The Graham Family
Thomas Graham, Private, Horse Transport, ASC
Charles Graham, Private, 1st Battalion, Bedfordshire Regiment

The Hales Family
Fred Hales, Lance Sergeant, 1/4th Northamptonshire Regiment
William Hales, Private, 101 Battalion, (Bucks and Berks) Machine Gun Corps
Jack Hales, Gunner, 54th Divisional Ammunition Column, RFA(T)
Joseph Hales, Private, 2/5th Battalion, Notts & Derby Regiment
George Hales, Lance Corporal, 23rd (Service) Battalion Royal Fusiliers

The Harman Family
Charles Harman, Lieutenant, 13th (Service Battalion), Middlesex Regiment
John Harman, Lieutenant, Royal Flying Corps*

The Holland Family
Ernest Holland, Private, 9th Battalion, Gloucestershire Regiment
Alfred Holland, Gunner, 104th Brigade, RFA

The Hooper Family
Edward Hooper, Lieutenant, 2nd Battalion, The Loyal North Lancashire Regiment
Henry Hooper, Lieutenant, 157th Heavy Battery, RGA

The Hosier Family
Frederick Hosier, Driver, 7th Horse Pontoon Park, RE
Joseph Hosier, Sapper, 70th Field Company, RE
Arthur Hosier, Lance Corporal 2nd Battalion, Bedfordshire Regiment

The Howlett Family
William Howlett, Private, 9th Battalion, West Riding Regiment
Walter Howlett, Private, 7th Battalion, Bedfordshire Regiment*

The Kempster Family
Joseph Kempster, Private, 693rd Agricultural Company, Labour Corps
Arthur Kempster, Private, Machine Gun Corps
Robert Kempster, Private, Machine Gun Corps

The Lay Family
Alfred Lay, Gunner, 386th Battery, RFA(T)
Arthur Lay, Driver, 386th Battery, RFA(T)
Sidney Lay, Private, 4th Battalion, North Staffordshire Regiment

The Loxley Family
Arthur Loxley, Captain, Royal Navy*
Vere Loxley, Captain, Royal Marine Light Infantry*
Gerald Loxley, Major, RAF
Reginald Loxley, Captain, RAF*

The Mapley Family
Ernest Mapley, Lance Corporal, Agricultural Company, Labour Corps
David Mapley, Private, 17th Battalion, Royal Sussex Regiment
Leonard Mapley, Gunner, 270th Brigade, RFA(T)

The Meager Family
Harry Meager, Sapper, Royal Engineers
Fred Meager, Sapper, Inland Water Transport Section, RE
Daniel Meager, Corporal, 1st Battalion, Grenadier Guards
James Meager, Driver, ASC

The Morgan Family
Shirley Morgan, Lance Corporal, 8th Battalion, Leicestershire Regiment
Lionel Morgan, Private, 1st Battalion, Hertfordshire Regiment*
Edwin Morgan, Private, 2nd Battalion, Bedfordshire Regiment*

The Mustill Family
William Mustill, Private, 1st Battalion, Northumberland Fusiliers
Henry Mustill, Private, Expenses Store, ASC
Edward Mustill, Private, Motor Transport Unit, ASC

The Parsley Family
Archibald Parsley, Private, 2nd Battalion, Bedfordshire Regiment
Frank Parsley, Driver, London Divisional Ammunition Column, RFA

The Penn Family
Charles Penn, Private, 4th Battalion, Suffolk Regiment
William Penn, Temporary Squadron Sergeant Major, ASC

The Porter Family
Nigel Porter, Lieutenant, 1/28th London Regiment (Artists Rifles)
Royden Porter, 2nd Lieutenant, 2nd Battalion, Honourable Artillery
Company*

The Rickard Family
Alfred Rickard, Driver, 311th Brigade, RFA(T)
George Rickard MM DCM, Sergeant, 2nd Battalion, Bedfordshire
Regiment

The Scott Family
Frederick Scott, Private, 753rd Area Employment Company, Labour
Corps
Harry Scott, Private, 12th Battalion, Norfolk Regiment
Charles Scott, Private, 3rd Battalion, Bedfordshire Regiment
Albert Scott, Private, 5th Battalion, Bedfordshire Regiment

The Seabrook Family
Francis Seabrook, Petty Officer, Royal Navy
Archibald Seabrook, Petty Officer, Royal Navy
Ernest Seabrook, Private, 2nd Battalion, Welch Regiment

The Talbot Family
Charles Talbot, Private, 1st Battalion, Bedfordshire Regiment*
Robert Talbot, Private, 1/1st Huntingdonshire Cyclists

The Teagle Family
Arthur Teagle, Private, 1st Battalion, Middlesex Regiment*
Thomas Teagle, Private, 2nd Battalion, Wiltshire Regiment*

The Waite Family
Stanley Waite, Sapper, 277th Railway Co, RE
William Waite, Lance Corporal, Machine Gun Corps*

The Welling Family (Little Heath)
Harvey Welling, Rifleman, 11th Battalion, Kings Royal Rifle Corps
Stanley Welling, Sergeant, 59th Machine Gun Corps

The Welling Family (Orchard End)
Walter Welling, Private, 6th Battalion, Royal West Berkshire
Regiment*
Arthur Welling, Private, 74th Company, Machine Gun Corps*

Appendix 2: Abbreviations

Acronym	Title
ADRIC	Auxiliary Division of the Royal Irish Constabulary
AEF	American Expeditionary Force
AIF	Australian Imperial Force
ANZAC	Australian and New Zealand Army Corps
AOC	Army Ordnance Corps
ARP	Air Raid Precaution
ASC	Army Service Corps
AVC	Army Veterinary Corps
BEF	British Expeditionary Force
CIE	Companion of the Most Eminent Order of the Indian Empire
CMG	Companion, Order of St Michael and St George
Coy	Company
CQMS	Company Quartermaster Sergeant
DAH	Disorderly Action of the Heart
DCM	Distinguished Conduct Medal
DSO	Distinguished Service Order
EEF	Egyptian Expeditionary Force
ERA	Engine Room Artificer
HAG	Heavy Artillery Group
HD	Home Defence
ICRC	International Committee of the Red Cross
IRA	Irish Republican Army
IWT	Inland Water Transport
KOYLI	Kings Own Yorkshire Light Infantry
MGC	Machine Gun Corps
MM	Military Medal
MPSC	Military Provost Staff Corps
MT	Motor Transport
NZRB	New Zealand Rifle Brigade
PoW	Prisoner of War
RAF	Royal Air Force

RAMC	Royal Army Medical Corps
RDC	Royal Defence Corps
Acronym	**Title**
RE	Royal Engineers
RFA	Royal Field Artillery
RFC	Royal Flying Corps
RGA	Royal Garrison Artillery
RHA	Royal Horse Artillery
RMA	Royal Marine Artillery
RMLI	Royal Marine Light Infantry
RN	Royal Navy
RNAS	Royal Naval Air Service
RNVR	Royal Navy Volunteer Reserve
TF	Territorial Force
VAD	Voluntary Aid Detachment
VAH	Valvular Disease of the Heart
WAAC	Women's Army Auxiliary Corps
YS	Young Soldiers

Appendix 3: Medical Categories

A	Able to march, see to shoot, hear well and stand active service conditions
A1	Fit for dispatching overseas, as regards physical and mental health, and training
A2	As A1, except for training
A3	Returned Expeditionary Force men, ready except for physical condition
A4	Men under 19 who would be A1 or A2 when aged 19
B	Free from serious organic diseases, able to stand service on lines of communication in France, or in garrisons in the tropics
B1	Able to march 5 miles, see to shoot with glasses, and hear well
B2	Able to walk 5 miles, see and hear sufficiently for ordinary purposes
B3	Only suitable for sedentary work
C	Free from serious organic diseases, able to stand service in garrisons at home
C1	Able to march 5 miles, see to shoot with glasses, and hear well
C2	Able to walk 5 miles, see and hear sufficiently for ordinary purposes
C3	Only suitable for sedentary work
D	Unfit but could be fit within 6 months
D1	Regular Royal Artillery, Royal Engineers, infantry in Command Depots
D2	Regular Royal Artillery, Royal Engineers, infantry in Regimental Depots
D3	Men in any depot or unit awaiting treatment

Acknowledgements

I would like to thank the following people, many of whom are relatives of the people whose stories are told in this book and who have dug around in their family photograph albums and archives and given me permission to use the information in this book. Particularly I would like to thank: Peter Addiscott, Vivienne Beaumont, Julie Blackley, Clive Blofield, Jane Cook, Robin Delderfield, Roger Emery, Jonathan Griffin, Karen Gunnell, Richard Hicks, Bert Hosier, Annie Jermain, Martin King, Frances Mathew, Sylvia Odell, Linda Pottinger, Janet Stupples, Andrew Sumner, Simon Thelwall, Mark Todd, Anthony Wagstaff and Roger Welling. I would also like to say a special thank you to Ray Smith, my co-author in *For Them's Sake*, who has assisted me with the research for this book. Finally, a big thank you to my wife, Rosemary, for proof-reading this book.

Additionally, I am indebted to the following organisations for allowing me access to their archives: National Archives of Australia, Berkhamsted Local History and Museum Society, British Library, British Newspaper Library, Canadian National Archive, General Register Office, Hertfordshire Record Office, National Archives, Northchurch Baptist Church, The Rector & Churchwardens of St Marys Northchurch.

Lightning Source UK Ltd.
Milton Keynes UK
UKHW010635181121
394145UK00002B/59

9 781803 690902